COMPANION TO THE INDUSTRIAL REVOLUTION

COMPANION TO THE
INDUSTRIAL REVOLUTION

Clifford Lines

Foreword by **Asa Briggs**

Consultant Editor: **Dr Barrie Trinder**

Facts On File

New York • Oxford • Sydney

COMPANION TO THE INDUSTRIAL REVOLUTION

For information contact:

Facts On File Limited
Collins Street
Oxford OX4 1XU
UK

or

Facts On File, Inc.
460 Park Avenue South
New York NY10016
USA

or

Facts On File Pty Ltd
Talavera & Kartoum Rds
North Ryde NSW 2113
Australia

A British CIP catalogue record for this book is available from the British Library

Library of Congress Cataloging-in-Publication Data

Lines, Clifford John.
    Companion to the industrial revolution / Clifford J. Lines.
        p.   cm.
    Includes bibliographical references.
    1. Great Britain—Economic conditions—1760–1860.   2. Great Britain—Industries—History.   I. Title.
HC254.5.L72   1990
338.0941'09'033—cc20

ISBN 0–8160–2157–0 (hc)   89–29633
ISBN 0–8160–2415–4 (pb)   CIP

Australian CIP data available on request from Facts On File

Facts On File books are available at special discounts when purchased in bulk quantities for businesses, associations, institutions or sales promotions. Please contact the Special Sales Department of our Oxford office on 0865 728399 or our New York office on 212/683–2244 (dial 800/322–8755 except in NY, AK or HI).

Photoset in North Wales by
Derek Doyle & Associates, Mold, Clwyd
Printed and bound in Great Britain by
Biddles Ltd, Guildford and King's Lynn

10 9 8 7 6 5 4 3 2 1

This book is printed on acid-free paper.

CONTENTS

FOREWORD

The one novel of Charles Dickens that focuses on industrial England, *Hard Times* (1854), has much to say both about the industrial environment and about industrial relations. It also has much to say about 'facts'. Coketown, where the action takes place, was 'a triumph of fact': 'it was a town of machinery and tall chimneys, out of which interminable serpents of smoke trailed themselves for ever and ever, and never got unveiled.' Mr Gradgrind, the schoolmaster in Coketown, believes that education is only about facts. 'Now what I want is facts,' he tells the boys and girls in the first sentence of the novel, set in a plain, bare monotonous vault of a schoolroom. 'Facts alone are wanted in life. Plant nothing else, and root out everything else.... Nothing else will ever be of service to them. This is the principle on which I bring up my own children ... stick to facts.'

It is fitting that this new *Companion to the Industrial Revolution* is published by Facts On File, although the facts that are set out in these pages are of a different order from Gradgrind's facts. Many of the latter were not really facts at all, as Dickens pointed out. They were humbug. At best, they represented only one side of the truth. Coketown was a mill town making textiles, and textiles figured prominently early in the industrial revolution. Yet there were different kinds of industrial communities, ranging from mining villages to the city of all trades, Birmingham.

Dickens was anxious too that fact should not destroy fancy. As far as early industrialization was concerned, it certainly did not do so. There was far more to the industrial revolution than grind – or smoke. In the 18th century there was a stimulus to the imagination, for example, in the sighs and sounds of Coalbrookdale, one of the cradles of the 18th-century industrial revolution, and in the famous iron bridge there across the Severn. It was possible to find romance, too, in the power of steam, particularly as expressed in the great locomotives built during the railway age, and in the triumphs of great inventors, engineers and entrepreneurs, men like James Watt, Thomas Telford and Matthew Boulton or George and Robert Stevenson.

By 1854, however, the British industrial revolution had passed through its first pioneering phases and some of the early romance had gone. Industry had established itself, and in many industries innovation had given way to routine. The new industrial environment and the new industrial towns and cities were taken for granted: they had lost most of their sense of shock. Machines too were taken for granted, though there were social critics who complained that much had been lost when they displaced human labour. There were still sharp divisions in society, and there was no unanimity that everyone in the country was better off than they had been before the smoke poured out of the chimneys. There were 'bad years' as well as 'good years' in an industrial society, years when unemployment was high and the profits of employers were cut. There were also different views of political economy and opposing forms of economic organization. Employers often, but not always, sang the merits of competition. Employees often, but not always, put their trust in cooperation. The new labour force called into existence by industrialization generated trade unions and developed the sense of a working class.

The dynamic behind the British industrial revolution was the expansion of markets at home and abroad. What happened was not planned centrally. It depended upon enterprise from below. Yet, for a variety of reasons, by 1854 the first official efforts to intervene in the processes of industrialization had already been made from above. The market was not left to itself. Thus, the Factory Act of 1847, following in the wake of earlier Acts in 1833 and 1844, limited the daily hours of work of young children and women in the textiles industry. Hitherto, much industrialization had depended upon them and many young children and women had been exploited. Now government – and inspectors – came into the picture. There were to be many later acts, culminating in a consolidated Factory Act of 1901.

Industrial society was more complex than previous societies and one more subject to change. It was a society, too, that identified economic, social and political problems, some of which had been present, unidentified, before industrial change began. At the same time, it was a society that offered solutions also, or at least the hope of solutions, even though they were no more acceptable to everyone in society than industry itself was. There were manifest conflicts of interests as well as of ideas. None the less, there was no way back. Industry had come to stay. The word industry had once been used to describe a human quality – hard work. By 1854, however, it referred to a sector of the economy, a sector that was compared and contrasted with agriculture or with commerce.

The growth of that sector, well advanced by 1851 – the year of the Great Exhibition in London's Crystal Palace, is well covered in the pages of this book. The main growth, however, had been not in London but in the provinces, and both Scotland and Wales had had industrial revolutions of their own. It is fascinating to go back and see some of the early industrial sites both in the countryside and in towns and cities. Population had risen at the same time as industrial output, both in London and the provinces, where there were great industrial cities like Birmingham, Manchester, Leeds, Bradford and Sheffield.

The facts set out in this book are not entirely statistical, however, even though in the 19th century the collection and analysis of statistics became increasingly important after the rise of industry, and statistical societies came into prominence. All the relevant national statistics were assembled in the pages of the successive editions of G.R. Porter's *Progress of the North*, the first edition of which appeared in 1837, the year Queen Victoria came to the throne.

Some of the most dramatic statistics relate to the 1780s, when the production of coal and iron, the key materials of early British industrialization, dramatically increased, and when steam power was first used to drive machines – notably in the rapidly expanding cotton textiles industry. National resources of coal and iron, hitherto imperfectly utilized, were given new significance by changes in technology, even though some of the basic resources on which the industrial revolution depended – in particular cotton – were imported from overseas. In the long wars with revolutionary France that began in 1793 Britain had a marked economic advantage. Between 1815, when the wars ended, and 1851 Britain further increased its lead both in production and trade. It was to lose its lead in production during the last decades of the 19th century when Germany and the United States forged ahead with industrial revolutions of their own.

During the 19th century, comparisons were frequently being made between the French Revolution, a political and social revolution, and the British industrial revolution, and comparisons have been made since between the British industrial revolution and later industrial revolutions in other countries, including Japan.

The first Englishman to make the term 'industrial revolution' popular was Arnold Toynbee, who gave a course of lectures to 'working men' in 1881 and 1882 on 'The Industrial Revolution of the Eighteenth Century', subsequently published in book form. Writing at a time when his fellow countrymen were living through a decade of intense social and economic ferment – and when foreign competition was much discussed, Toynbee selected for the attention of his audience those topics in industrial history that were associated not with achievement – the themes picked out earlier by Samuel Smiles, preacher of the gospel of work – but with social strain and disruption.

Later writers have often viewed things differently from Toynbee, although there has been no greater unanimity among historians than there was among contemporaries. C.P. Snow stressed the long-term importance of industrialization in raising the standard of living. Other writers argued that in the early stages of industrialization, in particular the workers, especially displaced traditional workers like the handloom weavers, were in many cases worse off. There were always optimists and pessimists among the observers and analysts. Not surprisingly, the debate turned not only on measurable quantities but on the quality of life. It engaged poets as well as employers and workers.

There is a strong case for restricting the use of the term 'industrial revolution' to over-all and once-and-for-all transformations in the whole lives of a society, and not using it to describe bursts of new economic activity. We can, in fact, distinguish between 'pre-industrial', 'industrial' and 'post-industrial' societies, the last of these – and the adjective is vague – being societies in which the proportion of industrial workers in the total population has fallen. Our own perspectives have changed in an age of computers and new technologies.

Science, too, which played a relatively small part in the industrial revolution of the 18th century, now propels much of the industrial and post-industrial system. Forms of power have changed too. Electricity was developed faster in Germany and the United States than it was in Britain. The changes in technology were mainly of British origin during the early stages of industrialization, but this was no longer so as other countries industrialized. And in some of the later industrial revolutions, for example those in Germany and Japan, the state played a different role.

Industrial growth in any age depends on capital investments as well as on new inventions, and in the late-18th century capital investment depended largely on the willingness of individuals to save and deploy funds instead of hoarding them or delighting in lavish consumption. There was no highly organized capital market. The first industrialists, most of whom were not themselves inventors, were often frugal and austere men content to pay themselves 'wages' rather than to dip into their profits. Their workers were not well paid, although they were paid more than in the traditional agricultural sector of the economy, and with very low direct taxation there was an almost complete absence of public investment. With the development of canals and railways shareholders increased in numbers, and there were important changes affecting the organization of companies in the second half of the 19th century.

Early manufacturers had to demonstrate other qualities, however, besides abstinence and frugality. They had to have the ability to see an opening and the drive to exploit it. In addition, before the rise of specialization in industrial management they had to be able to supervise and manage the daily operations of their enterprises. Lastly, they had to have a flair for selling, and there were some of them, like the potter Josiah Wedgwood, whose flair amounted to genius. The great ironfounder John Wilkinson, who helped to make Britain 'iron-conscious', became a legend in his own lifetime. The story spread that some years after his death he would rise from his famous iron coffin and visit his blast furnaces again. A large crowd gathered for his resurrection. There is a personal side to early industrialization which is as interesting as the statistics. And even when firms grew in size and employers came to rely on specialized managers personal factors still counted.

So, too, however, did systems of services, including banking and transportation, without which an industrial economy cannot operate effectively. The kind of society which emerged between the mid-18th and the mid-19th centuries had new attitudes, again never completely shared, not only to work but to credit and, above all, to time. We now require an effort of imagination to get back not only the pre-industrial society, but the kind of society that developed during those crucial years of change.

ASA BRIGGS
Provost of Worcester College, Oxford 1990

INTRODUCTION

The aim of this *Companion* is to answer questions about the Industrial Revolution for those who are interested in the places, people, ideas and technological changes which helped to make Britain the first industrial nation. It is intended to be of value to the non-specialist who wants to make a deeper study of the period or is interested in the industrial archaeology of the 18th and 19th centuries. It is also written as an *aide-mémoire* for students preparing for the GCSE, A-level or similar examinations.

Like all historical events, the Industrial Revolution is subject to a variety of interpretations, and every attempt has been made to describe the present-day views on such controversial subjects as child labour and the quality of life in the urban environments of the period. Inevitably a number of decisions had to be made and problems resolved before this *Companion* could be written. The first problem was the time-scale to be adopted since there is no general consensus on when the Industrial Revolution began and ended. Fundamental changes in the British economy and increases in the rate of growth were evident between 1740 and 1780, and it was in this period that a number of technological achievements were being introduced. There had been important discoveries before 1760, such as the smelting of iron ore with coke instead of charcoal, but information was disseminated slowly and there was a time lag of several decades before these developments were widely used. The starting date 1760 is, therefore, a convenient one, although entries have been included for relevant events which happened earlier.

One hundred years later Britain had been transformed from a country with a predominantly rural and agricultural population to one with over 50 per cent of the population living in towns and cities, and an economy based on industry and commerce. Technological improvements did not cease after 1860 but by that date Britain had undergone structural, political and social changes which amounted to a revolution.

A further problem which had to be resolved was the selection of material – what to include and, even more difficult, what to discard. After extensive reading a selection was decided upon which, in addition to essential information about industrial and technological developments and the people who made these possible, also includes organizations and events which affected the lives of working people, either directly or indirectly. So, for example, the introduction of the penny post is included, as is transportation as a system of punishment. Foreign policy decisions and political figures are included only if they have a direct bearing on industry or commerce, as had, for example, the American War of 1812–14 and the activities of Sir Robert Peel.

Interest in industrial history has increased considerably in recent years, partly inspired by a greater concern for the environment and the need to conserve what remains of our heritage. The Industrial Revolution has bequeathed to us a wealth of buildings, machines and other evidence which is worth preserving. The enthusiasm for industrial archaeology, coupled with the growth of leisure and the need to promote tourism, has resulted in some remarkable schemes to preserve the industrial heritage and create living museums where people can see faithful portrayals of life in the past. This interest in the visual evidence of the Industrial Revolution has been recognized in this *Companion* by providing information about places to visit associated with the entry, whether it is an exhibit in a museum or an industrial archaeological site. In addition, books have been recommended which should be consulted for a more detailed examination of the entry. These primary and secondary sources should be of value to students, particularly now that fieldwork is being given greater significance in schools and colleges, and course work involving research is an important part of the GCSE and the Scottish Standard Grade Certificate of Education examination.

This book is also designed for readers who do not live in Britain and some entries have been included to give overseas readers points of reference to the period, such as the monarchs of the time and details of the major towns mentioned in the text.

Maps and charts showing important statistics have been included in a separate section. There are contemporary illustrations and photographs of contemporary technological achievements throughout the book. Measurements are given in both the imperial and the metric systems, and a rate of exchange of £1 = US $1.70 has been used to convert British money into American dollars. A table is provided on page 262 showing the British currency of the time with its modern decimal equivalent.

Reorganization of local government in Britain in the 1970s brought about some boundary changes, particularly in Wales, where the new counties have Welsh names. The original names have been retained in the text. However, reference to industrial archaeological sites, museums and other places of interest have been given using the modern administrative terminology.

Cross-references are used extensively. When a word that has an entry of its own appears in the text, it is printed in SMALL CAPITALS the first time it occurs in the entry.

M* denotes a museum or site which is open to the public.

There is an extensive literature covering this period, including useful introductory paperbacks published by Shire Publications. I have found the following of particular value:

P. Mantoux, *The Industrial Revolution in the Eighteenth Century* (Methuen 1964).
Phyllis Dean, *The First Industrial Revolution* (Cambridge University Press 1979).
P.J.G. Ransom, *The Archaeology of the Transport Revolution 1750–1850* (World's Work Ltd 1984).
Asa Briggs, *Iron Bridge to Crystal Palace, Impact and Images of the Industrial Revolution* (Thames and Hudson 1979).
N. Cossons, *The BP Book of Industrial Archaeology* (David and Charles 1987).

This book would never have been written without the help and encouragement of a number of people. I am particularly grateful for the support I have received from Dr Barrie Trinder, whose scholarship and constructive suggestions resulted in numerous changes to the original draft. My thanks are also due to Valerie Gallard for typing the manuscript so efficiently. Although many people have helped me in a variety of ways, any omissions, inaccuracies or other shortcomings which this book may possess are entirely my responsibility.

A

Aberaeron

A new port, with a harbour completed in 1811, the town was created on the shores of Cardigan Bay by the Reverend Alban Jones Gwynne with money he inherited. It became a centre for the manufacture of agricultural tools and SHIPBUILDING, as well as carrying on a busy COASTAL TRADE in slate, limestone, coal, timber and grain.

Visit Aberaeron, Dyfed, Wales – harbour.

Act of Parliament Authorizing Transport Developments

In order to build a TURNPIKE ROAD, a CANAL, or later a railway line not on private land (see RAILWAY DEVELOPMENT), an Act of Parliament was needed and a public joint-stock company had to be set up. Because TOLL CHARGES were to be levied, Parliament required detailed statements on the route, bridges (see BRIDGES – ROAD), AQUEDUCTS and so on. An engineer was engaged to carry out a survey and after 1793 detailed plans had to be prepared for scrutiny by Parliament. Construction costs had to be estimated, together with likely traffic, revenues, water supply and consumption (in the case of canals). Lists had to be drawn up of landowners affected who agreed or disagreed with the scheme. The Bill had to be prepared with many detailed clauses and then presented to Parliament, supported by petitions and counter-petitions. In the Committee stages of the Bill expert witnesses would be called and counsel engaged, making the obtaining of an Authorizing Act extremely costly. After three readings of the Bill in the Commons and the House of Lords, the Act received the royal assent. Any changes which might be required later could be made only if approved by another Act of Parliament.

Adulteration of Food

In the early 19th century food adulteration became a problem, mainly because of the development of an organized food industry and the need for large quantities of food in the growing towns. Adulteration of food products had, however, been evident in the 18th century. Pepper had been adulterated with various materials such as mustard husks, pea flour and juniper berries. A substitute had also been found for China tea, on which a heavy duty had to be paid; the leaves of the ash tree were dried and cured on copper plates and then mixed with real tea leaves. Indian tea was 'regaled' by collecting used tea leaves from hotels and restaurants, stiffening them with gum and tinting them with black lead.

Frederick Accum (1769–1838), a German chemist living in Britain, exposed many of the tricks of adulteration in *A Treatise on Adulteration of Food and Culinary Poisons* (1820). He revealed that pickles owed their green colour to copper; bitter almonds containing prussic acid were used to give table wine a 'nutty' flavour; the rainbow colours of confectionery were obtained from poisonous salts of copper and lead; bread was loaded with alum; and the rind of Gloucester cheese acquired its rich orange colour from the addition of red lead. The book aroused public interest and the wrath of the food industry. Frederick Accum became involved in a charge of removing pages from books in the Royal Institute library and left England hastily.

Continued adulteration caused concern among doctors, and in 1850 the *Lancet*, an important medical periodical, announced the appointment of an Analytical and Sanitary Commission with two commissioners, an analytical chemist and a dietician. Between 1851 and 1854 the two commissioners published a series of articles reporting on the extraneous matter to be found in samples of foodstuffs bought at random in LONDON shops. They discovered that 49 loaves of bread from various sources contained alum, and coffee was invariably diluted with chicory, acorns or field beet. Other researchers found that publicans put froth on beer by doctoring it with green vitriol or sulphate of iron and that cocoa powder often contained a high proportion of brick dust.

In 1860 the first British Food and Drugs Act was passed. It gave county authorities the power to appoint analysts to control the quality of food, but it was administered half-heartedly and there was opposition from the food industry. A revised Act was passed in 1872 which required counties and boroughs maintaining police forces to appoint an analyst. A large proportion did and the suppression of food adulteration had begun.

J.C. Drummond and A. Wilbraham, *The Englishman's Food* (Cape 1958).

Agricultural Engineering

The development of MACHINES for use in agriculture was slow and taken up belatedly by farmers. In the 18th and early 19th centuries production of tools and machinery for use in agriculture was small-scale and limited to blacksmiths, wheelwrights and edge-tool makers. Tools were produced to meet a local demand and improvements were often suggested by local farmers or resulted from experiments by local smiths.

Agricultural engineering gradually emerged in the 19th century as a distinct manufacturing industry, particularly in market towns such as Stowmarket, Bedford and Lincoln, where foundries grew up to meet the needs of the farmers in the region. East Anglia was one area where new developments flourished. ROBERT RANSOME started making ploughshares at Norwich in the 1780s before moving to Ipswich in 1789. His factory expanded in the 19th century until it was one of the largest in Britain. Another early foundry was started by RICHARD GARRETT at Leiston in Suffolk in 1776. Other firms included Joseph Burrell of Thetford (1770), Woods and Co. of Stowmarket (1812) and R. Hunt of Earls Colne (1824).

THRESHING MACHINERY, invented in Scotland in 1786, became widespread fairly rapidly, but other inventions such as the SEED DRILL were found on few farms until the second half of the 19th century. STEAM ENGINES were introduced to power chaff cutters, root slicers and ploughs during the 1850s and 1860s but high costs confined them to the larger farms. The rise of steam engines on the farm was quickened by the coming of the railways (see RAILWAYS DEVELOPMENT). People became aware of the practical use of steam power for the first time.

Information about new machinery filtered very slowly to individual farmers. The founding of the ROYAL AGRICULTURAL SOCIETY in 1840 provided a showplace for agricultural machinery at its annual exhibition and a testing ground for new inventions. The GREAT EXHIBITION, 1851, gave farmers and engineers the opportunity to see new agricultural machinery, including the Cyrus McCormick reaper from the United States.

By about 1860, smiths and wheelwrights were limited to repairing machinery, and manufacture was in the hands of large firms using factory methods of production.

G.E. Fussell, *The Farmer's Tools* (Andrew Melrose 1952).

Air Coursing   See Coal Mining – Ventilation

Akroydon

A Halifax WORSTED manufacturer, Edward Akroyd built a 'model' village of two parallel terraces of BACK-TO-BACK HOUSES at Copley, in the Calder Valley south of Halifax in Yorkshire, between 1848 and 1853. In 1859 he began to build a second village adjacent to his Haley Mill, to the north of Halifax. The village was designed by an architect, George Gilbert Scott, who also built the church of All Souls near the village. Akroydon, as the village was called, is laid out in a square with a cross in the centre. The stone cottages were built in the Gothic style at Akroyd's request because 'it was the original style of the parish of Halifax'. Akroyd hoped that by providing good housing he would improve the moral condition of his workforce. He also believed that the idyllic rural village of mythology was a better place to live than an industrial town.

Visit Akroydon, Halifax, West Yorkshire.

Alum

A chemical used in the textile industry as a mordant to fix and diversify natural dyes on fabrics. In the 18th century it was extracted from aluminous shales which were roasted in large heaps in the open. Aluminous slate found at Whitby in Yorkshire was roasted and works were established near the town. Aluminous shales were also found in the waste materials from coal mines and CHARLES MACINTOSH started an alum works at Hurlet, Renfrewshire, in 1797. In 1808 a second factory was started at Campsie, Stirlingshire. In 1841 nearly 5,000 tonnes (5,600 US tons) were produced in Britain, with over 3,000 tonnes (3,600 US tons) coming from Whitby. In 1845 Peter Spence (1806–83), a chemist manufacturer, took out a patent for producing alum and copperas by digesting roasted iron pyrites and burnt shale in sulphuric acid. He set up a firm at Pendleton, near MANCHESTER, in 1847 and became the largest manufacturer of alum in the world.

Amalgamated Society of Engineers

This society was founded in 1851 from a number of smaller engineering unions. The subscription of one shilling (6 US cents) per week meant that only skilled workers could afford to join. The union was a model for other craft unions which were set up in the years that followed. Its example of having a London headquarters and a full-time paid secretary was copied by the other craft unions.

American War of Independence, 1776–83

A war in which the American colonists fought for their independence from the government of Britain. The war brought additional business to the IRON INDUSTRY and to other metal industries. The market for iron increased with the demand for large quantities of munitions, but when the war ended the demand dropped. The war also destroyed the tobacco trade on which GLASGOW's prosperity rested, but fears of American competition after the war proved wrong, and trade in some goods picked up, with orders for nails and hardware from the United States.

Anglican Church   See Church of England

Anglo-American War, 1812–14

A war that resulted from strained relations between Britain and the United States during the NAPOLEONIC WARS. The British ORDERS IN COUNCIL that barred neutral shipping from trading with French ports were resented in the United States, which retaliated in 1811 by passing the Non-Intercourse Act prohibiting trade with Britain. There was also alleged backing by the British for Indian raids on American settlements. The war seriously disrupted the COTTON INDUSTRY which depended on American cotton supplies. It is impossible to separate the need for arms from the IRON INDUSTRY created by the war with America from the need created by the Napoleonic Wars.

Anglo-French Treaty, 1786 (Also known as the Eden Treaty)

An important treaty for the COTTON and WOOLLEN INDUSTRIES since it opened up the French market to British textiles, subject only to an import duty of 12 per cent. In return cotton and woollen materials made in France were admitted to Britain, subject to similar duty. The treaty benefited Britain since factories in Lancashire and Scotland could produce a grade and quantity of goods at a lower price than their French counterparts.

Anglo-Irish Treaty, 1785

A proposed treaty between Great Britain and Ireland based on the principal of reciprocity, and including the equalizing of import duties on manufactured goods. Welcomed in Ireland, the treaty was greeted in England with anger. JOSIAH WEDGWOOD took the lead, and a committee was set up in London in 1785 called the GENERAL CHAMBER OF MANUFACTURERS. It attacked the treaty before it had been approved by Parliament, and issued circulars and pamphlets. After a series of amendments which considerably modified the Bill, it was talked out at the Third Reading.

Anti-Corn Law League

An organization set up in MANCHESTER in 1838 with George Wilson as president. It was a well-organized pressure group modelled on the Anti-Slavery League; it arranged lectures, prepared and distributed pamphlets and used the facilities of the PENNY POST of 1840 to canvas support. The League was essentially a middle-class movement, the counterpart of CHARTISM. Advocates of FREE TRADE such as RICHARD COBDEN and JOHN BRIGHT supported the cause, as did many business men who saw the League as a movement towards free trade. The election of the Conservatives under SIR ROBERT PEEL in 1841 was a setback for the League, since the CONSERVATIVE PARTY was committed to defending the CORN LAWS. However, duties on many farm products were abolished or reduced and the Corn Laws continued to be under fierce attack from the Anti-Corn Law League, which was the most powerful national pressure group the country had known.

In the end it was the Irish famine of 1845 (see HUNGRY FORTIES) that was the occasion for the repeal of the Corn Laws, although if there had been no famine other events, such as a depression, would doubtless have had the same effect. Peel formed a new ministry in 1846 and, supported by WILLIAM GLADSTONE, against opposition from the agriculturists led by BENJAMIN DISRAELI, repealed the Corn Laws. The Anti-Corn Law League had been a powerful force for repeal with its skilled oratory, mass meetings and persuasive arguments.

Antiquarian Paper

In 1770 the Society of Antiquarians commissioned a print of the picture of 'The Field of the Cloth of Gold'. The picture was too large for the single sheets of paper of the time and JAMES WHATMAN was asked to make special sheets large enough to allow the picture to be printed on one sheet. Larger moulds were designed and a team of eleven people was required to make the paper, which was called 'Antiquarian' paper. There was a large demand for this paper, especially from abroad, for maps and navigation charts, and it continued to be made by hand until 1936.

Apprentices Act, 1802   See Factory Act, 1802

Apprenticeship

The STATUTE OF ARTIFICERS 1563, set out regulations for apprenticeships which had to be observed by both the master and the apprentice. The INDUSTRIAL REVOLUTION broke down these rigid regulations and destroyed the spirit of the Statute. A long technical training was unnecessary for the limited skills required to operate the new MACHINES and apprentices were no longer thought of as young people training for a skilled trade. Many paupers were taken on as apprentices at very young ages and provided with low-level accommodation and wages, as well as being subject to the strict discipline required in the mills. This abuse of the system brought attempts in 1803–4 and 1813–14 to have the Statute restored. A Parliamentary committee investigated the situation but failed to reach a conclusion, and the Statute was repealed in 1814.

Aqueducts

Bridges built to carry CANALS over valleys, roads or other obstacles. The first was built by JOHN GILBERT and JAMES BRINDLEY in 1761 to carry the BRIDGEWATER CANAL over the River Irwell in Lancashire. The water was carried in a bed of puddled clay (a mixture of wet clay and sand, impervious to water), and a number of other aqueducts were also built in this manner by James Brindley, and by other engineers after his death. CAST IRON was first used to build the aqueduct at The Holmes on the Derby Canal in 1796; other cast-iron aqueducts followed, including one at Longdon, on the Shrewsbury Canal, and the PONTCYSYLLTE AQUEDUCT, which carried the Ellesmere Canal for over 1,000 feet (305 m) at a height of 126 feet (38 m) above the River Dee. In spite of the success of cast iron, masonry and brick continued to be used. The railway age brought a need for aqueducts to carry canals over the railway lines (see RAILWAY DEVELOPMENT).

Visit Llangollen, Clywd – Pontcysyllte Aqueduct (1805).
Merthyr Tydfil, Mid-Glamorgan – Pont-y-Cafnau, a cast-iron aqueduct.
Limpley Stoke, Wiltshire – Dundas Aqueduct on the Kennet and Avon Canal, built by John Rennie.

Arbitration Act, 1800

An Act requiring arbitration in all disputes about wages, payments for equipment and the delivery or quality of goods. Two arbitrators were to be appointed, one by each of the parties. If within three days the arbitrators could not reach a decision, the matter was to be settled by a JUSTICE OF THE PEACE who had no interest in the industry concerned. A similar law was passed in Scotland in 1803. The workers were more satisfied with the Act than the manufacturers, who campaigned for its repeal. Hostility from both magistrates and employers made the Act inoperative.

Archimedes

The first successful screw-driven STEAMBOAT, built in 1838. The principle of the Archimedes screw was well known and between 1833 and 1836 patents were taken out by four men for screw propellers. Francis Pettit Smith's propeller was most widely used and it was improved on by a Swede, JOHN ERICSSON, and used on the *Archimedes*. His design was the most efficient and considered by ISAMBARD BRUNEL to be the best for ships' propellers.

Arkwright, Sir Richard (1732–92)

One of the great entrepreneurs of the INDUSTRIAL REVOLUTION. He was born in Preston, Lancashire, the youngest of a large and poor family, and was apprenticed as a barber and wigmaker. With the help of John Kay, a clockmaker, he took out a patent in 1769 for a spinning frame, later called the WATER FRAME, which enabled WARP threads to be made of cotton instead of the more expensive linen which was used. The thread was coarse, but it formed the basis of cheap cotton CALICOES, which became very popular. The frame needed more power than human muscles could provide and at Arkwright's first factory, which was a converted house in NOTTINGHAM, the rollers of the spinning machine in 1769 were drive by a HORSE GIN. With the hosiers SAMUEL NEED and JEDEDIAH STRUTT, Arkwright set up a large, water-driven mill at Cromford in Derbyshire which employed over 300 workers. In 1775 Arkwright took out a patent for carding the cotton by means of cylinders turned by water power. In 1786, with DAVID DALE, he founded the NEW LANARK mills in Scotland.

There are doubts about the inventive skills of Richard Arkwright. Claims that he had obtained details of the spinning frame illegally were made by Thomas Highs. Arkwright's genius was as a successful entrepreneur and not as an inventor or mechanic. His cotton mills were remarkable examples of industrial organization which were copied by other manufacturers. His insistence on heavy premiums for using his patents and his claims to inventions that were not his own led to the early invalidation of his patents and the anger of the textile manufacturers.

Arkwright's empire reached its peak about 1784. After that date he failed to maintain his lead in the industry. He did not use the MULE, and by 1803, his son, who was running the three mills, was producing only cheap, coarse cloth. Richard Arkwright had, however, demonstrated the profitability of warp-spinning by water power and had induced others to follow his example. He craved the life-style of a rich landowner and was knighted in 1785. At his death he left half a million pounds ($850,000), an enormous sum at the time.

Visit Cromford, Derbyshire – Arkwright's mill and industrial housing. **M***

Matlock Baths, Derbyshire – The Masson Mill.

S.D. Chapman, *The Early Factory Masters* (David and Charles 1967).
R.S. Fitton, *The Arkwrights: Spinners of Fortune* (Manchester University Press 1989).

Armstrong, William George (1810–1900)

An engineer who built the first hydraulic crane and developed swing and lifting bridges. He constructed his first hydraulic crane by converting a crane owned by Newcastle Council at the works of a friend in NEWCASTLE-UPON-TYNE in 1846. He then set up his own firm at Elswick, near Newcastle, and converted more cranes. News of the performance of his cranes spread slowly but orders were received for two at the Albert Dock, LIVERPOOL, in 1848, and other orders followed, with 142 being made between 1848 and 1852. In 1858 William Armstrong turned his attention to the application of water power to lock gates (see LOCKS). He also built large bridges including the Tyne Swing Bridge in 1876 and Tower Bridge in 1894.

Army – To Prevent Civil Unrest

The ruling class relied on troops to keep order in the industrial towns when there were riots or signs of unrest. There was a deliberate policy of distributing troops in barracks in all parts of the country during the NAPOLEONIC WARS. In 1793 there were some 21,000 troops in 43 garrison towns and by 1815 there were over 150,000 troops in 155 barracks. The manufacturing towns were also garrisons with troops available at short notice when there was unrest or strikes. Troops were used on a number of occasions to restore order but there are also records of the military taking the side of the rioters. The local militia, a volunteer force, were particularly suspect.

Artificial Fertilizers

Superphosphates were first produced at a Deptford, London, works started by JOHN LAWES in 1841, using animal bones, which were later replaced by mineral phosphate. In Scotland factories were started at Carnoustie in 1846 and Aberdeen in 1852. Ground bones were treated with SULPHURIC ACID, while in a similar process local phosphatic nodules of coprolite were used instead of bones. A factory was set up on the Suffolk marshes at Bramford in 1854 and another in Shropshire at about the same time. By 1860 exports of superphosphates were beginning and the home market was expanding. By 1870 there were over 80 superphosphate works in Britain.

Artisans (Also known as Journeymen)

The name given to people who worked at a craft or trade. In LONDON, the largest centre in the world, there were few textile workers and the chief trades were shoe-making, building, tailoring, cabinet-making, printing, clock-making and baking. Skilled workers were also found in the provinces, among them the cutlers of SHEFFIELD, the jewellers of BIRMINGHAM and the CALICO pattern drawers. Artisans were distinguished from labourers and unskilled factory workers by their greater status and economic reward. The gulf between the small master and the journeyman in psychological and economic terms was less than that between the journeyman and the labourer, which was created partly by restricted entry to trades and by one group acquiring a privileged position. Artisans were often well organized with FRIENDLY SOCIETIES, TRADE UNIONS and recognized political interests.

The FACTORY SYSTEM brought a serious deterioration in the status and STANDARDS OF LIVING of groups of artisans as the number of unskilled jobs multiplied and apprenticeship schemes were abused or abandoned by the factory masters. Technical innovations and the superabundance of cheap labour wrecked the artisans' position. In general, in industries where much CAPITAL, skill and machinery were required the artisans were transformed into skilled workers. The millwright became an engineer, the smith a metal mechanic. Where juvenile and unskilled *labour could be used, artisans were also needed but became less secure and lost much of their status.*

J.L. and B. Hammond, *The Town Labourer 1760–1832* (Longman 1978).

Artisans' Homes

Skilled artisans had houses in the better parts of towns, usually with a yard at the back. Terraces of these houses can still be found in some towns, including the Islington and Chelsea areas of LONDON. Furnishings went beyond the basic needs to include pictures, books, floor covering and chests of drawers. The front room or parlour was not lived in except on special occasions. Scrubbng, scouring and polishing kept the outside and inside of the house clean and attractive, providing a 'decent' appearance. By the middle of the 19th century these houses had water laid on and might include a WATER CLOSET.

By the 1860s the TEMPERANCE MOVEMENT had influenced public opinion to the point where new housing estates could be sold more profitably if they excluded pubs. The Artisans', Labourers' and General Dwellings Company specialized in building drink-free estates such as Shaftesbury Park, London, and the houses were enthusiastically purchased by artisans who saw them as evidence of their rectitude.

S.D. Chapman (ed.), *The History of Working Class Housing* (David and Charles 1971).

Ashworth, Henry (1794–1880)

A cotton spinner whose father John built the New Eagly Mill north of Bolton, Lancashire, in 1793. With his brother Edmund, Henry expanded the mill and bought the Egerton Mill in 1829. Three rural industrial villages were built at Turton, Egerton and Bank Top. He adopted a strongly paternalistic attitude to his workers. They had to change their shirts twice a week, attend a place of worship on Sundays, be sober and sexually moral. Education was encouraged and wages for men were kept high so that their wives did not have to work. Cottages underwent regular inspections and were of a high standard, with piped water from 1835. Community buildings included schools, a library, several chapels, a newsroom but no public houses.

He was a founder of the ANTI-CORN LAW LEAGUE and became a friend of RICHARD COBDEN in 1837. He was an advocate of peace and reform, and wrote *Recollections of Richard Cobden and the Anti-Corn Law League*.

Visit Turton, Egerton and Bank Top near Bolton, Lancashire – Industrial villages.

A. Howe, *The Cotton Masters 1830–1860* (Clarendon 1984).
B. Trinder, *The Making of the Industrial Landscape* (Dent 1982).
R. Boyson, *The Ashworth Cotton Enterprise* (Clarendon 1970).

Astbury, John (1688–1743)

A pottery worker who experimented with clays from outside Staffordshire, including pipe clay from Bideford in Devon. He also experimented with ground flint as a wash on his pots, and later as one of the ingredients, in his works at Shelton.

B

Babbage, Charles (1791–1871)

A mathematician and inventor who wrote *Economy of Manufactures* (1833) and invented a calculating machine. In 1822 he made a model of a calculating machine that could add six-figure numbers, and he was given a government grant to develop his idea. In 1836 the grant was withdrawn and the device was never made. He attempted more advanced machines but they also remained unfinished. He invented the heliograph, a signalling device using mirrors to deflect sunlight, and the ophthalmoscope, a device for examining the interior of the eye.

Back-to-back Houses

Many WORKING-CLASS houses in industrial towns were built joined to another house at the back, so that a house in the middle of a terrace had three of its four walls shared by neighbouring houses. These back-to-back houses were built for cheapness and lacked good ventilation or lighting, since there could be outside windows only at the front of the house. Communal outdoor privies and stand water taps made sanitary conditions poor. With no back gardens the street at the front of the houses was used for hanging out washing, as a playground for the children and as a social meeting place for the residents.

Back-to-back houses were built in large numbers in LEEDS, BRADFORD, NOTTINGHAM and BIRMINGHAM. For building speculators back-to-back was the most economical form of housing for the poorest end of the market. Houses had to be let at low rents, hence land and building costs had to be low, and some of the cheapest land was around the urban core area, often consisting of low-lying, ill-drained sites.

Bacon, Anthony (1718–86)

An iron merchant who converted MERTHYR TYDFIL in South Wales from a village to an important centre for the iron-smelting industry. In 1765 he leased land with rich coal and iron mineral rights around Cyfarthfa, in partnership with William Brownrigg, and BLAST FURNACES were started. In 1780 he acquired the lease of the Hirwaun ironworks and in 1782 leased the CYFARTHFA IRONWORKS to FRANCIS HOMFRAY. He made a fortune during the AMERICAN WAR OF INDEPENDENCE by supplying the British government with artillery, and by 1782 he owned four prosperous ironworks in South Wales. He also had a partnership in a large estate in Virginia. His sons inherited his wealth and works but by 1814 they had sold their interests.

Baines, Edward (1774–1848)

The nonconformist (see DISSENTERS) editor of the *Leeds Mercury* in the 1840s, he was opposed to any form of state intervention in EDUCATION and advocated the end of government grants and regulations. He published an influential booklet in 1843, *The Social, Educational and Religious State of the Manufacturing Districts*, which deplored attempts to make education compulsory' and strongly advocated the voluntary system. He and his followers were called 'voluntaryists'. The movement lost ground in the 1860s and in 1867 it had a change of heart, and from then on supported compulsory attendance and rate support for schools.

Bank Charter Act, 1844

An Act restricting the BANK OF ENGLAND to issuing notes to the value of £14 million ($23.8m) without cover in the form of bullion. Above that figure all notes were to be covered by gold (75 per cent) and silver (25 per cent). The Bank of England was to have the sole right to issue notes, although banks already issuing notes could continue to do so. The Act checked over-lending by the COUNTRY BANKS but economic crises resulted in the Act being suspended on a number of occasions. The Act provided for the ultimate supremacy of the Bank of England, although effective central bank management took years to evolve.

Banking

Since the Middle Ages, the growth of business organizations and banking reflected their interdependence. The INDUSTRIAL REVOLUTION accelerated this process of growth and the banks contributed substantially to the expansion of industry, transport and commerce in this period. In 1750 there were less than a dozen banks in LONDON; by 1793 there were nearly four hundred. Outside London the number of COUNTRY BANKS also increased rapidly. In 1784 there were 120, in 1800 there were 370 and in 1810 at least 650. Country bankers were local men of substance whose credit could be trusted. They started issuing their own notes, but in 1793 the BANK OF ENGLAND restricted its own note issue and a panic followed. A number of country banks closed down but the others continued to issue notes, which in the early decades of the 19th century were accepted on the same terms as those issued by the Bank of England.

Early 19th-century banks were weak because of lack of control over note issues and the limitation of partners to a maximum of six. In 1821 Britain returned to the gold standard, under which the Bank of England must give gold in exchange for bank notes if requested to do so. Britain had abandoned gold in 1797 and created a paper currency which was not convertible. A financial crisis in 1825 resulted in the closure of 75 country banks, and 1826 an Act was passed allowing the formation of joint-stock banks provided they were over 65 miles (105 km) from London. This Act did not apply in Scotland where banking was on a sounder footing. The joint-stock banks could not issue notes under £5 ($8.5) in value. In 1833 joint-stock banks were allowed to be formed in London without being able to issue notes and the

restriction on the number of partners was lifted.

The BANK CHARTER ACT of 1844 passed by SIR ROBERT PEEL gave the Bank of England the sole right, eventually, to issue notes. A similar Act was passed in Scotland in 1845, but during severe slumps in 1847, 1857 and 1866 both Acts were suspended. In 1854 the joint-stock banks formed the London Clearing House to facilitate the transfer of cheques drawn on the Bank of England.

L.S. Pressnell, *Country Banking in the Industrial Revolution* (Oxford University Press 1956).

Bank of England

The first English joint-stock bank, established in 1694. In 1826 the Bank of England lost its monopoly of joint-stock banking outside London and in 1833 restrictions on the formation of joint-stock banks were also lifted in London. Bank of England notes were made legal tender in 1830, but the Bank did not achieve nationwide power until after the BANK CHARTER ACT of 1844. It was and is the government's bank and the custodian of the nation's gold reserves.

J.H. Clapham, *The Bank of England: A History, 1694–1914* (Cambridge University Press 1944).

Bank of Scotland

Established in 1695, one year after the BANK OF ENGLAND. In 1704 it was the first bank to issue £1 ($1.70) notes and as Scotland was not affected by the Bank of England's monopoly other joint-stock banks were also formed. All Scottish banks have retained the right to issue notes.

Barrow-in-Furness

A town in Cumberland which was created by the Furness Railway Company. In 1840 there was only a dilapidated quay from which iron ore from inland was shipped to South Wales and Staffordshire. In 1846 the Furness Railway was opened to carry slate and iron ore to Barrow and in 1849 the railway company began building cottages for its workers. The Barrow Building Society, founded in 1848 by James Ramsden, the Furness Railway Company's engineering director, played an important part in the building of the town. Large haematite iron ore reserves were found in the 1850s and smelting began in 1859 at Barrow. In 1866 the Barrow Haematite Steel Company was the largest steelworks in Britain. It used the BESSEMER PROCESS and had the advantage of local, non-phosphoric haematite iron ore.

Other rail links were made to enable Furness ore to be taken to County Durham, and further developments, including industry, docks, a jute mill and a shipyard, increased the size of the town. Its population was only 250 in 1841 but reached nearly 50,000 by 1881. The shipyards and jute mills attracted Scottish workers and Scottish-style tenements were built to house them. The decline in demand for iron in the 1880s and 1890s was partly compensated for by the takeover of the shipyard by Vickers, Son and Maxim in 1897.

Barton Aqueduct

Built by JOHN GILBERT and JAMES BRINDLEY in 1761 over the River Irwell, Lancashire, to carry the BRIDGEWATER CANAL. The water was carried over the valley in a stone channel lined with puddled clay (a mixture of wet clay and sand, impervious to water). It was considered a great wonder and attracted many sightseers. In 1893 the aqueduct had to make way for the Manchester Ship Canal. As a replacement the swing aqueduct was designed, which is in use today.

Bastilles

One of the names used by WORKING-CLASS people to describe the WORKHOUSES set up under the 1834 POOR LAW AMENDMENT ACT. The tall brick buildings surrounded by high walls looked like prisons and so acquired the name of the Bastille, the notorious prison in Paris stormed by the mob in 1789 at the beginning of the FRENCH REVOLUTION.

Bateman, John Frederick La Trobe (1810–89)

A water engineer who built a large number of dams in Britain. He was responsible for rebuilding the embankment to form the BILBERRY RESERVOIR in 1854. He was consulting engineer to MANCHESTER Corporation in the 1850s and in 1852 GLASGOW Council retained him to advise them on water supply. He recommended the use of Loch Katrine and work began in 1856. The water had to be conveyed 36 miles (58 km) to Glasgow with nearly a third of the distance through tunnels. An AQUEDUCT had to be built across the Duckray valley and Bateman used WROUGHT-IRON rectangular tubes and CAST-IRON open troughs on the approach embankments. The Loch Katrine works were completed in 1859 and are probably his most famous achievement.

Visit South of Aberfoyle, Central Scotland – aqueduct and conduit bridges.

Bazalgette, Sir Joseph (1819–91)

The engineer appointed in 1855 to the Metropolitan Board of Works to provide LONDON with a system of SEWERS. He built major sewers parallel with the river Thames on each side of it with pumping stations at intervals. The northern sewer ran to Barking in Essex, the southern to Crossness in Kent.

Beerhouse Act, 1830

This permitted virtually any householder, on payment of a small fee, to sell beer on his premises. The number of beerhouses (also known as Tom and Jerry shops) increased rapidly, and in GLASGOW in 1840 it was estimated there was one public house to every ten dwelling houses. WORKING-CLASS life was linked to drinking customs at meals, markets, fairs, baptisms, wedding and funerals. Drunkenness was apparent in the towns every Saturday night and temperance workers estimated that in 1830 more was paid per year on drink by a family than was paid in rent.

Beer Machine

A machine patented by JOSEPH BRAMAH in 1797 by which beer and other draught liquors stored in a cellar could be pumped up to the inn tap room.

Bell, Reverend Andrew (1753–1832)

An educationalist and CHURCH OF ENGLAND clergyman who conducted a MONITORIAL SYSTEM experiment in Madras which he described in 1797 in a book, *An Experiment in Education.* Using his ideas and in opposition to the work of JOSEPH LANCASTER, the Church of England set up in 1811 the NATIONAL SOCIETY (whose full title was 'the National Society for Promoting the Education of the Poor in the Principles of the Established Church'). Bell was made its superintendent.

Bell, Henry (1767–1830)

Born in West Lothian, Scotland, he was apprenticed as a millwright but later became a builder. In 1809 he began to experiment with STEAM ENGINES in boats and in 1812 built the *COMET*. This was the first steamer to run a commercial service in Europe, plying on the Clyde between GLASGOW and Greenock. It had been intended that it should travel as far as Helensburgh where Bell had a hotel, but there was no suitable landing place and Greenock on the opposite shore was used instead, with passengers being ferried across.

In 1820 he started to operate another steamer, the *Stirling Castle*, which he part owned, between Inverness and Fort Augustus. Later, when the CALEDONIAN CANAL was fully opened, the steamer operated between Inverness and Glasgow.

Bell, Patrick (1799–1869)

A Scottish clergyman who invented a successful REAPING MACHINE in 1828. At least 20 machines were made in the next four years but scythes and sickles continued to be used on many farms, particularly for hay-making. Bell's reaping machine was pushed from behind by a pair of horses and the grain was held by horizontal revolving rods to be cut. It was then sheaved and stooked by hand. Patrick Bell was honoured in Scotland for his services to agriculture and his machines were used in Europe and possibly reached the United States. The American reaping machines shown at the GREAT EXHIBITION, 1851, stimulated interest in Bell's reaper and reaping machines in general.

R. Brigden, *Harvesting Machinery* (Shire Publications 1989).

Belper

A village in Derbyshire in which JEDEDIAH STRUTT set up a water-driven spinning mill in 1778. The North Mill, which had a huge waterwheel 23 feet (7.0 m) in diameter, was added in 1786 and the West Mill in 1795. The mills were built using tubular framework. In 1803 the North Mill was burnt down. Jedediah Strutt rebuilt the mill using a rigid, fireproof framework. A round mill was built in 1813 and was designed so that an overseer could sit in the centre and see all the workpeople on the same floor from the same spot.

Like Richard Arkwright's CROMFORD, Belper was a model for the COTTON INDUSTRY, with workers' houses, an inn, a chapel and a TOMMY SHOP. In 1785 a SUNDAY SCHOOL was added and by 1815 there were nearly 1,500 employees at the mills. In 1835 Belper was described as a handsome town 'built of hewn stone, with streets flagged with the same, in regular houses on the most commodious plans'.

Some of the houses built by Jedediah Strutt for his workers can still be seen in Long Row and The Cloisters, and some of the mill buildings, including the North Mill, remain.

Visit Belper, Derbyshire – North Mill and workers' houses.

Bennet, Henry Grey (?–1836)

A Member of Parliament who promoted Bills in 1817, 1818 and 1819 to improve the working conditions of child chimney sweeps (see CHILD LABOUR – CHIMNEY SWEEPS). The Bills did not become law and

Bennet died before an Act was passed in 1840.

Bentall, E.H. and Co.

A firm of AGRICULTURAL ENGINEERS started at Goldhanger in Essex about 1808 by William Bentall, a jobbing ironfounder and farmer. A few years later the firm moved to Heybridge, near the seaward end of the Chelmer–Blackwater Navigation, which had been completed in 1797. William Bentall's reputation grew because he knew the problems of local farmers and could design agricultural implements to meet their needs. His principal invention was the Goldhanger plough which was sold in many parts of the country. Other implements were also made. His son, Edward, designed a patent broadshare and subsoil plough with shares of chilled CAST IRON, for which he took out a patent in 1852. The firm also made general castings such as grates, door scrapers and barge wheels. Overseas sales began in the 1850s, and in the 1860s the firm provided a school, housing and reading rooms for its workers.

J. Booker, *Essex in the Industrial Revolution* (Essex County Council 1974).

Bentham, Jeremy (1748–1832)

A reformer, philosophical radical and leader of Utilitarianism who, at the time of the 1832 Reform Act, demanded manhood suffrage for all men over the age of 21. His utilitarian philosophy was expressed in 1789 in *Introduction to the Principles of Morals and Legislation*. He believed that all laws should aim at 'the greatest good of the greatest number' and each law should be judged on its usefulness. He considered that punishment was evil and could be justified only if it prevented worse evils. He attacked the penal system and the Speenhamland System (see POOR LAW – SPEENHAMLAND SYSTEM). His philosophies greatly influenced FRANCIS PLACE, SIR ROBERT PEEL and many other social reformers of the first half of the 19th century.

Bentley, Thomas (1731–80)

A LIVERPOOL merchant and DISSENTER who became JOSIAH WEDGWOOD's partner at the ETRURIA WORKS in 1766. He was responsible for sales while Wedgwood concentrated on the production side of the business. Bentley was also a social reformer who was strongly opposed to the slave trade.

Bessemer Process

A process for making a raw material, MILD STEEL, invented by Henry Bessemer (1812–98), a professional inventor. Carbon steel had been made for centuries by a number of methods and for over 100 years using the crucible method developed by BENJAMIN HUNTSMAN. The process was small-scale and expensive so it was used only where it was essential; for example, to make edge tools. Bessemer set out to make carbon steel and WROUGHT IRON, but in the event made mild steel, which superseded wrought iron and today forms the greatest portion of all steel made. Bessemer blew air through molten iron in a converter and the oxygen in the air combined with the carbon in the iron to remove it as a gas. Bessemer had made a form of wrought iron – mild steel – but without the mixture of slag which had characterized wrought iron.

His invention was taken up by the ironmasters at DOWLAIS IRONWORKS and Ebbw Vale, both in Wales, but the results were a failure. After a great deal of investigation it was found that Bessemer had used an iron free from phosphorus (phosphorus in iron makes it weak and brittle), and had lined his converter with non-siliceous refractory, which prevented phosphorus entering the finished metal. Bessemer's reputation had suffered and he decided to set up in business himself, and started using his process in SHEFFIELD in 1858. Other firms followed and steel rails were first made in Sheffield in 1860. The scope of the process was limited by the need for haematite ores which came from small deposits in Cumberland. These had to be supplemented with large imports of ore from Sweden and Spain. Bessemer steel was also brittle, but this difficulty was overcome by adding a little manganese to the molten PIG IRON.

W.K.V. Gale, *The British Iron and Steel Industry: A Technical History* (David and Charles 1967).

Bickford, William (1774–1834)

A leather merchant in Cornwall who invented the miner's safety fuse. He was distressed by the injuries and high casualty rate among local tin miners at Camborne which resulted from the system of detonating gunpowder. By the end of the 18th century the fuse was made of goose quills inserted into one another and filled with powder. William Bickford's safety fuse used powder inserted into the centre of threads of cotton as they were spinning. The fuse was covered with a layer of tar and resin to seal and waterproof it. The advantages of this method were that the timing of the burn could be measured accurately and there was less risk of damage to the fuse. The fuse made the use of explosives much safer and it became very popular with the miners.

Thomas Davey, a Methodist miner, helped William Bickford to construct the machinery for making his fuses, and a factory was built near Camborne after Bickford's death.

Big Ben

1 The nickname given to EDMUND CART-WRIGHT's COMBING MACHINE, because the early machines had a jerking motion which looked like a boxer's actions. A popular prize fighter at the time had 'Big Ben' as a nickname and the expression was transferred to the machine.

In 1793 this was the only combing machine available and some improvements were made by John Hawksley in return for a quarter of the royalties. The machine was not capable of producing the finest combings but saved an enormous amount of labour, producing even, combed fibres without short lengths and irregular ends.

2 The name given, in error, to the clock tower attached to the Houses of Parliament in London. Big Ben is the great bell which tolls the hour and it was named after Sir Benjamin Hall, Commissioner of Works in 1858 when the clock was being made. Adjoining the first floor of the clock tower is a small room in which Members of Parliament (MPs) can be imprisoned. The other buildings which constitute the Houses of Parliament were erected between 1840 and 1888 and were officially opened in 1852.

Bilberry Reservoir

A group of master clothiers near HUDDERSFIELD decided in 1836 to have eight reservoirs built to regulate the flow of the rivers Holme and Colne. The reservoirs were needed to ensure a regular supply of water to water-driven textile machinery located in the Holme valley. The Act setting up the Holme Reservoirs Commission was passed in 1837 and GEORGE LEATHER was appointed to manage the construction. The first embankment to form the Bilberry Reservoir was completed in 1839 but repairs had to be made because it leaked.

In February 1852 the embankment partially collapsed and the flood water caused extensive damage. Eighty-one people lost their lives, four mills were destroyed and 17 seriously damaged, together with dye houses, cottages, bridges and two iron foundries. Over 7,000 people became unemployed, of whom over 2,000 were children. The Commission and the engineer were found guilty of gross negligence, and widespread interest in the disaster resulted in the collection of over £30,000 ($51,000) for the sufferers.

G.M. Binnie, *Early Victorian Water Engineers* (Thomas Telford 1981).

Bill of Exchange

An instrument of credit used by early industrialists. The supplier of goods (the MANUFACTURER) sent a bill to his customer for payment in anything from 3 to 12 months' time. The debtor signed the bill and returned it to the manufacturer. The endorsed bill could now be used like a bank note and subsequent holders of the bill could make use of it by endorsing it.

Because a bill of exchange arose out of a specific transaction it appeared at the time to have a stability which a banker's promissory note did not have. The more it circulated the greater the number of guarantors of its value as cash.

Birkacre Mill

A spinning mill built by RICHARD ARKWRIGHT in 1777 near Chorley in Lancashire. Among Arkwright's partners in the venture was JEDEDIAH STRUTT. In 1779 MACHINE BREAKERS attacked this mill among others, destroyed the machinery and burned down the works. Troops were called in and Richard Arkwright placed his CROMFORD mill in a state of siege. Birkacre was not rebuilt as a cotton mill.

Birmingham

The main industrial city of the West Midlands, which was a craft centre before the INDUSTRIAL REVOLUTION, using water power from several streams including the River Rea. It partly owed its rapid growth to the fact that it was free of guild and municipal restrictions on APPRENTICESHIP and employment. For centuries enterprising craftsmen had gathered to work in the metal trades and the resulting prosperity attracted lower-paid workers from the neighbouring villages. Small workshops produced a range of metal goods and brought prosperity to the town. In 1773 the streets were lit by oil lamps and by 1790 there were about 60,000 inhabitants. Despite its prosperity many streets were without pavements in the 1790s and workers were crowded together in three-storey tenements.

The main industries included the making of guns, jewellery, pins, screws, buckles and other forms of TOY TRADE ware. Although the STEAM ENGINE was developed at the SOHO WORKS to the north of Birmingham by BOULTON AND WATT in the 1770s, it was not applied on any significant scale to industries in Birmingham until the second half of the 19th century. This was because Birmingham manufacturing was based on a few, simple, hand-operated MACHINES, the stamp, the press and die

Birmingham, c. 1850. This view from the tower of St Philip's Church (now a cathedral) looks south towards New Street, which can be seen in the middle distance. The street edging the churchyard is Temple Row and the imposing houses which line it were the homes of middle-class people. In the distance can be seen the small workshops and crowded tenements where the working people lived. A few taller factory chimneys can be seen, but large works were uncommon. Most businesses employed less than 20 workers. (*Mary Evans*)

and the skilful application of the division of labour. For example, 50 different people were involved in the operation of making buttons. In the small workshops which were more common than large factories, masters and men worked alongside one another. Working hours were flexible and the quality of life for the workers was better than in many other industrial cities.

In 1801 there were 71,000 inhabitants. The number had more than doubled by 1841 and reached 296,000 in 1861. Housing for the increasing numbers of WORKING-CLASS families in the town began being built in the second half of the 18th century with the infilling of gardens and yards behind larger properties. These new dwellings were known as 'back-houses' and gave the central area of the town a high density of population. With industrial expansion the upper storeys of the large merchants' houses were converted into workshops and the backyards were lined with workers' cottages, making tiny courts of blind-back houses. Larger houses built at the end of the 18th century were in terraces with space behind for infilling.

A report by local doctors in 1836 stated that the working population lived in 2,030 courts which contained 12,254 tenements. Most houses were three storeys high and BACK-TO-BACK. The court had a wash house, an ash pit, a privy and often one or more pig-sties. Houses built in the 1860s and 1870s in what are now the inner suburbs all had a similar layout. A tunnel between two joining terraces led to an internal court with six to eight back-houses. The front terraced houses were built back-to-back and show the ingenuity of the builders in using every piece of available land. This tradition of court development was broken by the building bylaws in the Birmingham Improvement Act of 1876.

Visit Museum of Science and Industry, Newhall Street, Birmingham – steam engines. **M***
Curzon Street Station, Birmingham – built by Philip Hardwick, 1838.

E. Hopkins, *Birmingham: The First Manufacturing City* (Weidenfeld 1989).

Birmingham Riots

In 1791 UNITARIANS in BIRMINGHAM supported the FRENCH REVOLUTION and local Anglicans (see CHURCH OF ENGLAND) were incensed. A mob collected outside a hotel where supporters were celebrating the anniversary of the fall of the Bastille. The mob ransacked the houses of JOSEPH PRIESTLEY and other rich DISSENTERS. Two Unitarian and one Baptist meeting house were burned as well as over 20 houses and shops of dissenters. Troops restored order and four men were hanged. There is some evidence to suggest tacit support for the riots from prominent TORY magistrates and other members of the Establishment.

Birth Rate

The number of live births per annum for each 1,000 of the population. There is no conclusive evidence of a rise in the birth rate in the 18th century, although economic pressures probably encouraged larger families. Good harvests in the middle of the century and economic opportunities for children to work in industry towards the end of the century may have influenced the birth rate. So may the Speenhamland System (see POOR LAW – SPEENHAMLAND SYSTEM), and increasing urbanization seems to have encouraged earlier marriage, leading to larger families.

The birth rate increased after 1750 and reached its peak in the period 1780–1820. In the 1780s it was about 37.7 per 1,000. It remained at this level until 1810, after which it fell slightly until 1840 when a sharp drop set in, falling to 22–5 per 1,000. The causes of these changes are complex but higher STANDARDS OF LIVING in the mid-19th century may have accelerated the fall.

Biscuit Ware

Unglazed earthenware or PORCELAIN which has been fired only once. Biscuit ware was made at Derby from about 1770 using earthenware with no defects. Pieces with a defect were glazed and painted and then sold more cheaply. For a time biscuit ware went out of fashion, but it was reintroduced by WILLIAM COPELAND in 1846 using porcelain. It was called Parian porcelain, since it resembled marble from the Greek island of Paros because it was usually white. In 1860 the Wedgwood factory (see JOSIAH WEDGWOOD) introduced an improved Parian porcelain.

Black Country

The region centred on BIRMINGHAM which includes South Staffordshire, North Worcestershire and Warwickshire. The Black Country took its name from the blackened buildings and vegetation caused by the smoke of many chimneys. It developed a local culture of its own with several dialects and local traditions and was particularly renowned as the home of a variety of metal industries based on Birmingham.

The region became noted in the 18th century for the intense specialization of industries within different areas. Wolverhampton, an old-established market town, was the place for locksmiths and many other MANUFACTURERS. Stourbridge was the centre for glass-making, West Bromwich made springs, Walsall manufactured buckles, spurs and horses' bits, and nails were made at Sedgley, Gornal and Coseley. These industries, carried out in small workshops, did not lend themselves to factory production and the region was distinctive for the lack of mills and of the social problems which they produced.

During the period of CANAL construction the Black Country and Birmingham formed the heart of the English canal system. Between Birmingham, Wolverhampton, Stourbridge and the Tame Valley there was a network of canals linking the area with the ports on the Humber, LONDON, the Severn estuary and LIVERPOOL.

In the early 19th century the Black Country became the principal iron-making region in England. The heathlands became the centre for BLAST FURNACES and the numerous small coal mines were interspersed with spoil heaps, workshops and rows of cottages.

A visitor in 1843 thought the whole area was an interminable village. There were still considerable areas of woodland and a few fields of barley or corn survived.

Visit Black Country Museum, Dudley, West Midlands – industrial and domestic buildings. **M***

W.H.B. Court, *The Rise of the Midland Industries 1600–1830* (Oxford University Press 1953).

Black Damp (Also called choke-damp)

Carbon dioxide gas found in coal mines which suffocated miners and could cause death if those affected were not immediately removed to fresh air. Whereas FIREDAMP (methane gas) could cause an explosion and fire, the gases generated by the explosion formed black damp, which was heavier than air and rendered unconscious anyone knocked to the ground by the explosion. Suffocation from lack of oxygen could cause death very quickly. JOHN BUDDLE estimated that about one-quarter of the fatalities from firedamp resulted from the blast and the remaining three-quarters of the deaths were due to suffocation from the gases generated in the explosion.

Blaenavon

Thomas Hill of Stafford, Thomas Hopkins and Benjamin Pratt obtained a lease in 1789 to build an ironworks in the hills north of Pontypool in South Wales. The five furnaces were built on a sloping hillside so that they could be filled easily from the top. A tall water balance tower was also built and the weight of the water was used to move goods up and down the sloping site. In 1798 there were 350 workers and accommodation was provided nearby. Some homes had been built into the arches of a viaduct carrying a WAGONWAY, but the majority of the homes were built around a square. Between 1812 and 1832 terrace houses were built with three bedrooms. The works was connected by wagonway to other iron working sites and to the Monmouthshire Canal at Llanfoist.

Visit Blaenavon, Gwent – blast furnaces, water balance tower and housing. **M***

A. Burton, *Remains of a Revolution* (Deutsch 1975).

Blanketeers

HAND LOOM WEAVERS who organized a march from MANCHESTER to LONDON in 1817 to draw attention to the bad state of the COTTON INDUSTRY. They planned to walk with blankets on their backs and a petition to the Prince Regent in their arms. Of the 600 men who left Manchester only one reached London and presented his petition. The others were dispersed by the army.

R.J. White, *Waterloo to Peterloo* (Mercury Books 1963).

Blast Furnaces

Furnaces in which iron is smelted using iron ore, limestone as a flux and coke (originally charcoal). To reach the high temperatures required a blast of air is used. In the early furnaces this was supplied by bellows worked by hand or by a waterwheel, but when steam power was developed the blast was supplied by steam pumps (see STEAM ENGINES – PUMPING). The blast furnace was the basic unit of production of the IRON INDUSTRY and the period 1760–1860 saw the decline in demand for charcoal furnaces and the development of coke-burning furnaces. The use of coal as a fuel instead of charcoal brought about changes in the location of blast furnaces and made possible larger units of production, since coke could stand a greater weight of iron ore than charcoal without crushing.

Blast Furnaces – Charcoal-Burning

The earliest BLAST FURNACES burned charcoal as the fuel. The furnace was made of stone or brick with a stone lining. It was often built on a slope to make it easier to feed in the raw materials at the top. A charcoal blast furnace could make between 300 and 700 tonnes (336 to 784 US tons) of iron per year; they usually operated from October until May and

shut down when water, used to work the bellows, was low in the summer months.

Charcoal furnaces operated in Sussex, the Forest of Dean, Shropshire and elsewhere from Elizabethan times. In Scotland there were furnaces in the Highlands, in Inverness-shire and Argyllshire. As late as 1775 a charcoal furnace was built on the shores of Loch Fyne at a place now called Furnace. Scottish furnaces had been developed because of the shortage of wood in England. The use of coke instead of charcoal brought a slow decline to the charcoal blast furnace areas and the last furnace was put out at Ashburnham in Sussex about 1820.

Visit Taynuilt, Argyll, Scotland – blast furnace, 1753.
Ashburnham, near Battle, East Sussex – furnace and forge sites.
Broughton-in-Furness, Cumbria – Duddon blast furnace.
Charlcotte, near Bridgnorth, Shropshire – blast furnace.

Blast Furnaces – Coke-Fired

The first was developed by the COALBROOKDALE COMPANY in 1709, using the local 'clod' coal which coked into large lumps and had a low sulphur content. Coke was used exclusively at this site at least as early as 1718, but until 1750 no other ironmasters used coke, although the process was widely known. Coke was used when charcoal prices rose sharply in the second half of the 18th century and the demand for iron also increased. By 1775 coke smelting was superior to charcoal smelting (see BLAST FURNACES – CHARCOAL-BURNING), and the process became widespread. Many furnaces used water power but steam power permitted the ironmasters to operate the blast furnace almost all the year, increasing output and reducing unit costs.

There were 85 coke furnaces in Great Britain in 1788 and the number grew rapidly during the NAPOLEONIC WARS to 225 in 1805. In 1820 there were only 170 furnaces, as a result of the depression, but the number increased to 623 in 1847 and about 855 in 1860. In 1849, a worker from Ebbw Vale in Wales, George Pary, invented a bell and cone device for the top of a blast furnace. This allowed the hot waste gases to be led through pipes to heat hot-blast boilers, saving energy and improving furnace efficiency. The STEAM ENGINE helped to speed the diffusion of the new process and gave the ironmasters greater flexibility in the siting of blast furnaces. Coal and ore deposits helped determined the location and some areas, such as the West Midlands, were opened up by the IRON INDUSTRY. The size of the furnaces increased, as did output – to between 1,000 and 3,000 tonnes (1,120 to 3,360 US tons) per year in 1815, and 3.7 million tonnes (4.1 million US tons) in 1860.

Visit Ironbridge Gorge Museum, Shropshire – 18th-century blast furnaces. **M***
Morley Park, near Belper, Derbyshire – blast furnaces, 1780 and 1818.
Heage, near Belper, Derbyshire – Morley Park blast furnaces, 1780 and 1818.
   Moira, near Ashby-de-la-Zouch, Leicestershire – blast furnace, c.1804.

C.K. Hyde, *Technological Change and the British Iron Industry 1700–1870* (Princeton University Press 1977).

Bleach – Paper-Making

The use of chlorine as a bleach was first introduced in Europe about 1780, and in 1792 Clement and George Taylor, papermakers in Kent, obtained a patent for using chlorine to whiten rags for PAPER-MAKING. A similar process had been developed by William Simpson at his paper mill near Edinburgh in Scotland, a year earlier. Other paper-makers experimented with chlorine, and the use of bleaching spread rapidly. Bleaching powder was manufactured by CHARLES TENNANT in 1799 and, since it could be easily transported, was used on a wide scale by paper-makers. At times mistakes were made in the amount to be added, which resulted in paper disintegrating. When properly used, chlorine helped to ease the shortage of rags since it whitened some types of dyes used in coloured rags, making them suitable for paper-making.

Bleach – Textile Industry

The traditional bleaching method for cloth was repeated immersions in sour milk (lactic acid), followed by stretching the cloth out on tenterhooks in the open fields to allow the sun to complete the bleaching process over several weeks. The whole process lasted some seven or eight months. SULPHURIC ACID plants set up by DR JOHN ROEBUCK in BIRMINGHAM in 1746 and Prestonpans, Scotland, in 1749 resulted in the replacement of sour milk by diluted acid, which halved the time required for the bleaching process. CHARLES TENNANT's plant in GLASGOW began to make bleaching powder in 1799, and as a result bleaching took little more than a day to complete. A number of specialized bleach-works started manufacturing bleach commercially but very few of the MANUFACTURERS had any interests in spinning or weaving, although some were active as dyers and printers.

Blenkinsop, John (1783–1831)

A VIEWER at Middleton Colliery, LEEDS, who in 1811 patented the rack rail and pinion system, similar to that used on mountain railways today. He placed a toothed wheel between the two running wheels to engage in a toothed rail alongside one of the track rails. His cog engine could haul a load of 94 tonnes (105 US tons) at an average speed of 3 mph (5 kph). In 1812 he successfully operated his locomotives *Prince Regent* and *Salamanca* to pull loaded coal wagons from the colliery to a STAITHE on the River Aire. This was the first steam-powered railway to operate successfully.

Blind Jack of Knaresborough   See
Metcalf, John

Blister Steel

An early form of steel which was in use before the 19th century. Bars of WROUGHT IRON were covered with pieces of charcoal and then heated intensely for several days in a charcoal fire. The bars had a blistered surface when taken from the furnace. Further heat treatment and forging converted the steel to a form suitable for textile shear blades, cutlery and instrument-making.

Block Signalling

A system for avoiding accidents on the railways. The line was divided into sections and only one train was allowed in a section at a time. Confirmation that the section was clear and no longer blocked was given by ELECTRIC TELEGRAPH, which was introduced on the railways in 1839. Previously trains were separated from each other on a line by a time interval.

Blucher

A steam locomotive built by GEORGE STEPHENSON in 1814 to haul coal on the Killingworth Colliery WAGONWAY. It ran along CAST-IRON rails and led to the construction of other locomotives, including the *ROCKET*. It was distinctive in that it was the first locomotive with flanged wheels, running on edge rails, which did not use the rack and pinion system for haulage.

Boat People

The name used for the people who lived and worked on CANAL and river boats. In the early 19th century they possibly numbered 100,000. Some boats were crewed by a man and boy, the man to steer, the boy to guide the horse. On some canals, such as the LEEDS–LIVERPOOL, the Rochdale and the SHROPSHIRE, there were many family boats, as there were on long-distance routes such as the Grand Junction. Short-haul work, where crews changed boats often, was not suitable for family boats and the system was rare in South Wales, the BLACK COUNTRY, Ireland and Scotland.

The boats were long and narrow with a small cabin space in which the family lived. The boat people formed an independent community; they intermarried and sons took unofficial APPRENTICESHIPS on other boats. Boat children never received a regular education because they were always on the move. In THE POTTERIES families often

lived in a house and on a boat. Large families in small boat cabins meant squalor and disease, with the children being exploited.

George Smith (1831–95), a Leicestershire brick-yard manager and philanthropist, started a crusade to help the boat people in 1873. In 1875 he published *Our Canal Population. A Cry from the Boat Cabins,* and as a result of his work a Canal Boats Act was passed in 1877. Local authorities were to register and inspect boats used as dwellings and arrange for the education of the children. Few local authorities bothered to register boats and George Smith considered the Act inadequate. He continued to campaign until an Amending Act was passed in 1884 ordering local authorities to carry out regular inspections.

Bonawe

In 1762 Richard and William Ford, James Backhouse and Michael Knot took a lease on Bonawe, a site on the shores of Loch Etive in Argyllshire. The ironworks they established remained in production until 1866. The ore was shipped round the coast from England and power for the blast came from a waterwheel. The BLAST FURNACE was built against a hillside so that it could be filled easily from the top. The spot was very remote and houses had to be built for the workers. They were built as L-shaped tenements two storeys high with an outside staircase to the upper floor. Large storehouses also had to be built for the ore and fuel, and a quay was constructed for loading finished iron and unloading the ore.

Visit Bonawe, Taynuilt, Argyll, Scotland – blast furnace, houses, storehouses and other buildings.

Bone China

A type of PORCELAIN intermediate between a hard and a soft porcelain. It was first developed by JOSIAH SPODE I about 1791 using kaolin, china-stone and bone ash made from the burnt bones of cattle. This mixture produced a white paste of even translucency which could be marketed at a reasonable price, mainly because little was wasted during the firing process. The translucency is the result of the formation of a glassy material by a combination of bone ash and silica.

At first Josiah Spode's bone china was known as English Cornish china, and then as Stoke porcelain. The proportions of the ingredients have not changed. This form of porcelain is made almost exclusively in England and is sometimes called English China.

B. and T. Hughes, *English Porcelain and Bone China 1743–1850* (Lutterworth Press 1955).

Bottle Oven (Also called a biscuit oven)

An oven shaped like a very fat bottle, used for all types of pot firing and also for glazing and enamelling. These traditional ovens were developed in THE POTTERIES where coal was cheap. They used 2.5 lb (1.1 kg) of coal to fire 1 lb (0.45 kg) of clay, and wasted a great deal of energy as well as polluting the atmosphere with their smoke. In the oven the wares had to be heated for 40 to 50 hours and then allowed to cool gradually. Wares being fired were usually sealed in a protective case of fire clay, called a sagger, to keep them from contact with the smoke or dust resulting from the coal firing.

Experiments were begun in the second half of the 19th century to change the fuel to gas and improve the design of the oven. The first continuous circular kiln was patented in 1858 and the tunnel kiln was introduced some 20 years later.

Visit Gladstone Pottery Museum, Longton, Stoke-on-Trent, Staffordshire – bottle kilns and working museum. **M***
Ironbridge Gorge Museum, Shropshire – Coalport museum with bottle kiln. **M***
Portobello, Midlothian, Scotland – bottle kilns.
Kilmarnock, Ayrshire, Scotland – Longport pottery bottle kilns.

Boulton and Watt

A partnership set up in 1775 by MATTHEW BOULTON and JAMES WATT. Boulton was not an engineer but was able to provide entrepreneurial ability (see ENTRE-

PRENEUR) knowledge of the market and the CAPITAL required. James Watt possessed the inventive genius and held the patent for his STEAM ENGINE until 1800. The company did not manufacture steam engines for sale; instead they acted as consultants, designers and erectors of the engines for firms using their patents. The SOHO WORKS made only those parts requiring special care in manufacture, and other parts like cylinders were supplied by JOHN WILKINSON and other ironmasters.

When a Boulton and Watt engine had been erected, the owner had to pay Boulton and Watt a third of the estimated savings in fuel costs, as compared with a NEWCOMEN engine of the same HORSEPOWER. This made the engine expensive to use and some engineers infringed the patents with 'mongrel' engines. Others built the Watt engine without paying the necessary premium. By 1800 over 450 engines were in use in various parts of the country. Of these just over 300 were rotary engines and about 150 were for pumping.

In 1795 a new partnership was formed on a new site in Smethwick. This was the Soho Foundry, operated by Boulton, Watt and Co. with Matthew Boulton, his sons, James Watt and his two sons as partners. In 1800 the original partnership was terminated when James Watt's patent expired. The firm continued to make steam engines until it closed in 1850.

Sir Eric Roll, *An Early Experiment in Industrial Organisation: Boulton and Watt 1775–1805* (Cass 1968).

Boulton, Matthew (1728–1809)

The son of a silver stamper and piercer in BIRMINGHAM, Matthew Boulton was apprenticed in his father's business and took it over on his father's death in 1759. Two years later he raised sufficient CAPITAL to start building the SOHO WORKS on Handsworth Heath where waterwheels could be turned by Hockly Brook. The products made in the factory were wide-ranging and included buttons, coffee pots, buckles, Sheffield plate and other typical TOY TRADE goods. These products were produced in small workshops in Birmingham and Matthew Boulton's innovation was to supervise the manufacture of all these various items under the roof of a single large factory. Soho was described as a complete system of manufactories, where each worker had only a limited range of work without any need to change position and tools constantly.

Matthew Boulton was a brilliant ENTREPRENEUR, arranging the capital for new developments, organizing the labour needed and finding markets for the products. His partnership with JAMES WATT began in 1775 when the intricate valves required for Watt's STEAM ENGINE were made at the Soho Works. Matthew Boulton used steam engines to augment the limited water power and in 1780 set up coining presses, making coins for overseas countries. He started making copper coins for Great Britain in 1797 and supplied machinery for the new Mint built on Tower Hill in LONDON in 1805. He was a member of the LUNAR SOCIETY and his house at Soho was the meeting place for scientists. To his workpeople Matthew Boulton was a benevolent autocrat. He knew them personally and started a sick club to which workers subscribed a small amount according to their wages.

H.W. Dickinson, *Matthew Boulton* (Cambridge University Press 1937).

Bradford

A Yorkshire woollen town which was the fastest growing town in Britain during the first half of the 19th century. Its population rose from about 9,000 in 1760 to 13,000 in 1801, 26,000 in 1821 and 106,000 in 1861. The first woollen mills were built at the end of the 18th century, with about six in operation by 1800. The town had been connected to the LEEDS–LIVERPOOL CANAL in 1774 but industry was relatively slow to develop, partly because water power was limited and also because there was opposition from the wool weavers in the area to the introduction of WORSTED. COAL MINING was developed in the last decade of the 18th century and bands of ironstone in the mines resulted in the development of an ironworks at Low Moor.

Mills increased in number in the early 19th century with the development of worsted manufacture. The town later became known as 'Worstedopolis', because of the predominance of worsted manufacture. In 1810 Bradford was responsible for 25 per cent of the West Riding's production of worsted, and by 1881, 17 per cent of the workforce was employed in the industry. The number of mills increased from 39 in 1834 to 153 in 1851, but as late as 1838 there were 1,400 hand looms in the Bradford worsted district. The introduction of the STEAM ENGINE to drive machinery had compensated for the limited water power available. New fibres, especially alpaca and mohair, were introduced and in 1857 the firm of E. Cunliffe Lister began making silks, velvets and plushes. Engineering works also developed to produce the specialist machinery required by the mills. IRISH IMMIGRANTS found work in the town, and in 1861 only just over a quarter of the inhabitants had been born in Bradford.

Visit Industrial Museum, Moorside Road, Bradford – woollen and worsted exhibition in mill.

Bramah, Joseph (1748–1814)

A cabinet maker and extremely versatile engineer who invented a variety of important products. In 1778 he designed a WATER CLOSET and then invented an improved water cock used in the flushing system of lavatories. He went on to invent a burglar-proof lock, a fire engine and a planing machine. He became interested in the manufacture of machine tools and produced a number in his LONDON workshop. In 1795 he patented a hydraulic press, which was sold for crushing oil from vegetable seeds or used for baling wool and other light articles. He applied hydraulics to other MACHINES, including one for lifting gun carriages and another for driving piles, which he supplied to Woolwich Arsenal. His achievements were extensive and he can be said to be the originator of modern hydraulic power.

I. McNeill, *Joseph Bramah* (David and Charles 1968)

A. Jarvis, *Hydraulic machines* (Shire Publications 1985).

Brandreth, Jeremiah (1792?–1817)
(Otherwise known as Jeremiah Coke)

He was the leader of the unemployed Derbyshire FRAMEWORK KNITTERS who planned an insurrection to overthrow the government in 1817. Two or three hundred gathered at Pentridge in Derbyshire (see PENTRIDGE RISING), and set off to march to NOTTINGHAM, 14 miles (22.5 km) away. No support awaited them in Nottingham and a force of troops rounded them up before they reached the city. Brandreth and three others were hanged.

Brass

An alloy of copper with zinc or another base metal. The BRISTOL brass industry began when a mill was set up at Bristol by ABRAHAM DARBY I in 1702. In the next 50 years more mills were started in the area using copper from Cornwall and calamine (zinc carbonate) from the Mendip Hills in Somerset. The region was the centre of the industry during the 18th century and brass in sheet form was used in the production of pots and pans known as 'battery ware'. It was so called because the sheet was battered under water-powered hammers.

In the Bristol area the mills were sited along the River Avon and its tributaries and at other nearby locations – Keynsham, Saltford, Kelston and Warmley. There was also a brass mill in the Greenfield valley near Holywell in North Wales and mills at Cheadle and Macclesfield in Lancashire. By the early 19th century BIRMINGHAM was the chief centre of the brass industry. The metal was used extensively in the TOY TRADE of the city. Brass continued to be produced in the Bristol area until 1927, when the Keynsham mill was closed.

Visit Keynsham, near Bristol, Avon – mill remains and weir.
Industrial Heritage Centre, Camden Works, Bath, Avon – reconstructed brass foundry. **M***
Bewdley Museum, Bewdley, Hereford and Worcester – working brass foundry, waterwheel. **M***

J. Day, *Bristol Brass* (David and Charles 1973).

Brewster, Sir David (1781–1868)

A mathematician born in Jedburgh, Scotland, who investigated the properties of light. He published a number of papers, and invented the kaleidoscope in 1819. He also wrote papers on the chemistry of light and the phenomenon of polarized light. He shared with SIR CHARLES WHEATSTONE the introduction of the stereoscope.

Bridges – Hydraulic-Powered

Bridges moved by hydraulic power were first built in the second and third decades of the 19th century. One was positioned over the Rochdale Canal in MANCHESTER and was raised when a barge passed along the canal. Another was built by J.M. Rendell at Kingsbridge, Devon, and was raised by a hydraulic pump connected to a drum round which the lifting chains were wound. A double bascule bridge (that is, a bridge with two counterpoised sections which can be raised like a drawbridge) was built in 1839 to take the railway across the River Ouse at Selby.

I. McNeil, *Hydraulic Power* (Longman 1972).

Bridges – Iron

The Iron Bridge over the River Severn in Shropshire was built in 1779 to replace the ferry. Iron castings were manufactured at the COALBROOKDALE COMPANY nearby at ABRAHAM DARBY III's ironworks. From the first the Iron Bridge was promoted as a spectacle and it was considered one of the wonders of the age by contemporaries. The single arch had a span of over 100 feet (30.5 m) and the structure weighed 384 tonnes (423.4 US tons).

In 1796 an iron bridge was opened to traffic across the Wear at Sunderland. Each of the six ribs was made of 105 wedge-shaped iron boxes fitted together. It carried traffic high above the tideway and completed a route round the coast from NEWCASTLE to Teesside. A second iron bridge over the River Severn was built by THOMAS TELFORD in 1796, 2 miles (3.2 km) north of Coalbrookdale, near Buildwas Abbey. In 1816 JOHN RENNIE built an iron bridge over the Thames at Southwark, introducing CAST IRON as a structural material to LONDON.

Many more iron bridges were built in the first half of the 19th century, particularly during the building of the railways (see RAILWAY BRIDGES AND VIADUCTS). ROBERT STEPHENSON performed a brilliant piece of engineering with his High Level Bridge between Newcastle-upon-Tyne and Gateshead, which was opened in 1849. The railway was carried over the river on a series of iron arches supported on stone pillars, and a roadway was suspended from the arches. He also built two bridges made of WROUGHT-IRON tubes over the Conway estuary and the MENAI Straits in North Wales. ISAMBARD BRUNEL used iron for the ROYAL ALBERT BRIDGE at Saltash in 1859.

Visit Ironbridge, Telford, Shropshire – the first iron bridge.
Newcastle-upon-Tyne, Tyne and Wear – High Level Bridge.
Saltash, Devon – Isambard Brunel's Royal Albert Bridge.

N. Cossons and B. Trinder, *The Iron Bridge, Symbol of the Industrial Revolution* (Ironbridge Gorge Museum Trust/ Moonraker Press 1979).

Bridges – Road

A period of major bridge construction began in the latter years of the 18th century, mainly because of the increased traffic brought about by the turnpikes and the increase in trade. The Commission for Highland Roads (1803), with THOMAS TELFORD as engineer, built 1,200 bridges in 25 years in Scotland. Other important bridge builders included ROBERT MYLNE, Thomas Harrison (1744–1829), JOHN SMEATON and ISAMBARD BRUNEL. The Iron Bridge built in 1779 (see BRIDGES – IRON) marked the beginning of the use of iron in bridge building, although stone-arched bridges continued to be built. The need for very long spans led to the building of suspension bridges

(see BRIDGES – SUSPENSION), including those across the River Tweed in Northumberland (1820) and the MENAI Straits in North Wales (1826).

Visit Dunkeld, Perthshire – bridge built by Thomas Telford, 1809.
Edinburgh, Scotland – Dean Bridge, built by Thomas Telford, 1832.

Bridges – Suspension

The first to be made in Britain were over swift-flowing Scottish rivers. WROUGHT-IRON suspension chains were patented by Sir Samuel Brown, who built the Union Chain Bridge over the River Tweed in Northumberland (1820). His links were used by THOMAS TELFORD for the MENAI Straits Bridge in North Wales (1826), and they remained unchanged until 1939. ISAMBARD KINGDOM BRUNEL built a suspension bridge over the River Wye at Chepstow in 1852, and designed another across the gorge at CLIFTON in Bristol. It was opened in 1864, after his death.

Visit Clifton Suspension Bridge, designed by Isambard Brunel in the 1820s.
Loan End, near Berwick, Northumberland – suspension bridge, 1822.

Bridgewater Canal (Also known as the Worsley Canal)

A CANAL completed in 1761 from the coal mine owned by the DUKE OF BRIDGEWATER at Worsley to MANCHESTER, 8 miles (12 km) away. The canal crossed the River Irwell by an AQUEDUCT 40 feet (13 m) high. JAMES BRINDLEY was the engineer for the canal, which was the first of many with which he was associated. The canal was an economic success, since it halved the price of coal in Manchester and the increase in demand made the canal a very profitable undertaking. A passenger service was started in 1767.

Visit Worsley, near Manchester – canal and buildings.
Dockyard Road, Ellesmere Port, Cheshire – The Boat Museum. **M***

Bridgewater, Francis Egerton, Third Duke of (1763–1803)

The landowner responsible for building a number of CANALS including that from his coal mine at Worsley to MANCHESTER, known as the BRIDGEWATER CANAL. As a young man he travelled in Europe, where he probably saw canals such as the Canal du Midi in France. He inherited the Worsley Mine in 1757 at the age of 21 but found it was poorly served by transport and was badly drained. In 1759 he obtained an Act of Parliament permitting him to cut two canals. Work started the same year with JOHN GILBERT, the Duke's agent, as resident engineer and JAMES BRINDLEY as consulting engineer.

The success of the canal, which was the Duke's personal property, encouraged him to extend it. He was also the first person to promote the use of pleasure boats on canals. He had a personal 'gondola' to entertain visitors and he encouraged his friends to put their own pleasure craft on his canal.

Bright, Charles Tiltson (1831–88)

A telegraph engineer who was responsible for laying the UNDERWATER TELEGRAPH CABLE across the Atlantic. A series of failures between 1857 and 1866 were finally overcome in July 1866.

Bright, John (1811–89)

A cotton manufacturer of Rochdale in Lancashire, who was a QUAKER and strong advocate of FREE TRADE. With RICHARD COBDEN he led the ANTI-CORN LAW LEAGUE, set up in 1839, and in 1841 he left his family business to work full time as a politician. He was a great orator and an important member of the MANCHESTER SCHOOL. He was a frequent critic of foreign policy and never hesitated to follow an unpopular line if he felt it necessary.

Brighton System   See Co-operative Movement

Brindley, James (1716–72)

The son of a farm labourer who was apprenticed as a millwright. He used his practical skills to plan a route for the BRIDGEWATER CANAL, and he decided to build an AQUEDUCT over the Mersey and Irwell Navigation at Barton to carry the canal – the first time this type of structure had been built in Britain. He built many other canals and developed the idea of narrow canals and canal boats (see NARROW BOATS) with suitable LOCKS, bridges and tunnels. In 1766 he began work on a canal joining the Trent and Mersey rivers, giving direct communication by water between the North and Irish Seas.

As a canal consultant he was in much demand, since his reputation helped canal companies to secure finances and Parliamentary approval. There were complaints that he did not pay enough attention to the many developments with which he was associated. Up to his death he was incredibly busy, and according to JOSIAH WEDGWOOD was worn out by his hard work.

H. Bode, *James Brindley* (Shire Publications 1976).

Bristol

An important port for the slave trade in the 17th and 18th centuries. In 1750 Bristol had 50,000 inhabitants and rated second to LONDON for its trade, a position it had lost to LIVERPOOL by 1801. In that year it had 61,000 inhabitants whereas Liverpool had 82,000. Bristol lacked an industrial hinterland and its harbour was shallow and inconvenient. It lagged in port facilities until the early 19th century, when the docks were rebuilt and expanded by WILLIAM JESSOP. Further improvements were made by ISAMBARD BRUNEL in 1848, but as vessels increased in size towards the end of the 19th century Bristol's importance waned, and docks were built downstream at Avonmouth. By 1861 the port had a population of 154,000.

Visit Industrial Museum, Prince's Wharf, Bristol – Manufacturing equipment and history of the port. **M***

Bristol Riots

Unrest caused by the controversy over

Parliamentary reform in 1831. Riots began with the arrival of a new Recorder of Bristol, Sir Charles Wetherall, an opponent of reform in the Commons. Public buildings, including the Mansion House and Bishop's Palace, were destroyed or damaged. A cavalry charge restored order and four rioters were executed while 22 were transported.

Britannia Bridge   See Menai

British and Foreign Schools Society (Usually known as the British Society)

Founded in 1808 by Anglicans (see CHURCH OF ENGLAND) and nonconformists (see DISSENTERS) as an undenominational organization to train teachers in the intricacies of the MONITORIAL SYSTEM. The first government grant to EDUCATION in 1833 – £20,000 ($34,000) – was distributed through this Society and its Anglican rival, the NATIONAL SOCIETY. Subsequent grants were also dealt with in this manner.

British Association for the Advancement of Science

A society founded in 1831 and based at first mainly on the activities of geologists. The society aimed to increase public interest in useful knowledge and to inspire scientific discovery. The British Association still exists and is best known for its annual summer conference.

Brougham, Henry (1778–1868) (Created Baron Brougham and Vaux 1830)

A barrister and Member of Parliament who favoured legal reforms and slave emancipation. He wished to see the new MIDDLE CLASS fully represented in Parliament and agitated for the REFORM ACT, 1832. As Lord Chancellor he supervised the passage of the Act through the House of Lords. He helped to found London University in 1828 and also gave his name to a horse-drawn carriage built for him by Robinson of London in 1830. The Brougham, as the carriage was known, was short, with a body only 4 feet (1.2 m) long, giving room for two people. Larger versions were built later.

Brunel, Isambard Kingdom (1806–59)

Probably the greatest engineer of the INDUSTRIAL REVOLUTION. He was educated in Britain and France and set up as a civil engineer in 1830. In 1833, at the age of 27, he was appointed engineer to the Bristol–London Railway, later known as the Great Western Railway. He carried out some superb engineering work on the line, including the Box Tunnel and the terminus building at Bristol Temple Meads.

He persuaded the GREAT WESTERN RAILWAY COMPANY to build a steam boat to travel from Bristol to New York. The boat, the *GREAT WESTERN*, first sailed to New York in 1838 and made more than 60 crossings in the next eight years. A dry dock was built at Bristol for a sister ship, the *GREAT BRITAIN*, which was built with a screw propeller instead of paddles. His last great venture was the *GREAT EASTERN* a mammoth undertaking. Its launch on the Thames in 1857 took ten weeks, because the directors would not sanction the building of the hydraulic launching gear Isambard Brunel had designed.

In 1859 Brunel built a railway bridge, the ROYAL ALBERT BRIDGE, across the Tamar at Saltash between Devon and Cornwall. It was his last completed work.

Brunel conceived and executed his work on a grander scale than any other engineer, and at times this was a weakness. It resulted in the broad gauge (see RAILWAY GAUGES) of the railways he built; the more common smaller gauge was adopted nationally in 1846.

Visit Devon – Royal Albert Bridge across the Tamar.
Starcross, near Exeter, Devon – pumping house built by Brunel.
Great Western Railway from London to Bristol – numerous bridges, viaducts and other buildings.

L.T.C. Rolt, *Isambard Kingdom Brunel* (Longman 1957; Pelican 1970).

Brunel, Sir Marc Isambard (1769–1849)

The father of Isambard Kingdom Brunel and a well-known engineer. He worked in the United States for some years and submitted a winning design for a new Congress building in Washington, but the design was never used. He patented a number of inventions including an engine for a paddle steamer and a circular knitting machine. In 1801 he was commissioned to design equipment capable of producing at least 100,000 wooden pulley blocks per year for the Royal Navy. The machines he designed for this task were made by HENRY MAUDSLAY and the work was successfully completed. In 1843 he finished the dangerous task of boring the THAMES TUNNEL, the first tunnel in the world to be built in soft clay under a river.

Visit Science Museum, London – pulley block making machinery. **M***
Rotherhithe, London – Brunel's Engine House at the entrance to the tunnel, containing a pumping engine and other exhibits. **M***

R. Tames, *Isambard Kingdom Brunel* (Shire Publications, 1978).

Buchanan, Archibald (1769–1841)

The son of John Buchanan, RICHARD ARKWRIGHT's first agent in Scotland. He served his APPRENTICESHIP at the CROMFORD Mill, and he and his brothers James and George set up as merchants and dealers in cotton yarn. In 1785 the brothers built a cotton mill at Deanston in Perthshire and were concerned with a second mill built at Ballindallock in Stirlingshire in 1789. In 1793 they joined with James Finlay and Co. (see KIRKMAN FINLAY) to start more cotton mills.

Budding, Edwin Beard (1796–1846)

The inventor of the LAWN MOWER, which was first manufactured on a large scale by ROBERT RANSOME in 1832. The 19-inch (482-mm) roller mower was similar to those used today, using the same principle of rotary blades.

Buddle, John (1773–1843)

The son of John Buddle (1743–1806), who became an engineer and colliery VIEWER like his father. As an expert on COAL MINING in the North East he dominated the coal industry of that region in the first half of the 19th century. He was part owner of at least five collieries and introduced the first air pump in 1807. He was a major witness before a number of Select Committees and became Secretary of the Northumberland and Durham Coal Owners' Association in 1805. At the same time he also retained the respect of the miners, mainly because he shared their risks underground and helped to improve safety.

A UNITARIAN, he founded schools in colliery villages and a chamber music society in NEWCASTLE. His engineering expertise was also used outside coal mining. He was involved with the building of Seaham Harbour, Northumberland, in 1823–31 and improvements to Blyth Harbour, Northumberland, in 1837. In 1832 he surveyed the proposed route of the Durham and South Shields railway.

Burrell, Charles and Son

An AGRICULTURAL ENGINEERING firm started by Joseph Burrell in 1770 at Thetford in Norfolk. By 1800 a number of cultivating and sowing MACHINES were being made. The firm became famous for its STEAM ENGINES, which were used for agriculture in may parts of Britain. The first engine was a portable made in 1848, the same year in which the firm also built its first combined threshing and finishing machine (see THRESHING MACHINERY). In 1857 the firm demonstrated a portable steam engine for ploughing (see STEAM ENGINES – PLOUGHING). A steel windlass and tackle were attached to the engine, which was equipped with a winding drum. For the next 60 years steam ploughing was carried on sporadically throughout the country, often with a Burrell steam engine.

Buss, Frances Mary (1827–94)

A pioneer of education for girls, who was educated at Queen's College (see

GOVERNESS). She became headmistress of the North London Collegiate School in 1850 and set new standards in girls' EDUCATION.

Butler, Josephine (1828–1906) See
Prostitution

Butterley Company

An ironworks founded in 1790 near Belper in Derbyshire by BENJAMIN OUTRAM and WILLIAM JESSOP. From the first the firm was active in supplying CAST-IRON rails for TRAMWAYS, and ironwork for bridges, building and dockyards. During the NAPOLEONIC WARS the foundries turned out cannon and shot. After the war, STEAM ENGINES and water pipes were built and by 1831 Butterley was a large, integrated concern with iron mines, collieries, limestone quarries, four furnaces and a foundry. Nearly 1,500 men were employed and a model village was built between 1834 and 1860, called Ironville. In the 1860s, among its contracts was one for the WROUGHT-IRON work for St Pancras railway station.

Visit Ironville, near Alfreton, Derbyshire – model village.

C

Cadbury, John (1801–89)

A QUAKER who served an APPRENTICESHIP in the grocery business. In 1824 he took over the tea and coffee shop in BIRMINGHAM set up by his father, Richard. In 1831 he began to manufacture cocoa and chocolate, experimenting at first with a pestle and mortar. In 1847 he took his brother Benjamin into the workshop and the firm became Cadbury Brothers. The building at Bridge Street, Birmingham, had roasting ovens, a mill and other machinery. There was also a packing room where 20 girls worked. John Cadbury retired in 1861, handing over the business to his sons. George Cadbury, one of the sons, began to build the factory at Bournville in 1879, and in 1895 started to lay out a 'model village' for his work people.

I.A. Williams, *The Firm of Cadbury, 1831–1931* (Constable 1931).

Cage

The metal container in which miners and coal travelled up and down the mine shaft. The first cages were introduced in the 1840s and were held steady by guide rails down the side of the shaft. Before cages were introduced miners travelled up and down by grasping chains to which loops were attached for support.

Caisson

1 A water-tight chamber to hold water so that a canal boat could float in it to be lifted or lowered vertically or along an INCLINED PLANE.

One solution to moving canal boats from one water-level to another was to float the boat in a large water-tight caisson which was then raised or lowered using a counterbalance. A number of ingenious methods were adopted based on caissons. One of the earliest was built in 1796 on the Somerset Coal Canal at Combe Hay, where a caisson was raised vertically in a pit, using buoyancy. The experiment failed because the supporting masonry collapsed under pressure from the surrounding earth. On the Chard Canal (1842), caissons were employed to float the boats along three inclined planes. On the Monkland Canal in Lanarkshire an inclined plane was built at Blackhill in 1857, and the empty boats returning to the coal mines were floated in two caissons, which were carried along the inclined plane on a railway line. The last inclined plane lift to work in Britain was at Foxton on the Grand Union Canal. It used two counterbalanced caissons, each capable of floating a pair of NARROW BOATS, and it worked between 1900 and 1910.

2 A strong chamber for keeping out water while foundations of a bridge are built.

Chambers using compressed air were first used for constructing foundations in marshy ground by Sir Thomas Cochrane in 1830. Work was done in a special chamber at the bottom of the caisson, kept at the right pressure by compressed air. The workers were taken in and out of the chamber through an air lock. ISAMBARD BRUNEL used caissons for the building of the ROYAL ALBERT BRIDGE in 1859.

L.T.C. Rolt, *Navigable Waterways* (Longman 1969).

Caledonian Canal

A survey for a CANAL was made by JAMES WATT in 1773 to join Inverness and Fort William through the Great Glen. The cost killed the scheme until the NAPOLEONIC WARS, when its strategic value in providing a sea passage for northern Scotland without risk from storms or French privateers became an important consideration. THOMAS TELFORD surveyed the route, which consisted of 20 miles (32 km) of hilly country requiring a number of LOCKS. The canal was opened in 1822 but was not fully completed until 1847.

Visit Corpach, Highland Region – entrance locks.
Glen Loy, Mount Alexander, Torcastle, Highland Region – aqueducts.

Calico

A plain white cloth imported from Calicut in India in the 18th century. A duty of 6 pence (3 US cents) per yard (0.91m) had to be paid on the cloth, which British spinners wanted to avoid by making the cloth themselves. RICHARD ARKWRIGHT'S WATER FRAME made it possible to make calico using a cotton WARP, whereas previously it could be made only with a linen warp, which made it inferior to the import.

Calico, a cotton dress-fabric, was printed by using patterned rollers to which the dye was applied by hand. The drive shaft for the rollers can be seen on the right connected to the machinery by a number of huge cogs. The rollers of the machine on the left have a belt drive also operated by the drive shaft from the steam engine. (*Elton Collection: Ironbridge Gorge Museum Trust*)

JEDEDIAH STRUTT, Richard Arkwright and some NOTTINGHAM cotton spinners successfully promoted an Act in 1784 known as the Calico Act, to limit the duty on British-made calico to 3 pence (1.5 US cents) per yard (0.91m) when printed.

Canal Association

An Association set up in 1855 to give the waterways a sense of unified purpose. It was founded under the leadership of the Aire and Calder Navigation and until its formation there had never been a national waterways body. The Association became a permanent organization to watch railway legislation and promote canal interests. In 1858 there were 40 members including some of the railway-owned CANALS. Sub-committees investigated aspects of canal management and the standardization of bylaws. The Association lasted until the canals were nationalized in 1948.

Canal Carrier Acts, 1845, 1847

Acts passed to help canal companies to compete with the railways. The 1845 Act made it possible for the companies to act as carriers as well as providing the routes, the idea being to strengthen the canal system by allowing more co-operation and amalgamation. The 1847 Act allowed companies to borrow money to set up a carrying department, so that they could provide an alternative service to the railways.

Canal Mania

The first CANALS produced large profits for the owners and shareholders and as a result people rushed to speculate in canal shares, producing a canal mania in the last decade of the 18th century. Between 1791 and 1796, 51 new canals were authorized by Parliament, and before long central England had a network of inland waterways. Because of speculation the date and place of promotion meetings were kept secret for as long as possible, so that a limited number of people 'in the know' could buy up all the shares. Some values doubled in a week and many people buying shares borrowed heavily

from banks. The war with France in 1793 and the failure of a number of banks dampened speculation, which in any case was less evident in Scotland.

Canals

The first canal in England was built to carry coal from ST HELENS to LIVERPOOL. It was a navigable cut, paralleling the course of the SANKEY BROOK NAVIGATION and drawing its water supply from it. It was opened in 1757 and was eventually joined to the Mersey by a LOCK in 1762. The building of the BRIDGEWATER CANAL in 1759 was the beginning of the canal era. By the end of the century a network of canals covered the Midlands and the North of England. After 1768 BIRMINGHAM was able to receive and send goods overseas by water. In Scotland the Forth and Clyde Canal was started in 1768 and others quickly followed. By the 1820s the canal network carried a large amount of trade, including coal, timber, grain, limestone and manufactured goods. In addition some canals provided passenger services. Canals were still being built in the 1830s, including the Birmingham and Liverpool Junction Canal and the Macclesfield Canal.

Canal construction was not uniform. Wide canals were built north of the rivers Trent and Mersey, with narrow ones in the Midlands where water supply was more difficult. Where gradients were steep and money scarce, as in Shropshire and the South West, smaller TUG-BOAT CANALS were built. Lack of uniformity made it necessary to trans-ship long-distance cargoes and the canal network was never an integrated system. Early canals tended to follow the contours of the land, whereas those built later were more direct and often involved flights of LOCKS.

Freight did not desert the canals when a railway was opened. By lowering tolls canals were able to compete with the railways. Many were bought by railway companies and allowed to decline, although some were promoted – if only to compete with rival railway companies. Some, such as the Aire and Calder, remained independent, but although freight continued to be carried on all the canals during this period, maintenance was poor and the network stagnated.

Visit Kennet and Avon Canal Centre, Devizes, Wiltshire – exhibition. **M***
Gloucester – National Waterways Museum. **M***

L.T.C. Rolt, *Navigable Waterways* (Longman 1963).
P.J.G. Ransom, *The Archaeology of Canals* (World's Work Ltd 1979)
P.L. Smith, *Discovering Canals in Britain* (Shire Publications 1989).

Canals – Contribution to Economic Growth

The most important commodity carried on the CANALS was coal. The DUKE OF BRIDGEWATER said that a canal would prosper if it had 'coals at the heels of it', and the most prosperous canals were those linking coal mines with towns and cities along their routes, such as the BRIDGEWATER, the TRENT AND MERSEY and the Coventry cànals. Canals allowed coal to reach the consumers at lower prices, which reduced costs to MANUFACTURERS and made goods cheaper to produce. There were also large savings in manpower and HORSEPOWER. A single horse could drag 50 tonnes (56 US tons) along a canal, 30 tonnes (33.6 US tons) along a navigable river, 8 tonnes (8.96 US tons) along iron rails and 2 tonnes (2.2 US tons) on a macadam road.

The second most important commodity carried was limestone, which was used as a flux in smelting iron, or burned in kilns to produce the lime used as fertilizer or mixed with mortar to make cement. Limestone was important on the Peak Forest Canal and the LEEDS–LIVERPOOL CANAL, among others. Timber was carried on the canals, and in agricultural areas corn and other grains were carried to feed the industrial towns of Lancashire, the Midlands and Central Scotland. In areas with ironworks, such as South Wales and the Midlands, iron was carried on the canals, while the Trent and Mersey, Staffordshire and Worcestershire canals carried china clay, flint, pottery and glass.

The canals also carried merchandise such as shop goods and parcels. These were transported in FLY BOATS by haulage firms including PICKFORDS. These lightly loaded vessels were hauled day and night by relays of horses and operated to a timetable.

M.E. Ware, *Canals and Waterways* (Shire Publications 1987).

Canals – Passenger Traffic

Passenger traffic on canals started in 1767 when converted barges were used on the BRIDGEWATER CANAL between Manchester and Altrincham. The service was later extended along the full length of the canal. In Ireland passenger services were started on the Grand Canal in 1780 and in Scotland passengers were carried on sections of the FORTH AND CLYDE CANAL in the 1780s. Other canals also carried passengers, and road coaches connected with some of the services. A STEAM BOAT service was started from Inverness to Fort Augustus on the CALEDONIAN CANAL in Scotland in 1820, and in 1822 steamers between GLASGOW, Oban, Fort William and Inverness used the Crinan and Caledonian canals en route. On the Paisley Canal in the 1830s long, light passenger boats were introduced to travel at speeds about 10 mph (16 kph). On the Forth and Clyde Canal swift, horse-drawn passenger boats were introduced in 1828 and the journey from Glasgow to Falkirk, a distance of 24.5 miles (39 km) took three hours.

Passenger boats were more successful when linked to river services. There were services from 1797 on the Cromford Canal between Cromford and NOTTINGHAM, and this service provided a connection along the River Trent to Gainsborough and Hull. In 1830 two fast passenger boats were used on the Knottingley–Goole Canal, but some areas, such as South Wales and the English Midlands, had few passenger services compared with the number offered in Central Scotland and North West England.

Canal passenger traffic ended when it faced competition from the railways, although horse-drawn passenger boats were still running on the Bridgewater Canal in the 1860s, and steamer services continued on the Crinan Canal until 1929 and on the Caledonian Canal until 1939.

Canals – Railway Competition

Passenger services on the CANALS were quickly withdrawn when the railways were built but freight traffic, especially heavier goods, was not affected so badly, and if the tolls were reduced traffic often increased. There was, however, the loss of lighter merchandise and parcels which were transferred to the railways. The CANAL CARRIERS ACT, 1845, enabled canal companies to act as carriers, and railway companies began buying canals or merging their companies to provide a joint service. A few canals were filled in and converted into railways, such as the Croydon Canal in south LONDON, with West Croydon station built on the site of the canal basin. Some canals, such as the Grand Junction, retained their independence and part of their freight traffic.

Canal Towns

Towns which owed their importance and growth to the building of CANALS. They became established at points where the canals joined the river navigations. They were distinctive settlements with a number of common features. Normally basins, LOCKS, quays and warehouses were constructed close to the junction of the waterways with cottages for the workpeople. To service the boats there were also smithies, boatyards and rope walks. Some of the towns became popular resorts, with hotels, flower gardens and regattas to attract visitors.

At Runcorn, where the traffic from the BRIDGEWATER and TRENT AND MERSEY CANALS reached the Mersey, quays, basins and warehouses were constructed, and for a time it was a fashionable bathing resort. Stourport-on-Severn in Worcestershire developed from a hamlet into a town after the construction of a canal basin in 1768 linking the Staffordshire and Worcester Canal with the navigable River Severn. Like Runcorn, Stourport was a resort for a time. At Shardlow in Derbyshire, near the junction of the Grand Trunk Canal with the River Trent, a trans-shipment point grew up where goods were moved between river and canal craft. Basins and warehouses and then buildings where vessels could be serviced were constructed and a canal village grew up, distinct from the original one.

A deep-water channel from the River Aire to the River Ouse at Goole was built in 1826 and the company which owned it, the Aire and Calder Navigation Company, created a new town around two wet docks. The streets were wide, there were spacious bonded warehouses and low terraces of houses. Cities such as BIRMINGHAM, MANCHESTER and Oxford also developed important functions as canal towns, with dock and warehouse facilities as well as industrial growth close to the canals.

Visit Stourport-on-Severn, Hereford and Worcester – warehouses and merchants' homes.
Shardlow, near Derby – wharves, warehouses and basins.
Ellesmere Port, Cheshire – The Boat Museum. **M***

J.D. Porteous, *Canal Ports: The Urban Achievement of the Canal Age* (Academic Press 1978).

Canal Tunnels

To build the CANAL network, tunnels totalling 45 miles (72 km) in length had to be made. They had to be both horizontal and straight, and shafts had to be dug to provide ventilation. Work proceeded slowly – the Standedge Tunnel in the Pennines, 5,698 yards (5,210 m) long, took 17 years to complete. Tools were simple and the only lighting was by candles. Brick was used for the lining and early tunnels had no towpath, being just wide enough to take the NARROW BOATS. Later, towpaths were made only through short tunnels; where there was no room for a horse, chains or wire were placed on the walls so that boatmen could haul themselves along. Before STEAM BOATS appeared, LEGGING or SHAFTING were common ways of moving the boats through the confined space of the tunnels.

Tunnels passing through mining regions sometimes suffered from subsidence and maintenace was a constant problem. A tunnel was constructed on the GRAND TRUNK CANAL

(Trent and Mersey) at Harecastle in Staffordshire in 1775. It was 2,880 yards (2,633 m) long but had no towpath, and was for single-line traffic. As the freight carried on the canal increased the tunnel became a bottleneck. THOMAS TELFORD built a second tunnel between 1824 and 1827, using bricks made on the spot, and pumping water out of the rocks with a STEAM ENGINE. The new tunnel allowed only one boat at a time but it did have a towpath.

Visit Blisworth Tunnel, North-amptonshire – the longest canal tunnel still in use.
Dudley, West Midlands – Dudley tunnel.
Marsden, West Yorkshire – Standedge canal tunnel.
Otley, West Yorkshire – Bramhope tunnel memorial.

Canning

The use of tin plate for food canning was patented by Peter Durand in 1810. His invention was used by BRYAN DONKIN, an inventor and engineer, who, with partners, set up a cannery in Bermondsey. The cans were sealed with solder and the firm supplied preserved meat and soup to the British Navy during the ANGLO-AMERICAN WAR, 1812–14. The industry grew, and heat sterilization was carried out in baths of boiling calcium chloride solution after 1841. Canning was done by hand and in the 1840s an expert canner could fill and seal 60 canisters per day.

Capital

The stock of money which is required for developing and carrying on a business. In the late 18th century the demand for capital increased as the simple and cheap machinery, as well as the accommodation required to start up a business, gave way to more advanced machinery, STEAM ENGINES as a source of power and specially designed buildings where production could take place.

In the early days of the INDUSTRIAL REVOLUTION it was possible to set up a business with relatively little capital. ROBERT OWEN, for example, started with £100 ($170) borrowed from his brother, and with this he went into partnership with a mechanic. The capital required by the early industrialists was not obtained by forming joint-stock companies as it would be today. Until the middle of the 19th century there were no laws to protect individual investors, to ensure that their liability was limited to the amount they invested. To obtain sufficient capital, businessmen formed partnerships and capital was acquired from the savings of a few wealthy landowners or built up by the industrialists from profits.

The most intensive capital investment was made in the cotton textile spinning industry (see COTTON INDUSTRY) as a result of technological changes and increased demand. There was also considerable capital investment in the IRON INDUSTRY. For example, the DOWLAIS WORKS was started in 1760 with a capital of £4,000 ($6,800). This was obtained from investors who became partners in the company. Most coke furnaces required individual investments of over £1,000 ($1,700), a very large sum of money at that time.

In the 1830s and 1840s heavy industry, the railways and public utilities needed large quantities of capital and it was then that joint-stock companies began to flourish.

Cardiff

A relatively small settlement in the 18th century with a population in 1801 of 1,800. The building of the GLAMORGAN CANAL in 1794 made Cardiff the chief outlet for the iron and coal of the inland mines and ironworks, and by 1841 the population had grown to more than 11,000. The first dock was built in 1839 and the Taff Valley Railway from MERTHYR TYDFIL provided another means of communication with the inland valleys after 1841. As trade expanded so did the need for banks, insurance offices, warehouses and additional dock space. The East Dock was opened in 1859, and by 1861 the population had reached 33,000, making Cardiff the most important town in Wales.

Visit Bute Street, Cardiff – Welsh Industrial and Maritime Museum. **M***
Cathays park, Cardiff – National Museum

of Wales with coal mine equipment and other industrial displays. **M***

Carpenter, Mary (1807–77)

A penal reformer who opened a RAGGED SCHOOL in BRISTOL in 1846. She wrote *Juvenile Delinquents* in 1853, which helped to change the law so that magistrates could send children to reformatories instead of prisons. She started her own reformatory in 1852.

Carron Ironworks

Three men were responsible for founding this Scottish ironworks. They were SAMUEL GARBETT, a MANUFACTURER from BIRMINGHAM, JOHN ROEBUCK, a businessman, and William Cadell, a local ironmaster. Samuel Garbett was the mastermind and he carefully selected a site in 1759 near the Firth of Forth, with water power and close to coal, iron and limestone. The first two BLAST FURNACES were lit in 1760 and the main business was casting, with the cannon as the chief product. Bar iron was imported to be used at ROLLING MILLS at Cramond for making into nails. The AMERICAN WAR OF INDEPENDENCE gave a new impetus to the gun trade, and the carronade, a short cannon with a big bore, was made in large numbers after 1778. Other products included agricultural implements, household utensils, stoves, kettles and fire grates. In 1792 about 2,000 people were employed and the furnaces consumed 800 tonnes (896 US tons) of coal, 400 tonnes (448 US tons) of iron ore and 100 tonnes (112 US tons) of limestone per week.

During the NAPOLEONIC WARS sales of ordnance increased substantially, and even in the slump which followed the war the Company was still making a profit through contracts with the East India Company and the armed forces. In 1829 there were four blast furnaces with an output of 300 tonnes (336 US tons) per week. The firm's trade was depressed after the railway boom (see RAILWAY – IMPACT ON THE ECONOMY), and faced competition from new ironworks in the West of Scotland and around MIDDLESBROUGH. New and more efficient furnaces were erected in the early 1870s and further improvements were made in the 1880s, with a large extension in 1883. By the beginning of the 20th century the firm was making gas appliances, cooking apparatus, building materials and a range of foundry goods.

Visit Larbert, Stirlingshire – Carron Ironworks.

R.H. Campbell, *Carron Company* (Oliver and Boyd 1961).

Cartwright, Reverend Edmund (1743–1823)

The younger son of a NOTTINGHAM gentleman, Edmund Cartwright became a country parson. In 1785 he invented a weaving machine which could be operated by horses, a waterwheel or a STEAM ENGINE. The POWER LOOM was produced in large numbers in the following decades and brought unemployment and much hardship to the HAND LOOM WEAVERS. In 1791 a MANCHESTER mill was burned down after installing a few of Cartwright's looms as an experiment, and Cartwright was forced to close his own works at Doncaster and move to London to continue with his inventions. He was eventually given a grant of £10,000 ($17,000) by the government and retired to farm in Kent.

Cartwright, Major John (1740–1824)

The founder of the HAMPDEN CLUBS and elder brother of EDMUND CARTWRIGHT. He undertook evangelical tours in 1812, 1813 and 1815 to the industrial North and to Scotland to promote support for reform. He opposed any incitement to damage property and believed that reform would come by means of the MIDDLE CLASSES. He obtained signatures for his reform petitions and sowed the seeds for provincial Hampden Clubs. These grew rapidly in 1816, but he was remote from the WORKING-CLASS reformers and out of touch with those who advocated active demonstrations and more radical measures. The movement gradually faded away as more militant leaders came forward.

Cassimere Cloth

A fine woollen cloth introduced in a patent taken out by FRANCIS YERBURY in 1766. This light-weight cloth required a very fine yarn which was produced in the West of England, making that region's reputation for woollen cloth. The material became popular at the end of the 18th century, but demand declined in the first decades of the 19th century.

Cast Iron

An iron alloy containing carbon. It is a crystalline metal, easily melted and capable of being cast molten into moulds, the shape of which it takes when cold. It cannot be forged, rolled or shaped either hot or cold, nor can it be welded. It will stand heavy crushing loads but it is brittle and poor in tension. BLAST FURNACES produced cast iron and in that form it was poured into moulds to make firebacks, household utensils, cannon and small arms. Much of the machinery of the early 19th century was made of cast iron. It was also used for iron bridges (see BRIDGES – IRON), frames for buildings and the pipes of SEWER and water systems.

Catch Me Who Can

A steam locomotive built by RICHARD TREVITHICK. During the summer of 1808 he rented a piece of ground at what is now Euston Square in LONDON, erected a high fence and laid down a circular track. The engine pulled trucks and Trevithick charged the public a shilling (8 US cents) for a ride at 12 mph (19 kph). Track trouble caused many breakdowns and it was regarded by the public as a stunt. After the show closed Richard Trevithick abandoned any interest in developing a locomotive.

Catholic Emancipation Act, 1829

The Act gave Catholics (see ROMAN CATHOLICISM) equal civil rights with other religious groups. They could become Members of Parliament and hold public office, except as Lord Chancellor or Viceroy of England. In 1836 a Marriage Act allowed Catholics and nonconformists (see DISSENTERS) to be married in their own churches. Previously, only CHURCH OF ENGLAND clergy had been able to marry people legally.

Cavendish, Henry (1731–1810)

A scientific investigator of electricity who spent most of his time and his considerable fortune on his experiments. He successfully exploded oxygen and hydrogen electrically to produce water, an experiment which was the first event in atomic science. The Cavendish Laboratory in Cambridge is named after him.

Census of Population

A census carried out every ten years since 1801, except for 1941 (during the Second World War). The first census was so successful that its scope was subsequently increased to give a great deal of information about 19th-century society. The census highlighted the growth of the industrial towns and of the shift from a rural to an urban society.

From 1841, census returns were drawn up by enumerators who wrote the information on printed sheets, household by household. The enumerators' returns cannot be made public for 100 years, which means that at the present time they are available for 1841–81. These returns provide a basis for enquiry into the social conditions of Victorian towns and the domestic lives of the people. The returns for 1841–81 are mainly on microfilm and can be found at county and city record offices and larger public libraries. Photocopies of specific pages can be purchased from the Public Record Office in London.

J. West, *Town Records* (Phillimore 1983).

J.S.W. Gibson, *Census Returns (1841–1881) on Microfilm: A Directory to Local Holdings.* (Federation of Family History Societies 1986).

Chadwick, Sir Edwin (1800–90)

The self-educated friend of JEREMY BENTHAM. He joined the Poor Law Commissioners in 1832 and was largely responsible for the evidence collected to form the basis of the POOR LAW

AMENDMENT ACT, 1834. The Act was identified with Edwin Chadwick, who became secretary to the three Commissioners with responsibility for operating the new Poor Law. In 1842 he presented the *Report of the Poor Law Commissioners into the Sanitary Condition of the Labouring Population of Great Britain*. This report brought into the spotlight the terrible domestic conditions of the workers in the industrial towns, country towns and villages. A Royal Commission called the HEALTH OF TOWNS COMMISSION was set up under Chadwick's guidance, which investigated 50 towns and produced reports in 1844 and 1845.

In 1848 Edwin Chadwick headed the Board of Health and had to deal with the CHOLERA epidemics of that year and 1849. The Board was attacked by local authorities and Chadwick was suspected of being a socialist and opposed to private enterprise. Chadwick retired to private life in 1854 and the Board of Health was abolished. He had been responsible for the first efforts at slum clearance and for improving sanitary conditions so that cholera was stamped out.

R.A. Lewis, *Edwin Chadwick and the Public Health Movement, 1832–1854* (Longman 1952).

Chain Shops

Workshops where iron chains were made, with the links hammer-welded by hand. These workshops were common in the Cradley Heath area near Dudley in the BLACK COUNTRY. The demand for WROUGHT-IRON chains increased rapidly in the early 19th century. They replaced the hemp rope used by the Royal Navy and were used for the MENAI Straits suspension bridge. They were also used as chain drives in machinery and had a wide range of uses on the railways.

Winding chains were used in some coal mines from about 1800, particularly in Shropshire where there was a chain-making industry. They were used less after the introduction of the CAGE and wire winding rope in the 1840s.

Visit Black Country Museum, Dudley, West Midlands – reconstructed chain shop. **M***

Avoncroft Museum of Buildings, near Bromsgrove, Hereford and Worcester – reconstructed chain shop. **M***

Chaldron

A measure of coal which in NEWCASTLE had a weight of 53 cwt (2693 kg or 2.97 US tons). In LONDON a chaldron weighed about half as much as in Newcastle. To carry this amount of coal, chaldron wagons were built. In North East England these had a trapdoor in the floor, so that the coal could be discharged down a chute into a waiting vessel.

Champion, Richard (1743–91)

A QUAKER merchant in BRISTOL who became a partner in WILLIAM COOKWORTHY's Bristol porcelain works. In 1773 he took over the company and the exclusive rights to manufacture HARD-PASTE PORCELAIN from English materials. His attempt to extend the Cookworthy patent after 1782 met with opposition from JOSIAH WEDGWOOD and other Staffordshire potters, but the patent was extended until 1796. Richard Champion lost his American trade during the AMERICAN WAR OF INDEPENDENCE and in 1778 his ships were captured by the French, making him bankrupt. He sold his patent and the manufacture of hard-paste porcelain began at NEW HALL in 1781. After a short spell as deputy paymaster-general, he emigrated to the United States in 1784.

Chance, Robert Lucas (1782–1865)

A glassmaker who bought the Spon Lane glass factory in Smethwick, in the Midlands, in 1824. His uncle, John Robert Lucas Chance, was proprietor of the NAILSEA GLASS HOUSE in BRISTOL. The Spon Lane works began to manufacture SHEET GLASS in 1832, with North America as the main market. Home sales increased after 1837 and the next year Robert Chance's nephew James Timmins Chance (1814–1902) patented a method for smoothing and polishing glass. Two sheets of glass were bedded on a damp leather surface and rubbed one upon the other with emery powder placed between them. The firm also took up the manufacture of glass for telescopes and camera lenses in 1848.

Chaplin, William (1787–1859)

A STAGE COACH proprietor who was the son of a coachman. He built up a business hiring out stage coaches and operating mail coaches for the Post Office. The firm became the largest of its kind, with five coach yards in LONDON and 1,300 horses. Among the places served by stage coaches which he owned were BRISTOL, BRIMINGHAM and MANCHESTER. He worked in co-operation with other proprietors, who had responsibility for horsing the coaches over certain sections of the routes.

Chapman, William (1749–1832)

A CANAL engineer who worked during the early years of his career in Ireland. On the Kildare Canal there, in about 1788, he built a skew bridge – that is, a road-carrying bridge crossing a waterway at an oblique angle. He later worked with WILLIAM JESSOP and in 1797 he designed a steam dredger to deepen the channel of the River Orwell at Ipswich. The dredger was built in 1805–6 with a BOULTON AND WATT engine, and later he was consulted by ROBERT FULTON about an engine for his boat, the *Clermont*. In 1812 he designed a system for a locomotive to haul itself along a chain laid between rails. The scheme was a failure but the locomotive had a distinctive feature; four of its six wheels were mounted on a swivelling bogie. This was the first use of a swivelling bogie for locomotive wheels, which had previously been fixed.

Charlestown

A harbour created by JOHN SMEATON near St Austell in Cornwall in 1791, at the request of the landowner, Charles Rashleigh. The harbour included a curved pier, a wet dock in which ships could be moored at all states of the tide, a shipyard, cottages, warehouses and other buildings. It became a busy centre from which china clay was shipped to LIVERPOOL for use in THE POTTERIES.

Visit Charlestown, St Austell, Cornwall – Shipwreck and Heritage Museum, original harbour and buildings. **M***

Charlotte Dundas

A STEAM BOAT built by WILLIAM SYMINGTON in 1802 for Lord Dundas, governor of the FORTH AND CLYDE CANAL Company. In 1803 it towed two sloops along the canal for 19.5 miles (31.4 km) in a headwind, demonstrating the value of steam as a source of power for boats. The *Charlotte Dundas* had a horizontal engine driving a single paddle wheel near the stern. It was a great success as a tug boat, but the wash from the paddle wheel churned up the banks of the canal, and the boat was not used because of the cost which would be incurred repairing the banks.

Visit Grangemouth Museum, Scotland – rudder of the *Charlotte Dundas*. **M***

Chartism

A movement which began in 1836 when WILLIAM LOVETT formed the London Working Men's Association. It was not a national movement, but a series of local and regional movements which took its name from the petition which became known as the PEOPLE'S CHARTER. There were six points in the Charter: universal manhood suffrage; vote by ballot; annual Parliaments; constituencies with equal numbers of voters; abolition of property qualifications for MPs; and payment for MPs.

The movement received its impetus from the Midlands and industrial North. Areas of greatest discontent also included the West Country textile industry and towns dependent on a single industry. The movement was the rallying flag for many WORKING-CLASS grievances including the agitation provoked in the North by the new Poor Law (see POOR LAW AMENDMENT ACT). For some ten years the Chartist Movement gave the poor a chance to agitate against the position they held in the squalor of industrial towns. Large numbers of working-class people were willing to follow any movement that offered radical change. There was considerable discontent due to a variety of causes, and the workpeople were willing to be swept along by any movement which promised a better life. The leaders had different views on how to achieve their objectives. William Lovett believed in peaceful persuasion but others in the movement, including those led by FEARGUS O'CONNOR, editor of the *Northern Star*, took a more vigorous line. Other Chartist leaders included FRANCIS PLACE, Thomas Attwood, Joseph Stephens and JOHN FROST.

The government showed restraint, but rejected a second petition in 1842. There were strikes in the West Midlands and Lancashire but the leaders failed to organize the violent actions they advocated. Revolutions in Western Europe in 1848, the Irish famine (see HUNGRY FORTIES) and financial crises alarmed the government and special constables were recruited. A master petition was delivered by the Chartists containing less than 2 million signatures; there were some arrests, and ridicule resulted in the collapse of the protest and the end of Chartism.

Increasing prosperity and the lack of strong MIDDLE-CLASS support weakened the movement although its six points were ideas for the future and all but one, annual parliaments, eventually became law. Chartism was an important movement assisting the transformation of the labouring poor into a working class and acting as a peaceful safety valve in contrast to the revolutions in Europe. It stimulated interest in the TRADE UNION MOVEMENT and the movements for EDUCATION, public health and TEMPERANCE.

J.T. Ward, *Chartism* (Batsford 1973).

Chartist Land Company

A company formed in 1845 by FEARGUS O'CONNOR to provide settlements for rural smallholders. As CHARTISM declined as a political movement the Land Company flourished. Subscriptions were raised through branches all over the country and the plots of land were distributed by ballot. Each cottage stood in a 4-acre (1.6-ha) plot, and each village had a school for use by adults as well as by children. The first estate at Heronsgate, near Rickmansworth, Hertfordshire, was completed in 1847. Other estates were built at Charterville in Oxfordshire, at Dodford in Worcestershire and at Snigs End and Lowbands in Gloucestershire.

The Land Company collapsed in 1851 because of financial difficulties, and other owners bought the cottages.

Visit Charterville, near Minster Lovell, Oxfordshire – original housing.
Heronsgate, near Rickmansworth, Hertfordshire – original housing.

A.H. Hadfield, *The Chartist Land Company* (David and Charles 1970).

Chat Moss

A peat bog near MANCHESTER which had to be crossed by the LIVERPOOL AND MANCHESTER RAILWAY. It stretched over a distance of 5.5 miles (9 km) and posed a problem which was solved by GEORGE STEPHENSON. He built the railway on a foundation of brushwood hurdles and branches of trees, using the same method as was used by road builders like THOMAS TELFORD. On this section of the line wooden cross-sleepers were used instead of stone blocks.

Chelsea Porcelain

PORCELAIN made at the Chelsea Porcelain Manufactory, founded *c*.1742 by Thomas Briand. The firm flourished with aristocratic patronage under Nicholas Sprimont, and developed a fine-ground paste which was glazed with a brush. After 1758 bone ash was added to make the porcelain harder and whiter. The works closed in 1783, having been bought by the DERBY PORCELAIN MANUFACTORY 13 years earlier.

Cherokee Clay

Clay found in South Carolina, which JOSIAH WEDGWOOD used in small quantities and investigated as a possible large-scale clay source for his pottery works. In discussions with people who knew South Carolina he found that the clay had to be taken 300 miles (483 km) overland, which made transport costs very high. He sent his agent, Mr Griffiths, to South Carolina, but it appears he eventually decided it would be too expensive to carry the clay to England. Small amounts are known to have been used in the 1770s in the making of Jasper vases, which were highly priced products.

Child Labour – Chimney Sweeps

It was a common practice in the 18th century for a young child to be trained to climb inside chimneys and sweep them. The working conditions and hazards appalled many people. In 1817 it has been calculated there were about 400 masters and 1,000 boy sweeps, of whom half worked in LONDON. The children were often paupers, apprenticed to their masters by the parishes (see PARISH APPRENTICES); some were sold by their parents, with the highest prices for the smallest children. A few girls, usually the sweep's children, were also employed – two girls swept the chimneys of Windsor Castle.

The children were apprenticed at ages between 4 and 8. Their work was dangerous and unhealthy, with sores developing on elbows and knees. Chimneys in large mansions and public buildings were the most dangerous because the soot collected in the flue and the child could be smothered.

The first Act to reduce the chimney sweeps' misery was passed in 1788, but it was ineffective, as there was no machinery to enforce it. Bills brought before Parliament in 1817, 1818 and 1819 were never passed, and the first Act of significance was in 1834. This said that boys under 14, unless apprentices, could not be employed; apprentices had to be over 10 years of age and had to have two months' trial, during which time the apprentice could withdraw. An Act of 1840 was not effective and it was not until 1875 that Lord SHAFTESBURY was able to pass an effective Act. By that time fewer chimneys were being built that boys could climb and machinery was available to do the cleaning.

Child Labour In Factories

Children of the poorer CLASS worked from a very early age before the INDUSTRIAL REVOLUTION, either on the land or in cottage industries, and often for long hours in unhealthy surroundings. To the factory owners they were particularly valuable since they could be disciplined easily, could carry out simple repetitive operations and were very cheap. SIR ROBERT PEEL had over a thousand in his mills, some of whom were paupers, supplied by parishes which were only too glad to get rid of them.

Conditions in the factories were bad and the working day was at least 14 hours. Accidents were common and discipline very strict. Some factories operated the machinery day and night, so that one shift of children used the beds vacated by the next shift. The principal sanction available to the factory owner and the foreman was beating, although some employers prohibited it. Workers and parents were often responsible for the harsh treatment of children, and factory masters often made the workpeople responsible for recruiting and disciplining juvenile workers. Parents were able to increase the family income by recruiting their own children, reinforcing the tradition of family employment. Employers such as JEDEDIAH STRUTT sometimes took very young children to oblige parents who were already working at their mills.

Although children in factories were often treated harshly, the children of UPPER-CLASS parents received savage punishments at the public and grammar schools of the time. Abuse of child labour diminished only gradually in the first half of the 19th century. The FACTORY ACTS of that period were confined to the textile factories and legislation was only gradually extended to other occupations.

The development of the EDUCATION system helped to remove children from the labour force. The 1870 Education Act gave voluntary schools slightly higher grants and allowed school boards to be set up to build schools, paid for partly out of the rates (a local authority tax on property). Between 1870 and 1876 over

1,600 Board schools were built. The 1880 Education Act made school compulsory for all children aged 5 to 10. If by the age of 10 they had reached a satisfactory educational standard, they could leave to do half-time work in factories; otherwise school was compulsory until the age of 13.

J. Walvin, *A Child's World* (Penguin 1982). J.T. Ward, *The Factory System, Vol. 2. The Factory System and Society* (David and Charles 1970).

Child Labour In Mines

Much information about the treatment of children working in the COAL MINES comes from the Royal Commission which made a report in 1842. Boys were employed in all parts of the country, girls in Scotland, South Wales, Lancashire, Cheshire and the West Riding of Yorkshire. Children were employed as TRAPPERS, to fill the skips and carriages and as pushers (hurriers) of the carriages. Often they were harnessed to the carriage and dragged the heavy load behind them crawling along on all fours. Some of the worst conditions were suffered by apprentices from the WORKHOUSES. Hours underground were very long, with 12 hours per day for 6 days a week common, although 18 hours a day were recorded in some pits. The MINES ACT, 1842 eliminated some of the worst aspects of the system and prohibited the employment of women, girls and boys below the age of 10 underground.

China Clay (Also known as kaolin)

A fine, white clay used for making PORCELAIN and found in large deposits inland from St Austell in Cornwall. A QUAKER chemist, WILLIAM COOKWORTHY, was the first person to appreciate the importance of the Cornish clay. His monopoly of the process from 1768 delayed the use of china clay by other porcelain makers, although it could be used for earthenware.

Quarrying developed in the second half of the 18th century and the clay was taken by sea and canal to THE POTTERIES. In 1800 about 2,000 tonnes (2,240 US tons) were mined. This had expanded to 10,000 tonnes (11,200 US tons) by 1830 and 65,000 tonnes (72,800 US tons) by 1858.

Visit St Austell, Cornwall – Wheal Martyn Open Air Museum of the China Clay Industry. **M***

K. Hudson, *The History of English China Clays* (David and Charles 1966).

Cholera Outbreaks

A major outbreak of cholera in 1831–2 was followed in 1845 by an epidemic sweeping across Europe and reaching Britain in 1848. Cholera, spread from polluted water supplies, was no respecter of social CLASS. It affected the rich, although it was more likely to afflict the poor. It was known that the cholera epidemics were linked with water and bad sanitation but there was no understanding that cholera was a specific infection from a self-propagating micro-organism. LONDON was hit by two waves of the disease in late 1848 and the summer of 1849. About 80,000 people died from cholera during the epidemic, nearly four times as many as in the 1831–2 outbreak. The recommendations of the GENERAL BOARD OF HEALTH for lime washing, cesspool clearing and avoidance of filth were made in ignorance of the true nature of the epidemic. The Board did what it could and made more people aware of the dangers of poor sanitation.

N. Longmate, *King Cholera* (Hamish Hamilton 1966).

Christian Socialism

A movement led by F.D. Maurice, Charles Kingsley (who wrote *The Water Babies*) and Thomas Hughes (who wrote *Tom Brown's Schooldays*). These young men founded the movement in 1848 to promote social reform through SELF HELP. They gained support from MIDDLE-CLASS people and agitated for the expansion of the CO-OPERATIVE MOVEMENT, SLUM clearance and adult EDUCATION.

Church Attendance

In 1851 the government caried out a

RELIGIOUS WORSHIP CENSUS, which showed that a large proportion of the population of England and Wales were neither church people nor of any other religion. At least half the people, mostly from the WORKING CLASSES, did not go to church or chapel. A number of social deterrents reduced congregations. Poor people could not afford to rent a pew, they lacked good clothes, and in large towns the social gulf between rich and poor limited attendance to the 'respectable' MIDDLE and UPPER CLASSES. Religion was associated with CLASS and many of the churches were mainly middle- and upper-class institutions.

Church of England (Also called the Anglican Church)

The ESTABLISHED CHURCH of England, with churches in nearly every village that were the responsibility of a vicar or a curate. Politically the majority of the clergy in the Anglican church were supporters of the Establishment and the TORY party. By about 1836 changes within the Church of England began to be apparent. Anglican champions of social reform appeared among the clergy and new parishes were created in industrial districts where previously there had been no church. Old churches were repaired and new ones built. Between 1840 and 1870 over 1,700 new churches were built and 7,000 rebuilt. There was an evangelical fervour to help the labouring population through clothing clubs, parochial schools and other organizations. A number of leading Anglicans, including RICHARD OASTLER, supported WORKING-CLASS reforms. Nevertheless, working- and MIDDLE-CLASS people who wanted a closer identification with the organization and control of the church had to turn to the dissenting religions (see DISSENTERS).

W.R. Ward, *Religion and Society in England, 1790–1850* (Batsford 1972).

Circular Knitting Needle

A patent for this was taken out by MARC BRUNEL in 1816, although the machine was probably not his invention. It knitted tubular fabrics, but these were not suitable for use as shaped stockings until a machine producing a rib stitch was invented in 1847 by Matthew Townsend. The rib stitch made it possible to produce non-fashioned seamless hose of reasonable elasticity. In 1855 A. Paget of Loughborough invented a power-driven circular knitting machine.

Civil Engineers, Institution of

The Institution was founded in 1818 and THOMAS TELFORD became the first president in 1820. There was no great dividing line between civil and mechanical engineers, and until the Institution of Mechanical Engineers was created in 1847 both groups helped to build up the prestige of the Institution of Civil Engineers, which was able to establish recognized standards only very slowly. The Institution became an important forum for the exchange of ideas and the dissemination of knowledge and was joined by many distinguished engineers, including ISAMBARD BRUNEL, JOSEPH WHITWORTH, Henry Palmer, BRYAN DONKIN, and SIR WILLIAM FAIRBAIRN.

Clapham Sect

A group of middle-class Anglicans (see CHURCH OF ENGLAND) within the EVANGELICAL MOVEMENT, many of whom worshipped at Clapham parish church in south LONDON, where the Reverend John Venn was rector. They had a sense of moral responsibility and possessed both intellect and wealth. The sect played an important part in the anti-slavery movement and members also believed in improving the condition of the poor and encouraged religious education. The sect was influential in starting the Church Missionary Society in 1799. The movement flourished between about 1792 and 1813.

Clark, C. and J. Ltd

A shoe firm founded by Cyrus Clark (1801–66) in 1821. Cyrus Clark, a QUAKER, set up in business with a partner, Arthur Clothier, in Street, Somerset, making sheepskin rugs and tanning leather. In

1825 James Clark (1811–1905), Cyrus's brother, entered the business and began making slippers out of the short-fleeced skins which were unsuitable for rug-making. Making shoes and slippers was essentially a handcraft with the two main operations done as outwork (outside the factory). Uppers cut at the factory were sent out to binders who sewed the pieces together and then returned them to the factory. The stitched uppers, together with soles, were then given to shoemakers who finished the job.

In 1856 the Singer Company of America persuaded the firm to take a treadle sewing machine which could be used for closing uppers. An improved machine, the Blake sewer, was introduced during the next year and the mechanization of the boot and shoe industry had begun. The firm is still in operation in Street.

Visit Street, Somerset – Clark's shoe factory and model village.

K. Hudson, *Towards Precision Shoemaking* (David and Charles 1968).

Class

The development of the use of the word 'class' in a social sense belongs to the period 1770–1840, when society was being reorganized as a result of the INDUSTRIAL REVOLUTION. The economic changes of that period gave the opportunity for individual SOCIAL MOBILITY, and created an awareness that social position could be made rather than merely inherited. Before the rise of industry, writers spoke of 'ranks', 'orders' and 'degrees' in a hierarchical society shaped like a pyramid, with the 'common people' at the base.

With the onset of the Industrial Revolution and the new social system, social divisions were described by the use of specific terms such as lower classes, middle classes and higher or upper classes (see the following entries). The term 'working class' was not in common use until the 1840s. It implied productive or useful activity, whereas 'middle class' suggested a hierarchy. (The increasing number of merchants, bankers and MANUFACTURERS regarded themselves as 'middle class', with the implication that there were also lower and higher classes.) In *Capital*, KARL MARX identified three great social classes: wage-labourers, capitalists and landlords. This division later became simplified into the bourgeoisie and the proletariat. The division of the classes into sections, with the middle class divided into lower and upper and the working class into skilled, semi-skilled and labouring, did not come until the 1860s.

The confusion which occurs in the use of the word 'class' is further complicated by these divisions, and it is probably best to regard the terms as potentially helpful descriptions rather than as dogmatic facts.

R.J. Morris, *Class and Class Consciousness in the Industrial Revolution, 1780–1850* (Macmillan 1979).

Class – Middle

The development of the factory and the growth of commerce made it necessary to employ managers, clerical staff, foremen and supervisors. New professional groups also emerged, such as draughtsmen, engineers, chemists, statisticians and other qualified personnel. These groups formed the expanding middle CLASS; the factory system had interposed a new element between the owners of CAPITAL and the workers who produced the goods. In 1851 about 18 per cent of occupied adult males belonged to this middle class, and the middle class of this period helped to finance the railways and overseas investments. They were distinguished by their EDUCATION, religious affiliation, life-style and level of income.

The top echelons of the middle classes mingled with the aristocracy and included bankers, merchants, engineers and businessmen. The lower middle class consisted of shopkeepers, innkeepers, clerks, school teachers and the lower ranks of the professions. They were either connected with trade or performed some paid service, and considered themselves as 'respectable' people who did not have to live by their manual labour. They were very class-conscious and had houses in suitable locations which were well furnished. Most middle-class people kept servants, and this defined their status and rank as superior people. Central to their way of life was their home and the sanctity of the family.

H. Perkins, *The Origins of Modern English Society 1780–1880* (Routledge and Kegan Paul 1969).
G. Crossrick (ed.), *The Lower Middle Class in Britain* (Croom Helm 1977).

Class – Upper

In the early 19th century, national economic policy decisions were taken by the nobility and gentry, or by those who owed their power to the hereditary ownership of large estates. Wealthy people outside this group, such as the families of RICHARD ARKWRIGHT and JEDEDIAH STRUTT, used their money to build up large estates so that they could secure their position in the upper CLASS.

Landowners fell into two groups, the aristocracy (or nobility) and the gentry. About 300 families owned large estates and were titled, forming the closely knit aristocracy. Lesser landowners, the gentry, often performed leadership tasks at a local level as village squires or JUSTICES OF THE PEACE and in similar positions. Most of their time, however, was spent in leisure pursuits. They were joined by the PEELs, Strutts and others who obtained their wealth from industry but abandoned middle- or lower-class habits to take on the culture of the landed gentry – although it often took two generations to be accepted.

The self-confidence and authoritarian attitude of the upper class and their EDUCATION and life-style set them apart from other groups.

Class – Working

The growth of industry produced a distinctive working CLASS with attitudes to life and work different to those of the mill owners. There was a great gulf established between manual and non-manual occupations and between master and employee. In some of their statements, members of the UPPER CLASS provide proof that they regarded working-class people as different from themselves – as 'lower orders' always condemned to a particular station in life, as servants, mill-hands or manual workers.

At the same time there was a great diversity within the working class. There was a hierarchy, with highly skilled artisans at the top, such as cabinet makers and, in the 19th century, engine drivers. They merged with lower middle-class groups such as shopkeepers. Below them in the hierarchy were the skilled workers such as tailors and building trades craftsmen. Below them came the labourers and semi- or unskilled workers. This group was often ostracized by the skilled workers, who considered themselves socially superior.

See also WORKING-CLASS FOOD.

E.P. Thompson, *The Making of the English Working Class* (Penguin 1971)

Classical Economics

The economic theories of ADAM SMITH, JOHN STUART MILL, DAVID RICARDO and THOMAS MALTHUS became known as classical economics. These men believed that the community as a whole benefited from free competition and that individuals were motivated by personal ambition. They stressed the importance of the development of manufacturing and of labour productivity. They believed that wages were determined by the demand for and supply of labour, and that saving was a form of investment and was determined by the rate of interest. Classical economics still continues to influence economists in many parts of the world.

Clay Cross Ironworks

A firm established after coal and ironstone were discovered by GEORGE STEPHENSON during the cutting of a tunnel for the North Midland Railway. The company was formed in 1837 with George and ROBERT STEPHENSON, GEORGE HUDSON and others as shareholders. In 1846 the furnaces were built and local iron was used at first, although later Northamptonshire ore was brought in. The company later owned iron mines in Northamptonshire and Oxfordshire.

Clayton and Shuttleworth

An AGRICULTURAL ENGINEERING firm at Lincoln, started in 1842 by Nathaniel Clayton (1811–90) and his brother-in-law, Joseph Shuttleworth (1819–83). One and a half acres (0.6 ha) of low-lying land by the river belonging to Joseph Shuttleworth were reclaimed and a forge was built, with work for 12 men making portable STEAM ENGINES. In 1851, six years after it started, 126 portable engines had been produced and as a result of good publicity at the GREAT EXHIBITION another 209 were sold in that year. In 1857 the company claimed that it had made 2,400 portable steam engines and had sold 500 in 1856 alone. The works employed 940 men, and by 1861, 15 engines were being produced each week.

Clegg, Samuel (1781–1861)

A gas engineer who had worked as an assistant to WILLIAM MURDOCK. He purified gas by adding lime to the water through which it passed. He invented the gas meter and an improved gas burner, and put up the first gas lamp in Westminster. By 1816 LONDON had 26 miles (42 km) of gas mains.

Clement, Joseph (1779–1844)

A tool-maker who worked for JOSEPH BRAMAH at HENRY MAUDSLAY's workshop in 1817, making precision hand-tools. His most important contribution to engineering was the standardization of screw threads in 1828. He also made self-acting tools of great precision, especially a planing machine patented in 1825 and a constant speed lathe patented in 1827.

Clifton Suspension Bridge

Designed by ISAMBARD BRUNEL in the 1820s, the bridge was not opened until 1864, after his death. It crosses the gorge of the River Avon at Bristol. THOMAS TELFORD competed with Brunel for the design and in 1831 a modified design was accepted, but money ran out after the foundation was laid. After Brunel's death in 1859 interest was renewed, and a new

The Clifton Suspension Bridge. In 1829 designs were invited for a bridge to span the Avon Gorge at Bristol. Isambard Brunel submitted four designs and in 1831 he was appointed to construct the bridge. The foundation stone was laid in 1836 but progress was slow because the money ran out. When Brunel died in 1859 the two supporting piers had still not been completed. A new company was formed by some of the important members of the Institution of Civil Engineers and Brunel's design was modified. The bridge was opened in 1864 but it cannot be considered as entirely the work of Brunel as was the Royal Albert Bridge at Saltash in Devon. (*Mary Evans*)

company was formed by some members of the INSTITUTION OF CIVIL ENGINEERS.

Visit Clifton, Bristol – suspension bridge over the Avon gorge.

Clough, Anne Jemima (1820–92)

An educationalist who pioneered education for girls. She opened a girls' school in LIVERPOOL in 1841, and later one at Ambleside in the Lake District. She became head of the first hall of residence for women at Cambridge in 1871 (see UNIVERSITIES).

Clyde Ironworks

BLAST FURNACES were set up on the River Clyde near GLASGOW in 1786 by Thomas Edington and John MacKenzie to manufacture bar iron, iron products and pig iron. The works was only 3 miles (4.8 km) from Glasgow and close to coal and ironstone deposits.

Coach Services

From the time of Henry VIII, before wheeled coaches were introduced, travellers were accustomed to ride post – that is, hire horses at post houses from the post master, who was usually an innkeeper. The post master kept a horse for the use of post 'boys' (mostly older men) who carried official mail and papers. The Post Office had a monopoly of post horses until 1780, and from that date extra revenue was obtained by charging a fee for a licence for horses let out for hire.

With the introduction of mail coaches many post boys were made redundant and the post chaise service was developed, whereby travellers could hire a post chaise, a pair of horses to pull it and a post boy as rider, on a mileage basis. The post chaise was capable of carrying two passengers and some luggage. Persons who travelled in this manner were said to be 'travelling post' or posting. Inns acted as post houses and the post boys wore distinguishing colours to identify their allegiances. Posting was a fast means of travel with fierce rivalry between competing post houses.

The development of wheeled vehicles to carry passengers was closely linked with improvements on the roads which resulted from the TURNPIKE system. By the 18th century coaches to carry passengers had been introduced. They were primitive devices which were originally pulled throughout each journey by the same team of horses. In 1734 relays of horses were used to service the NEWCASTLE to LONDON coach, reducing the journey from 12 days to 9. The rehorsing of coaches at carefully spaced stages, usually inns, became general and stage coach services were extended to link the main towns. Stages were at about 10-mile (16-km) intervals and at each stage a four-horse coach needed a fresh relay of horses and one spare. The stage coach services speeded up journey times and in their heyday, between 1815 and 1835, stage coach firms employed over 3,000 coaches and averaged a speed of 10 miles (16 km) per hour. Over 100,000 horses were needed and there was employment either directly or indirectly for over 30,000 people.

Mail was still carried by post boys on horseback or, rarely, by mail cart in the early 1780s. JOHN PALMER was authorized in 1784 to arrange a trial, at his own expense, to carry mail on a fast coach guarded by an armed man, between London and BRISTOL. The service was successful and was extended to other routes. Passengers were allowed to travel by mail coach, and the service was extended to most roads in Britain and the main routes in Ireland in the 1790s. By 1814 there were 82 coach routes and the mail coaches provided fast services with the protection of an armed mail guard.

The rapid expansion of the railway network (see RAILWAY MAIL COACHES) towards the end of the 1830s resulted in the transfer of mail to trains and the contraction of mail coach services. The last service to operate to London, from Norwich, closed in 1846, although mail coaches in some rural areas continued to run into the 1860s. Some of the terms used by the coach services, such as 'coach', 'guard', 'up' and 'down' (for coaches up to London, or down to the country), were taken up by the railways and are still in use today.

A. Bird, *Roads and Vehicles* (Longman 1973).

Coalbrookdale Company

An ironworks sited in a small valley in the Severn gorge of Shropshire close to deposits of iron ore and coal. In 1708 ABRAHAM DARBY I took over the lease of the furnaces at Coalbrookdale, and operations began the next year after repairs had been carried out. In 1709 the first use was made of coal instead of charcoal for smelting, using local clod coal which was suitable for making coke. The Company expanded to other nearby sites and the Darby family continued to run it until 1849. The Company continued to operate until 1929 when it became a subsidiary of Allied Ironfounders Limited. A museum was opened on the site in 1959 and now includes other nearby sites as the IRONBRIDGE GORGE Museum.

Visit Ironbridge Gorge Museum, Ironbridge, Shropshire – remains of the original furnaces, and Museum of Iron. **M***

A. Raistrick, *Dynasty of Ironfounders: The Darbys of Coalbrookdale* (Longman 1953; David and Charles 1970).

Coal Combines

Organizations of coal masters aimed at fixing the price of coal in GLASGOW and regulating mine output to prevent the flooding of the market with cheap coal. COAL MINING companies were assigned quotas and a joint selling agency, the Glasgow Coal Company, was set up. The agreement operated from 1 January 1791 and lasted about three years; then new pits were sunk and new mines on the Monkland Canal could sell coals much cheaper in Glasgow. A second Combine was set up in 1813, but in the revival of trade after the depression of 1815 the agreement was ended.

Coal Drop

A device invented by William Chapman of NEWCASTLE about 1800 and used on STAITHES to transport coal from the wagons to the hold of the boat. The device used pulleys and weights to lower and raise the wagon in a frame.

Coal Mining

In 1760 coal was mined in several areas of Britain, but the mines were small, often with horizontal shafts into a valley side. Less than a dozen men were employed in most pits, although a few of the larger ones employed 60–70. The most important area was the North East, with coal shipped round the coast to LONDON and other towns. The better pumping facilities which the STEAM ENGINE provided meant that deeper pits were sunk, and canal construction increased demand by cutting transport costs. Expansion of the industry was very rapid in the 19th century, with an output of 49.4 million tonnes (55.3 million US tons) in 1850. MACHINES were not used on a large scale and picks and shovels were used at the coalface. The most important changes were the use of power-driven machinery for winding, shaft sinking and surface activities. Even these advances came slowly; the introduction of CAGES, for example, did not take place on a large scale until the 1840s.

Visit Chatterley Whitfield Mining Museum, Stoke-on-Trent – museum and underground trips. **M***
Scottish Mining Museum, Lady Victoria Colliery, Newtongrange, Midlothian. **M***
Cefn Coed Colliery Museum, Blaenant Colliery, Neath, West Glamorgan. **M***

A.R. Griffin, *Coalmining* (Longman 1971).

Coal Mining – Ownership

The right to mine coal was vested in the owner of the surface land, but difficulties arose when the land was common or copyhold (tenants had safeguards of tenure). Landowners quickly asserted their rights when mineral wealth was likely to be present. As landlord of nearly all the manors in east Glamorgan, the Marquess of Bute owned the mineral rights to the minerals beneath the commons. In Scotland the Dukes of Buccleuch and Hamilton found themselves the owners of many mines.

The Duke of BRIDGEWATER drew a considerable amount of his income from mining rights and the Church, particularly the Bishop of Durham, also owned a number of collieries.

Some landowners developed their own mines; some preferred to lease the land to others. In South Wales, the Midlands, Yorkshire and Cumberland many mines were leased to ironmasters. In the Forest of Dean, where the mineral rights were owned by the Crown, residents had the right to mine coal, but as mines became deeper in the 19th century a number of capitalists (see CAPITAL) took over. (In fact some residents still have the right to mine coal there, but on a small scale.)

Coal Mining – Ventilation

Early mines used a fire basket, which was placed in the shaft of the mine known as the upshaft. Air was drawn down the downshaft as hot air was expelled from the upshaft. After about 1760 the air was directed around the working by the use of doors. This was known as 'air coursing' and was introduced by James Spedding. The work of directing the flow of air by doors was done by very young children. They were known as door TRAPPERS; children aged between 5 and 8, girls and boys, were employed to sit by a door in the mine all day, closing it every time someone passed through.

In 1787 an underground furnace was installed at a pit in the North East, with a chimney on the surface, and the fire basket was no longer needed. There was still the risk of an explosion or fire and several did occur. Very few collieries were well ventilated until the mid-19th century, when mechanical ventilation was introduced. In 1807 a steam-driven air pump (see STEAM ENGINES – PUMPING) was used at a colliery to extract air. Some air pumps forced air into the mine. Fans were also used, but they were relatively slow. One, invented by William Furness of LEEDS in 1837, rotated at a speed of between 100 and 300 revolutions per minute. The first successful steam-driven fan was installed at the top of a shaft of a colliery near Paisley in Scotland in 1827. From the 1830s the larger collieries were

ventilated by air pumps, but the smaller ones continued to use ventilation furnaces into the 20th century.

One mechanized device which was widely adopted in the 1860s and 1870s was the waddle fan. It revolved slowly at about 70 revolutions per minute and drew air from the mine up the upcast shaft. These fans ranged from 9 feet (2.3 m) to 45 feet (13.7 m) in diameter, and some were still in use in 1947.

Visit Bitton, near Bristol – mine ventilating furnace.
Chatterley, Whitfield Mining Museum, Stoke-on-Trent – ventilation fan. **M***

Coal Mining – Villages

In the 18th century mining villages were built in many coalfields. These villages were very isolated, particularly in Northumberland, Durham, South Wales and Scotland. In the Midlands they were more likely to be close to industrial or agricultural settlements. The houses were built in rows, similar to those of the industrial towns, with primitive sanitation and water supply. In the first half of the 19th century miners' houses were much the same in all coalfields, with 'two up and two down' (two rooms upstairs and two rooms downstairs).

The public house was of central importance to the mining village, particularly since in the early 19th century it was the only non-religious building in which communal activities could take place. Chapels were also important village centres and had a considerable influence, since many miners' leaders were Methodists (see METHODISM). The village shop was often run by the colliery owner, or someone with whom he had an arrangement, as a TOMMY SHOP, with part of the miners' wages being paid in kind.

Visit Deri, Mid-Glamorgan – Welsh mining village.
Moira, near Ashby-de-la-Zouch, Leicestershire – miners' houses, built c. 1811.
Leasingthorn, County Durham – miners' houses.

Coal Owners' Association

An association founded in Northumberland and Durham in 1805. JOHN BUDDLE was appointed as secretary the next year and it became known as the Joint Northumberland and Durham Coal Owners' Association. Its prime objective was to maximize profits. This was done by restricting output, controlling labour costs and eliminating price competition. The quantity of coal marketed by each colliery was agreed and approved annually and there were heavy fines for excess sales. In some years the members failed to agree the quantities, but prices were regulated too and measures standardized. The Association also represented the coal owners' interest to the government. The owners condemned strikes and combinations of employees, but never doubted the appropriateness of their own Association.

M.W. Flinn, *The History of the British Coal Industry: Vol. 2, 1700–1830* (Oxford University Press 1984).

Coalport

The place where coal from the Shropshire Canal was transferred to boats on the River Severn, near the COALBROOKDALE COMPANY. In 1795 a PORCELAIN factory was founded by JOHN ROSE at Coalport. Coal and fireclay were delivered by CANAL to the works and waterborne china clay and china stone could be unloaded at the factory's wharf, having been shipped from Cornwall via the River Severn. In 1799 John Rose bought the Caughley works from THOMAS TURNER and transferred it to Coalport in 1814.

Efforts were made to improve the quality of the BONE CHINA and in about 1822 feldspar china, hard and brilliantly white, was introduced. This enabled the firm to produce one of the most translucent ceramics ever made in England. In 1820 John Rose introduced a leadless glaze for which he obtained a medal.

During the period 1820–40 Coalport was one of the most important potteries in Britain. In 1926 the Coalport works and employees were transferred to the Cauldon Works at Shelton in North Staffordshire. In 1958 production moved to Fenton and in 1967 Coalport joined the Wedgwood Group.

Visit Coalport China Works Museum, Ironbridge, Shropshire. **M***

G.A. Godden, *Coalport and Coalbrookdale Porcelains* (Barrie and Jenkins 1970).

Coal Trade – South Wales

Until the NAPOLEONIC WARS, when the IRON INDUSTRY grew rapidly, the trade in coal in South Wales was the most important industry. Land sales were never large and most of the trade was by sea and relatively local, covering Ireland, Cornwall, the Channel Islands and the Bristol Channel ports. Anthracite was sent to Kent to use in the hop-drying kilns, and small amounts of coal went to Portugal and France. The main uses of the coal were in copper mines in Cornwall and the lime kilns of Ireland. The opening of the CANALS resulted in cheaper coal after 1796 and an increase in the trade of Swansea, Neath and Llanelly.

Newport developed trade with BRISTOL and the Devon and Cornish ports, and by 1820 it was the most important port for coal in Wales. Demand increased for the smokeless steam coals after 1840, once they had been shown as ideal for small, tubular marine boilers. The port of CARDIFF handled large quantities of this coal and the development of the steamship (see STEAMSHIP COMPANIES) brought new markets in France. The quantities exported from Cardiff increased rapidly from 3,580 tonnes (4,000 US tons) in 1837 to 918,877 tonnes (1,029,000 US tons) in 1857.

Coastal Trade

In 1768 some 580 places in England and Wales were able to receive goods sent by water. The majority were small seaports such as Rye in East Sussex and Lyme Regis in Dorset. The boats used for coastal trade were small and could reach quays in shallow creeks as well as at larger harbours. The transport of coal dominated the coastal trade for over 350 years with a fleet of vessels sailing between the North East coast and the large cities, particularly LONDON. The second most important cargo was corn, followed by raw materials including raw wool.

Coastal shipping was also a means of transport for passengers in the summer months, with regular sailings from such places as London to Margate and from Leith in Scotland to London. Sailing ships inevitably were affected by the direction and strength of the wind and services were irregular, producing shortages and gluts of such things as coal in London. Throughout the 19th century coastal shipping, in terms of tonnage, was far more important than shipping tonnage engaged in overseas trade.

After 1812 passenger services on steamers (see STEAM BOATS) developed rapidly; by 1821 there were 188 steamships and by 1853, 639. At first the steamships were small and low-powered, which limited them to short distances in estuaries and along the coast. Coastal passenger steamship services achieved their greatest importance in the 1840s, with links between 90 ports and harbours. Steam power was adapted more slowly to goods traffic than to passengers. There was no sense of urgency before the railways were built (see RAILWAY DEVELOPMENT), and goods carried were high in value relative to weight. Merchants sent them by a variety of means, including wagons, CANALS and coastal steamer, to reach their ultimate destination. Irish produce was shipped to England and Welsh ports, and cattle and sheep were sent from Scotland to London by sea, arriving in better condition (unless there was a severe storm) than by other means of transport.

Passenger traffic dropped sharply after the railways had been built and services were curtailed. Nevertheless, sea competition had a widespread effect on railway rates, and seaborne coal continued to be of great importance into the 20th century. The small harbours were no longer able to take the larger vessels being built and deep channels had to be provided for the larger harbours.

Cobbett, William (1763–1835)

A radical politician who printed a political journal, the *Political Register*. He was the leader of the opposition from 1815 to 1821 and strongly resented Lord Liverpool's repressive measures. In 1821 he began to publish *Rural Rides*, in which he described the misery of the agricultural workers. He fought to improve the conditions of the WORKING CLASSES and strongly supported the FACTORY ACT, 1833. No other writer attacked the Anglican clergy (see CHURCH OF ENGLAND) in his works as ruthlessly as did William Cobbett, and he was prepared to use his journalistic skills to challenge the social system when he judged the conditions of the working classes warranted it. He considered CHILD LABOUR 'unnatural' and regarded the factory workers of MANCHESTER as producers who had lost their independence and rights.

G.D.H. Cole, *Life of William Cobbett* (Collins 1947).

Cobden, Richard (1804–65).

A MANUFACTURER of CALICO in MANCHESTER who, as a RADICAL, became a strong advocate of FREE TRADE. With JOHN BRIGHT he led the ANTI-CORN LAW LEAGUE, set up in 1839. He believed that free trade in corn would give manufacturers prosperity, cheapen the price of food, make British agriculture more efficient and encourage a new era of international friendship and peace. After his election to Parliament in 1841 he put the case for CORN LAW reform. He gave his name to the Cobden Treaty of 1860, a commercial treaty which, on a reciprocal basis, reduced duties between Britain and France.

Coltman, John (1727–1808)

A Leicester hosier who experimented successfully with the SPINNING JENNY and then with RICHARD ARKWRIGHT'S WATER FRAME to spin WORSTED. Enough money was raised by him, in partnership with others, for machines to be made in 1785. However, after two weeks of riots in Leicester, the town corporation forbade the operation of the machines within 50 miles (80.5 km) of the town. Coltman moved to Bromsgrove in Worcestershire, where his nephew had a small cotton mill. The mill turned over to worsted spinning and experiments were made with combing by power (see COMBING MACHINES). Coltman's nephew cheated him by selling machines to other manufacturers and the partnership was dissolved.

John Coltman was a leading UNITARIAN and started a Philosophical Society in Leicester about 1780.

Combination Acts, 1799, 1800

Before 1799 workers grouping themselves together to reduce hours or raise wages were considered illegal, but combination was allowed against masters who did not obey the law. By 1799 the government was concerned about the spread of ideas from the FRENCH REVOLUTION and decided to act against workers' demands. An Act was passed by WILLIAM PITT outlawing combinations of workers to press for more pay or shorter hours. People who tried to induce workers not to work, took part in illicit meetings or gave money for the organization of such meetings were also threatened with imprisonment.

The haste with which the first Act was passed brought petitions of protest from all parts of the country, and an amended bill was introduced. The 1800 Act was an improvement on that of 1799. Power to convict had to be given by two magistrates instead of one. Arbitration was also introduced and if the two arbitrators could not agree then a JUSTICE OF THE PEACE would make the binding decision. The Act forbade combinations among masters but this was ignored.

The novelty of the Acts was that they provided for summary trial and conviction, giving employers instant redress against individuals threatening collective action. The workers' activities were driven underground, although some workers' societies continued to have peaceable relations with employers. The Acts were repealed in 1824 when it was realized that combinations had not been suppressed, especially in the skilled trades. Employers also recognized that the presence of the laws had made labour relations difficult.

Combing Machines

Combing textile fibres cleans and removes short fibres and makes the fibres lie in a parallel formation. For centuries combing was done by hand and then in 1792 EDMUND CARTWRIGHT invented a wool-combing machine. It was only partly successful because the quality of the combing was poor. Other machines were invented in the 1820s and 1830s, but it was not until 1846, when J. Heilmann of Mulhouse took out a patent in Britain for a machine, that combing became fully mechanized. Other patents were granted in the 1850s, notably one which was taken out by G.E. Donisthorpe and S.C. Lister for what became known as the Lister comb. Another inventor, James Noble, patented a machine in 1853, and this is the one which is most commonly used for combing today.

Comet

The first STEAM BOAT to operate a commercial service. It was designed by HENRY BELL in 1812 and operated along the Clyde. Competition from other vessels resulted in it being transferred to the GLASGOW–Fort William service, and it was wrecked in 1820.

Visit Science Museum, London – engine of the *Comet*. **M***

Committee of Manufacturers

A committee set up in 1782 by cotton MANUFACTURERS to protect themselves from the actions of their employees. They persuaded Parliament to pass laws making it a capital offence for workers to damage their looms, destroy goods or go on strike.

Committee on the Woollen Trade

A committee set up in 1806 to enquire into the woollen trade, following the petitions and unrest by the CROPPERS and weavers in the first years of the 19th century. The workers argued that the STATUTE OF ARTIFICERS should be reinstated so that APPRENTICESHIP schemes could operate as they had in the past. The Committee was not prepared to be impartial and became an investigating tribunal. Account books were seized and the croppers were branded as a dangerous, organized force. The Committee did, however, compile some valuable statistics about the industry.

In 1809 the protective legislation in the WOOLLEN INDUSTRY was repealed and the croppers and weavers were further disadvantaged.

Companies Act, 1844

An Act requiring all companies to be registered and to publish a balance sheet. The Act did not apply to companies such as the railways which had been approved by Parliament. It did, however, check speculation and systematize company procedures.

Conservative Party

One of the two major political parties in Britain which, according to BENJAMIN DISRAELI in 1872, had as its principles to maintain the institutions of the country, to uphold the Empire and to ameliorate the condition of the people.

The accession of George II in 1760 restored the Tories (the original name of the party) to favour, but it was not until the leadership of WILLIAM PITT after 1783 that the Tories began a period of predominance which lasted until 1830. By the 1820s the party was divided into two sections, the progressives who followed George Canning and the reactionaries who looked to the Duke of Wellington. After Canning's death in 1827 the party split and some of his disciples, including WILLIAM GLADSTONE, drifted into Liberalism (see LIBERAL PARTY). The word 'Conservative' was first used in an article in 1830 and quickly took the place of 'Tory', which had been in existence for over 150 years.

SIR ROBERT PEEL revived the party's fortunes after the passing of the REFORM ACT, 1832, which Conservatives had opposed. Peel was returned as prime minister in 1841, but the party was split in 1845 over the abolition of the CORN LAWS. Peel then resigned, taking the Peelites with him and leaving the rest of the party under the leadership of Lord Derby and

Disraeli. Benjamin Disraeli carried through the Electoral Reform Bill of 1867, and in 1874 was returned to office with the first clear Conservative majority since 1841. Until 1886 when they lost the general election, the party was responsible for the passing of a number of Acts for the improvement of social conditions.

Continental System

Attempts by Napoleon to stop Britain's trade with Europe during the NAPOLEONIC WARS. The System had been initiated when the war started in 1793 but it was ineffective until 1807, when most of Europe was under French control. Trade was hit severely at first and low grain imports led to high bread prices, unemployment and disturbances in a number of towns. The strains imposed on Europe were also very great. Customs duties on imported goods fell drastically and France needed some of the products of British colonies, which were forbidden. The Continental System was unpopular with the French MIDDLE CLASS as well as with the people of Europe overrun by France.

In 1809 Napoleon introduced a system of trade licences and the blockade began to break down. British exports in 1812 were 28 per cent higher than in the previous year, and after his disastrous retreat from Moscow Napoleon was unable to control trade in Europe.

Cookworthy, William (1705–80)

A QUAKER chemist in Plymouth who developed a process which cleaned Cornish CHINA CLAY or kaolin of impurities, so that it could be used for making HARD-PASTE PORCELAIN like that made in China. He searched Cornwall for suitable clays and became aware of the Cornish soapstone deposits. The superintendent of the St Austell tin mines, John Nancarrow, drew his attention to the white clay near the works, which was found to be identical with the kaolin used in China. William Cookworthy evolved a satisfactory method of purifying the clay and took out a patent in 1768. His monopoly of the process until 1796 delayed its use by other porcelain makers, although it could legally be used for earthenware. He also found the fluxing element of porcelain, known as *petuntse* by the Chinese, which became known as china stone in Britain. He started a small factory at BRISTOL in 1763 and shortly afterwards another at Plymouth. In 1773 he sold his interests in the Bristol firm to RICHARD CHAMPION.

Co-operative Movement

A movement which started in 1820 and took the form, at first, of non-violent societies of workers who wished to transform society by setting up primitive communist communities based on equality, labour and co-operation. The Co-operative Societies set up at this time needed CAPITAL to built their communities, and many of the 500 or so Societies aimed to acquire this capital by the 'Brighton System' of Dr William Kay. This consisted of the members purchasing from a common store, the profits of which would be used to purchase more commodities and, in time, manufactured goods. In this way the community would provide for all its needs in food, clothing and housing.

The failure of the GRAND NATIONAL CONSOLIDATED TRADES UNION and other WORKING-CLASS schemes resulted in the winding-up of many, but not all, of the Co-operative Societies. The movement was provided with a new emphasis in 1844 when the ROCHDALE PIONEERS opened a co-operative shop in the Lancashire town of Rochdale. The shop was a retail outlet, buying in bulk and selling to members of the public at large. Profits were used to buy further stock and keep prices low for the consumers. By 1851 there were 930 Societies similar to that at Rochdale.

The Co-operative Societies had their greatest strength in the industrial Midlands and North, with a number in the LONDON area. They provided opportunities for working people to gain experience of running the affairs of the community on democratic lines. Members of a Society were entitled to vote for the management committee which was responsible for running the society.

The Co-operative Wholesale Society was set up in Manchester in 1863 to buy goods centrally in bulk for co-operative shops to sell. The next step, in 1872, was for the Wholesale Society to undertake the production of goods to be sold in the stores. The number of shops increased steadily to reach 1,000 in the 1880s.

J. Bailey, *The Co-operative Movement* (The Party, 1952).

Copeland, William Taylor II (1797–1868

Son of William Taylor Copeland I, he acquired the SPODE Pottery in 1833 and took a Mr Spencer Garrett as his partner. He gathered around him a group of sculptors and artists who made the firm particularly well known for its statuettes and figurines. He became an important public figure, being a London alderman and Lord Mayor in 1835. He later became CONSERVATIVE MP for Stoke-on-Trent. When Spencer Garrett retired in 1847 the firm was managed by the Copeland family.

Copper and Brass Industries

BRASS is an alloy of copper and zinc, normally containing more copper than zinc, so the availability of copper is highly significant for its production.

Improved methods of casting brass and the introduction of the stamping process (used for making many brass goods, including buttons) about 1769 gave the industry an impetus, with BIRMINGHAM as the centre. By 1795 about 1,000 tonnes (1,120 US tons) of brass were being used there annually. Overseas trade flourished in the second half of the 18th century, particularly to India and the East. During the NAPOLEONIC WARS demand for brass declined and there was a period of depression. Buckles made of brass were replaced by shoestrings, and demand increased only later in the century when new ideas were found for the use of brass and copper, such as brass bedsteads, carpenters' tools and equipment for sanitation and water supply.

Apart from the demand for copper for

the brass industry, it was needed for the sheathing of ships' hulls. It was first used on warships in 1761 and later for merchant vessels. The opening up of copper mines in South America after 1830 provided the British manufacturers with large amounts of cheap ore which helped them to capture markets in Europe and North America.

H. Hamilton, *The English Brass and Copper Industries* (Cass 1967).

Copper Mining

The main centre was Cornwall where production trebled between 1750 and 1770, with about 90 mines in the county producing copper. The Cornish Copper Company improved the harbour at Hayle for importing coal, timber and iron from the mines, and for exporting copper. Mining costs were high because NEWCOMEN steam engines were needed in pits to pump out water. The first WATT engine began work in 1777, but mining in the county was already depressed by the discovery of large deposits of ore at PARYS MOUNTAIN in Anglesey. By 1788 the mines in Anglesey were controlled by THOMAS WILLIAMS, the 'Copper King', and to export the ore the port of Amlwch was improved. Copper mining also took place in North Staffordshire and at Alderley Edge in Cheshire.

R.L. Atkinson, *Copper and Copper Mining* (Shire Publications 1987).

Copper Smelting

Traditionally smelting took place in South Wales around Swansea and Neath. Coal was cheap and the copper could be sent from Cornwall by sea, with return cargoes of coal to fire the NEWCOMEN engines at the mines. The banks of the rivers Tawe and Neath were lined with copper smelthouses which polluted the surrounding area. A model industrial village was built in 1768 by Robert Morris, called Morriston. Ore was also smelted in Lancashire, near Warrington and at ST HELENS, using ore brought in by CANAL. The Greenfield Valley in Flintshire was another smelting area. A ROLLING MILL was built and by 1796 THOMAS WILLIAMS

had six smelters in the valley using water power. There were also smelters at Cheadle and Macclesfield in Lancashire at the end of the 18th century.

Corf

A container for carrying coal; originally a basket made of hazel wood, corves were later made of wood and iron. They could hold up to about 1.5 cwt (76 kg or 1.7 US cwt) of coal. Corves were dragged underground, mounted on wooden runners or sledges. Girls and boys were used for this heavy work, often crawling on all fours. Later the corves were placed on wheeled trams hauled by ponies or horses. One of the last pits to use corves was at Whitehaven, Cumberland, where they were abandoned in 1975.

Visit National Mining Museum, Lound Hall, Haughton, Retford, Nottinghamshire – corves on display. **M***

Corn Laws

Laws prohibiting the import of corn until the home price reached a specified amount. These laws had a long history, but the 19th-century agitation against them was directed at the 1815 Act, which fixed at 80 shillings ($6.8) the price below which corn could not be imported. In times of hardship the price was allowed to drop but fluctuations hit the WORKING CLASSES, whose wages were not adjusted accordingly. The Corn Law was believed to make the price of bread abnormally high and it became the symbol of political unrest with the founding of the ANTI-CORN LAW LEAGUE in 1838. In the 1841 election SIR ROBERT PEEL with the CONSERVATIVE PARTY was returned to power, pledged to defend the Corn Laws for the agriculturists.

A severe famine in Ireland in 1845 (see HUNGRY FORTIES), following the failure of the potato crop, caused many deaths, much hardship and emigrations and persuaded Peel that the Corn Laws must be abolished. He resigned when a bill to modify the Corn Laws was not supported by two of his colleagues and returned to office a few months later in 1846 to repeal the Laws. Shortly afterwards he was defeated and compelled to resign. The collapse of British agriculture, which had been confidently predicted, did not take place; instead there were 30 years of great agricultural prosperity.

Cort, Henry John (1740–1800)

An inventor who discovered the method for converting PIG IRON into WROUGHT IRON by separating the coal from the iron in the smelting process. The flames from the coal were deflected or reverberated down on to the iron in a REVERBERATORY FURNACE. He took out patents for PUDDLING and rolling in 1783; these processes took place after the reheating of the pig iron, which was then stirred with iron rods until the carbon and impurities had been burned away. It was then passed between iron rollers which speeded up the process and allowed larger quantities to be produced more quickly than in the past. His process made a single operation of puddling, hammering and rolling, which were previously disconnected.

Henry Cort also successfully developed the ROLLING MILL using grooved rollers to make iron shapes which were not flat, such as rails. Financial misfortune resulted in the loss of his patent right in 1790 for the reverberatory furnace, and as a result the process was able to spread rapidly.

R.A. Mott, *Henry Cort: The Great Finer. Creator of Puddled Iron* (Metals Society 1983).

Cost of Living

Careful analysis of prices of basic foodstuffs, clothing and household goods such as candles and coal provides broad tendencies in living costs. The crude statistics suggest that after 1755 there was an increase in living costs which reached a peak after 1790 until about 1813, as a result of the NAPOLEONIC WARS. Peaks within this trend were due to exceptionally bad harvests in 1766, 1782, 1795, 1800 and 1812. The cost of living fell between 1813 and 1823, when it increased again due to bad harvests, before falling steadily until 1845. The poor harvest of that year brought a sharp increase in the living costs for two years before further falls occurred in the 1850s.

A.J. Taylor, *The Standard of Living in Britain in the Industrial Revolution* (Methuen 1975).

Cotman, John Sell (1782–1842)

A member of the Norwich School of painters who was inspired by some of the industrial developments of his age, particularly the works along the valley of the Severn at COALBROOKDALE. He made sketches of TELFORD's AQUEDUCT at Chirk and Bedlam Furnace near Madeley, both in Shropshire, and of a coal shaft overlooking Coalbrookdale.

F.D. Klingender, *Art and the Industrial Revolution* (Paladin 1968).

Cotton Industry

Cotton is a natural fibre found in the seed boll of the cotton plant. In the 18th century it was imported from the West Indies and the American Colonies.

The cotton textile industry had been founded in Lancashire (see COTTON INDUSTRY – LOCATION in the 17th century, producing a woven cloth that was a mixture of cotton and linen. The two basic processes involved were spinning and weaving, with the spinning process the first to be transformed by MACHINES during the second half of the 18th century. By the middle of the 18th century a large proportion of the population of Lancashire and the adjacent counties was dependent on the cotton industry. The region saw the evolution of a capitalist CLASS (see CAPITAL), and it is not surprising that improvements to machinery (see COTTON INDUSTRY – MACHINERY) were first made there. Many of the early inventions were designed for cotton and did not work well with other fibres.

Cotton was cheap, despite the cost of bringing it from overseas, and there were fewer regulations and restrictions in the industry than in the older-established woollen and linen districts. The cotton industry had a greater freedom to expand and develop and by 1802 the industry accounted for between 4 and 5 per cent of the national income of Great Britain. By 1812 it had risen to between 7 and 8 per cent and had outstripped the WOOLLEN INDUSTRY in national importance. There was a boom in mill building between 1780 and 1788, and by the latter year there were at least 208 mills in operation. The number of workers in the industry increased rapidly, reaching 100,000 spinners and 250,000 weavers and auxiliaries by 1812.

By 1830 more than half the value of British home-produced exports (see COTTON INDUSTRY – EXPORTS) consisted of cotton textiles. Not a great deal of capital was needed to start production, and the demand for the product expanded rapidly as overseas markets were developed. It was a highly localized industry which benefited from economies of scale and encouraged innovation.

S.D. Chapman, *The Cotton Industry in the Industrial Revolution* (Macmillan 1972).
C. Aspin, *The Cotton Industry* (Shire Publications 1981).

Cotton Industry – Exports

Until 1815 there was a rapid growth in the sale of cotton piece goods and yarn to North America, Europe and the West Indies, although wartime problems caused changes in the markets from year to year. By 1810 cotton had replaced wool as the most important British export and by 1815 provided the country with 40 per cent of its total income from exports. This level was sustained with some fluctuations until the 1850s. After 1815, exports to Europe and North America continued to increase, but the growth of industrialization in the more advanced countries resulted in cotton falling as a proportion of total exports. This was partly due to a tariff imposed by the United States in 1815 and the removal of restrictions on the export of machinery (see COTTON INDUSTRY – MACHINERY) from Britain in 1843. Exports increased to the less developed world and by 1860 India was taking 31 per cent of British cotton cloth exports.

Cotton mills at Manchester. During the 19th century, cotton mills became progressively larger, depending for their strength on a cast-iron frame. They were built of brick with considerable areas of glazing supplemented by gas lighting. This sketch was made in 1835 and shows a seven-storey structure built close to a canal which would have been used to transport coal, chemicals and cotton to the mill and to distribute the finished rolls of cotton cloth. (*Mary Evans*)

Cotton Industry – Location

The COTTON INDUSTRY developed in the 18th century in three main districts: North West England, centred on MAN-CHESTER; the Midlands, centred on NOT-TINGHAM; and the Clyde Valley in Scotland, between Lanark and Paisley. The pre-eminent reason for location in these regions was the availability of water power from streams flowing from the Pennines or Scottish Uplands. In the Midlands, which included Derbyshire, Staffordshire, Leicestershire, Northamptonshire and Warwickshire, there were concentrations of cotton spinning mills in Nottingham and district, around Matlock and in the Dove Valley between Ashbourne and Uttoxeter. These concentrations were partly the result of the initiatives taken by such men as LEWIS PAUL, JAMES HAR-GREAVES, RICHARD ARKWRIGHT and William Strutt (see W.G. AND J. STRUTT).

At first the Midlands was the most important area but it had lost its early leadership by the end of the 18th century. There are a number of reasons for the decline. The isolation of the Derbyshire mills made transport costs high and delivery dates uncertain, outweighing the possible advantages conferred by complex water power and cheap labour. The Midlands failed to keep pace with Lancashire and West Yorkshire in taking on the MULE, and attempts to adopt the mule forced some Nottinghamshire and Derbyshire firms to go bankrupt. Lancashire developed important external economies, such as specialist textile machinery makers who were based in Manchester and Stockport, and LIVERPOOL developed as the cotton port for Lancashire. The Midlands could, however, import through LONDON and raw cotton could reach the mills by water, and it was nearer the markets of London and the South.

The fashion trades of Nottingham suffered from loss of business during the NAPOLEONIC WARS, whereas the high price of wool induced some people to buy the cheaper cotton clothes which were made in Lancashire. Bankruptcies reduced the number of Midlands firms, but others, such as Strutt's, survived into the 19th century.

Visit Lewis Textile Museum, Blackburn, Lancashire – machinery and other relics. **M***

S.D. Chapman, *The Early Factory Masters* (David and Charles 1967).

Cotton Industry – Machinery

Some of the early cotton spinners like ROBERT OWEN were also machinery makers. The first MULES were principally made of wood, with the shafts and spindles of WROUGHT IRON and the pinions and wheels of CAST IRON and BRASS. These machines were made by local wood workers. The first concern specializing in the making of cotton machinery was the firm of Dobson and Rothwell, of Bolton, Lancashire, in 1790. Henry Houldsworth, owner of mills near GLASGOW, carried on as a cotton and machine maker until the 1820s, but by the 1830s engineers had developed the machine tools required to make the machinery, and specialist firms grew up. These were located in the cotton-producing regions and could respond to changes in design and techniques as they occurred.

W. English, *The Textile Industry* (Longman 1969)

Cottonopolis   See Manchester

Cotton Spinners' Associations

Associations founded in the 1790s as benefit clubs, giving unemployment and sickness benefits to members in return for a small weekly subscription. They continued even after the COMBINATION ACTS were passed and in 1810 they were very effective during a strike in MANCHESTER, distributing strike pay to thousands of striking workers.

Country Banks

To meet the needs of businessmen who needed CAPITAL, country bankers began operating in various parts of the country in the 18th century. They were usually traders, financial intermediaries or collectors of government revenue. By 1784 there were more than 100 country banks and 10 years later the number had trebled. They played a vital part in economic progress as money lenders, suppliers of cash and custodians of deposits. They also transferred money to areas for investment, such as the Midlands and the North.

Most country banks were small with few reserves. In 1826 the joint-stock monopoly of the BANK OF ENGLAND was broken and joint-stock banks could be formed, at first outside LONDON and later in the capital. The country banks lost their ability to issue notes and they gradually disappeared as they were replaced by joint-stock banks. Although unable to cope with major crises, the country banks played an important part in the industrial development of Britain.

L.S. Pressnell, *Country Banking in the Industrial Revolution* (Oxford University Press 1956).

County and Borough Police Act, 1856

An Act of 1839 encouraged JUSTICES OF THE PEACE to appoint special constables, but by 1853 only 22 counties had taken advantage of the Act. The 1856 Act made it compulsory for the counties and boroughs (towns granted special privileges by royal charter, such as SHEFFIELD, Warrington and Brighton) to set up police forces, and three inspectors of constabularies were appointed with powers to check their efficiency. Grants for the setting up of these police forces were given by the central government to local authorities, but boroughs with a population of less than 5,000 maintaining separate police forces were not eligible for the grant. Overall power was effectively in the hands of Whitehall.

A similar Act, the County and Burgh Police (Scotland) Act, was passed for Scotland in 1857.

V. Bailey (ed.), *Policing and Punishment in Nineteenth Century Britain* (Croom Helm 1981).

Courtauld, George (1761–1823)

A UNITARIAN who started as a silk throwster in Spitalfields, LONDON, in 1782. He later moved to America and farmed in Kentucky, marrying Ruth Minton before returning to England in 1794 to work in silk mills in Kent. In 1799 he set up a silk mill at Pebmarsh in Essex to manufacture CRAPE, a hard, stiff silk which later became fashionable for mourning clothing. He later abandoned this mill and converted a flour mill at Braintree in Essex in 1809, where he employed large numbers of pauper girls who were looked after by his four daughters. In 1814 he patented a silk spindle which was used at his works. In 1818, with his son SAMUEL COURTAULD III in charge of the factory, he crossed the Atlantic again to live in Ohio, where he died.

Courtauld, Samuel III (1793–1881)

Born in Albany, New York, he grew up to help his father GEORGE COURTAULD at the Braintree, Essex, silk factory. He took over the business in 1817, built a new factory at Braintree and converted mills at Halstead and Bocking near Braintree for the silk industry. A STEAM ENGINE was introduced at Bocking in 1825 and POWER LOOMS followed in the 1830s. By the 1840s some 2,000 people were employed at the three mills and a variety of silk materials were made. The main activity was the manufacture of mourning CRAPE, which became fashionable in the second half of the 19th century and was the main dress material worn, particularly by UPPER- and MIDDLE-CLASS women, for months or even years after the death of a relative.

In the 1880s the demand for black crape dropped and the firm began to sell coloured crapes as well. New machinery and better dyeing equipment were introduced by George Courtauld IV (1830–1920) in 1894, and in 1905 the firm began making artificial silk (rayon) at a factory in Coventry. The firm improved the processes and the lower-priced product brought the firm success.

D.C. Coleman, *Courtaulds, An Economic and Social History* (Clarendon 1969).

Coventry

An industrial town in the West Midlands with a population of about 15,000 in 1790. It had been an important medieval centre with a wool industry, but this declined and the weaving of silk ribbon became the major industry. Another industry of the city was watch- and clock-making. The population of 16,000 in 1801 rose relatively slowly compared with other industrial towns, reaching 41,000 in 1861.

It is possible that George Eliot's masterpiece *Middlemarch* (1871–2), set in a mythical community in the Midlands, was based on Coventry.

The cycle industry was started in Coventry in 1868 by a firm which became known as the Coventry Machinists Company. The first British all-metal high bicycle was produced in 1870 and patented as the Ariel. Tricycles were also manufactured and in 1881 the production of these machines was more important to the city than the bicycle trade. Coventry developed as the cycle capital of the world and attracted component MANUFACTURERS like John Boyd Dunlop. He moved his factory making pneumatic bicycle tyres from Ireland to Coventry in 1888, to be near the heart of the trade.

In the 20th century the city was to become a major centre of the automobile and motorcycle industries.

Visit Herbert Art Gallery and Museum, Coventry – ribbon looms and winding machines. **M***
Museum of British Road Transport, Coventry – mainly Coventry-made cars and motorbikes. **M***

Crank and Flywheel Mechanism

An invention patented by James Pickard in 1780 to convert the pumping action of the early STEAM ENGINE into rotary motion. This enabled a steam engine to turn wheels and drive machinery. To avoid using the patent JAMES WATT patented his SUN AND PLANET GEAR in 1781. This was used on BOULTON AND WATT steam engines until Pickard's patent ran out in 1794.

Crape

The English word from the French *crêpe*, a thin, gauze-like fabric of highly twisted silk which has been crimped to give a minutely wrinkled surface. It became identified as the material, dyed black, to be worn when in mourning and at funerals. The fashion started with royalty in the 18th century, when Italian or Norwich crape was worn. Conspicuous grief for death became a symbol of social status among private families who took their example from royal protocol. In Victorian times mourning clothes were a boom industry. Widows wore black for a year and a day and then wore part black. Mourning for a child or parent lasted 12 to 15 months, with crape worn for at least the first six months. Household servants went into mourning with their employers. QUEEN VICTORIA had a remarkable enthusiasm for crape, dressing her daughter Beatrice at the age of three (1860) in a long, black, silk and crape dress.

Crawshay, Richard (1739–1810)

The son of a Yorkshire farmer who ran away from home, became an apprentice and won money in a lottery. He became a partner in the CYFARTHFA IRONWORKS in South Wales in 1777 and effectively owner in 1786. He introduced HENRY CORT's PUDDLING process in 1787 and expanded the business, making himself rich and famous and earning the nickname of the 'Iron King'. He was the chief promoter and shareholder of the GLAMORGAN CANAL, opened in 1794. By 1803 he owned six furnaces and employed 2,000 men at Cyfarthfa. He founded a dynasty of ironmasters who passed on the business to sons for several generations.

Visit Cyfarthfa Castle Museum, Merthyr Tydfil, Mid-Glamorgan – home of the Crawshay family, exhibitions of iron from the works and family relics. **M***

J.P. Addis, *The Crawshay Dynasty: A Study in Industrial Organisation and Development, 1765–1867* (University of Wales 1957)

Crawshay, William I (1764–1834)

The son of RICHARD CRAWSHAY, he took charge of the selling agency in London until his father's death in 1810. He has been called 'the uncrowned Iron King', since he was the architect of the prosperity at CYFARTHFA in South Wales during the difficult years after the NAPOLEONIC WARS. He bought out the other partners and became sole owner between 1817 and 1819.

Crawshay, William II (1788–1867)

He became sole owner of the South Wales CYFARTHFA IRONWORKS on the death of his father, WILLIAM CRAWSHAY I, in 1834. During his period the works grew considerably. He built Cyfarthfa Castle in 1825 and had a strong interest in the Taff Vale Railway (1841). He bequeathed his iron interests to his sons, giving the Cyfarthfa Works to Robert Thompson Crawshay (1817–79). His sons carried on the business until taken over by Guest, Keen and Nettlefold in 1902.

Creamware

Cream-coloured earthenware introduced about 1760 by JOSIAH WEDGWOOD. The material used was CHINA CLAY mixed with flint, with a transparent lead glaze added. Queen Charlotte, wife of King George III, ordered a tea-service of the material and Wedgwood renamed the earthenware 'Queen's Ware'. It was popular as an alternative to Delft ware, and factories making Delft pottery closed. Creamware was decorated with painting, TRANSFER PRINTING and moulding.

Crewe   See Railway Towns

Cromford

A settlement near Matlock in Derbyshire, which was developed by RICHARD ARKWRIGHT in 1771 with a large cotton mill to house his WATER FRAME. Water power for the spinning machines was provided by a stream, the Bonsall brook, and by the Cromford SOUGH, which drained a nearby lead mine.

Cromford was the forerunner of the mills and factories which were an essential part of the INDUSTRIAL REVOLUTION. It was the first of the cotton factory villages, and Richard Arkwright's ideas were copied by a number of other factory masters. Advertisements for workers at the mill appeared in the *Derby Mercury*, with the emphasis on craftsmen, since the new technology depended on their skills. A village was built by Arkwright to attract workers to the rather remote valley. There was a Greyhound Inn as well as terraced houses, a church and shops. A large part of the workforce consisted of women and children, some of whom were pauper families, and the mill operated day and night under the careful personal supervision of Richard Arkwright.

While two of the six storeys of the Cromford Mill have not survived, its scale and style can be assumed by examination of Richard Arkwright's Masson Mill (1784), nearby on the River Derwent at Matlock Bath. Masson Mill can be viewed only from the outside but the Cromford site has been developed by the Arkwright Society and tours can be made of the mill area. There are also important transport remains nearby, including the Cromford Canal and High Peak Railway with an INCLINED PLANE.

Visit Cromford, near Matlock, Derbyshire – industrial village. **M***

Crompton, Samuel (1753–1827)

A Bolton weaver who invented, in great secrecy in 1779, a machine which incorporated some of the features of the SPINNING JENNY and of RICHARD ARKWRIGHT's WATER FRAME. It spun a strong, fine and soft yarn which could be used in all kinds of textiles, but was particularly suited to the production of muslins, which were then imported as an expensive luxury. Samuel Crompton's spinning machine, being a cross-breed, became known as the MULE. By 1792 DAVID DALE at NEW LANARK was using water power to drive the mule, and within ten years mules with nearly 500 spindles were in operation.

Crompton's invention brought great wealth to the country and established Bolton as the world centre for the spinning of fine cotton yarn. Unfortunately, Crompton lacked business ability and his machine was not patented, making him very bitter when he saw the fortunes being made from it. ROBERT PEEL offered him a partnership in his textile business, which he refused. A BLEACHING business which he started failed because of bad management by his sons, and Crompton died relatively poor.

Cropper (Called a shearman in the West Country)

The name given to a skilled worker in the WOOLLEN INDUSTRY whose task was to take a piece of cloth from the fulling mill, cut it with shears while it was still wet, and cut it three times more after it had been teaseled, dried and stretched. The cropper's skill was in the central operation when the surface or nap of the cloth was raised and had to be trimmed by shears weighing 40 lb (18 kg) and measuring 4 feet (1.2 km) in length. These operations required that croppers worked in workshops and controlled the finishing processes, putting them in a strong position to organize themselves and keep out unskilled labour. The main threat to their livelihood was the GIG MILL, which had been invented in the 16th century and operated on a very limited scale. A larger threat in the late 18th century came from the shearing frame, which dispensed with the need for skilled craftsmen.

Mill owners who tried to introduce the gig mill had their mills destroyed and in LEEDS they dared not introduce them. Mills were also attacked in Somerset in 1797 and in Wiltshire in 1802. Attempts by the croppers to reinstate the STATUTE OF ARTIFICERS failed, and in 1809 all protective legislation was repealed. In 1812 shearing frames and gig mills were destroyed by LUDDITES in the West Riding of Yorkshire, and 4,000 soldiers were brought in to keep order. Mills were attacked and rioting took place in other areas, followed by arrests, threats, betrayals and public hangings. The croppers lost their livelihood and by the 1820s few skilled men were required, since the machinery made the operation

suitable for boys and a small number of unskilled men.

Crowley Ironworks

An ironworks established about 1682 by Ambrose Crowley III (1658–1713) at Sunderland. Later with partners he moved to a site on the river Derwent, a tributary of the Tyne just west of NEWCASTLE. This site was developed in 1707 and had direct access by boat to the sea. The works was extensive and included two steel furnaces, an iron forge, and blade and SLITTING MILLS. Naval contracts included orders for a range of iron goods such as axes, chisels, shovels, hinges, anchors and 108 different kinds of nails. The family also had a house, warehouses and a wharf at Greenwich in LONDON.

Ambrose Crowley's son John took over the business on his father's death, and other members of the family took over when he died. The firm developed in the 18th century using local coal and charcoal, water power and Swedish bar iron. The works used a form of the DOMESTIC SYSTEM, in that the nailers worked with their apprentices in shops or 'stalls' provided by the firm within one part of the factory buildings. Other nailers worked in their own homes as outworkers. The firm had a system of compulsory contributory insurance against death, sickness and old age, and a clergyman, doctor and schoolmaster were maintained jointly by the firm and its employees.

The depression following the NAPOLEONIC WARS forced the firm to reduce output, there was a lack of vigorous leadership and the works was sold in 1863.

M.W. Flinn, *Men of Iron. The Crowleys in the Early Iron Industry* (Edinburgh University Press 1962).

Crucible Steel

A process for making steel invented by BENJAMIN HUNTSMAN.

Visit Abbeydale Industrial Hamlet, Sheffield – crucible steel furnace. **M***

Cubitt, Sir William (1785–1861)

A civil engineer who started as a millwright in Norfolk. In 1812 he became a partner at ROBERT RANSOME's Ipswich works, and then moved to LONDON in 1826. He worked on CANALS in the Oxford area and took over from the ageing THOMAS TELFORD as engineer to the Birmingham and Liverpool Junction Canal. He carried out improvements to Ellesmere Port and worked on river and coal navigation schemes in his native East Anglia. In 1839 he completed the West Bute Dock at CARDIFF. He was also an important railway engineer, working on the London–York line and building the Wakefield–Lincoln railway, which was then extended to Boston.

Cultivator (Also known as a grubber, scarifier or scuffer)

An agricultural machine used to break up soil and clear it of weeds, roots or large stones. John Finlayson, an Ayrshire farmer, produced a self-cleaning grubber in 1820, the first to be forged entirely in iron. The implement was subsequently improved by James Kirkwood of East Lothian and Arthur Biddell of Essex in the 1830s. Biddell's scarifier was built by RANSOME's and received the gold medal of the ROYAL AGRICULTURAL SOCIETY. By about 1860 the cultivator was used extensively.

Curr, John (1756–1823)

An engineer who introduced L-section rails (called plate) into a colliery in SHEFFIELD in 1777. Because the rails were flanged, wagons with unflanged wheels could run along them. The rails were laid so that their upright flanges ran along their inner edges, between the wheels. He also designed a wheeled TRAM in 1787 which could run on the rails underground, be loaded with coal and be brought up the mine shaft without being unloaded at the pit bottom. To hold the tram steady in the mine shaft he placed guide rods down the side of the shaft. The tram was suspended on wooden cross-bars with rollers at either end which ran on the guide bars. His guide-bar system was not widely adopted.

Cutlery Industry   See Sheffield

Cyfarthfa Ironworks

Ironworks established near MERTHYR TYDFIL in South Wales in 1765 by ANTHONY BACON and William Brownrigg. In 1777 Bacon was joined by RICHARD CRAWSHAY, who took over the works in 1786 on Bacon's death. CORT's PUDDLING process was introduced the next year and by 1797 there were four furnaces in operation. In 1799 the largest waterwheel in Britain was installed there, to be supplemented in the next decade by STEAM ENGINES. By about 1810 the works employed 1,500 men, and by 1815 it had the largest output of any ironworks in the country. In 1830 there were 13 furnaces and 5,000 men.

Visit Cyfarthfa Castle Museum, Merthyr Tydfil, Mid-Glamorgan – ironmaster's house and iron museum. **M***

Cylinder Boring Machine

Early guns had a cored hole in the barrel which a boring tool, turned by a waterwheel, opened out and smoothed. The barrel had to be of equal thickness in cross-section or it was liable to burst. The method had only a limited success and a greatly improved boring system was introduced by Jan Verbruggen at the Royal Woolwich Arsenal in 1770. (Jan Verbruggen came to England from the Netherlands, where he had worked for the Dutch Admiralty.) By his method a solid cannon casting was rotated horizontally between bearings and the stationary boring head was advanced by a toothed rack on the boring bar. James Wilkinson took out a patent for a similar machine in 1774 but five years later the patent was revoked when it was realized the machine was based on Verbruggen's, which Wilkinson probably saw operating on the Continent.

The boring of cylinders for the early STEAM ENGINES was carried out using the original boring device for cannon, but the method failed to give the degree of precision JAMES WATT required. The cylinder for Watt's engine was of a small size, and in 1775 James Wilkinson probably bored it on the Verbruggen machine. It proved to be accurate enough to solve Watt's difficulties. He boasted that the machine was accurate to within the 'thickness of a thin sixpence', which would be an enormous margin of error by today's standards. Soon other firms were using similar machines and Jan Verbruggen's boring machine remained in use at Woolwich unti 1842.

In the mid-19th century a large vertical boring mill was built at the SOHO WORKS and used to bore four cylinders for ISAMBARD BRUNEL's *GREAT EASTERN*. Each cylinder bore was 7 feet (2.1 m) in diameter.

L.T.C. Rolt, *Tools for the Job* (Science Museum 1986).

Cylinder Printing Press

A press invented by Thomas Bell in 1783. He used copper cylinders for printing fabrics, which were a great improvement on the practice of stamping fabrics by hand using printed plates. One revolving cylinder press could print material as fast as a hundred workmen using engraved plates.

D

Dale, David (1739–1806)

A Scottish businessman and a strict Presbyterian who was the co-founder, with RICHARD ARKWRIGHT, of the NEW LANARK spinning mill in 1786. The mill took power from the river Clyde but it was located in a sparsely populated rural area, so David Dale built a model village near the factory and offered houses at a low rent. A number of families were attracted to the area, chiefly from the Highlands; Edinburgh and GLASGOW sent several hundred pauper children. Dale looked after his apprentices, providing food, clothing and EDUCATION. His daughter married ROBERT OWEN in 1799.

David Dale had a number of other interests. In partnership with JAMES MONTEITH he established cotton mills at Blantyre in Lanarkshire in 1787, and with other partners built a mill at Catrine in Ayrshire and Newton Stewart in the south of Scotland. In 1783 he established the first turkey red dye works at Barrowfield. He also played an important part in the formation of the GLASGOW Chamber of Commerce.

Visit New Lanark, Lanarkshire – mill and model industrial village. **M***

Dalton, John (1766–1844)

A chemist and meteorologist who devised a hygrometer to measure humidity and argued that air is a mixture of gases and not a single compound. In 1803 he described the atomic theory – that matter consists of indivisible atoms which are indestructible and merely rearrange themselves in chemical reactions.

Dandy Cart

A low truck in which a horse, normally used for pulling coal wagons, could ride when the wagons ran down steep inclines under their own momentum. The cart was fixed behind the wagons and the system was used at one or two locations until the beginning of this century.

Dandy Roll

A cylinder frame with a woven wire cover which helped to press out the water from wet paper pulp and improved the sheet formation. It was patented by John and Christopher Phipps, paper-makers with mills at Dover. Later, watermarking patterns were sewn on the woven wire.

Darby, Abraham I (1678–1717)

A QUAKER ironmaster who was a partner in a BRASS works at BRISTOL before moving to COALBROOKDALE in Shropshire. In 1709 he produced PIG IRON smelted with coke instead of charcoal at his ironworks. The use of the process spread slowly, partly because the iron was impure and could be used only in the production of castings. The discovery led to the gradual development of foundries on the coalfields instead of in forest regions such as Sussex. Abraham Darby leased the Coalbrookdale works in 1708 and became an active member of the Quaker community in the region. Many of the workpeople he employed were Quakers, which helped to give the works a 'family' atmosphere.

Visit Ironbridge Gorge Museum – a large working museum of the early iron industry. **M***

B. Trinder, *The Industrial Revolution in Shropshire* (Phillimore 1981).
A. Raistrick, *Dynasty of Iron Founders: The Darbys and Coalbrookdale* (Longman 1953; David and Charles 1970).

Darby, Abraham II (1711–63)

The son of ABRAHAM DARBY I, he took over the complete management of the COALBROOKDALE Ironworks in 1745 on the death of RICHARD FORD. In 1748 he built wooden WAGONWAYS and new furnaces where PIG IRON could be made suitable for conversion into bar iron. A QUAKER, like his father, he took a great interest in the social needs of his workpeople. Houses were built for them and Friends' Meeting Houses in 1745 and 1759.

Darby, Abraham III (1750–89)

The grandson of ABRAHAM DARBY I, he took control of the COALBROOKDALE COMPANY in 1769 and expanded it, as well as rebuilding the old furnace. The firm had been making cylinders, pump parts and pipes for NEWCOMEN'S STEAM ENGINE since the 1720s, and this practice continued under Abraham Darby III.
Probably he is best remembered for the IRON BRIDGE over the River Severn which was erected in 1779. In this

venture he was joined by JOHN WILKINSON and Thomas Harries, who owned much land on the west side of the river. In 1788 the Society of Arts presented their gold medal to Abraham Darby in recognition of his achievements in building the Iron Bridge.

Darby, Abraham IV (1804–78)

The great-great-grandson of ABRAHAM DARBY I. With his brother Alfred he took over the management of the COALBROOKDALE COMPANY in 1830. They made some important changes, improving the furnaces and introducing NEILSON's hot blast method in 1838. From 1830 to 1850 the engine shop and foundry produced a succession of bigger and better engines. The plate mill could produce iron for boiler plates 5 feet (1.5 m) wide, larger than anywhere else in the country. A wire mill was built in 1834 and the works rapidly expanded, employing about 2,000 men,
Houses were built for the workers using shale from one of the ironstone waste heaps to make bricks. A voluntary sick club was started and surplus funds were used to build a school in 1846 to serve 700 children.
Abraham Darby IV left the works in 1849 to manage the Ebbw Vale and Brymbo Ironworks. The tradition of caring for the workers continued; a school of art was founded in 1856 and a literary and scientific institution was built in 1859.

Darby, Francis (1783–1850)

The son of ABRAHAM DARBY III and father of ABRAHAM DARBY IV, he was a manager of the COALBROOKDALE Works from 1810 until his death. His main interest was in art and he was responsible for the Company developing art castings. He introduced artistic designers who produced designs for rails, balconies, gates and other ornaments in CAST IRON.

Darwin, Erasmus (1731–1802)

A doctor, scientist, poet and philosopher, he founded the Derby Philosophical Society in 1782. He designed a FLINT MILL for JOSIAH WEDGWOOD and was abreast of all the advanced scientific thought of his time. He was a leading spirit of the LUNAR SOCIETY and wrote some influential poetry called 'Botanic Garden' in 1789–91. The title is rather misleading since the poems embrace the whole field of knowledge and its industrial applications.

His poetic imagery appealed to his contemporaries although he has been ridiculed for his flamboyant style. Here is a short section from the 'Botanic Garden', in which he describes the operations in RICHARD ARKWRIGHT's cotton mill at CROMFORD:

> *First with nice eye emerging*
> *Naiads cull*
> *From leathery pods the vegetable wool;*
> *With wiry teeth revolving cards release*
> *The tangled knots, and smooth the rovell'd*
> *fleece;*

He was the grandfather of the author of *The Origin of Species*, Charles Darwin (1809–82).

Davenport, John (1765–1848)

A master potter who established a works at Longport, near Burslem in THE POTTERIES in 1794. In 1806 he patented a type of art glass having a design made up of a coating of many-coloured powdered glass applied to the surface. The pottery produced earthenware and a wide range of coloured domestic ware as well as vases and a few figures. A PORCELAIN factory was added in 1820, making porcelain similar to that at Derby, with tea and dessert services as a staple product. In 1830 he employed 1,400 workers and had many commissions from royalty and the gentry. He was elected MP for Stoke-on-Trent in the Potteries from 1832 to 1841, and his sons continued the business until it closed in 1882.

T.A. Lockett, *Davenport Pottery and Porcelain, 1794–1887* (David and Charles 1972).

Davy, Sir Humphry (1778–1829)

A Cornishman who became a brilliant scientist. He is best known as the inventor of a SAFETY LAMP, which was successfully tried in the Hebburn Colliery near Newcastle in 1816. He also became well known in social and scientific circles for the lectures he gave at the Royal Institution. In 1810 he demonstrated the carbon arc at one of the lectures. This electric arc light was obtained with a very large battery of voltaic cells, probably as many as 2,000. He had demonstrated that a glow of light could be obtained by the resistance of a conductor to electric current, but at that time there were no practical applications possible.

Dawson Wheel

A notched wheel invented in 1791 by William Dawson of Leicestershire. It was used in the textile knitting industry and led to the use of power for driving knitting machines.

Death Rate

The number of deaths per thousand of the population. Estimates suggest that the death rate fell steadily after 1740, from 35.8 per thousand to an average of 21.1 between 1811 and 1820. It then began to rise again to reach 23.4 in the 1830s, before more or less remaining constant at 22 per thousand.

The main reason for the fall towards the end of the 18th century was the rise in the STANDARD OF LIVING. The rise in the death rate in the early 19th century was connected with the growth of the towns. Over half the deaths were from infectious diseases, the product of overcrowding, dirt and ignorance; sanitation systems could not keep pace with the expansion of the towns and in the first half of the 19th century the urban environment was deteriorating. In 1839 the Registrar-General reported that 20 per cent of the total death rate was caused by consumption, a disease normally associated with poverty and overcrowding. His report also showed that the death rate was particularly high among children. Improvements did not come until the 1870s.

Derby Porcelain Manufactory

A pottery established in 1756 by William

Duesbury (1725–86), a PORCELAIN enameller. He bought the CHELSEA PORCELAIN factory in 1770 and the Bow porcelain works in 1775. The firm started making Crown Derby ware in 1784 and there was a considerable trade in smelling-bottles, toothpick cases, plaques for mounting as brooches and cuff links. Derby was the first porcelain factory to decorate with pictures in the style of oil paintings. The factory closed in 1848.

J. Twitchett, *Derby Porcelain* (Barrie and Jenkins 1980).

Detroisier, Rowland (1800?–34)

A self-taught Lancashire cutter who became a political lecturer and reformer. He established some of the first MECHANICS' INSTITUTES in England. He believed in the benefits of a general EDUCATION and was an eloquent speaker. In 1831 he was made secretary of the National Political Union to press for reforms.

Dickens, Charles (1812–70)

A novelist from a poor home who worked as a reporter before achieving success as a writer in 1836. He wrote extensively about LONDON and vividly portrayed the SLUMS, poor schooling and many aspects of the life of the industrial WORKING CLASSES. He drew the attention of his generation to some of the problems which had arisen from the rapid urbanization and LAISSEZ-FAIRE attitudes of the time.

In *David Copperfield* and *The Pickwick Papers* Dickens gives a vivid description of coaching. The refusal of the magistrates to make Oliver Twist, in Dickens' novel of the same name, become an apprentice chimney sweep (see CHILD LABOUR – CHIMNEY SWEEPS) may have helped the passing of the 1840 Act, since the novel was published in 1838–9. He also attacked the legal system for its incompetence and greed and wrote a pamphlet exposing the anachronistic PATENT LAWS.

Visit Dickens House Museum, 48 Doughty Street, London WC1. **M***

R.J. Cruickshank, *Charles Dickens and*

Early Victorian England (Pitman 1949).

Dickinson, John (1782–1869)

A stationer in the City of London who was also an inventor and took out a patent in 1809 for a PAPER-MAKING machine. It was called Dickinson's cylinder mould machine and a number of improvements were made to it, including the addition of a vacuum trough to help draw off water from the wet sheet. In the same year he bought the Apsley Mill in Hertfordshire and in 1811 he purchased the Nash Mill near Hemel Hempstead. He successfully developed a paper-making business and in 1815 introduced STEAM-HEATED CYLINDERS to dry the wet pulp. Three other mills came under his control and by 1838 his mills were turning out 41 tonnes (45.9 US tons) of paper each week. He was probably the pre-eminent paper maker in Britain between 1810 and 1860.

Disraeli, Benjamin (1804–81)

The son of a christianized Jew who entered Parliament in 1837 as a Tory RADICAL (see CONSERVATIVE PARTY). He wished to see the aristocracy work to help the mass of the people, but did not want to give power to the WORKING CLASSES. He disliked the commercial MIDDLE CLASS and supported the landlord class in trying to retain the CORN LAWS. He was a novelist and in *Sybil; or, the Two Nations* he urged the need for an aristocratic revival to solve the problems of the times.

Visit Disraeli Museum, Hughenden Manor, High Wycombe, Buckinghamshire. **M***

R. Blake, *Disraeli* (Methuen 1969).

Dissenters

People whose religious beliefs were at variance with those of the CHURCH OF ENGLAND and who separated from it because they did not wish to conform – hence the term nonconformists, also used of dissenters.

During the Commonwealth (1649–60) the Church of England was

disestablished and there was an increase in the number of independent sects. These, like the Presbyterians in Scotland, had the protection of Parliament under Oliver Cromwell, a Puritan. The chief of these dissenting sects were the Congregationalists or Independents. The movement had grown during the Civil War (1642–9) and was particularly strong in LONDON, East Anglia and towns in the South West. The Baptists formed another dissenting sect and were much persecuted after the Restoration of the monarchy in 1660.

The 17th century also witnessed the growth of small groups whose members believed in direct spiritual guidance. These groups were rallied by George Fox and his followers and became known as QUAKERS. Another small group, the UNITARIANS, were joined by many Presbyterians in the 18th century.

The changes brought about by the INDUSTRIAL REVOLUTION in the second half of the 18th century were largely ignored by the Church of England, and a new group of dissenters emerged – the followers of METHODISM. They were led by JOHN WESLEY and appealed directly to the WORKING CLASSES, who assembled in large crowds to hear him preach. Although he never broke with the Church of England the Methodists formally separated in 1795, four years after his death.

Dissenters in general believed in personal probity and honesty and considered luxuries and idleness to be twin evils. These qualities, among others, made them skilful business people. Their social isolation drew them together into closely knit communities where there was mutual trust and help for members in difficulty. Business partnerships were reinforced by kinship and marriage within the sect. As a result of their hard work and thrift, dissenters became some of the key agents of economic growth during the Industrial Revolution.

Dissenting Academies

Schools developed by the DISSENTERS or nonconformists who, because they were not members of the CHURCH OF ENGLAND, were excluded from Oxford and Cambridge (see UNIVERSITIES), as well as major schools such as Eton (see SCHOOLS – PUBLIC). The restrictions on schooling were reinforced by the exclusion of nonconformists from Parliamentary careers and civil and military office. Many nonconformists were well established in business, BANKING and industry. There was a sense of social alienation, strengthened by lack of access to institutions and other groups which could promote business interests.

The dissenting academies provided an excellent commercial EDUCATION with a practical emphasis which included foreign languages, mathematics, accounting and science. The education they provided contrasted with the rigid, authoritarian approach of the GRAMMAR SCHOOLS and helped to establish the conditions in which the INDUSTRIAL REVOLUTION could take place, as well as training some of the ENTREPRENEURS, mechanics and technical innovators who pioneered it.

Docks

The working area of a port or harbour where ships are unloaded and loaded. There are three main types of dock; wet docks with entrances that can be closed; tidal docks with unclosed entrances; and dry or graving docks to contain a vessel which is out of the water for repairs. Wet docks are needed where there is a rise and fall of tides over about 10 feet (3 m); entrance is usually by means of a LOCK and the water-level inside remains unchanged. LONDON, LIVERPOOL and BRISTOL are three ports where wet docks had to be built. Tidal docks are built where there is only a small tidal range, as at GLASGOW, while dry docks were built at a number of ports where repairs were carried out.

Dock construction requires very strong stone and concrete side walls and sufficient space for warehouses, cranes and other equipment for loading and off-loading ships. At Liverpool and other ports the docks were enclosed by a high wall and few gates to provide security.

The growth in trade towards the end of the 18th century resulted in the need for more docks and better harbours.

Extensive excavations at Liverpool extended the docks to over 50 acres (20.2 ha) by 1824. The most extensive developments were in London, which had only two wet docks in 1800. The bottleneck in the movement of goods was solved by excavating wet docks downriver from the Tower of London. The loop in the Thames made by the Isle of Dogs was cut at its narrowest part by the West India Dock, opened in 1802. Nearer the Tower of London, the London Dock was built in 1805, and further downstream the Grand Surrey Basin, forerunner of the Surrey Commercial Docks, was opened in 1807. St Katherine's Dock near the Tower was approved in 1824, with a design by THOMAS TELFORD.

In Liverpool, dock expansion was considerable between 1824 and 1860 under JESSE HARTLEY. There were over 200 acres (80.9 ha) of docks in 1860. The Albert Dock, completed in 1845, was surrounded by large enclosed warehouses.

Visit Albert Dock, Liverpool – Merseyside Maritime Museum. **M***

J. Pudney, *London's Docks* (Thames and Hudson 1975).

Doherty, John (1797–1854)

A cotton worker who settled in MANCHESTER in 1816 and led a successful strike of the cotton spinners in 1829. He helped to form the NATIONAL ASSOCIATION FOR THE PROTECTION OF LABOUR in 1830 and edited their journal, *The Voice of the People*. He wanted the WORKING CLASSES to organize their own EDUCATION, and he saw the development of MACHINES as inevitable. He argued that machinery must be under the direction of the working classes and that the ultimate goal of human effort was not wealth but freedom.

Domestic System

The organization of manufacturing before the introduction of the FACTORY SYSTEM during the INDUSTRIAL REVOLUTION. By the middle of the 18th century the domestic system displayed a number of distinctive characteristics.

(a) Very little CAPITAL was needed to start a business – many workers' capital consisted of no more than a loom or a set of tools. Enterprises requiring capital were mainly confined to the IRON INDUSTRY and COAL MINING. Much capital was invested in materials which were handled by merchants, many of whom were also MANUFACTURERS.

(b) The family was the most important work group, but it was not a self-contained unit. A weaver, for example, required yarn from at least three spinners to be kept fully occupied. Production units were small and based on the home or the workshop, with some workers employing others as apprentices or journeymen (apprentices who had completed their APPRENTICESHIP).

(c) In the textile and metal trades production was carried out by outworkers who were paid by the piece. Some manufacturers employed over 1,000 outworkers who were scattered over a wide area.

(d) Processes were relatively simple and men and women could move easily from one occupation to another and between industry and agriculture.

(e) Workers were free to determine their hours of work. They could regulate their workday and working week, subject always to the need to make a living.

(f) Working conditions in the home were generally poor and children were expected to work from an early age.

(g) Workers were frequently in debt, borrowing from their employers in time of need and placing themselves under an obligation to the employer until the debt was repaid.

(h) There were many sources of industrial conflict, often caused by dishonesty in the employer or by the worker when dealing with raw materials or the finished goods.

(i) Under-employment rather than periodic unemployment was very common, mainly because employers spread work lightly over a large number of workers to ensure there would be no shortage of labour if demand increased.

(j) There were large numbers of poor people who were semi-employed or who had no regular means of employment.

Donkin, Bryan (1768–1855)

An inventor and manufacturer of PAPER-MAKING moulds, who started as a millwright apprentice. He was responsible for setting up the first paper-making machine at FROGMORE MILL in Hertfordshire, based on drawings provided by Nicholas Robert, the inventor. The first machine in 1803 was not successful and the FOURDRINIER brothers, who had financed the experiment, set up an engineering works for Bryan Donkin in Bermondsey. A machine built at the works in 1804 was further improved by Donkin, and by 1807 the first paper-making machine in the world was running successfully.

With partners he set up a CANNING factory in 1810 in Bermondsey, which was also a success. By 1815 he had turned his interests to civil engineering, and became a founder member of the INSTITUTION OF CIVIL ENGINEERS.

Doulton, Sir Henry (1820–97)

The son of John Doulton (1793–1873), who started a small pottery in Lambeth, LONDON, in 1815. In the 1820s the firm extended its output to make terracotta garden ware and chimney pots. Henry Doulton joined the firm as a thrower and in 1846 introduced the manufacture of glazed pipes for sanitary ware and the making of earthenware sinks for WORKING-CLASS homes. There was a considerable expansion in demand for sanitary ware in the 1840s, and the firm played an important part in providing the materials for sewage disposal (see SEWERS). From 1862 the firm produced SALT-GLAZED WARES with blue decorations, in addition to PORCELAIN and fine BONE CHINA for domestic use.

D. Eyles, *Royal Doulton 1815–1965* (Hutchinson 1971).

Dowlais Ironworks

Ironworks set up in 1759 on heathland near MERTHYR TYDFIL, South Wales, by Thomas Lewis and partners. JOHN GUEST became manager in 1767 and a partner in 1782. On his death in 1787 his son Thomas took charge until 1792. In 1801 the firm introduced CORT's PUDDLING process, and concentrated on WROUGHT IRON. The company expanded during the NAPOLEONIC WARS and had three BLAST FURNACES in operation. After the war there was further expansion, and a build-up of orders from the railways in the 1830s and 1840s.

Apart from the CYFARTHFA works Dowlais was the largest in the country, and it continued to prosper under SIR JOHN GUEST. By 1843 the output was 70,000 tonnes (78,000 US tons) annually and 7,000 people were employed. The neighbourhood benefited from the Guest family's philanthropy, and schools, a church and a library were built. The works had a contributory medical scheme and in 1853 a savings bank was started. After Sir John Guest's death in 1852 Dowlais was administered by a board of trustees.

Visit Dowlais, near Merthyr Tydfil, Mid-Glamorgan – stable block and remains of blowing house.

Dredging Equipment

A STEAM ENGINE made by BOULTON AND WATT was used as a dredge at Sunderland in 1796, and JOHN RENNIE developed a steam dredger with a bucket chain in 1804. This method of dredging spread to other harbours in the first half of the 19th century.

Drummond, Thomas (1797–1840)

An engineer and surveyor, born in Edinburgh, who invented LIMELIGHT, known as the 'Drummond Light'. He also invented an improved heliostat, an instrument for throwing rays of light in a given direction which was used in surveying. After 1831 he became interested in politics, having met HENRY BROUGHAM, and in 1835 he became under-secretary at Dublin Castle and virtually Governor of Ireland.

Dundee

Scottish textile and engineering town with an important LINEN industry in the 18th century. After the ACT OF UNION there was a policy of encouraging the WOOLLEN INDUSTRY in England and linen in Scotland. There was a linen bounty paid on exported linen between 1732 and 1832 and the industry flourished, using local flax or flax from the Baltic. Between 1793 and 1806 steam-driven mills were built in the town. In the late 1820s flax became scarce and in 1822 jute was introduced. By 1833 the first sample of jute carpeting was produced and demand increased for it, both dyed as a floor covering and for sacking.

The switch to jute was not rapid; firms retained their FLAX SPINNING and weaving and manufactured jute materials as well. The jute industry was stimulated by the interruption in flax supplies during the Crimean War (1854–6). In the 1850s Dundee began making textile machinery for export, and machinery was installed in a Calcutta jute mill in 1855. Competition from India became severe and Dundee, which had not diversified its industrial structure, faced fierce competition from 1875 to 1914, when the jute industry recovered by meeting the First World War demand for sandbags.

The population was 26,000 in 1801 and reached 63,000 in 1841, 90,000 in 1861 and 140,000 in 1881. Distinctive tenement blocks were built in the second half of the 19th century. The tenements had four storeys with gallery access to economize on staircases. Most families had a 'home of two rooms, although some had three, with two or more families sharing a stairway and lavatory. The tenements were built of stone by speculative firms using money invested by the MIDDLE CLASSES.

Visit Tay Jute Works, Lochee Road, Dundee.
McManus Galleries, Albert Square, Dundee – local industrial history. **M***

Dyeing

In the 18th century dyes were made from natural substances such as roots, saffron, woad and madder. In the 1790s GEORGE MACINTOSH set up a works at Dalmarnock in central Scotland to produce turkey red dye on a vast scale, using lichens as the vegetable source. For many hundreds of years dyes had been fixed on fabrics by using alum as a mordant. As most natural dyes were in the red range, colour diversification was obtained by variation of the mordants with which the dyes were applied. For example, green was obtained by double-dyeing with indigo (blue) and yellow (fustic).

By the 1850s it was considered that there could be a shortage of natural dyes because they were obtained from a limited number of crop plants. The first synthetic dyes were not introduced until the 1860s, following experiments by SIR WILLIAM PERKIN, who produced an aniline dye in 1856 by synthesizing coal tar. New aniline colours were quickly developed in Britain and in France. From 1860 to about 1880 initiatives in the dye industry came from those two countries. Natural colour materials were still used; in 1870 the UK imported over 10,000 tonnes (11,200 US tons) of madder. A rapid expansion of the British dye industry was needed if synthetic dyes were to be produced in the amounts required by the textile industry.

The industry failed to respond to the need, the major developments took place in Germany and Britain had to import large quantities of German dyes. The failure of the British dyestuff industry to keep pace with Germany has been attributed to the lack of technical training in the UNIVERSITIES, the attitude of the government and the general absence of vision, which exemplified a loss of 'industrial spirit'.

S. Grierson, *Dyeing and Dyestuffs* (Shire Publications 1989).
D.W.F. Hardie and J.D. Pratt, *A History of the Modern British Chemical Industry* (Pergamon 1966).

Dynamometer

A simple, spring-operated instrument used for measuring the pulling power required for ploughs. It was invented by Samuel Moore, Secretary to the Royal Society of Arts in the 1780s, and enabled farmers to determine the best plough for their land. The instrument had a dial and as the horse pulled forward all the tension was passed along the meter; the draught, or pulling power, was indicated by a pointer mounted on the dial.

E

Eddystone Lighthouse

The third lighthouse on the Eddystone Rock outside Plymouth harbour, Devon, was built by JOHN SMEATON in 1759. He used shaped stones, each of which dovetailed into its neighbour. He also used a strong cement to hold the stones together. The lighthouse remained in position for 120 years and was then dismantled because of erosion of the rock under its foundations.

Visit Plymouth, Devon – part of the Eddystone Lighthouse, built by Smeaton on Plymouth Hoe.

Eden Treaty See Anglo-French Treaty, 1786

An artist's impression of the Eddystone lighthouse as it looked *c.* 1845. This was the third lighthouse to be built on the dangerous reefs guarding the entrance to Plymouth harbour. The first lighthouse was destroyed in 1703 only five years after it was built. The second, built partly of timber in 1709, lasted for 46 years before it burnt down. John Smeaton was responsible for the third lighthouse which was built between 1756 and 1759. He used granite blocks, dovetailed together and locked to each other by wooden pins and marble plugs. The ball on top of the cupola was screwed into place by Smeaton himself. It stood 70 feet (21.3 m) above the rock and the light was provided by 22 tallow candles. After 120 years the lighthouse was replaced because the sea had destroyed the cement and undermined the rock used for the foundations. The stump was left in position and the upper half was re-constructed on Plymouth Hoe. (*Mary Evans*)

Education

Provision for elementary schools throughout England was made in a Bill of 1807, which was rejected by the House of Lords. Apart from CHARITY SCHOOLS, the main education available at that time was financed by two organizations. The first, formed in 1808, was the BRITISH AND FOREIGN SCHOOLS SOCIETY and was supported by rich WHIGS and QUAKERS. The other, founded in 1811, was the NATIONAL SOCIETY for Promoting the Education of the Poor in the Principles of the Church of England. Some churchmen and members of the UPPER CLASSES did not

encourage the poor to become literate, believing that education for WORKING-CLASS people should be limited to making them more useful workpeople. This view was not shared by others, including working-class parents who supported privately run DAME SCHOOLS and the SUNDAY SCHOOL movement.

In 1818 about one in four poor children was receiving some kind of education. The position was worst in the rapidly growing industrial towns, where there were often no schools. In 1833 the government gave a grant to be divided between the British and Foreign and the National societies. This grant was raised in 1839 and inspectors were set up to examine the work of the schools. By 1840 about two-thirds of the female population and half of the male could not sign their names on their marriage certificates.

Dr KAY-SHUTTLEWORTH, the chairman of a committee set up by the Privy Council, opened a private training college for teachers in Battersea, London, in 1840, which was handed over to the National Society in 1843. Subsequently several other training colleges were formed. In 1854 a practising teacher could earn the title of registered teacher, which provided a status and a wage paid by the government. The 1870 Education Act was eventually to lead to all children receiving some full-time elementary education. It provided for school boards to be set up to build schools, which were to be paid for partly out of rates (a local authority tax on property). School fees of a few pence a week were charged, but poorer parents could be excused from paying.

The 1880 Education Act made it compulsory for children aged 5 to 10 to go to school. They could then leave to work half-time in factories if they had reached a certain standard of education; otherwise they had to stay at school until they were 13.

M. Sanderson, *Education, Economic Change and Society in England, 1780–1870* (Macmillan 1983).

Electric Cables

Underground cables became necessary to carry ELECTRIC TELEGRAPH signals in urban areas, and in the 1840s and 1850s methods of insulating and protecting them were explored. At the same time UNDERWATER TELEGRAPH CABLES also required protective materials. In 1848 THOMAS HANCOCK coated wire with gutta-percha, but in time the material perished. Unsuccessful attempts were then made to insulate telegraph wires with bitumen. Lead-covered cable was introduced in 1850, and the practice of identifying multi-strand cables with different colours for each strand was introduced in 1852. Later in the century rubber was used successfully as an insulating material.

Electric Generator

Within two years of MICHAEL FARADAY describing to the Royal Society the interaction of electric and magnetic fields to produce mechanical motion (1831), a simple, rotating coil generator had been demonstrated to the BRITISH ASSOCIATION. Generators began to be made commercially in LONDON and in 1857 a steam-driven generator with an output of 1½ kW was used to produce a light, using an arc lamp. The equipment was installed in the South Foreland Lighthouse in 1858 and worked successfully. Nevertheless, generators capable of giving satisfactory service over long periods had still to be designed.

Electric Telegraph

This was developed in Britain by William Cooke and CHARLES WHEATSTONE after Cooke had seen an instrument operated in Heidelberg, Germany. A patent was obtained in 1837 and it was demonstrated to the directors of the GREAT WESTERN RAILWAY. The line from LONDON to Slough was connected up in 1842, using an instrument with two needles and based on a code. In 1845 the electric telegraph attracted public interest when a suspected murderer was arrested in London. He had boarded a London-bound train at Slough and the telegraph had been used to signal to London that he was on the train. He was tried, found guilty and hanged.

In 1846 Cooke and Wheatstone formed the Electric Telegraph Company, and they had installed some 4,000 miles (6,437 km) of telegraph by 1852. In 1851 a cable was laid under the Channel linking Britain with France. After several attempts, a cable was laid under the Atlantic between Britain and the United States in 1866 (see UNDERWATER TELEGRAPH CABLE).

Electroplating

First developed by GEORGE RICHARDS ELKINGTON and his cousin Henry in 1840 for the electro-deposition of silver or gold on base metals such as copper or BRASS. The earlier method of plating was to coat the metal with mercury and then to rub the surface with gold or silver and mercury in the form of a stiff paste, until a smooth coating had been applied. Finally the article was heated on a charcoal fire to drive off the mercury before burnishing the surface. Electroplating rapidly replaced the old method and there was a large demand for silverplated jugs, spoons and teapots and for goldplated jewellery from the increasing numbers of the MIDDLE CLASSES.

Elkington, George Richards (1801–65)

The inventor who, with his cousin Henry, pioneered the technique of ELECTROPLATING. He started as an apprentice in a BIRMINGHAM small-arms factory and later became its owner. In 1840 he, with his cousin, took out a patent for electroplating metals with silver or gold. In the same year a patent for an electromagnetic machine was taken out by John Stephen Woolrich, who set up a factory in Birmingham. The Elkingtons took over the patent and set up a large workshop in Newhall Street, Birmingham. They also patented their ideas in France and after 1850 electroplating replaced the early methods of coating base metals with gold or silver. George Elkington also established a COPPER-SMELTING works in Pembury, South Wales, providing schools and housing for his workers.

Elliott, Ebenezer (1781–1849)

A SHEFFIELD ironworker who started a business in 1821. He became active in CHARTISM but withdrew when the Chartists repudiated the movement for the repeal of the CORN LAWS.

Emigration

Small numbers of people emigrated from the UK to the American Colonies and West Indies in the 18th century, and after the AMERICAN WAR OF INDEPENDENCE skilled workers, including potters, were encouraged by American firms to emigrate. For some years after the founding of Sydney Cove, Australia, in 1788 as a convict settlement the number of free emigrants to Australia was negligible, although by the end of the century the government was anxious to attract emigrants to Australia and offered free land and a free supply of (convict) labour, as they had done in the American Colonies 50 years earlier. In the 1820s the British government and charitable organizations began making small grants to poor, unemployed people, to help them to emigrate. Skilled workers did not qualify; until 1824 it was a crime to 'seduce' an artisan to emigrate and there were many prosecutions to prevent the free flow of labour.

Planned emigration to Australia was started in the 1830s by Edward Gibbon Wakefield, and the numbers increased in the 1840s, encouraged by Caroline Chisholm, a ROMAN CATHOLIC philanthropist who founded a Family Colonisation Loan Society in 1849. Writing at the time, CHARLES DICKENS provided a happy haven for Wilkins Micawber in Port Middlebay (Melbourne) at the end of *David Copperfield* (1849–50).

Developments overseas proved a powerful influence in accelerating or reducing the flow of emigrants. The discovery of gold in Australia between 1848 and 1851 and in California in 1849 attracted immense crowds of immigrants. A new and better life with the chance to become rich were 'pull' factors, but there were also 'push' factors. Emigration fluctuated according to the state of trade; unemployment drove up the flow of emigrants and the TRADE UNIONS sometimes used their funds to help people in depressed regions or trades to emigrate. One of the strongest 'push' factors was the Irish famine of 1845 (see HUNGRY FORTIES). In the years that followed some 2 million Irish people emigrated to America. By the 1870s emigration was at the rate of nearly 90,000 every year, and this figure more than doubled during the depression of the 1880s.

T. Coleman, *Passage to America* (Penguin 1974).

Employment of Children   See Child Labour

Engels, Friedrich (1820–95)

A German socialist philosopher who was the son of a cotton manufacturer with mills in Germany and MANCHESTER. Friedrich Engels moved to Manchester in 1842 to complete his training as a cotton merchant and was shocked by the social divisions there, which he thought could result in a revolution between 'masters and men'. He met KARL MARX in 1844 and corresponded and worked with him for the rest of his life. He wrote *The Condition of the Working Classes in England* in 1844 as an indictment of the industrial society he observed in Lancashire. From 1854 until 1870 he worked in his father's firm in Manchester while financing and encouraging Karl Marx.

Enginewright

A highly skilled craftsman who looked after the pumps and other machinery at a colliery. When steam was introduced the enginewright developed into an engineer but often kept the old title. Both GEORGE and ROBERT STEPHENSON were enginewrights for collieries in North East England.

Enterprise

The first packet steamer (see STEAM BOATS) to cross the oceans from Falmouth to Calcutta via Capetown. The journey took 113 days in 1825 and during that time the ship was under steam for 64 days. The twin-cylinder engine was made by HENRY MAUDSLAY.

Entrepreneur

The entrepreneur in business is responsible for obtaining the CAPITAL required and organizing production by efficiently using the inputs such as labour and raw materials, deciding on the rate of output to meet demand and introducing innovatory techniques when necessary to maximize profits.

RICHARD ARKWRIGHT was a brilliant entrepreneur and kept his fixed capital working for 24 hours a day by using two 12-hour shifts. He organized a large workforce and used methods which were to become part of the factory system. Large works such as COALBROOKDALE and MATTHEW BOULTON's SOHO WORKS were training grounds for apprentices, and their skilled labourers were sought after by other MANUFACTURERS. Men like JOSIAH WEDGWOOD produced goods for which there was a demand; they employed travelling salesmen, chose works managers with great care and marketed their goods at home and overseas. The INDUSTRIAL REVOLUTION produced people who could organize industrial enterprise on a large scale to exploit the expanding market at the time.

P.L. Payne, *British Entrepreneurship in the Nineteenth Century* (Macmillan 1979).

Ericsson, John (1803–89)

A Swedish-born American engineer who designed the locomotive *Novelty*, which competed at the RAINHALL TRIALS in 1829. He designed other locomotives and experimented with a rotary STEAM ENGINE in conjunction with F.B. Ogden, the United States Consul in LIVERPOOL, and a pioneer of steamship operations in the USA.

By 1833 John Ericsson was experimenting with various types of stern propellers for CANAL boats. In 1835 he designed a screw propeller, and two years later a high-pressure steam engine directly coupled to the propeller shaft. In association with Mr Ogden he had a vessel built for experimental purposes and launched on the Thames in 1837. The trials attracted the attention of an American canal builder, Robert E. Stockton, who ordered an iron-hulled steam canal tug to be built using the engine and propeller. The tug was named after the owner and despite its small size of 70 feet by 10 feet (21.3 m by 3 m) it crossed the Atlantic under sail, and operated for many years as a canal tug.

John Ericsson's design was used for the ARCHIMEDES in 1838, and in the next year he emigrated to the United States, becoming an American citizen in 1848. In 1849 he built the *Princeton*, the first metal-hulled, screw-propelled warship and the first to have the engines below the waterline. His skills as a naval engineer were used in the American Civil War when his ship the *Monitor* defeated the Confederate ship *Morrimack*. After the Civil War he continued his work as a designer and inventor.

W.C. Church, *The Life of John Ericsson* (London 1890).

Established Church

The church recognized by the state as the official religion. In England it is the Church of England; in Scotland it is the Church of Scotland, which is Presbyterian. There is no established church in Wales; the Church of Wales was dis-established in 1920. The monarch must be a member of the Church of England and the church can change the form of worship only by consent of Parliament. Two archbishops and 24 Church of England bishops sit in the House of Lords. The Church of Scotland is free from Parliamentary control and has much looser links with the state.

Etruria Works

A pottery works built in 1769 by JOSIAH WEDGWOOD, to the south of Burslem and just northeast of Newcastle-under-Lyme in THE POTTERIES, to replace another site known as the Bell Works. The new factory was on the Ridge House Estate where the TURNPIKE ROAD from Leek to Newcastle-under-Lyme crossed the TRENT AND MERSEY CANAL. The building faced the canal and a bell was set in a cupola to summon workers to the works.

Nearby Wedgwood built Etruria Hall, a mansion for himself which was completed in 1770.

Visit Wedgwood Museum, Barlaston, Stoke-on-Trent – examples of Wedgwood porcelain. **M***

Evangelical Movement

The work of JOHN WESLEY was part of what is called the 'Evangelical revival'. It was a protest against the frivolity and excesses of society in the latter part of the 17th century and the worldliness of church during the 18th century. The Evangelicals were puritan in outlook and fundamentalists in their attitude to the Bible. Evangelical clergymen such as John Wesley delivered rousing sermons which moved many in the audience to tears and other emotional scenes.

From about 1738 clergy, supported by sympathetic churchgoers, preached of the need for salvation. GEORGE WHITEFIELD was one of the leaders of the Evangelicals although in time he became a formidable opponent of John Wesley. John Fletcher, vicar of Madeley in Shropshire, was a strong supporter of Wesley and a holy, as well as a humble, parish priest. Salina, Countess of Huntingdon (1709–91), tried to extend the Evangelical revival to those of her own CLASS. She used her own money to build chapels and a college for the training of ministers. Her organization, over which she presided with a rod of iron, became known as 'Lady Huntingdon's Connexion'. The effects of the revival were widespread and Sunday was given a greater significance.

The Wesleyans broke away from the ESTABLISHED CHURCH and formed a separate religious denomination, METHODISM, in 1795. Evangelicals who remained with the established church were treated with a good deal of hostility, but the exemplary behaviour of the Evangelicals gradually broke down opposition. They tended to form themselves into groups in certain centres. One group was based in Cambridge. Another group formed in Somerset under the leadership of HANNAH MORE. The most famous of all Evangelical groups was based at Clapham and known as the CLAPHAM SECT.

The Evangelical revival of the 18th century found expression as practical Christianity in the 19th. The Evangelicals considered the slave trade a disgrace and it was William Wilberforce and his friends at Clapham who persuaded Parliament that slavery should be abolished in 1833. The Evangelicals were also active in other areas; an Anglican Mission was started in India after 1813, while in 1799 the RELIGIOUS TRACT SOCIETY had been started by Hannah Moore to bring cheap religious literature to the poor. The Evangelicals stirred the conscience of the people by their practical Christianity and the exposure of social injustices.

Exports

In 1775 over 70 per cent of British exports went to Europe, but Europe's share dropped to about 30 per cent by 1798 during the NAPOLEONIC WARS. In the same period exports to North America rose from 11 per cent to 32 per cent and Americans still preferred British manufactures after the AMERICAN WAR OF INDEPENDENCE. Exports to the West Indies increased in the 18th century from 5 per cent in 1750 to 25 per cent in 1798. The volume of all exports increased until the Napoleonic Wars, when there was a slump, but a rapid upsurge followed after about 1820, the result of a vast increase in the quantities of textiles and other goods exported. Between 1820 and 1850 the value of exports increased nearly four times despite falls in export prices. Because of a deterioration in the terms of trade, Britain had to export twice as much by quantity to earn the same amount of imports in 1860 as in 1800. This was mainly due to falls in the price of cotton, the major export, caused by steep falls in production costs and in the price of raw cotton.

F

Factory Act, 1802 (Also known as the Health and Morals of Apprentices Act)

Introduced by SIR ROBERT PEEL SENIOR to improve the conditions for apprentices – mainly children in factories (see CHILD LABOUR – FACTORIES). The Act applied only to large factories, especially the spinning mills, where the APPRENTICESHIP system was abused severely by some MANUFACTURERS. The Act had clauses detailing rules for workshop hygiene and limitations on the hours of work. Work could not exceed 12 hours per day and could not take place after 9 p.m. or before 6 a.m. All apprentices had to be taught reading, writing and arithmetic in their work hours and religious instruction was compulsory every Sunday. Girls and boys were to sleep in separate dormitories with no more than two children sharing a bed. Inspectors were to be appointed to visit the factories, of whom one was to be a local magistrate, the other a CHURCH OF ENGLAND clergyman.

The Act was too vague and people were employed without apprenticeships to avoid it. The inspectors were not anxious to quarrel with the employers and the system was allowed to lapse in some districts. The Act, however, although ineffective, did lay the foundations for future industrial legislation and was a step away from the policy of LAISSEZ-FAIRE.

Factory Act, 1833

The first effective Factory Act, because it provided for full-time inspectors. It applied only to the textile industry and even then not to silk mills. Children under 9 could not be employed and hours of work for children under 13 were limited to 9 per day and 48 per week, with 2 hours' compulsory education for children aged 9 to 11. (In practice this was ignored because of lack of schools.) Night work was not permitted for workers under 18 years of age.

Factory Act, 1844

This Act applied only to textile factories, and limited women and young persons aged 13 to 18 to not more than 12 hours' work a day. Children under 13 under work 6½ hours a day with time for EDUCATION. The age children could start work was lowered from 9 to 8. Dangerous machinery was to be fenced in and accidents reported to the doctor.

Factory Act, 1847

This Act limited the hours of work for women and young people to 10 hours a day and 58 per week. This was later amended to 10½ hours per day. The Act applied only to parts of the textile industry.

Factory Act, 1850

This applied to the textile industry and limited hours for women and young persons to within the period 6 a.m. to 6 p.m., with a 1-hour meal break. The Act put an end to the shift system, which had made inspection difficult. There was to be a 2 p.m. finish on Saturdays.

Factory Act, 1853

The Act prohibited the use of child labour in the textile industry for shift work and laid down that children were to be employed only from 6 a.m. with 1½ hours for meals. (Children had not been mentioned specifically in the 1850 Act.)

Factory (Extension) Act, 1864

Special safety regulations were laid down for six dangerous industries which included match-making, pottery and cartridge-making. The existing FACTORY ACTS were extended to apply to other industries as well as to textile mills and mines.

Factory (Extension) Act, 1867

Factory regulations extended to all places employing more than 50 people.

Factory Act, 1874

The minimum working age raised to 9. Women and young people were to work no more than 10 hours a day in the textile industry. Children up to age 14 were to work for only half a day.

Factory Act Workshops (Consolidation) Act, 1891

The safety and sanitary regulations were extended to include workshops and the minimum working age was raised to 11.

Factory Act, 1901

The minimum working age raised to 12.

Factory System

The organization of production into units employing more people than the workshops or workers' homes of the DOMESTIC SYSTEM. The first factories used water power and were located where this power was available. They housed a large number of MACHINES which required many workers to tend them. When steam power was introduced more machinery could be driven and factories became larger, with hundreds or even thousands of workers. This concentration of workers in one place resulted in the growth of towns close to the factories. The factory system also produced a division of labour and strict regulations for the workers. There were health and social problems arising from large numbers of people living and working in close proximity.

The factory owners formed a new class of ENTREPRENEURS with considerable powers and wealth. All these features distinguished the factory system from the small workshops and rural, home-based industrial structure which it replaced. The factory system did not dominate industry in the first half of the 19th century, because domestic and small-scale workshops survived in large numbers and employment in them expanded. In the 1830s and 1840s the factory system was still mainly confined to the textile industry. By 1840 the term was a convenient label for a complex of social attitudes and assumptions. Factory life was, for thousands of workers, their social experience of industrialism. It was a new way of life which did not, in its early days, undermine the family unit. Ironically it was the FACTORY ACT, 1833 which broke the kinship system, with adults and children working different length days.

J.T. Ward, *The Factory System, Vol. 1. Birth and Growth* (David and Charles 1970).

Fairbairn, Sir William (1789–1874)

A Scottish engineer who founded the firm of engineering millwrights, Fairbairn and Lillie, in MANCHESTER in 1817. He designed more efficient line shafting to transmit power to the fast-running textile machinery. This resulted in an orderly and carefully planned grouping of MACHINES in the workshops. He also invented a machine for riveting boiler plates by steam power in 1838. In the 1830s he concentrated on SHIPBUILDING, first in Manchester and then in 1835 at Millwall on the River Thames, where his ironworks employed 2,000 men. He wrote a number of learned papers and books including an account of the construction of the BRITANNIA BRIDGE and the Conway tubular bridge, industrial biographies, *Iron, its History, Properties, etc.* and *Mills and Millwork*.

Family – As Economic Unit

The pre-INDUSTRIAL REVOLUTION textile family was an economic unit. This continued to operate in the early FACTORY SYSTEM; the skilled man hired his own assistants, who were members of his family. As POWER LOOMS were introduced the team necessary to work the looms could not be confined to family units, and the unrest and strikes of the 1820s were partly to protect the economic relationship between parent and child. Factory legislation, starting with the FACTORY ACT, 1833 split the hours of child labour from those of adults and recommended educational provision for the children. The 1840s and 1850s factory legislation further increased the split between home and factory, and began the surrender of the family's traditional training function to the beginnings of an educational system.

Faraday, Michael (1791–1867)

The son of a poor blacksmith who became the founder of the electrical engineering industry. He was largely self-taught, and attended the lectures given by SIR HUMPHRY DAVY at the Royal Institution. He became Davy's assistant and accompanied him on a European tour. He demonstrated electromagnetic induction in 1831 and pointed the way to the conversion of mechanical into electrical power. He also promoted the idea that the atom was the centre of force, and inaugurated the Christmas lectures at the Royal Institution which are still popular today. Michael Faraday blended theory and experiment and many of his discoveries were not put into use until some years after his death.

Fellows, Samuel (1687–1765)

A FRAMEWORK KNITTER who became a hosier and pioneered the concentration of textile production in NOTTINGHAM. He established a workshop with apprentices and began to specialize in silk hosiery. New knitting techniques for making eyelet holes prompted him to build a factory where the innovations could be developed. Other hosiers followed his example so that by the time RICHARD ARKWRIGHT arrived in Nottingham in 1769, small factories had been developed by innovators who wanted some degree of secrecy for the methods they were using.

Female Reform Societies

The first societies for women were set up in 1818 and 1819 in the cotton towns of Blackburn, Preston, Bolton, MANCHESTER and Ashton-under-Lyne. The increased use of female labour during the NAPOLEONIC WARS had given women a measure of self-confidence and independence. Further female political unions were formed with chairwomen, committees and other officers. Between 1815 and 1835 there were a number of independent TRADE UNION actions among women workers, including a strike of 1,500 female card-setters in the West Riding of Yorkshire in 1835. There was no question of these societies seeking female suffrage. Their role was limited to giving moral support to the men, making banners and caps of liberty, passing resolutions and swelling the numbers at meetings. In their actions they were strongly supported by WILLIAM COBBETT and other reformers.

Fielden, John (1784–1849)

A factory reformer who was a cotton MANUFACTURER in Yorkshire. As an MP he introduced the FACTORY ACT, 1847, which restricted the hours of work for women and young persons in textile factories to 10 a day.

Fines

Fines were imposed to keep discipline in both the DOMESTIC and FACTORY SYSTEMS. There was a need for factory discipline because of the young age and inexperience of the workforce, who were not accustomed to factory methods. Employees who left work without permission could be prosecuted. The STRUTTS used 'small fines' to enforce discipline. They were called forfeits and were punishments for such offences as theft of mill property, failure to do the work as required, destruction or damage of mill property and misconduct outside working hours. The forfeits were taken from earnings and records show that at the Strutt mills the percentage of total earnings forfeited was small, although it could cause hardship.

Finlay, Kirkman (1773–1842)

The son of James Finlay, a yarn merchant in GLASGOW. In partnership with the Buchanan brothers (see ARCHIBALD BUCHANAN), the firm took over the Catrine Mills in 1802 and the Ballindalloch Mills in 1808. James Finlay and Co. became the largest firm in the trade and Kirkman became an MP in 1812. The firm is still operating, the only survivors of a time when the manufacture of cotton was Scotland's chief industry.

J. Finlay, *James Finlay and Co. Ltd 1750–1950* (Jackson 1951).

Firedamp

The name given to methane gas found in some coal pits and formed from the decay of vegetation during the Carboniferous period. The gas is retained under pressure in seams and if ignited can cause an explosion and fire. The most effective remedy is good ventilation (see COAL MINING – VENTILATION). The deeper pits in Northumberland and Durham were prone to firedamp, and 643 colliery explosions were recorded between 1835 and 1850. The dangers from firedamp led to the invention of the SAFETY LAMP.

Fireproof Mills

Towards the end of the 18th century a number of mills burned down, including the Albion mills in LONDON in 1791. Early mills were built with a wooden framework and floors and the machinery was liable to overheating resulting in serious fires. The first move towards fireproof mills was the putting up of buildings at Derby and Milford in 1792–3 for William Strutt (see W.G. AND J. STRUTT), which had CAST-IRON uprights but cross-beams of wood. Strutt also built his West Mill at Belper in 1793–5 with a similar construction. The first fireproof mill was built by Messrs Marshall, Benyon and Bage at Shrewsbury in 1796 for the production of LINEN. No wood was used in the construction, the beams being of iron with the floors supported by brick arches. The mill was five storeys high and was followed by two more at LEEDS between 1802 and 1804 and another at Shrewsbury in 1804–5. William Strutt used iron frames to rebuild his North Mill at Belper, after it burned down in 1803.

Fireproof mills were more expensive to build and were adopted only slowly, and numerous industrial buildings were poorly constructed of wood throughout the 19th century.

Visit Belper, Derbyshire – Strutt's North Mill.

Flax Spinning

Flax, the fibres of which are used for making LINEN, was grown extensively in Scotland in the 17th and 18th centuries. In 1780 probably 250,000 people were employed spinning and weaving the material, and linen production was Scotland's main industry. Counties as far north as Orkney grew considerable quantities of flax, but difficulties of transport resulted in the industry flourishing best in coastal areas with communications by sea.

The west central area around Paisley and the Clyde Valley moved to cotton spinning in the 1780s and the linen industry became concentrated on the east coast, with the main areas in 1820 being in Angus, Fife and Perthshire. Hand spinning was taken over by MACHINES, although at first the machinery was only capable of spinning coarse yarns and fine yarns were still spun by hand until the 1820s. Factories were built at Arbroath, Brechin, Forfar, Cupar, Dunfermline and Kirkcaldy, but the industry was centred on DUNDEE.

In England the manufacture of linen became an important industry in LEEDS. Flax had been grown locally to the east of the town and the spinning and weaving of the cloth took place at Knaresborough, in the valleys of the Upper Nidd and Washburn using local water power.

JOHN MARSHALL was responsible for the development of the industry at Leeds. He leased a watermill to the north of the town in 1789 and began spinning flax yarn. In 1793 he perfected a series of processes for producing linen thread and yarn, and built a mill at Water Lane in Leeds. The town had the advantage of local coal and access via Hull to imported flax from northeast Europe. In 1838–40 John Marshall had the Temple Mill built at Leeds in an Egyptian style. John Marshall and Company continued as flax spinners until 1886, when the mill was closed.

P. Baines, *Flax and Linen* (Shire Publications 1985).

Flint Mill

A mill used for grinding flint into a powder, for use as a whitener in the PORCELAIN industry. The problem of some silica getting into the lungs was solved by grinding under water until the mixture was creamy. It was then run off and agitated before settling. The last process was drying in a kiln. This operation was based on patents taken out in 1726 and 1732 by Thomas Benson of Newcastle-under-Lyme.

Visit Cheddleton, Staffordshire – operational flint mill *c*.1760.
Hanley, Staffordshire – Etruscan bone and flint mill, 1857.

Fluid Glaze

A glaze consisting of a mixture of lead and flint into which BISCUIT WARE was dropped before a second firing. It was developed by a Tunstall potter, Enoch Booth, about 1750. He also improved cream-coloured wares by mixing local clay, Devon and Dorset clay and flint.

Fly Boat

A fast boat used on the CANALS to carry shop goods, parcels and other miscellaneous freight as part of a regular service. Fly boats were popular on the SHROPSHIRE CANAL and linking canals in the Midlands and THE POTTERIES. Their services were intended to compete with road transport and win traffic from other canals. To achieve this less tonnage was carried than on normal boats. PICKFORDS had extensive schedules from LONDON to MANCHESTER and LIVERPOOL, from

BIRMINGHAM to Leicester and from Birmingham to Stourport (for Bristol). The boats ran to a timetable and had regular stops on the way. Horses on fly boat services were changed along the route. The fly from Birmingham to Ellesmere Port on the river Mersey took place twice weekly and took 29 hours to cover the 110-mile (177-km) journey – 3.8 mph (6.1 kph). On this journey horses were changed five times.

Fly Frame

A MACHINE used in the processing of cotton to prevent uneven winding caused by excessive power transmission to the bobbins as they filled. It was patented by Henry Houldsworth of MANCHESTER in 1826.

Fly Van

A light, horse-drawn coach used by carriers to carry freight. Fly vans ran to fixed schedules and provided a fast service.

Fogging   See Nail Making

Food Riots

Sporadic food riots took place in different parts of Britain during the second half of the 18th century and the first two decades of the 19th century. A further outbreak took place during the potato famine of 1846–7 in the peripheral regions of North East Scotland and Cornwall.

The causes of these riots are complex and were related to regional patterns of industrial development as much as to the growth and development of internal trade. The 1846–7 food riots took place in small communities which were in rural settings and where it was assumed farmers and dealers were profiteering. Apart from these, however, the food riots were mainly the collective actions of town ARTISANS and industrial workers. Only in rural Wales did the yeoman small farmers join the rioters. Rioting was a strategy employed by industrial workers in defence of their STANDARD OF LIVING. As contributory factors, there were the

growth of capitalist farmers (see CAPITAL) and large merchants, which undermined local markets for food, as well as some dislocation in supplies following the increased demand for food resulting from industrial growth.

Poor harvests and dislocation of supplies due to war also led to unrest. A number of MANUFACTURERS gave relief during food crises in the 18th century and it was with this sort of background that the Speenhamland System (see POOR LAW – SPEENHAMLAND SYSTEM) was introduced in 1795, to subsidize wages in relation to the price of bread. By the end of the century food price levels were steadily rising and in the heavily capitalized growth industries, such as coal, iron and textiles, the workers shifted their tactics from rioting to wage bargaining. The manufacturers after 1800 forced through wage reductions, and used troops to protect their property during the disturbances which followed.

After the NAPOLEONIC WARS there was a period of depression, low grain prices and improved communications with better retail and wholesale outlets. As a result food rioting practically stopped, although riots did occur at LIVERPOOL in 1855 and LONDON in 1860–1 and 1866–7.

A. Charlesworth (ed.), *An Atlas of Rural Protest in Britain, 1548–1900* (Croom Helm 1983).

Ford, Richard (1689–1745)

The manager of the COALBROOKDALE Ironworks from 1717 until 1745. A capable businessman, he expanded sales and worked closely with ABRAHAM DARBY II from 1732. Although both Richard Ford and Abraham Darby were QUAKERS they began manufacturing cannon in 1740. In 1742 a STEAM ENGINE was introduced to work the pumps, which returned water to the mill pond after it had passed through the waterwheel.

Forth and Clyde Canal

An Act was passed in 1768 forming the Forth and Clyde Navigation Company. Work was started, directed by JOHN SMEATON, but the money ran out before the CANAL was finished, and it was not opened from the Forth to the Clyde until 1790. The Company then became prosperous, with the carriage of both goods and passengers, and the canal had considerable economic importance for the industries of central Scotland.

Fourdrinier, Henry (1766–1834) and Sealy (1766–1847)

Brothers who were pioneers of mechanized paper manufacture. The first MACHINE for PAPER-MAKING which produced a continuous roll of paper was invented by a Frenchman, Nicholas Louis Robert (1761–1828). He obtained a patent in 1798 with the backing of St Leger Didot (1767–1829), owner of a printing firm. Didot asked his brother-in-law, an Englishman called John Gamble, to take out a patent for the machine in England where there was likely to be a better chance of getting the machine improved. Gamble came to England in 1801 and showed some rolls of paper produced on the machine could make continuous rolls of paper and decided to build one at a mill they owned in Hertfordshire, called the FROGMORE MILL.

The first machine was erected by BRYAN DONKIN in 1803, but it did not work well. He made several improvements and after 1807 a number of the machines were sold. The machine could produce 600 lb (272 kg) of paper ever 24 hours, or almost 100 tonnes (112 US tons) a year, nearly three times as much as the average production of a hand-made mill at the time.

The Fourdrinier brothers failed to obtain all the royalties owed to them and became bankrupt in 1810. By 1830 half the paper manufactured in Britain was being made on a Fourdrinier machine.

Fowler, John (1826–64)

A pioneer of steam ploughs (see STEAM ENGINES – PLOUGHING), who at first had his ploughing engines built by other firms. In 1858 he was awarded a prize at the Royal Show as the first man to make ploughing by steam cheaper than horse ploughing. In 1863 he set up his own works in LEEDS,

and in 1864 steam ploughing trials were held and Fowler gained first prize. He died in a hunting accident later that year. The firm prospered for the next 70 years, mainly on its sales of steam ploughing systems.

Fox, James (1789–1859)

A self-taught engineer who was supplied with CAPITAL by a country parson, who employed him as a butler, to set up in Derby as a MANUFACTURER of improved textile machinery of his own design. He had first to design and construct the MACHINES to make his textile machinery, and for this task he made a lathe in 1814 and a planing machine with advanced features. The success of these machine tools was such that he began to manufacture them for sale at home and abroad.

Visit Birmingham Museum of Science and Industry – planing machine and lathe made by James Fox. **M***

Fox Talbot, William (1800–77)

The inventor of a method of making a photograph called a calotype. The image was fixed with chemicals on paper which was rendered with translucent wax, and positive copies could be made from this negative. The advantage of his invention was that it was much faster than the daguerreotype method then in use, and copies could be made from the original negative. He took out a patent in 1841 and continued to improve his invention. In 1852 he engraved a photograph on a steel plate and in 1854 gave photographs a gloss by using albumen.

Visit Lacock, near Chippenham, Wiltshire – Fox Talbot Museum of Photography. **M***

J. Hannavy, *Fox Talbot*, (Shire Publications 1976).

Frameshop

A workshop in which the early hand-knitting frames were operated by knitters. Sometimes these workshops formed the third floor of a building with the homes of the knitters beneath.

Visit Sutton Bonnington, Hinckley, and Shepshed, Leicestershire – frameshops. Ruddington, Nottinghamshire – Ruddington Framework Knitters' Museum, frameshop with hand frames. **M***

Framework Knitters

Workers in the domestic textile industry who operated a stocking or hosiery frame. Work was usually done in the knitters' homes or adjacent workshops, where the stocking frames were operated by members of the family. Middlemen called bag hosiers acted as agents between the framework knitters and the merchant hosiers. They distributed yarn and forwarded the finished goods to the warehouses, working on a commission basis. The stocking frame, though a complicated mechanism, was not difficult to operate and young people of 10 or 12 could become skilled in six or nine months. Some framework knitters built up small amounts of CAPITAL and became hosiers, employing apprentices and building workshops.

The development of factory production in the second half of the 18th century brought deterioration in the STANDARDS OF LIVING of those engaged in the unskilled work. Those on more skilled work mainly lived in NOTTINGHAM and, being in local contact with framesmiths and merchant hosiers, were able to develop new meshes and garments on the versatile stocking frame. There was considerable discontent in the villages, where the workers were reluctant to enter the mills with their strict discipline and regular working hours. In 1807 an old-established Framework Knitters Company was revived at a time when wages were declining. The depressed state of the knitters exploded into LUDDITE machine smashing in 1811–12. In 1811 there were some 29,000 stocking looms in the country and 50,000 workers. Like the HAND LOOM WEAVERS, the framework knitters were slowly to decline into poverty as production was taken over by powered machines. Less than 5,000 remained in 1901.

M. Palmer, *Framework Knitting* (Shire Publications 1984).

Free Trade

The ability to trade with other countries without encountering artificial restrictions like tariff barriers. British attitudes to trade in the 18th century were based on the Mercantilist (see MERCANTILE SYSTEM) theory of protection.

Writers such as ADAM SMITH, DAVID RICARDO and RICHARD COBDEN argued for free competition. They were opposed by many MANUFACTURERS, farmers, shippers and government agents who raised revenue from tariffs. WILLIAM PITT simplified and reduced tariffs, but the war with France and the economic crises which followed prevented any further movement towards free trade. The CORN LAWS of 1815 reversed the trend, but WILLIAM HUSKISSON lowered tariffs and modified the NAVIGATION ACTS while president of the Board of Trade between 1823 and 1827.

In 1841 SIR ROBERT PEEL became prime minister, determined to restore prosperity after the slump at the end of the 1830s. He reduced tariffs on imported manufactured goods and raw materials, but did not go far enough. Further reductions were made in his 1845 budget, and the Corn Laws were repealed in 1846. GLADSTONE continued the free trade policy as chancellor of the exchequer after 1853 and most remaining duties were removed in his 1860 budget, with only small duties remaining on 48 items for revenue purposes. In the same year a free trade treaty was negotiated with France, and so by 1860 Britain had become a free trade country.

N. McCord, *Free Trade* (David and Charles 1970).

French Revolution

A revolution which started in France in 1789 with the storming of the Bastille. The overthrow of the monarchy and aristocracy followed, and some British RADICALS such as JOSIAH WEDGWOOD welcomed the revolution. Fear that the ideas might spread across the Channel encouraged repression by the British government from 1792, with a series of measures which culminated in the COMBINATION ACTS of 1799 and 1800.

Friendly Societies

Benefit clubs first grew up in the 17th and 18th centuries; members contributed regularly to them as a form of insurance against sickness and death. Some of the early societies were really TRADE UNIONS in disguise, especially during the time of the COMBINATION ACTS. Friendly societies were especially common in Lancashire and the other industrial regions. There were 700,000 members in England in 1800 and 925,000 in 1815. Some societies were based on a mine or a mill and some were supported by employers, but the majority were not. They were viewed with caution by the magistrates who suspected, often correctly, that their funds were used to provide strike pay.

They gained full legal recognition in 1824 and grew rapidly in the 1830s and 1840s. Some, like the Manchester Unity of Oddfellows and the Foresters, were very large. In 1842 a Registrar of Friendly Societies was appointed and the home secretary laid down that all societies should be enrolled.

The friendly societies were agents not of social change but of social adjustment, a form of SELF HELP by the WORKING CLASSES. They formed part of the subculture out of which the trade unions grew, and in which trade union officers were trained.

P.H.J.H. Gosden, *The Friendly Societies in England, 1815–1875* (Manchester University Press 1960).

Friendly Societies Act, 1793

An Act which gave some protection to the increasing number of FRIENDLY SOCIETIES. By registering with magistrates the societies protected their funds at law in the event of officers defaulting. A large number of societies did not register, through either hostility to the authorities,

parochial inertia or the need for secretiveness.

Frigger (Also spelt 'friggar')

A glass object of various forms made by a glass-maker in his own time and for his amusement, as a home decoration or for sale. These objects were usually made from molten glass left over at the end of the day. In some regions they were made on Saturdays when the works was closed. On Sunday each factory group paraded with its accomplishments in the town centre, stopping at each public house to have the pieces voted on. The most popular piece received a prize and possibly factory production followed. They were made in many English regions in the late 18th and early 19th centuries, especially at NAILSEA GLASS HOUSE. They included bells, hats, walking sticks, ships, tobacco pipes and rolling pins.

Frogmore Mill

The mill in Hertfordshire, sometimes called Two Waters Mill, at which the first satisfactory MACHINE for PAPER-MAKING was developed and became a commercial success. The mill is still in operation, producing paper and card from waste materials.

Visit Frogmore Mill, Hemel Hempstead, Hertfordshire.

Frost, John (1784–1877)

The leader of about 4,000 men who marched on Newport, Monmouthshire, in 1839 to release a number of Chartists (see CHARTISM) imprisoned there. The marchers were beaten back by soldiers and police and 24 were killed. John Frost was captured and transported. He eventually returned to England, and lived to the age of 93. He served much of his transportation sentence at Port Arthur in Tasmania, where he witnessed the brutal treatment of prisoners which he described on his return.

Fry, Elizabeth (1780–1845)

A QUAKER prison reformer married to

John Fry, another Quaker. As a girl of 17 she taught poor children in Norwich, her home town. In 1817 she founded the Association for the Improvement of Female Prisoners in Newgate, LONDON, after a visit to the prison there. With a group of followers she helped organize classes for women prisoners, providing them with clean clothes and reading the Bible to them. In 1840 she founded the Institute of Nursing Sisters in London, to train nurses to care for poor people in their own homes. She was also active in getting better conditions for convicts transported to Australia.

J. Rose, *Elizabeth Fry* (Macmillan 1980).

Fulton, Robert (1765–1815)

An American artist, born in Pennsylvania, who came to England to study art in 1787 and became fascinated by the CANALS and STEAM BOATS. He abandoned art to become an engineer, and in 1796 published *A Treatise on the Improvement of Canal Navigation*. After promoting his ideas on small canals in France he started work on a submarine. It was called *Nautilus* and was built in France in 1800 for the war with Britain. It was never used and was eventually dismantled.

Robert Fulton returned to England in 1804 and then went to the United States, where he built the paddle steamer *Clermont* in 1807. It had a BOULTON AND WATT engine to drive six paddle wheels. This ship was the first commercial steamer in the world with a regular pasenger service between Albany and New York, a distance of 150 miles (240 km). The journey took 32 hours and was commercially successful. By 1813 Robert Fulton had three boats carrying passengers down the river.

H.W. Dickinson, *Robert Fulton* (John Lane 1913).

Fustian

A coarse, twilled cotton cloth which was woven in Lancashire in the 17th and 18th centuries. The cloth was then sent to LONDON for BLEACHING, printing and marketing. The WARP threads of the cloth were made of flax to provide the strength required. In 1841 FEARGUS O'CONNOR appealed in his newspaper, the *Northern Star*, to 'the fustian jackets, the unshaven chins and blistered hands of true working men'. Fustian was evidently a cloth associated with WORKING-CLASS people. Fustian manufacture continued throughout the 19th century and fustian cutting (trimming the nap) was a specialist trade in Lymm, near MANCHESTER, in Warrington and elsewhere.

G

Garbett, Samuel (1717–1805)

A brass worker with little EDUCATION, who became a wealthy merchant and the partner of JOHN ROEBUCK in his BIRMINGHAM laboratory. He assisted Roebuck in the development of SULPHURIC ACID manufacture, iron making, COAL MINING and salt manufacture in Scotland. The failure of a Birmingham partner made him bankrupt in 1772.

Garrett, Richard (c. 1805–66)

The grandson of the founder of a firm of edge-tool makers and gunsmiths at Leiston in Suffolk. In 1778, when the works started, six or seven men were employed at the village forge. In 1806 the firm started to build THRESHING MACHINERY and SEED DRILLS. In 1836, the year before his father died, Richard Garrett took over the firm, which employed 500 men and manufactured patent STEAM ENGINES, threshing machinery, corn and seed drills and manuring machinery. With others he helped to found the ROYAL AGRICULTURAL SOCIETY in 1938. By 1866 there were 600 men on the payroll making various types of steam engines, seed drills and an improved threshing engine invented by Richard's son.

Visit Leiston, Suffolk – Long Shop Museum, with a history of the Garrett engineering works. **M***

R.A. Whitehead, *Garrett 200. A Bicentenary History of Garretts of Leiston, 1778–1978* (Bookman Publications 1978).

Gas, Light and Coke Company

The first company to sell gas to private customers from a central generating station. The Company was founded in 1812 by Frank Winsor, and SAMUEL CLEGG was brought in as a gas engineer. By 1814 the parish of St Margaret's, Westminster, was lit by gas and there were more than 26 miles (41.8 km) of underground mains

in LONDON a year later. The gas was transmitted through iron street mains to houses and public buildings where, at first, it was used solely for lighting. By 1823 there were three rival companies at work. The gas burned from what was known as a fish-tail burner until the 1840s, when air was mixed with the gas to increase its efficiency.

Gas Lighting

Gas for lighting was first introduced by WILLIAM MURDOCK in 1792, and in 1802 it was adopted at the SOHO WORKS in BIRMINGHAM. Its use spread rapidly to the larger towns during the period from 1810 to 1840. Gas supply companies were founded in GLASGOW in 1817, Edinburgh in 1818 and Paisley and DUNDEE in 1823. By that year 52 English towns were also lit by gas and by 1859 there were nearly 1,000 gas works.

Until the 1880s gas lighting was very imperfect, consisting of a yellow flame which heated the air, blackened the ceiling and used large quantities of gas. This was changed when the gas mantle was perfected and lighting became much more efficient.

Visit Biggar, Lanarkshire – gasworks, an outstation of the Royal Museums of Scotland. **M***
Fakenham, Norfolk – gasworks (1846).
Fulham, London – gas holder (1830s).

T. Williams, *A History of the British Gas Industry* (Oxford University Press 1981).
D. Gledhill, *Gas Lighting* (Shire Publications 1984).

Gauge Act, 1846   See Railway Gauges

Geach, Charles (1808–54)

The founder of the Midland Bank, who began by working as a junior clerk at the BANK OF ENGLAND. He helped establish two local banks in BIRMINGHAM in 1836, and after lending money to save an iron company from bankruptcy became the sole owner in 1844. He also invested in the Park Gate Iron Works which specialized in making rails. In 1851 he retired from banking to concentrate on iron production and become an MP.

General Board of Health

Set up in 1848 by th PUBLIC HEALTH ACT with EDWIN CHADWICK and LORD SHAFTESBURY as members. The Act provided for local boards of health to be set up on the request of the General Board of Health where the DEATH RATE exceeded 23 per thousand (the national average was 21), or where one-tenth of the inhabitants petitioned for a board. The local boards had powers to borrow money and levy a rate to finance sanitary improvements. LONDON was allowed to have its own scheme and the adoption of the Act was largely voluntary. Ratepayers in many areas did not want to spend money on these services and there was no effective machinery to carry out the Act, which was the responsibility of a variety of bodies ill-equipped for the task. There was strong opposition to central control and the Board of Health was abolished in 1858, Edwin Chadwick having been retired on a pension in 1854.

General Chamber of Manufacturers

A committee of manufacturers set up in London in 1785, which successfully attacked the proposed ANGLO-IRISH TREATY. In 1786 the Chamber was divided over a commercial treaty with France. The leaders of the new industries, such as JOSIAH WEDGWOOD, were in favour of measures which made unlimited commerce easier. They trusted their better techniques when faced by competition and did not approve of protectionism, whereas MANUFACTURERS of the older industries, such as wool, were in favour of a protectionist system.

General Union of Trades

An organization set up in MANCHESTER in 1818 to unite workers in different trades into one union, to support one another for their mutual advantage. The

organization was short-lived and an attempt to set up a 'Philanthropic Society' in its place failed.

George III (1739–1820)

King of Great Britain and Ireland from 1760 to 1820. He believed the monarch had the right to control the composition of governments and rigidly interpreted his right in relation to the American colonists. His attitude proved unyielding at times when compromise might have succeeded. He was an inept and obstinate man who interfered in government, promoting discredited administrations such as that of Lord North and disliking the old Whig families intensively. He accepted WILLIAM PITT the Younger in 1784 because he disliked Charles James Fox, the contender for the premiership, and it was under Pitt that there was a national revival. In 1765 he had the first of many bouts of madness which resulted in a slow physical deterioration. In 1808 he was unable to read or write and the next year he became blind. From 1811 his long spells of insanity resulted in the appointment of his eldest son as Regent.

George IV (1762–1830)

Regent 1811–20 and king of Great Britain and Ireland 1820–30. He had become well known as Prince Regent before becoming monarch. As Prince Regent his life-style brought contempt from all CLASSES of society, and during his reign the monarchy sank even lower. He lacked responsibility and lived the life of a libertine. His secret marriage to Mrs Fitzherbert (1756–1837), a ROMAN CATHOLIC, created a scandal in 1785, and his official marriage to Princess Caroline of Brunswick in 1795 was a fiasco.

Friction between the king and his ministers did not enhance his popularity. In 1822 he tried to exclude George Canning from office as foreign secretary and attempted to thwart his foreign policy. In 1827–8 he distributed appointments without consulting his ministers, and in 1829 was opposed to CATHOLIC EMANCIPATION. He consented to the Act only because his ministers were not dismayed at his threat to abdicate.

In the last years of his life he suffered from failing health and delusions. His main contribution was to the architecture of the time, in having the Royal Pavilion built at Brighton in 1784.

Visit Brighton, East Sussex – Regency pavilion and exhibition. **M***

C. Hibbert, *George IV* (Allen Lane 1975).

Gig Mill

A MACHINE consisting of teasels fixed into a revolving drum, used to raise the nap on wool cloth. The machine was probably introduced in a simpler form earlier, and was prohibited by a statute in the middle of the 16th century. In the late 18th century the clothiers claimed that the gig mill was different from the original model and the statute did not, therefore, apply to it. The CROPPERS thought differently, knowing that the gig mill enabled a man and a boy to do in 12 hours what a man working by hand took 100 hours to do. The croppers brought actions against the use of gig mills and the introduction of some of these machines led to riots. Mills were burnt down in Somerset in 1797 and in Wiltshire five years later. Machines were broken up in the LUDDITE riots of 1812, but the gig mill, together with the shearing frame, brought about the decline of the croppers by the 1820s.

Gilbert, John (1724–95)

He worked as an apprentice at the Boulton hardware works, Snow Hill, BIRMINGHAM. There he met and became friendly with MATTHEW BOULTON, the son of the owner of the works.

John Gilbert's elder brother Thomas (1720–98) became Lord Gower's land agent at Trentham and legal agent for Lord Gower's brother-in-law, the DUKE OF BRIDGEWATER. Thomas introduced to the duke his brother John, who became land agent for the duke's Worsley Estate. In 1759 Thomas introduced JAMES BRINDLEY to the duke, who made him consultant engineer for the building of the CANAL which was to be known as the BRIDGEWATER CANAL. John Gilbert was appointed resident engineer for the project and was responsible for raising much of the CAPITAL required.

With his brother and Lord Gower, he formed Earl Gower and Company to develop the earl's east Shropshire mineral resources. He helped build the Donnington Wood Canal in east Shropshire, with branch canals to limestone quarries and navigational SOUGHS to the canal mines. He was involved as committee member with both the Shrewsbury and SHROPSHIRE CANALS and subscribed to the TRENT AND MERSEY CANAL. He made a navigational sough into the Speedwell lead mine in Derbyshire between 1774 and 1778, and was also involved with his son John in the canal carrying firm of John Gilbert and Company. Towards the end of his life he worked on INCLINED PLANES, including one for the underground levels at the Worsley Colliery.

Thomas Gilbert became Member of Parliament for Newcastle-under-Lyme in 1763 and as a Parliamentary reformer secured a POOR LAW ACT in 1782 which became known as Gilbert's Act.

Gilbert's Act, 1782   See Poor Law – Gilbert's Act, 1782

Gillinder, William (1823–71).

A glassmaker born at Gateshead in County Durham, who worked in BIRMINGHAM making paperweights at George Bacchus and Son. He emigrated to the United States in 1853 and at first worked at the New England Glass Company, before buying the Franklin Flint Glass Works in Philadelphia in 1861. The firm was continued after his death by his two sons.

Gladstone, William Ewart (1809–98)

A politician and four times prime minister. He supported the FREE TRADE policies of SIR ROBERT PEEL when vice-president of the Board of Trade between 1841 and 1846. He was chancellor of the exchequer 1852–5 and 1859–66, and in his first budget reduced import duties. He sent RICHARD COBDEN in 1860 to negotiate the Cobden Treaty with France, which lowered duties on imports from Britain and almost abolished all duties on French manufactures coming into Britain.

H.C.G. Matthew, *Gladstone 1809–1874* (Oxford University Press 1986).

Glamorgan Canal

The MERTHYR TYDFIL ironmasters, RICHARD CRAWSHAY and FRANCIS HOMFRAY, promoted an Act of Parliament to build this CANAL. The Act was passed in 1790 and the canal, linking the ironworks and coal mines of the Merthyr Tydfil district with the coast, was finished in 1794. It extended from near the Crawshay ironworks at CYFARTHFA and reached the sea at CARDIFF. It was dependent on WAGONWAYS for much of the traffic, but a quarrel between the ironmasters caused problems. The other ironmasters complained that the Crawshays, as the biggest shareholders, were running the canal for their own benefit. As a result the Penydarren Railway was built from Merthyr to Abercynon, parallel with the canal. The canal was busy in the first six decades of the 19th century and the building of the Taff Vale Railways in 1841 did not immediately affect the canal, but by the 1860s tonnage fell sharply.

Visit Whitchurch, South Glamorgan – section of the canal.

Glasgow

In the first decades of the 18th century Glasgow developed an important tobacco trade, and by the 1770s more than half the tobacco brought to the United Kingdom passed through Glasgow. It was an entrepôt trade with re-exports to France, Germany, Italy, Holland and Norway. The LINEN industry which had grown up around the town switched over to cotton cloth production in the 1780s and cotton mills were built.

Glasgow was not accessible to shipping, and trade was handled by Greenock and later Port Glasgow. Improvements to the river by David Logan, the engineer to the Trustees of Clyde Navigation, were carried out in the 1840s and 1850s, when quays were built and the river dredged. The launch of the *COMET* in 1812 heralded a new era in SHIPBUILDING, and by 1835 half the tonnage of steam ships (see STEAM BOATS) built in Britain were built on the Clyde. Whereas the textile industry had benefited from the chemicals for BLEACHING produced at the ST ROLLOX CHEMICAL WORKS by CHARLES TENNANT after 1799, the shipbuilding industry was closely linked with the production of iron and steel and the development of marine engineering. The decline of the Scottish COTTON INDUSTRY in the 1850s came at a time when shipbuilding was expanding and Glasgow had become the business centre for the shipbuilding industry downstream.

The town grew rapidly from a population of 77,000 in 1801 to 420,000 in 1861, and WORKING-CLASS housing of very low standard was built to meet the rising demand. By 1857 the city centre was an unhealthy, overcrowded ghetto with levels of population density from 500 to 1,000 per acre (1,200–2,400 per ha). The area was a breeding ground for CHOLERA and typhus and after 1866 the city, through an Improvement Trust (see IMPROVEMENT ACTS), began to improve conditions by pulling down the worst of the SLUMS. Municipal house building began in the late 1880s, but overcrowding was common and the building of substandard tenement blocks was to continue until well into the 20th century.

Visit Heathbank Museum of Social Work, Milngavie, Glasgow – reconstruction of a slum street. **M***
Museum of Transport, Kelvin Hall, Glasgow – early road carriages and model boats. **M***

H. Hamilton, *The Industrial Revolution in Scotland* (Cass 1966).
D. Daiches, *Glasgow* (Deutsch 1977).

Glass Cone – English

A coal-fired furnace developed in the 17th century for making glass. It was about 80 feet (24.2 m) high, with an open top and a base 40 feet (12.2 m) in diameter. The furnace was situated in the centre of the floor and the glass was formed in glass pots, with each furnace having between four and ten of these pots. Flames and smoke were directed around the glass pots and discharged into the central chimney. A long gallery opened at one end into the cone and completed glass was placed in it to cool.

Visit St Helens, Lancashire – Pilkington Glass Museum, models only. **M***
Lemington, near Newcastle-upon-Tyne – glass cone.
Catcliffe, near Sheffield – restored glass cone (1740).
Redhouse Glass Works, near Stourbridge, West Midlands – glass cone.

Glass – Crown

The most common glass in windows in the 18th and early 19th centuries. It was a small, round sheet of glass with a 'crown' or 'bull's eye' in the middle. The crown was at the point where the blow-iron was removed when making the glass.

Glass Industry

The main ingredient of glass is silicon dioxide, which is found in many types of sand. Very high temperatures are needed to fuse the silicon, but by adding soda ash (Na_2CO_3) the melting temperature can be reduced. The substance obtained is then soluble in water, but adding limestone as a stabilizer makes the glass non-soluble. These three ingredients, sand, soda ash and limestone, are cheap and occur in many parts of Britain. Large quantities of fuel, however, are also needed. Originally wood was used, but in 1615 a royal proclamation was made forbidding the use of wood as a fuel in glass-making because timber supplies for warships were becoming scarce. The glass-making centres in the wooded areas of southern England and Staffordshire closed down and new centres developed close to supplies of coal. By the end of the 18th century a REVERBERATORY FURNACE was in use, operating within a GLASS CONE.

One of the main areas of the glass industry in the 17th century was the North East coalfield. Sir Robert Mansel made NEWCASTLE-UPON-TYNE his centre after 1615 and used local coal, with sand and soda ash shipped in from LONDON. The PLATE GLASS which was made was sent by coastal vessels to London and other towns, but the transport costs were high because of the fragile nature of the product. The industry therefore grew up in other areas where there was local coal and markets were more accessible than those for Newcastle glass. Glass made in the Midlands in the 17th and 18th centuries had a local market as well as one in London. Stourbridge became the main centre, with 520 glassworkers in the town at the end of the 18th century. BIRMINGHAM made high-quality glass and new firms were formed in the first decades of the 19th century. In 1832 the Smethwick firm of Chance and Hartley (later Chance Brothers) in the BLACK COUNTRY started making SHEET GLASS using the cylinder method, and the firm went on to improve the polishing and grinding processes.

During the 18th century the glass industry developed in southwest Lancashire, at Stockport, and the construction of the SANKEY BROOK NAVIGATION encouraged expansion of the industry at ST HELENS, where cheap coal was available. The Ravenhead works with a huge casting hall was built in 1773 for making plate glass, and the manufacture of CROWN GLASS was started in the town in 1792. The demand for window glass rose in the late 18th century, when windows for houses became larger, but the WINDOW TAX limited demand until the tax was reduced in 1823 and abolished in 1851. In 1825 the ST HELENS CROWN GLASS COMPANY was formed, and a plant was built next to a glass works started by John William Bell three years earlier. In 1829 WILLIAM PILKINGTON, one of the partners in the Crown Glass Company, began to take an active part in the management of the company.

The glass industry flourished during the building boom of the early 19th century and in 1836 the Union Plate Glass works was built at St Helens with a large casting hall. Technical improvements reduced costs and the reduction of the duty on glass in 1836, followed by the duty's abolition in 1845, together with the increased demand for new houses, encouraged the expansion of the industry during the second half of the 19th century.

Visit Pilkington Glass Museum, St Helens, Merseyside – processes and models. **M***

Science Museum, London – glass technology gallery. **M***

R. Dodsworth, *Glass and Glassmaking* (Shire Publications 1982).

Glass – Optical

Both scientists and manufacturers helped to improve optical glass-making in Britain. In 1758 an optician obtained a patent for achromatic lenses made by cementing concave and convex lenses together. Large reflecting telescopes were also developed in 1848 when a plant was set up by the firm of Chance Brothers at BIRMINGHAM.

Visit Smethwick, West Midlands – Chance's glassworks.

Glass – Plate

The manufacture of plate glass reached England from France in 1773 and three years later it was being made near ST HELENS in Lancashire, in a casting hall which was one of the largest industrial buildings of that time. Once the glass was molten in specially made crucibles it was cast on a copper table. As early as 1789 a BOULTON AND WATT STEAM ENGINE was used for the grinding and polishing processes. The demand for window glass for new houses and other buildings increased rapidly after 1821 and a new CROWN GLASS company was set up at St Helens in 1826. Later another works was built in the town, the Union Plate Glass Works, but expansion and new developments were limited until the repeal of the excise duty on glass in 1845 and the removal of the WINDOW TAX in 1851.

Glass – Sheet

An improved method of making sheet glass other than CROWN GLASS was introduced in 1832 by William Chance and his brothers, at their Smethwick works in the BLACK COUNTRY. A cylinder of glass was formed and then slit lengthways, reheated and unrolled as a flat sheet. It was cheaper and produced larger sheets than the earlier crown glass

method. The Chance brothers devised a grinding process in 1838.

Gooch, Daniel (1816–89)

An engineer, who, at the age of 21, became the first locomotive superintendent of the GREAT WESTERN RAILWAY. He worked in the foundry and pattern shop at the Tredegar Ironworks in South Wales and was then appointed to his post as superintendent by ISAMBARD BRUNEL. He was ordered to produce engines and took the *North Star*, built by ROBERT STEPHENSON, as his model. He insisted on standardization and quality control and used the most powerful engines available. In 1840 Swindon was chosen as the site for his locomotive works and he produced there a number of powerful locomotives, including the *Great Western*. In all he designed 340 engines. In 1840 he took out a patent for cladding iron wheels with steel to give them a longer life, and in the same year he became a director of the Great Eastern STEAMSHIP COMPANY, resigning from the Great Western Railway. He returned as chairman in 1865 and was responsible for the boring of the Severn Tunnel in 1886.

Goodyear, Charles (1800–60)

An American who experimented with rubber to improve its capacity to withstand extremes of temperature. A process for this was discovered and called vulcanization, and Goodyear took out a US patent in 1841. There was a strong prejudice against rubber in the United States and Goodyear tried to sell his process to CHARLES MACINTOSH without success. Samples of the rubber he had sent to Charles Macintosh were given to THOMAS HANCOCK, who worked out a method to manufacture them and obtained a patent in 1843, two months before Charles Goodyear. By 1858, when Thomas Hancock's patent expired, vulcanization had proved successful for such things as footwear, waterproof clothing, valves, conveyor belts and hoses.

Gordon, David (?–1830)

An engineer and inventor who made three or four STEAM COACHES with mechanical legs between 1824 and 1830. The number of breakdowns was high and the vehicles moved only at a walking pace.

Gordon Riots

In 1780 Lord George Gordon, head of the Protestant Association, petitioned Parliament not to relax anti-Catholic laws (see ROMAN CATHOLICISM). The House of Commons refused to debate the issue, which provoked riots directed against Catholic shops and the homes of wealthy Catholics. The BANK OF ENGLAND was attacked and there was arson and theft. After much delay by the authorities the army was called in to restore order. Some 700 people lost their lives and much property was destroyed.

Gott, Benjamin (1762–1840)

A Yorkshire clothier who, with his partners, built a wool mill in LEEDS in 1792. The mill was planned on a large scale with four storeys and an L shape. The site, at Bean Ing beside the River Aire, was called Park Mills. Despite a disastrous fire in 1799 the mill flourished and expanded, and houses were built nearby for the workers. A BOULTON AND WATT STEAM ENGINE was added in 1793, probably the first to be erected in a mill in Yorkshire.

Benjamin Gott introduced broadcloth manufacture into the county. Broadcloth is a fine material, woven with a plain weave, and had previously been made only in the West of England. He also introduced Spanish wool into the trade at the end of the 18th century, and by 1802 he was the largest clothier in the country. GAS LIGHTING was installed at the mill between 1808 and 1810, and by 1830 he employed 1,120 workers. At that date only part of the spinning was mechanically powered; much was still done by HAND LOOMS. This mixture of mechanical power and human effort has since earned Gott the title of 'Industrial half-Revolutionary'.

Governess

A woman employed by a Victorian MIDDLE-CLASS family to teach their children. The occupation was almost the only career open to the unmarried middle-class girl. A Governesses' Benevolent Institution was founded in 1843 for their protection and in 1848 it opened Queen's College, London, for girls over 12 years old, who could later train to become teachers. The curriculum was very unusual for the time, including English literature, botany, chemistry, philosophy, mechanics and modern languages. Students of the College included FRANCES MARY BUSS, who became headmistress of the North London Collegiate School in 1850, and Dorothea Beale, headmistress of Cheltenham College for Young Ladies in 1858.

Grand Alliance

An association of coalowners in the North East of England, founded in 1726, which lasted for over a century. Its purpose was to create a powerful union of coalowners which would attract other proprietors to join. They wished to secure as great a share of the market as possible, and to achieve this purpose they bought up collieries and took out leases. Of the nine new collieries opened on the Tyne between 1726 and 1750, the Grand Alliance controlled eight. The Alliance was designed to restrict output and raise the price of coal. The members were often related through marriage and remained active as owners and lessees in the industry. By purchasing or leasing land between collieries and the River Tyne, the Grand Alliance could control the movement of coal to the river, and therefore the price.

As the coalfield expanded in the second half of the 18th century the Alliance found it difficult to control the trade. It was difficult to get coalowners on the River Wear to work in concert with those on the Tyne and the strength of the Alliance faded.

Grand National Consolidated Trades Union

The first attempt to bring together all

types of worker in one TRADE UNION. It was promoted by ROBERT OWEN and JOHN DOHERTY in 1834. The membership quickly rose to half a million and a strike was proposed for an 8-hour day. It is doubtful if the half a million members ever paid any dues to the GNCTU. In March 1834 the authorities charged six Tolpuddle labourers (see TOLPUDDLE MARTYRS) with administering unlawful oaths for seditious purposes, and sentenced the men to seven years' transportation. Employers organized a series of lock-outs and the demands for strike pay seriously affected the GNCTU. These and other actions by the employers and the authorities left the constituent unions of the GNCTU in disarray.

Even before its formation Robert Owen had become unhappy with the militant attitude of the members, and looked instead to employers and the government to improve the working conditions of the workers. He was unable to influence the unionists. Seven months after its formation the GNCTU was transformed into a mild and ineffective organization, the British and Foreign Consolidated Association of Industry, Humanity and Knowledge. Like its predecessor, this also soon collapsed.

Grand Trunk Canal   See Trent and Mersey Canal

Great Bandana Gallery

A large workshop at a dye works in GLASGOW in which 16 large hydraulic presses were erected in 1818. The factory printed patterns on cotton bandanas – handkerchiefs brightly coloured with white or yellow spots. In the process the cotton was dyed turkey red and then placed in the presses with a solution of chlorine to bleach out (see BLEACH – TEXTILE INDUSTRY) the areas of pattern which were to be left white. Four men operated the MACHINES and could convert over 19,000 yards (17,373 m) of cloth into bandanas in a 10-hour shift.

Great Britain

A steamship built to the design of ISAMBARD BRUNEL and launched in 1843 in the dry dock at BRISTOL, which had been built for it. The *Great Britain* was designed to carry 250 passengers, 130 crew and 1,200 tonnes (1,344 US tons) of cargo. Like other steamships of the period, it had six masts and sails. It had an iron hull and was fitted with a propeller with six

The launching of the *Great Britain*, 19 July 1843. Isambard Brunel's iron ship was built between 1839 and 1843 in a dry dock at Bristol specially made to accommodate her enormous bulk. The dock was flooded to allow the ship to float out for the launching by Prince Albert. The *Great Britain* was the first all-iron, screw-propelled merchant ship on the North Atlantic run and could accommodate 252 passengers, 130 crew and 1,200 tonnes (1,320 US tons) of cargo. (*Mary Evans*)

blades. The maiden voyage to New York took place in 1845 and the next year the ship ran aground on the Irish coast, eventually being salvaged to operate between LIVERPOOL and Melbourne, Australia. Damaged by gales in 1886, she reached Port Stanley in the Falkland Islands, where she remained until 1970. In that year conservationists returned the hull to the original dry dock at Bristol, where the ship was restored and is now a tourist attraction.

Visit Industrial Museum, Bristol – *Great Britain* restored, in the original dry dock. **M***

E.C.B. Corlett, *The Iron Ship* (Moonraker Press, 1980).

Great Eastern

A steamship (see STEAM BOATS) built on the Thames for ISAMBARD BRUNEL by JOHN SCOTT RUSSELL in 1858. The ship was very large with an iron hull, two paddle wheels and a screw. It was not a success as an Atlantic passenger liner, partly because there were not enough passengers to fill the 4,000 berths, and the engines were uneconomic. The biggest mistake was the underestimation by some 75 per cent of the quantity of coal required to drive the paddles and screw engines of the ship at the designed speed of 14 knots. It was used to lay the UNDERWATER TELEGRAPH CABLE in 1866.

Great Exhibition, 1851

An idea of a number of businessmen and PRINCE ALBERT, the husband of QUEEN VICTORIA. The exhibition aimed to show the world's technical and industrial achievements. A glass exhibition hall, called the Crystal Palace, was designed by JOSEPH PAXTON and erected in Hyde Park, LONDON. It was made of iron and wood, with nearly 300,000 panes of PLATE GLASS. The exhibits came from many parts of the world, with 7,351 exhibitors from the British Isles and 6,556 from other countries. They consisted of examples of industrial achievements together with foodstuffs, handicrafts and raw materials. The exhibition was open for 141 days and attracted over 6 million

visitors. The Crystal Palace was taken down after the exhibition had closed and rebuilt in South London, where it was destroyed by fire in 1936.

A. Briggs, *Iron Bridge to Crystal Palace* (Thames and Hudson 1979).

Great Western

A steamship built by ISAMBARD BRUNEL, with a wooden hull and engines which drove paddles. The maiden voyage to New York was in 1838 where she arrived on the same day as a rival, the SIRIUS. The *Great Western* took 15 days to cross the Atlantic, the *Sirius* 19. The *Great Western* ran a regular transatlantic service for eight years before being sold to the West Indian Steam Packet Company. The ship was broken up in 1857.

Green Glaze

While THOMAS WHIELDON was JOSIAH WEDGWOOD's partner (1754–9), he encouraged Wedgwood to improve and innovate, using his interests in research as much as possible. By 1750 a clear lead glaze in liquid form had been devised and potters were experimenting to colour it with pigment. In 1759 Josiah Wedgwood developed a green glaze which could be laid on white or cream-coloured BISCUIT WARE. To obtain green pigment, oxide of copper was heated until it fused into a glassy material which, when cooled, was ground to a powder. Wedgwood's success at providing a deep green glaze was used in making fruit and vegetable shapes, plates, dishes and tableware which included fruit baskets. He did not patent his glaze, which was copied by other potters who undercut his price, but his designs remained unique and helped to make the firm world famous.

Visit Hanley, Stoke-on-Trent, City Museum and Art Gallery – examples of Wedgwood's green glaze ware. **M***
Barlaston, Stoke-on-Trent – Wedgwood Museum. **M***

Greg, Samuel (1758–1834)

A Belfast man who moved to MANCHESTER

as a cloth dealer. He built the Quarry Bank Mill at Styal in Cheshire in 1784, 11 miles (17 km) from Manchester. The mill was run on paternalistic lines and a village was built near the works with a school, chapel, MECHANICS' INSTITUTE and other amenities. His sons and daughters worked in the business, the daughters being responsible for the large number of pauper girls employed on the WATER FRAMES. By 1815 Samuel Greg was trading with Italy, France, North America, Russia, Germany and South America. After his death the firm continued to expand under the management of his sons.

Visit Styal, near Wilmslow, Cheshire – Quarry Bank Mill, a working museum. **M***

M.B. Rose, *The Gregs of Quarry Bank Mill* (Cambridge University Press 1986).

Guardians

Groups set up by the POOR LAW AMENDMENT ACT, 1834, to supervise poor relief and run WORKHOUSES in the unions which were formed by groups of parishes. Each parish elected guardians to serve on the board of a union, and these elected bodies were known as Boards of Guardians. They were effective in seeing that the Act was carried out in the South of England, but in the North some Boards refused to put men who were temporarily unemployed into workhouses and continued to give them outdoor relief in the form of cash payments.

Guest, John (1772–87)

An ironmaster who became manager of the DOWLAIS IRONWORKS in 1767. He became a partner in 1782 and died in 1787, passing on the management to his son Thomas.

Guest, Sir John Josiah (1785–1852)

The son of Thomas Guest and grandson of JOHN GUEST, he became master of the DOWLAIS IRONWORKS in 1807. In 1815 he became the largest shareholder in the Company, and in 1832 he became MP for MERTHYR TYDFIL. He took an active interest in the local community, which depended for its existence on the ironworks. In 1833 he married Lady Charlotte, a daughter of the Earl of Lindsey, which gave him access to the higher ranks of society. By that time Dowlais Ironworks had 18 furnaces working, with orders pouring in from the railways. Dowlais shared in the prosperity and the Guest family was one of the most progressive in South Wales. A library and church were built as well as schools. Over 7,000 people were employed in 1847 at the works, which produced 70,000 tonnes (78,400 US tons) annually.

Visit Dowlais, near Merthyr Tydfil, Mid-Glamorgan – stable block and remains of blowing house.

Gurney, Sir Goldsworthy (1793–1875)

A Cornish doctor who moved to LONDON in 1820. He designed a series of steam carriages from 1825 onwards and established a steam carriage factory. In 1827 he patented a STEAM COACH with the outside passenger seats on top of the boiler and the inside seats in front of it. In 1829 a steam drag towing a carriage did a trial run from London to Bath and back. The next year one of his drags was fitted with CAST-IRON wheels and used on a tram-road at Hirwaun in South Wales. In 1831 a public passenger service between Cheltenham and Gloucester was started, using the drag to tow a coach. The fare was half of that charged by stage coaches (see COACH SERVICES), but the TURNPIKE trusts disliked steam vehicles and increased their tolls. Goldsworthy Gurney abandoned steam carriages and returned to his interest in medicine and science.

T.R. Harris, *Sir Goldsworthy Gurney* (Trevithick Society 1975).

H

Hackney Cab

The earliest vehicles for hire were usually discarded, private, four-wheeled coaches in poor condition. In 1805 licences were given for the operation of nine hackney cabriolets (hence 'cab'), a small carriage with a folding leather hood with room for only one fare. An improved vehicle to carry two passengers, the Davies cab, was licensed in 1825. In 1833 a cab was designed by Joseph Hansom, the Hansom cab. A better cab was patented by John Chapman and the company owning Hansom's patent bought out the Chapman patent. It was this 'Hansom' cab which operated for the next 70 years.

Hackworth, Timothy (1786–1850)

A railway engineer appointed in 1825 on the recommendation of GEORGE STEPHENSON to take responsibility for the engineering shops of the STOCKTON AND DARLINGTON RAILWAY. He made improvements to the locomotives based on his practical experience. He first introduced the spring safety valve which allowed steam to escape. He also designed an improved wheel, cast in two parts to reduce risk of breakage. Various other improvements were made by him including the design of the *Royal George* in 1827, the most powerful locomotive of its day and used for hauling coal traffic. He drove *Sans Pareil* at the RAINHILL TRIALS in 1829, but the engine had a leaking boiler and failed. Nevertheless, it was most the most formidable challenge to the ROCKET.

Visit Shildon, County Durham – Timothy Hackworth Railway Museum. **M***
Science Museum, London – *Sans Pareil*. **M***

R. Young, *Timothy Hackworth and the Locomotive* (Shildon, 'Stockton and Darlington Railway', Jubilee Committee 1923).

Haigh Ironworks

An ironworks started by the Earl of Balcarres (1752–1825), who entered into partnership in 1788 with an ironfounder in Wigan, James Corbett, to exploit a forge and coal on his estate. Iron furnaces were built in 1789 and the Earl's brother, Robert Lindsey (who knew nothing of the business), was brought in to organize the ironworks. The works was sited on the Liverpool Canal and made casings, machinery and arms during the NAPOLEONIC WARS. In the post-war recession the firm developed as a foundry and engineering works. After 1856 it concentrated on the manufacture of mining machinery until it closed in 1884.

Hall-i'-the-Wood

A 15th-century house which was the home of SAMUEL CROMPTON, at Bolton, Lancashire. It is now a folk museum containing the furniture and a spinning wheel which were used at the time of Samuel Crompton.

Visit Hall-i'-the-Wood, near Bolton, Lancashire – Museum of the Crompton family. **M***

Hall, Joseph (1789–1862)

Ironfounder who experimented with WROUGHT IRON and observed that in CORT's process the hearth of the PUDDLING furnace was lined with sand. Some of this formed slag when in contact with the molten metal and some of the iron was lost. Joseph Hall experimented and accidentally found, about 1830, that iron oxide in waste slag, heated with PIG IRON, boiled over. The iron left in the furnace was a refined form of wrought iron and the boiling mixture was the result of carbon in the iron reacting with iron oxide to form carbon monoxide. The process was known as pig boiling or WET PUDDLING. It was a faster and more economic process than that invented by Cort.

W.K.V. Gale, *Iron and Steel* (Moorland Publishing 1977).

Hampden Clubs

Clubs set up in 1812 by MAJOR JOHN CARTWRIGHT. The clubs flourished in the North, where the subscription was a penny a week. Support came from skilled workers who saw the clubs as centres where their RADICAL views could be aired. The SPA FIELDS MEETING of 1816 alarmed the government, habeas corpus was suspended and the Seditious Meetings Act passed to suppress reforming societies and clubs. The clubs abandoned their radical attitudes and built up reading societies with permanent newsrooms in the larger centres.

Hancock, Joseph (1711–91)

A metal worker who developed a process for coating thick copper with thin silver by fusion. The process had been discovered by Thomas Boulsover in 1742. The product was known as Old Sheffield Plate, and after about 1765 there was a rapid growth in the production of SHEFFIELD-plated articles. This production lasted for about 100 years, until it was replaced by depositing silver or gold by electrolysis.

Hancock, Robert (1730–1817)

A ceramic engraver of copper plates who developed ceramic TRANSFER PRINTING in the 1760s. He took the process from Battersea in LONDON to the WORCESTER PORCELAIN COMPANY, where he worked with THOMAS TURNER from 1772 to 1774. Turner then went to Shropshire and founded the Salopian Works at Caughley.

Hancock, Thomas (1786–1865)

An engineer who experimented with a rubber shredding machine in 1820 and found it produced a mass of solid rubber. Improving the device, he was able to make rubber cylinders which could be compressed in iron moulds into any shape and size. He was also able to produce rubber sheets by slicing sections from a block. In 1846 he manufactured rubber road-vehicle tyres, which were solid and attached to a metal hoop by flanges. Two years later he invented a machine that coated wire with gutta-percha. This was not entirely successful since in time the gutta-percha decomposed.

Hancock, Walter (1799–1852)

A steam carriage (see STEAM COACHES) engineer and designer, who designed a wheel for use on steam omnibuses in the 1820s. The wheel was very strong; it was later used for gun carriages and became known as the artillery wheel. He also patented a steam boiler and ran an omnibus service. In 1824 he patented a STEAM ENGINE using rubber bags in place of conventional cylinders and pistons. This operated well at low pressures but was unsuited for high-pressure work. He went on to build a steam carriage, the *Infant*, which ran from LONDON to Brighton and back in 1831. Like other steam carriage ventures it had a short life, but Walter Hancock was undeterred and built the *Automaton*, which ran until 1940. In 1836 his steam carriages worked various routes in London without any accidents, and over 12,000 people were carried. Steam carriage services never developed whereas those of horse-drawn omnibuses did.

Hand Loom Weavers

The traditional process of weaving by hand on simple wooden looms was undermined in the first decades of the 19th century by the introduction of POWER LOOMS. The increase in output was dramatic. A skilled hand loom weaver could produce two pieces of shirting in a week. By 1833 a relatively unskilled power loom weaver, helped by a young girl, could produce 18 to 20 pieces in the same period. The change to power loom weaving was a gradual one, but as more and more looms were steam driven, the hand loom weavers began to experience poverty. Their skills were no longer needed, and machine smashing by LUDDITES was partly caused by the distress being experienced by the hand loom weavers. Their death was a slow one. In 1833 there were still 210,000 cotton hand loom weavers, compared with 192,000 in all other textile mills, but by 1850 few remained.

The redundant workers found employment mainly in factories or in other textile weaving. For the hand loom weavers near towns factory work, particularly on power looms, was available but some did not take it up. Weavers in the countryside some way from factories had fewer opportunities for work in industry. Some older weavers found employment in mills doing tasks which were not mechanized, such as looming and twisting, while others used their skills to weave silk, LINEN or mousseline-de-laine (a dress fabric made of cotton and WORSTED). Some weavers turned to agriculture for a livelihood while others became coal miners. No precise date can be given for the disappearance of hand loom weavers; a few were still to be found in the 1880s.

D. Bythell, *The Handloom Weavers* (Cambridge University Press 1969).

Hand Loom Weavers Commission

A Parliamentary enquiry set up in 1839 to investigate the problems of the HAND LOOM WEAVERS. The report issued in the next year highlighted the destruction of the craft. Their pay was worse and their hours longer than were those of any other group of workers. The Commission recommended the repeal of the CORN LAWS or EMIGRATION as possible cures. Hand loom weaving for woollen cloth continued as late as the 1880s, but the decline in other sections of the industry came 20 or 30 years earlier.

Hanway's Act, 1767

An Act of Parliament proposed by James Hanway (1712–86), which stated that LONDON children under 6 years of age living on the parish (that is, who were paupers) were to be boarded out not less than 3 miles (4.8 km) away at not less than two shillings and sixpence (21 US cents) per week. Parish authorities with large numbers of children in their care

saw the Act as a means of sending them to the cotton mills of Lancashire, Derbyshire and Nottinghamshire, and children aged 7 and upwards were sent as apprentices. This helped to solve the labour problem of the COTTON INDUSTRY.

Hargreaves, James (*c.* 1719–78)

A weaver who invented the SPINNING JENNY in his cottage at Stanhill, Lancashire, in about 1764. His machine allowed a number of cotton threads to be spun at once, greatly increasing the output of the spinners. Fears that the jenny would result in unemployment led to attacks on Hargreaves' home in 1768, during which his furniture and some 20 jennies were smashed. Hargreaves left the district and moved to Nottingham where he went into partnership with Thomas James. For some years they had a relatively successful cotton spinning business, but Hargreaves had delayed taking out a patent for his machine and was too late to prevent copies being made in large numbers. He was actively involved in spinning until his death, although he never made a fortune from his invention and died practically unknown.

Visit Stanhill, near Blackburn, Lancashire – Hargreaves' cottage.

Hartley, Jesse (1780–1860)

A civil engineer who was dock surveyor at LIVERPOOL 1824–60. He was responsible for the development of Liverpool's dockland, which he separated from the city by a wall. His masterpiece, Albert Dock, opened in the 1840s and was surrounded by a set of warehouses. He built the Victoria Tower at the entrance to Salisbury Dock in 1848, giving it a six-faced clock and a bell to ring out warnings. He was also engineer for the Bolton and Manchester CANAL and railway.

Visit Albert Dock, Liverpool – Merseyside Maritime Museum. **M***

Hawksley, Thomas (1807–93)

The son of a NOTTINGHAM MANUFACTURER

who was apprenticed to a local architect and surveyor. About 1830 he was appointed to construct the Trent Waterworks. He designed a system with a constant supply, which was a relatively new idea, and subsequently he designed pumped water supplies for over 18 English towns and two in Europe. In 1850 he designed a catchment scheme in Lancashire, using filters to obtain pure water for LIVERPOOL. Five reservoirs were built to serve the city and for a few years Liverpool obtained an uninterrupted supply.

Visit Kensington Gardens, London – pavilion at north end of Serpentine designed by Thomas Hawksley in 1858 as a pumping station.

Health of Towns Association

An association formed in 1844 by Dr Southwood Smith and others to instruct audiences in the basic principles of ventilation, drainage and civic and domestic cleanliness. Lectures and pamphlets were used and in many towns working-class groups set up associations. Although the association was a powerful instrument of propaganda, EDWIN CHADWICK remained apart from it, using it indirectly to spread his own ideas.

Health of Towns Commission

Set up in 1843 following the publication of EDWIN CHADWICK's *Report on the Sanitary Condition of the Labouring Population of Great Britain* in 1842. Under the director of Edwin Chadwick (although he was not himself a member) the Commission made reports on a number of towns. It produced a first report in 1844 and a second the next year. The reports explored the technical and administrative possibilities for improving the health of the urban population and made recommendations that local authorities should have wider powers in sanitary matters. The authorities should be obliged to supply water for domestic use, clean the streets, scour the drains and SEWERS and extinguish fires. The supply of water should be extended to all dwelling houses and should be constant rather than intermittent as it had been in

the past. The Commission paved the way for the PUBLIC HEALTH ACT, 1848.

Heathcoat, John (1783–1861)

The inventor in 1809 of a lace-making machine known as the bobbin net or bobbinet machine. The machine formed the foundations of an extensive lace industry after it had been improved by John Lever and others in 1813. John Heathcoat started a factory in Loughborough, Leicestershire, in 1805, which was broken into by LUDDITES in 1816 and the machinery destroyed. He moved to Tiverton in Devon and built a large mill using water from the River Exe. He also invented machinery for plaiting or braiding and for the mechanical ornamentation of lace fabrics. He was MP for Tiverton from 1832 to 1859.

Visit Nottingham Industrial Museum, Wollaton Park, Nottingham – lace machinery. **M***

Hedley, William (1779–1843)

The designer of a locomotive with the wheels linked by gears to check them from slipping when a heavy load was being hauled. To reduce damage to the track two locomotives were made about 1815, each mounted on two four-wheeled bogies, similar to those designed by WILLIAM CHAPMAN. When the line was relaid as an edge railway they went back on to four wheels again. They were in use until 1860 and are now known as the *PUFFING BILLY* and *WYLAM DILLY*, although originally they carried no names.

Visit Science Museum, London – original *Puffing Billy*. **M***
Royal Scottish Museum, Edinburgh – original *Wylam Dilly*. **M***

P.R.B. Brooks, *William Hedley, Locomotive Pioneer* (Tyne and Wear Industrial Monument Trust 1980).

Helmshore

The site of an 18th-century woollen mill in Lancashire called the Higher Mill, and of a later cotton mill. A woollen cloth-fulling mill was built at Helmshore by the Turner family in 1789 using local stone.

The fulling process involved pounding the cloth in a trough for two days with heavy wooden fulling stocks operated by a waterwheel. During the process there was considerable shrinkage which was followed by scouring (removing the grease). Urine provided in large pots by the workers was used for this, and then the cloth was washed before being stretched on tenterhooks to dry. Teasels were rubbed across the surface to raise the nap so that it could be removed by CROPPERS. Later the Turner family built a second mill to spin cotton using CROMPTON'S MULE.

The stone upper and lower mills are now arranged as a working textile museum. The mills contain the original fulling stocks, waterwheel, tenterhooks and rotary GIG MILLS containing teasels, as well as a collection of early textile machinery including mules, a SPINNING JENNY and ARKWRIGHT'S WATER FRAME. The lower mill has a magnificent mule floor.

Visit Textile Museums, Helmshore, Rossendale, Lancashire – working museum in original mill buildings. **M***

Herculaneum

A pottery in LIVERPOOL, started in 1756 by Richard Chaffers (1731–65), to manufacture soft-paste soapstone porcelain (see PORCELAIN – SOFT PASTE) for domestic tableware. This method was abandoned in the early 1770s in favour of one using bone ash. In 1793 another factory was set up, later called the Herculaneum Pottery. All kinds of tableware were made in dead-white BONE CHINA. The factory closed in 1840. Pottery made in it is known as Liverpool ware.

A. Smith, *Liverpool Herculaneum Pottery, 1796–1840* (Barrie and Jenkins 1970).

Highland Commission for Roads

Set up by Act of Parliament in 1804 as the result of a survey carried out by THOMAS TELFORD the previous year. In his report he urged the building of new roads and bridges as a means of developing the Highlands and restraining EMIGRATION. The Act offered state aid, paying half the cost, the remainder to be raised locally.

Highways Acts

An Act of Parliament in 1555 made road maintenance in England the responsibility of the parishes. Parishioners were obliged to spend four consecutive days working on the roads, providing their own tools and horses and carts if they owned them. Each parish appointed two surveyors of highways to supervise the work. This system of 'statute labour' worked none too well, and in 1654 road rates were introduced to pay for labour. For many parishioners money payments replaced physical labour.

Statute labour had always proved inadequate to deal with busy main roads passing through a parish, especially if the parish was small and poor. This problem was overcome after 1663 when Parliament authorized three TOLL gates on the Great North Road. Further TURNPIKE Acts followed and in 1706 the first turnpike trust was set up. Turnpike trustees had the power to erect gates, collect tolls, appoint surveyors and demand statute labour or its equivalent in money, and were responsible for repairing the roads. Turnpike road surveyors included JOHN METCALF, THOMAS TELFORD and JOHN McADAM.

Acts in 1766 and 1773 gave parishes the power to nominate a paid surveyor. Magistrates could appoint a surveyor of their choice and order the parish to pay him if the parish failed to appoint an unpaid surveyor annually. Some magistrates never appreciated this power and were also reluctant to enforce an order which put a further burden on poor parishioners. The law was implemented in larger parishes, but there was no co-ordination between parishes and the surveyor was unlikely to have experience of road engineering. Often he was given a small honorarium, which was sometimes a means of paying a pension to an incapacitated local worthy.

The 1835 Highways Act abolished the obligation of local people to repair the roads by their own labour and established the use of salaried officials and hired labour for highways repairs, paid for out of the rates (local taxes). The parishes could combine with others to form highway districts in the interests of economy, but few wanted to surrender their autonomy. There were some 15,000 highway parishes reponsible for maintaining more than 100,000 miles (160,930 km) of roads.

In 1888 the Local Government Act set up county councils with responsibility for main road maintenance, and in 1895 the last turnpike trust was dissolved.

Hill, Sir Rowland (1795–1879)

Introduced the postage stamp and was responsible for the development of a national postal service. He analysed the cost of sending letters and found that while transit costs were small, administration costs were very high. In 1837 he published his view that a prepaid flat rate of one penny should be charged irrespective of distance. The government disliked the idea but Parliament was subjected to a propaganda campaign, partly instigated by the BANKING house of Baring Brothers.

The PENNY POST became law and the service began to operate in 1840. The railways provided a new means of sending mail and the Post Office increased its business rapidly. Rowland Hill was eventually made secretary to the Postmaster-General, and when he retired he was belatedly awarded a life pension.

Hoffman Kiln

A circular brick kiln for firing pottery and for burning limestone to make lime, introduced to Britain in 1858 by a German engineer, Friedrich Hoffman (1818–1900). The kiln had a tall central chimney and contained radiating chambers which could be used in a continuous succession, making a form of continuous kiln.

Visit Bridgwater, Somerset – two Hoffman kilns.
Llanymynech, Powys – Hoffman kiln.
Minera, Clwyd – Hoffman kiln.

Homfray, Francis (1726–98)

An ironmaster in Worcestershire and at Broseley near COALBROOKDALE. With his three sons, JEREMIAH, Thomas and SAMUEL, he settled at MERTHYR TYDFIL, South Wales, in 1782 and leased the CYFARTHFA IRONWORKS for two years. In 1784 he started an ironworks at PENYDARREN. He was one of the promoters of the GLAMORGAN CANAL.

Homfray, Jeremiah (1759–1833)

The son of FRANCIS HOMFRAY, with partners he started the Ebbw Vale Ironworks in Wales in 1789. He prospected for minerals in South Wales and had an interest for a time in other ironworks. He had financial difficulties and was made bankrupt in 1813, with the result that he went to live in Boulogne to avoid paying his debtors.

Homfray, Samuel (1761–1822)

An ironmaster and the younger brother of JEREMIAH HOMFRAY. He became manager of the PENYDARREN WORKS in Wales in 1789 and was one of the chief promotors of the GLAMORGAN CANAL, which was opened in 1794. He also promoted the TRAMWAY from Penydarren to Abercynon and established the Tredegar Ironworks in 1800 and the Aberdare Works in 1801.

Visit Abercynon, Mid-Glamorgan – Penydarren tram-road.

Hornsby, Richard (1790–1864)

An AGRICULTURAL ENGINEER who, with Richard Seaman, set up a works at Grantham in Lincolnshire in 1815 to make SEED DRILLS, THRESHING MACHINES and other agricultural implements. The firm won a ROYAL AGRICULTURAL SOCIETY medal for a portable STEAM ENGINE in 1848, which was a great commercial success. There were similar awards for a corn and seed drill at the GREAT EXHIBITION, 1851. The drill used india rubber for the seed tubes and had rack and pinion steering. In 1854 the works had 34 furnaces, and 14 steam engines were in production simultaneously. In 1859 the firm started making ploughs and self-binding harvesters for the home and overseas markets.

N.R. Wright, *Lincolnshire Towns and Industry 1700–1914* (Society for Lincolnshire History and Archaeology 1982).

Horrocks, John (1768–1804)

A QUAKER who set up a cotton spinning mill in Preston, Lancashire, in 1786. He started by using SPINNING JENNIES before building more mills and using the MULE, which made it possible to manufacture muslin. He brought prosperity to Preston, and his brother Samuel (1766–1842) joined him. The firm became known as Horrocks, Miller and Co., and by 1812 there were eight mills with 107,000 mules producing cotton goods.

Horse Gin

A horse harnessed to a capstan so that as the horse moved round in a circle the mill machinery rotated. RICHARD ARKWRIGHT used this form of power in 1769 in his first factory in NOTTINGHAM. The gins were cheap to install and were used to work carding engines and MULES. It is possible that they were the most common kind of power in use in the second half of the 18th century.

Horsepower

The INDUSTRIAL REVOLUTION diminished but did not extinguish the use of horses and ponies as a source of power. They were used in mines and quarries to drive winding gear or raise drainage buckets throughout this period. Horses were needed to haul coal along WAGONWAYS, and they were valuable pieces of property that needed to be safeguarded by the wagoners, who were dependent on contracts and owned the animals. In 1827 the wagoners of Pontop Colliery in South Wales formed a FRIENDLY SOCIETY called the Pontop Colliery Wagon Horse Collection. Benefits were paid in respect of the illness, accident to or death of one of the horses. Humans were not included in the insurance!

Horses, mules and ponies were used underground from about 1763 and continued in use until recent times. As late as 1924 over 65,000 pit ponies were at work underground, and it is only since the Second World War (1939–45) that ponies have ceased to be used underground in mines.

Technically one horsepower is the amount of power required to raise 33,000 lb (14,969 kg) one foot (0.3 m) in one minute.

Hot Blast

A system which increased the output and speed of production of BLAST FURNACES. It was patented by JAMES NEILSON in 1828. He discovered that preheating the blast going into the furnace lowered fuel consumption, increased output and speeded up the process. The fuel savings brought by the hot blast method increased Scotland's competitive position after about 1830. Raw coal could be used in the furnaces, saving the cost of coking it, and the sulphur normally removed by coking was removed in the furnace slag by the higher temperatures. Scotland became the lowest cost region in Britain at this time and high profits were common.

English and Welsh ironmasters were slow to adopt hot blast, although many switched over in the 1840s. In 1844, J.P. Budd of the Ystalyfera Ironworks in South Wales used waste heat from his furnaces to heat the blast. He went on four years later to use waste heat to make steam for the STEAM ENGINE. Virtually all furnaces were using hot blast by 1860.

Howard, James (1821–89)

The son of John Howard, an ironmonger and agricultural implement maker of Bedford. With his brother Frederick he produced a Champion all-iron plough in 1841, for which they won first prize at the Royal Show. The firm took out 70 patents between 1851 and 1881 covering all kinds of cultivating, harvesting and steam machinery. A factory was built in 1856 called the Britannia Works, located beside the navigable River Ouse and with its own railway sidings. Three cupola furnaces produced molten iron from PIG IRON and this was run off into ladles mounted on trucks, to be distributed to the moulders via an internal railway system. Like some other AGRICULTURAL ENGINEERING firms, Howard's progressed from a small ironmonger's business to a large factory.

Howard, John (1726–90)

A prison reformer who was concerned with the poor conditions and unjust treatment of prisoners. His account of what he had seen in prisons, *The State of Prisons in England and Wales*, published in 1777, shocked public opinion. Howard proposed that gaolers, instead of running prisons for their own profit, should be paid, and inspectors appointed. Prisoners should be classified according to their age, sex and offence, provided with proper clothes and sanitation, and receive wholesome food. Some of his proposals were written into the Penitentiary Houses Act of 1779 but few were ever carried out.

Huddersfield

A woollen town in West Yorkshire noted for its cloth. Its prosperity began in the second half of the 18th century, when the WOOLLEN INDUSTRY was carried out in the villages of the area under the DOMESTIC SYSTEM. Huddersfield became the centre of the trade and a cloth hall was built in 1766–8. Small mills using water power from the River Colne stretched along the river and by 1801 the town had a population of 7,000. By 1811 Huddersfield was linked to the cross-Pennine CANAL system and steam power began to replace the waterwheels. By the mid-1830s there were 45 woollen mills in the town and 42 in the neighbouring parish of Almondbury. Using the JACQUARD LOOM, the town became noted for its high-quality fine cloth, which sometimes had fancy weaves and was popular for waistcoats.

Huddersfield began to grow rapidly after the railway (see RAILWAY DEVELOPMENT) had been built in the mid-1840s. The magnificent railway station with its classical façade of Corinthian-style columns was built by the Huddersfield Railway Company in 1847. It was designed by J.P. Pritchett and is the most imposing building in the town. After it was built the central area around the terminal was redeveloped. There is also a very fine town hall built in 1875, but the cloth hall was demolished in 1930 and only a few fragments can still be seen in Ravensknowle Park.

During the second half of the 19th century rows of closely packed terraced houses were built close to the large, rectangular woollen mills. The industrialized valley floor of the River Colne has not changed a great deal in the last hundred years; many of the mills are still standing, although not all are now used for textile production.

Visit Tolson Museum, Ravensknowle Park, Huddersfield, West Yorkshire – textile looms, relics of the Luddite riots and of the social history of the town. **M***

Hudson, George (1800–71)

Sometimes known as the 'Railway King', he was a businessman who became chairman of the York and North Midland Railway Company in 1840. By a series of amalgamations he controlled the railways from the River Tyne to BRISTOL, 1,500 miles (2,414 km) of track and £30 million ($51 million) in capital. He concealed losses, which accelerated during the trade depression of 1847–8, and became bankrupt. By 1849 he had resigned his chairmanships and was ruined.

Hungry Forties

A series of bad harvests started in 1837 and trade stagnation resulted in considerable suffering for the WORKING CLASSES during much of the 1840s. The COST OF LIVING was increased by import duties on grain, butter, tea, sugar and other foods. The Irish potato famine of 1845 brought starvation and death; over 700,000 people died in Ireland between 1845 and 1850. Nearly one million emigrated following the failure of the potato crop. This period of economic distress encouraged CHARTISM and hastened the repeal of the CORN LAWS.

Hunt, Henry (1773–1835)

A wealthy gentleman farmer and reformer, known as 'Orator Hunt'. He was the chief speaker at PETERLOO in 1819, where he was arrested and sentenced to two years in prison. While in prison he wrote his *Memoirs*. He was the foremost public orator of the reform movement until the passage of the REFORM ACT, 1832.

He was elected to Parliament in 1830 and remained loyal to manhood suffrage, attacking the 1832 Reform Bill as being a betrayal. Vain and bombastic, he wore a white top hat when addressing meetings and liked to be known as the 'Champion of Liberty'.

Huntsman, Benjamin (1704–76)

A clockmaker who developed a process about 1742 to produce better quality steel for clock springs and pendulums. His CRUCIBLE process used coke in furnaces to heat Swedish BLISTER STEEL with fluxes in clay crucibles. The intense heat burned all the impurities away and the molten steel was then poured into iron moulds. The steel was hard and could be used for razors, penknives and edge tools. The process played an important part in the development of many industries, including engineering.

Benjamin Huntsman did not patent his invention and had to work in great secrecy. About 1770 he set up a small steel works at Attercliffe near Sheffield. The SHEFFIELD cutlers tried, unsuccessfully, to limit the use of his process, but knowledge of the process spread slowly, and it was not used extensively until the end of the 18th century. His son carried on the business and the steel became famous all over the world. The making of this cast-steel, as it was called, was a costly, small-scale process which was not improved until the BESSEMER PROCESS was introduced in 1856.

Humanitarianism

A movement which sought to correct the social distress of the period, particularly the conditions of the working people and their children. The movement was supported by ROBERT OWEN, the EARL OF SHAFTESBURY, William Wilberforce (the founder of the anti-slavery movement) and factory reformers such as RICHARD OASTLER and JOHN FIELDEN.

Huskisson, William (1770–1830)

President of the Board of Trade 1823–7. A minister with FREE TRADE ideas who reduced tariffs on the import of manufactured goods and raw materials. He modified the NAVIGATION ACTS, introduced a sliding scale for the import of corn, negotiated a number of reciprocal treaties with foreign countries to reduce trade barriers and was active in repealing the COMBINATION ACTS. He was killed by stumbling in front of the ROCKET in 1830 at the opening of the LIVERPOOL AND MANCHESTER RAILWAY.

Hydrometer

An instrument used to measure the specific gravity of liquids such as beer and spirits. A number of instruments were developed by Benjamin Martin and others in the 18th century and an instrument made by John Sikes was chosen by the Excise in 1803. The instrument was valuable in costing liquids and identifying the malts which were most economic to the brewers.

I

Improvement Acts

Acts of Parliament which gave local authorities powers they had requested to carry out certain improvements to their towns. The Acts were promoted by the local authorities and were costly undertakings. Between 1785 and 1800 there were over two hundred Improvement Acts dealing with street lighting, paving, providing watchmen and water supply. By the Acts, local Improvement Commissioners were given financial powers which were often very limited. Instead of following schemes for large-scale changes over the whole locality, they improved the better residential districts. Nevertheless, improvements were made, especially in the prosperous ports such as LIVERPOOL, BRISTOL, NEWCASTLE-UPON-TYNE, Portsmouth and Southampton.

In the 19th century the rapid increase in the population of the towns resulted in social and sanitation problems which could not have been solved by Improvement Acts even if the local authorities had been willing to promote them. Some larger towns did obtain Improvement Acts; NOTTINGHAM, by an Act in 1845, stipulated the width of the streets, alleys and courts, and Liverpool in 1846 made regulations about SEWERING and draining of houses.

In 1847 Parliament passed several Acts which enabled a town to incorporate into one Improvement Act clauses covering a variety of services such as gas, water and other improvements, thereby saving itself trouble and expense. The PUBLIC HEALTH ACT, 1848 set up local Boards of Health with powers which, if adopted, would avoid the expense and time involved in passing local Improvement Acts. Unfortunately the Central Board was powerless to force town authorities to comply and some took no effective action. Nevertheless, the Act was adopted in some 200 places including a number of industrial towns where sanitary measures were specially needed, such as Bolton, MERTHYR TYDFIL, Wakefield and Wolverhampton. Some towns, including LEEDS and BIRMINGHAM promoted Improvement Acts of their own to maintain their independence.

After the Board was abolished in 1854 towns continued to make improvements, encouraged by grants and loans with low rates of interest from the government.

Inclined Plane

A steep slope along which rails were laid to haul boats or wagons on TRAMWAYS from one level to another. In the early 1800s steam power was introduced to replace the horses previously used to haul up the load. TUB BOATS were used in conjunction with CANAL inclined planes, and in some cases the tub boats had wheels permanently fitted so that they could be hauled up and down on rails.

Visit Ironbridge Gorge Museum, Shropshire – Hay inclined plane. **M***
Cromford and High Peak Railway, Derbyshire – Middleton and sheep pasture inclined planes.

Income Tax

A tax first introduced in 1798 by WILLIAM PITT as a temporary measure to help pay for the NAPOLEONIC WARS. It was abolished in 1816 and reintroduced in 1842 by ROBERT PEEL. The rate at that time was 7d (5 US cents) in the pound on incomes of £150 ($255) a year or over.

Industrial Revolution

The changes in British industry, and their impact on the economy and society, which occurred in the period from approximately 1760 to 1860. The process was long and complicated, not sudden and violent as most revolutions are. It was a change from the DOMESTIC SYSTEM of production to the FACTORY SYSTEM – from small-scale to larger-scale industry. Steam (see STEAM ENGINES) as a new source of power and the development of new MACHINES were paralleled by improved means of communication by land and water. The revolution produced a new class of capitalist owners (see CAPITAL) who became very rich. It also produced masses of wage-earners in factories and mines who grouped together to form the WORKING-CLASS movement. The Industrial Revolution gave Britain a start of several decades over other countries, where industrial development began later, and consequently gave it enormous advantages for the expansion of trade and the opening up of new markets.

The reasons for the revolution occurring are not fully understood. Britain had certain advantages over Continental Europe. There were rich deposits of coal and iron, a long tradition of commercial BANKING, population growth, internal peace and security, and a burst of inventions and technological improvements. Professor D. Eversley (in Jones and Mingay's book – see below) has postulated that between 1750 and 1780 the number of households in the middle income range (£50–£400 a year – $85–$680) rose from 15 per cent of the population of England to 20 per cent or even 25 per cent. The foundation of the Industrial Revolution was laid by the sale of articles of everyday life, such as cotton and iron goods, to this MIDDLE CLASS of consumers.

P. Mantoux, *The Industrial Revolution in the Eighteenth Century* (Methuen 1964).
P. Mathias, *The First Industrial Nation* (Methuen 1969).
P. Deane, *The First Industrial Revolution* (Cambridge University Press 1979).
E.L. Jones and G.E. Mingay (eds), *Land, Labour and Population in the Industrial Revolution* (Edward Arnold 1967).

Industrial Wages

The wages paid in industry were generally higher than those in agriculture throughout the Industrial Revolution, although in industrial counties such as Warwickshire the differential was lower than in rural counties such as Suffolk. A farm labourer in 1770 earned on average 5–6 shillings (42–50 US cents) per week in winter and 7–9 shillings (59–76 US cents) in summer. A cotton weaver earned 7–10 shillings (59–85 US cents), a Wilton carpet-maker 11 shillings (93 US cents) or more and a NEWCASTLE miner 15 shillings ($1.27). FRAMEWORK KNITTERS were poorly paid, earning less than 6 shillings (50 US cents) per week.

By 1795 industrial wages had increased more rapidly than those in agriculture, widening the gap still further. During periods of recession such as 1793 and 1816 the wages of some factory workers fell dramatically, especially for weavers, who were too numerous as a result of an influx of country labourers used to low wages.

Infant School Society

Founded in 1824 with Samuel Wilderspin as its organizer of schools. The Society had taken as its inspiration the work of ROBERT OWEN at NEW LANARK, where an infant school had been a successful addition to the mill. The Society, and others that were formed, emphasized moral and intellectual character and moved away from Robert Owen's enlightened views. During the 1840s and 1850s infant schools combined formal scripture lessons with reading, writing, arithmetic, physical exercise and play.

Insurance

In 1720 two corporate bodies, the Royal Exchange and London Assurance Companies, received charters to do business in marine insurance. They later extended their business into fire risk. Both companies appointed agents and their business, at first predominantly with houses and shops, became increasingly industrial. The Phoenix and the Sun Fire Offices were established in the late 18th century, and by 1800 the Phoenix, the Sun and the Royal Exchange were the biggest insurance companies. In the provinces there were other companies, such as the Norwich Union (1797) and, in Edinburgh, the North British (1809). Life assurance policies were also issued by the Royal Exchange and other companies on a small scale, but the first company to base its policies on statistical life tables was the Equitable Life Assurance Society, founded in 1762.

The growth of overseas trade brought about a steady increase in insurance business. British merchants exporting cargoes insured them in LONDON, and Lloyds of London had almost a monopoly of insuring the ships in which the cargoes sailed. Other rival ports, especially Amsterdam, lost their international business through war after 1780, and by the end of the NAPOLEONIC WARS the main insurance market was based in London, where it remained unchallenged throughout the 19th century. The evolution of London as the world's main centre of insurance, BANKING and finance was a feature of the dominance of British shipping in world trade.

International Trade

Foreign trade helped the development of the INDUSTRIAL REVOLUTION by:

(a) creating a demand for British manufactures;

(b) giving access to raw materials, especially cotton;

(c) providing less developed countries with the purchasing power to buy British goods;

(d) providing an economic surplus in the form of profits which were used to invest in further developments;

(e) helping create an institutional structure which included a money market and INSURANCE, necessary for commercial development;

(f) promoting the growth of large towns and industrial centres where specialization of production could take place. The growth of LIVERPOOL and GLASGOW was almost entirely the result of foreign trade.

Inventions

Many of the so-called inventions of the period were really improvements and adaptations. They were often adjustments made by workers or, occasionally, MANUFACTURERS. Some experiments had distant futures not realized by the inventors. For example, JAMES WATT's 'governor', which ensured constancy of speed with load by automatically controlling a valve in the steam-inlet pipe, was the forerunner of automation.

Very few men were professional inventors. Most were skilled craftsmen or engineers who developed an idea by trial and error. Some were remarkably naive, and unscrupulous ENTREPRENEURS copied their ideas before they were patented or because the inventor made no attempt to take out a patent. Some of the most successful inventions were developed as the result of a partnership between a successful entrepreneur and an inventor; for example, that between BOULTON AND WATT.

Inventors sometimes delayed progress because of the restrictions caused by patent rights, which usually lasted for fourteen years. James Watt's STEAM ENGINE was not free to be copied without paying a royalty until 1800 because of this tight control of the patent.

Irish Immigrants

Irish immigrants between 1790 and 1810 included a number of Protestants and particularly Ulstermen abandoning their declining textile mills for MANCHESTER, GLASGOW, Barnsley, Bolton and Macclesfield. After 1810 immigrants were mainly Catholic peasants driven out in large numbers by crop failures, such as that of the potato crop in 1821–2 and 1845 (see HUNGRY FORTIES). Irish labour was essential for the INDUSTRIAL REVOLUTION, partly because it was cheap and partly because the immigrants were prepared and able to do the heavy digging of harbours, docks, CANALS and roads. By 1830 Irish labourers in large numbers were to be found engaged in a variety of manual tasks, including NAVVYING.

In 1841 approximately 400,000 Irish immigrants were living in Britain, attracted there by the better job opportunities and higher wages than those in the rural areas of Ireland. About a third of the people in Manchester were Irish and they were to be found in large numbers in LONDON and the other industrial towns. Their wages and living conditions were miserable and they formed an alien element within the labouring poor, being absorbed only slowly by WORKING-CLASS communities. There was some antagonism, particularly when it was assumed that the CHOLERA OUTBREAK of 1849 was due to the squalor of the Irish sections of the mining towns.

Irish immigrants were strong supporters of English RADICALISM, but because they were members of weak unions their voice was seldom heard.

Ironbridge Gorge

The steep-sided valley of the River Severn southeast of Shrewsbury in Shropshire is often referred to as the birthplace of the INDUSTRIAL REVOLUTION. During the 17th century there were BLAST FURNACES smelting local iron ore with charcoal in the valley, and one of these furnaces was leased by ABRAHAM DARBY I in 1708. The next year he successfully used coke instead of charcoal as a fuel for smelting iron. The company he started at COALBROOKDALE prospered, and some of the iron goods produced helped to set in

motion the sequence of events which became the Industrial Revolution. The IRON BRIDGE from which the gorge takes its name was erected in 1779, and was the first CAST-IRON bridge.

The bridge and its surroundings attracted a number of artists as well as tourists, although the gorge was no longer the picturesque wooded region it had once been. Instead, the slopes were littered with spoil tips and other evidence of industry which, with the clouds of smoke and steam and the flames of the furnaces, suggested hell to some visitors. By present-day standards it would have been considered an unplanned development creating a visual eyesore and producing pollution on a large scale. To contemporary eyes it was both fascinating and awe-inspiring.

Visit Ironbridge Gorge Museum, Shropshire – working museum of the area and its industries. **M***

N. Cossons and H. Sowdon, *Ironbridge: Landscape of Industry* (Cassell 1977).
B. Trinder, *The Industrial Revolution in Shropshire* (Phillimore 1981).

A view of Coalbrookdale with its iron works 'for casting cannon'. This engraving after a painting was published in 1788. The steep slopes of the gorge form a backcloth for the smoking chimneys of the furnaces. Cannon ready for shipment can be seen on the far bank close to the water wheel. (*Elton Collection: Ironbridge Gorge Museum Trust*)

Iron Industry

Like the COTTON INDUSTRY, the manufacture of iron was revolutionized in the last quarter of the 18th century. Unlike cotton it had been developed as a capitalist industry (see CAPITAL), with workers paid a wage and working at a 'works'. It achieved economies by INVENTIONS which used raw materials more efficiently, or by switching raw materials (for example, from charcoal to coal when timber became scarce). The product, iron, depended on the growth of industries which could use it; in other words, the demand was derived. It also depended for its development on the STEAM ENGINE, both as a source of power and because large amounts or iron were used in the engines' construction. The development after 1775 of JAMES WATT's rotative steam engine gave the works power for the ROLLING MILLS and hammers.

Large-scale production began to appear in regions where coal and iron were to be found, and by 1806, 87 per cent of PIG-IRON production was located in the coalfields. Demand increased rapidly and by 1810 the iron industry generated about 6 per cent of the British national income. Plants became large and the ironmasters operated on a vast scale, with interests in collieries, mines, landing stages, foundries and forges. Growth accelerated in the railway age (see RAILWAY DEVELOPMENT) after 1830, and the iron industry was the most important single consumer of coal. The industry supplied a cheap and tough material which industry and transport needed in large quantities, and any reduction in the price of iron affected a whole range of other industries.

The HOT BLAST process was the most important advance in the smelting sector during the period 1830–70. It was responsible for substantial improvements in BLAST FURNACE productivity and costs, particularly in Scotland where fuel costs were drastically reduced. The challenge to the supremacy of WROUGHT IRON came from Henry Bessemer in 1856. His new BESSEMER PROCESS provided MILD STEEL, and after some initial problems a few firms started making Bessemer steel in

1860. The open-hearth steel process, slower but more accurate than the Bessemer, was introduced at the end of the 1860s and the demand for steel increased rapidly.

T.S. Ashton, *Iron and Steel in the Industrial Revolution* (Manchester University Press 1963).
C.K. Hyde, *Technological Change and the British Iron Industry, 1700–1870* (Princeton University Press 1977).
W.K.V. Gale, *Ironworking* (Shire Publications 1981).

Iron Industry – Charcoal Forge

To make WROUGHT IRON, the CAST IRON from the CHARCOAL FURNACE was refined at a forge, where it was placed in a finery furnace and then reheated in a chafery furnace. Both furnaces used charcoal as a fuel and water-powered bellows to provide a blast of air. The bars of wrought iron were then forged under a huge hammer (also water-driven) and were then either taken to a SLITTING MILL to be cut into small rods or to a blacksmith for shaping. Edge tools also had to be ground.

Visit Abbeydale Industrial Hamlet, Sheffield – 18th-century industrial hamlet with crucible steel furnaces, tilt hammers, forges and workmens' cottages. **M***

Iron Industry – Charcoal Furnace

Before coke was used in BLAST FURNACES the heat was obtained from charcoal. Charcoal, iron ore and limestone (used as a flux to promote the formation of slag) were mixed together to form a 'charge' which was put into the top of the blast furnace. Iron collected at the bottom of the furnace and the slag floated on top. The slag was drawn off and then molten iron was allowed to run out into a sand bed to cool as CAST IRON.

Iron Industry – Integrated Ironworks

In an integrated ironworks the iron which is produced passes through forges, foundries and ROLLING MILLS to become iron products such as girders, pipes and boiler plates. The integrated mill processes the raw material and then manufactures finished iron products. By the second decade of the 19th century large integrated ironworks dominated the industry. They had five or six BLAST FURNACES, for which they required large quantities of iron ore and coal. Some companies owned COAL MINES and ore deposits to supply their integrated works. Three of the largest were the CARRON IRONWORKS, the COALBROOKDALE COMPANY and the CYFARTHFA IRONWORKS. The tendency throughout the 19th century was for the number of integrated works to increase at the expense of the smaller producers.

Iron Industry – Iron-hulled boats

The first WROUGHT-IRON barge was launched on the River Severn by JOHN WILKINSON in 1787, and an iron barge was used to carry coal on the Firth of Clyde in Scotland in 1816. The first STEAM BOAT with an iron hull was the *Aaron Manby*, built in 1822 at Tipton, Staffordshire, and taken in sections to LONDON for assembly. A second boat, the *Marquis Wellesley*, started a service on the River Shannon in Ireland in the 1820s.

In 1829 the SHIPBUILDING firm of Cammell Laird began building iron ships at Birkenhead, and iron-hulled steam boats were being built on the Clyde by the 1830s. In 1839 the Admiralty ordered the first iron-hulled naval steamer, the *Dover*. However, experiments showed that iron plates were likely to splinter in battle, and no more warships were built of iron until HMS *Warrior* was launched in 1861.

The potential of the STEAM ENGINE could not be fully realized until the hulls of ships were built completely of iron. After the GREAT WESTERN had proved the importance of transatlantic services, its owners and designers planned a much more ambitious vessel completely made of iron, unlike the *Great Western*, which had a traditional wooden hull. ISAMBARD BRUNEL designed this vessel, the GREAT BRITAIN, as an all-iron merchant ship with screw propulsion for the Atlantic service, and it was launched in 1843. The ship was built in a dry dock that had been specially constructed to accommodate her enormous bulk. Both the original dry dock and the restored *Great Britain* can be seen in BRISTOL. By the 1850s merchant ships were being built with iron hulls, and iron was replacing wood for decks and other fittings.

Visit Industrial Museum, Bristol – dry dock, *Great Britain* and other forms of early transport. **M***

Iron Industry – Iron Ploughs

Ploughs with the share and the coulter made of iron were common in the 18th century, but they were not very efficient implements; moreover, each part was made separately, so there was no uniformity and a new part had to be made each time a replacement was needed. In 1770 John Brand of Lawford, Essex, made the first iron plough. It was heavy, distinctive in having only one handle and became known as the Suffolk iron plough. The lighter Norfolk plough had only an iron mouldboard and a WROUGHT-IRON share, the rest being made of wood. ROBERT RANSOME obtained a patent in 1785 for a tempered CAST-IRON ploughshare which became very popular. He took out another patent in 1803 for a chilled shoe – the chilling process hardened the edge of the shoe so that it remained sharp. Probably his biggest contribution was the standardization of plough parts at his Ipswich factory. In 1840 Ransom's was making ploughs with iron parts bolted to wooden bodies, and in 1843 the firm made its first all-iron plough, the YL.

Iron Industry – Iron Rails

Iron rails were first used in the Severn Gorge area in 1767, having been cast at COALBROOKDALE. Previously rails had been made of wood, but they wore quickly when iron wheels were introduced. The rails were 'edge' rails, designed for use with flanged wheels. JOHN CURR invented the L-section rail or plate on which wagons with plain, unflanged wheels could run, and by the early 19th century these plates were in use in most parts of Britain (except the

North East, where there was a long tradition of flanged wheels).

WROUGHT IRON was first used for rails in 1808 at collieries near Edinburgh and at about the same time at Tindal Fell in Cumberland. The rails consisted of square bars 9 feet (2.7 m) long. In 1820 John Birkinshaw of the Bedlington Iron Works, Northumberland, took out a patent for the construction of wrought-iron rails by passing them between rollers while hot. The rails were wedge-shaped, and later T-shaped. The first line to use the rails was that from the colliery to Bedlington Iron Works, a distance of 3 miles (4.8 km). ROBERT STEPHENSON saw the potential of the rails and on his advice they were adopted by the STOCKTON AND DARLINGTON RAILWAY COMPANY. John Birkinshaw's process was used extensively when the railway network was being built.

Visit Ironbridge Gorge Museum, Shropshire – early rails. **M***
Cyfarthfa Castle, Merthyr Tydfil, South Wales – early rails. **M***

C.F. Dendy Marshall, *A History of British Railways Down to the Year 1830* (Oxford University Press 1971).

Iron Industry – Iron Rolling See
Rolling Mills

Iron Industry – Location

The last decades of the 18th and the first two decades of the 19th century saw a considerable shift in the location of the IRON INDUSTRY and in the balance between the major regional centres of the industry. The locational change was due to a change in fuel from charcoal to coke and the development of the new techniques of PUDDLING and rolling (see ROLLING MILLS).

One of the major producing areas, Shropshire, expanded considerably in the 1750s, using coke PIG IRON to produce WROUGHT IRON. Five new works were built within 7 miles (11.2 km) and the output of the furnaces increased from 25 tonnes (27.6 US tons) a week in the 1790s to 40–50 tonnes (44–55 US tons) a week ten years later.

The most remarkable increase towards the end of the 18th century occurred in South Wales, particularly around MERTHYR TYDFIL, between 1759 and 1765, when the DOWLAIS, Plymouth and CYFARTHFA WORKS were started. The district had local coking coal, iron ore and water resources and the ironmasters quickly adopted Henry CORT's puddling process. By 1815 the Merthyr works, which by then also included PENYDARREN (1784), produced 35 per cent of Britain's iron output, with Shropshire producing only 12.5 per cent.

Another area which developed during the NAPOLEONIC WARS was Staffordshire, where there was good coking coal, ore, limestone and fireclay in close proximity. A local deficiency of water power was overcome by using steam power to provide the blast and work the rolling mills. The CANAL system of the BIRMINGHAM area provided cheap transport, and in 1815 Staffordshire together with South Wales accounted for two-thirds of pig iron production.

Scottish iron production started in 1759 with the building of the CARRON IRONWORKS, but for 20 years it was the only company. Although there were ten works by 1800, seven of them in West Scotland, output was only 9 per cent of the British total and by 1825 it had dropped to 5 per cent. The HOT BLAST method considerably increased production in Scotland since it lowered costs and made the region competitive with the rest of Britain. Eleven new works were started and production of 30,000 tonnes (33,000 US tons) of pig iron in 1830 jumped to 1 million tonnes (1,120,000 US tons) by 1860.

Production in the North East did not keep pace with South Wales and the other major regions, and in 1860 only about one-tenth of the total output came from Northumberland and Durham, with smaller outputs from Lancashire, Cumberland, Shropshire and South Yorkshire.

Ironmasters' Associations

Commercial undertakings and agreements in which the ironmasters combined to their mutual advantage. There are reports of monthly meetings at

Stourbridge in the BLACK COUNTRY as early as the 1720s. Meetings were held regularly in the Midlands at different centres, and by 1790 there was a weekly dinner in the Ironmasters' Room at the Union Tavern in BIRMINGHAM. Major producers in South Yorkshire and Derbyshire formed a Friendly Association in 1799 and quarterly meetings were held in Wales in 1802.

There was no national body of ironmasters, although the industry organized itself on a national basis in times of crisis, such as that caused by the proposal to impose taxes on coal in 1796, 1806 and 1819. A national association was set up in 1808 but little was achieved. Other national meetings were held in 1813 during the dislocation of trade caused by the ANGLO-AMERICAN WAR, but again, no agreement was reached on the suggestion of price fixing. In 1840–2 output was deliberately restricted, with virtually no exceptions, as a result of the severity of the 1839–42 slump. Success was therefore achieved not by price control but by output control.

J

Jacobins

Originally the term was used for a society of French revolutionaries who met in the house of a Jacobin convent. During the FRENCH REVOLUTION the term crossed the Channel to be used to describe groups of English extremists. The outbreak of the French Revolution was seen by some as the dawn of European liberty, and the reform movement increased in popularity, fuelled by THOMAS PAINE's *Rights of Man*. The LONDON CORRESPONDING SOCIETY was set up in 1792 and universal manhood suffrage was demanded. The government, under WILLIAM PITT, reacted by outlawing Paine, and the London Corresponding Society was fatally weakened. The TWO ACTS were passed in 1795 and Jacobinism went underground. By 1797 some of the extreme Jacobins had come to despair of constitutional agitation and saw their only hope in a *coup d'état*. Further oppression followed with the COMBINATION ACTS, but Jacobin ideas persisted. They were based on the popular belief that all men are capable of reason, and that deference and distinction of status were an affront to human dignity. These ideas were passed on to the Chartists (see CHARTISM).

Jacquard Loom

A loom worked with a system of punched cards which allowed elaborate patterns to be woven. A number of Frenchmen invented the system and in 1801 Joseph Marie Jacquard (1752–1834) improved on it. A British patent was taken out in 1817.

The jacquard loom was used in its early days mainly in the silk industry; later it was used in the weaving of fine LINEN, cotton and WORSTED materials. It was not evident in large numbers in Britain until the 1820s, when it was improved and made more compact so that it could be used in the cottage industry as well as in factories. In 1832 there were 600 jacquard looms in COVENTRY. In 1841 Hooton Deverill, a NOTTINGHAM lace-maker, adopted the loom for lace-making so that it was possible to reproduce the traditional patterns of hand-made lace in wide and narrow pieces.

James, William (1771–1837)

An estate agent and colliery owner who superintended the building of the Stratford-upon-Avon CANAL in Worcestershire and spent large sums of money on the River Avon navigation. He was also one of the earliest advocates of a railway system in England. In 1819–20 he planned to extend the line of the Stratford

Canal by a tram road to Moreton-in-Marsh in Gloucestershire. The Stratford and Moreton Railway was completed in 1826, a year after the Stockton and Darlington RAILWAY, but by this time William James was not involved. He projected and surveyed many miles of railway in the Midlands, the West Country, Kent and the North West. In the 1820s his scheme for a railway between MANCHESTER and LIVERPOOL was the beginning of a campaign which resulted in the building of a line in 1830.

He was one of the first to advocate the use of locomotives and to realize the vast possibilities of carrying passengers by rail. He has been called the 'Father of Railways'.

Visit Stratford-upon-Avon – Stratford and Moreton Railway wagon standing on original track and site close to the canal basin; brick viaduct crossing the River Avon used as footpath.

Japanning

Varnishing to give a black, glossy finish to ornaments, household goods and jewellery. The practice of japanning tin-plate is said to have started in Pontypool in Wales and was introduced into the Midlands about 1720. Looking for a new material which was heat-resistant and would bear japanning or lacquering, the japanners introduced papier mâché about 1750. In 1772 a japanner, Henry Clay, introduced PAPER WARE made from layers of paper glued to a core which was later removed. This proved ideal for japanning and a variety of trays and other household articles were made.

Japanning was simple, much being done by unskilled women, girls and boys using lamp-black, turpentine, oils, pitch, resin and wax. The industry used stamping machines and drying ovens, and many products fetched high prices in LONDON and elsewhere. The trade spread to Wolverhampton where its centre was OLD HALL. The industry relied on public taste and was prosperous until the middle of the 19th century.

Jardine, James (1776–1858)

An engineer to the Edinburgh Water Company and the builder of the Union Canal. He was also the first person to determine the mean level of the sea. In 1823 he built a pipeline with a diameter from 20 inches to 15 inches (508 mm to 381 mm) to carry water from springs south of Edinburgh to the city. With THOMAS TELFORD as chief designer, he also built the Glencorse Dam, in the Pentland Hills about 8 miles (12.9 km) south of the city, to provide a storage area for the water supply.

Jenner, Edmund (1749–1823)

A doctor who practised in the west of England. He knew of the local tradition that milkmaids who caught cowpox were immune to smallpox, and he experimented with the inoculation of people with cowpox. He coined the word 'vaccination', from the Latin *vacca* (cow), for this inoculation. Vaccination was quickly accepted because there was a great fear of smallpox and in some parts of Europe vaccination was made compulsory. In the USA his method was taken up by Benjamin Waterhouse (1754–1846) of the Harvard Medical School, and Edmund Jenner received a letter of commendation in 1806 from the President of the USA, Thomas Jefferson.

Visit The Chantry, Church Lane, High Street, Berkeley, Gloucestershire – former home of Edmund Jenner with memorabilia. **M***

Jessop, William (1745–1814)

A canal engineer who built, among other CANALS, the Grand Junction Canal linking London with the Midlands, and the Cromford Canal in Derbyshire. With THOMAS TELFORD, he built the PONTCYSYLLTE AQUEDUCT to carry the Ellesmere Canal over the River Dee. In 1799 he recommended the formation of the first railway company, the SURREY IRON RAILWAY. Between 1800 and 1809 he remodelled BRISTOL harbour, creating a huge wet dock, and diverting the river along the New Cut. He became a partner in the BUTTERLEY COMPANY in 1792, joining BENJAMIN OUTRAM and others. The Company owned mines and quarries near the Cromford Canal and were iron founders and engineers.

C. Hadfield and A.W. Skempton, *William Jessop, Engineer* (David and Charles 1979).

Jones, Griffith (1683–1761)

The vicar of Llanddowror in Carmarthenshire who started CIRCULATING SCHOOLS in Wales about 1730.

Joule, James Prescott (1818–89)

The son of a brewer in Salford, Lancashire, he began work in the family business at the age of 15. In 1847 he published a paper which established a precise relationship between heat and work. Regardless of the type of heat-engine used, the amount of work it could perform for a given amount of heat supplied to it was limited. He went on to measure the mechanical equivalent of heat as accurately as possible. His work paved the way for the conservation theory, the first law of thermodynamics: energy, like matter, can be neither created nor destroyed.

Justice of the Peace

A person appointed to administer justice, sometimes called a magistrate. In 1195 Richard I commissioned certain knights to ensure that the peace was observed by everyone. The idea developed in the succeeding centuries and the knights became known as 'custodes pacis' or 'keepers of the peace'. Their authority was gradually enlarged and by the 14th century they were empowered to deal with most offences. An Act of 1361 formally recognized them as justices of the peace.

In the 18th and 19th centuries justices of the peace were usually country gentlemen or parsons who mainly protected the interests of the UPPER CLASSES and of the MANUFACTURERS. For many years in the 18th century manufacturers were excluded from becoming magistrates, and it might be assumed that the justices therefore dealt fairly with the workpeople. However, the squires and parsons regarded the WORKING CLASS as a menace to property and order, and therefore had their grievances to bias their decisions. In some respects the manufacturers understood their workers, and on such issues as the COMBINATION ACTS the magistrates were sometimes more hostile than the masters.

When factory owners became magistrates, however, few had sympathy with the workers. The only magistrates in Caerphilly and MERTHYR TYDFIL in 1826 were two ironmasters who employed four or five thousand workers apiece and were constantly trying workers for offences against themselves. A parson magistrate informed the Home Office in 1817 that two men who had distributed pamphlets by WILLIAM COBBETT had been well flogged at the whipping post under the VAGRANCY laws. The magistrates upheld the TRUCK SYSTEM and ignored the fact that the Combination Laws applied to the factory owners as well as the workpeople. They took the attitude that if the masters would not obey the law there was nothing they could do to enforce it.

The appointment of JPs was a form of political patronage. It was an honour within reach of local businessmen, and magistracies were readily granted as favours. By the 1860s JPs in the agricultural counties were mainly gentry; in the industrial counties, gentry and manufacturers; and leading tradespeople and councillors in the boroughs. The highly nonconformist county of Huntingdon had no magistrate DISSENTERS until 1873, and it was not until 1884 that the first working-class magistrate was appointed.

K

Kay, John (1704–64)

A Lancashire reed-maker for the weaving industry who became an inventor. His first INVENTION in 1730 was a new process for carding and roving mohair and WORSTED. In 1733 he improved the hand loom shuttle by mounting it on wheels and making it possible to throw the shuttle across the loom more easily and faster. His invention, known as the fly or flying shuttle, was a labour-saving device which enabled a weaver to make a wide cloth previously requiring two weavers. Mechanical difficulties and opposition from workers, who saw their jobs threatened, prevented the fly shuttle from coming into general use until the 1750s. John Kay settled in France in 1747 because of financial difficulties. He encountered hostility when he visited England and died in poverty in France.

Kay-Shuttleworth, Sir James Phillips (1804–77)

The secretary of the Committee of the Privy Council on Education, 1839. This body had the task of supervising the proper use of Parliamentary grants to EDUCATION, and this was done by appointing inspectors. In 1840 he opened a teacher training school in Battersea which he later handed over to the NATIONAL SOCIETY. He was responsible for the introduction of the pupil teacher scheme in 1846 and supported the foundation of more teacher training colleges. As a result some 40 colleges were opened in England and Wales by the early 1850s, which helped to give teachers a professional training and a status which Kay-Shuttleworth encouraged. As a result the MONITORIAL SYSTEM, with its narrow and inefficient method of teaching, disappeared.

Keel

1 A small cargo-carrying vessel used on rivers and inland waterways, mainly on the east coast of Britain. The main cargo carried was coal, and on the Tyne and the Wear in North East England this was the only cargo. On these rivers keels were propelled by oars, but a single, square mainsail was available. The size of the keels was determined by the waterway on which they operated. On the Tyne they were about 40 feet (12.2 m) long with a beam of 19 feet (5.8 m). They carried just over 21 tonnes (23.5 US tons) of coal. During the 1790s there were an annual average of 338 keels working on the Tyne and 452 on the Wear. Their number declined in the 19th century as colliers began to load directly from STAITHES on the rivers.
2 The central ridge on the under-surface of a ship, designed to increase the stability of the vessel.

Keir, James (1735–1820)

A Scot who studied medicine at Edinburgh University and served seven years in the army before settling in West Bromwich, in the Midlands. He founded the TIPTON CHEMICAL WORKS in West Bromwich in 1782. The factory was to supply alkali to the soap-makers, but later it made soap as well as red and white lead and metal window-sashes. Locally the Tipton Chemical Works was regarded as a wonder. It was extremely profitable and about 1794 James Keir and his partner, Alexander Blair, purchased a colliery near Dudley to supply their works with coal. Keir was a serious student of chemistry as well as a man of action who developed a successful new industry in the West Midlands.

Kelvin, Lord William Thomson (1824–1907)

A scientist who contributed to electromagnetic theory, thermodynamics and geophysics. He was responsible for stimulating much of the scientific progress and practical industrial advance from about 1850. In 1855 he became involved in the design and construction of the first successful transatlantic UNDERWATER TELEGRAPH CABLES.

Kirkcaldy

A LINEN-spinning centre in the 18th century, with spinning carried out as a cottage industry in the surrounding countryside. The number of mills increased in the 19th century and POWER LOOMS were established in 1821, reducing the number of outworkers. In the 1840s the town became an important jute-spinning centre and in 1847 the allied industry of linoleum manufacture, using a jute base, was introduced. This was to expand and make the town well known throughout the world.

L

Labour Aristocracy

Craftsmen and others who improved their STANDARD OF LIVING at a faster rate than the majority of the WORKING CLASS during the 19th century were sometimes known as the labour aristocracy. They included printers, cutlers, blacksmiths, wheelwrights, cabinet-makers and railway engine drivers. Their skills were in increasing demand and they benefited from industrialization as much as the MIDDLE CLASS.

R.Q. Gray, *The Aristocracy of Labour in Nineteenth Century Britain* (Macmillan 1981).

Labour – Recruitment for Early Mills

The scarcity of labour in the early cotton mills was partly the result of a general shortage in the manufacturing districts. It was also due to the reluctance of the workers to enter factories, where discipline was strict and the hours long and tedious. A third reason was the remoteness of some mills, such as the CROMFORD Mill, from centres of population. The NAPOLEONIC WARS also aggravated the situation by taking men into the army.

Wages in spinning mills were higher than those of farm labourers but not sufficient to attract workers from regular employment in the towns. To attract and retain a labour force the factory masters used a number of inducements. The most common was the provision of housing at low rents. At Cromford, RICHARD ARKWRIGHT built cottages set behind a broad avenue of trees with lawn borders and allotment gardens nearby. This housing was far more attractive than that being built in nearby NOTTINGHAM at the time. With large gardens, allotments, milking cows and similar rural amenities, workers were attracted to environments with a rural setting.

Subsidies were also used. Coal and other provisions were subsidized and cheap or free medical care was provided. In some cases employment elsewhere was provided for the fathers and husbands of the main mill labour force, who were the wives and children. Richard Arkwright owned a paper mill at Cromford and employed many men building Willersley Castle, his country home nearby.

The larger MANUFACTURERS also created communal facilities such as churches, markets, schools and public houses. Some mill owners gave the workers what they thought was good for their souls, but Arkwright gave them what they wanted.

Labour – Supply and Demand

The early, water-driven factories were situated in remote rural areas and were constantly short of labour. They could obtain hundreds of pauper children but few adults, because local people regarded the factory as a kind of WORKHOUSE. To obtain labour the mill owners had to provide housing and other facilities, offer high wages and promise work for all the family (see LABOUR – RECRUITMENT FOR EARLY MILLS).

Steam power changed the picture. Factories could be located in or near towns to which labour could be attracted, so the labour force was no longer the employer's responsibility. It could move between employers and be discarded in times of slump or when MACHINES were introduced as a substitute. A wage-earning class was formed which, at times, aired its grievances with strikes and MACHINE BREAKING.

Labour requirements varied. Outworking was common in the textile industry, but where powered machinery was used labour was confined to factories, with large numbers employed. In 1815 there were between 1,600 and 1,700 workers at NEW LANARK, and 1,000 workers at a mill was not uncommon.

Lady Huntingdon's Connexion See Evangelical Movement and George Whitefield

Laissez-faire

A term first used by the 18th-century French economists known as the Physiocrats. They believed that the state should not interfere with the natural order of supply and demand, and they influenced British economists such as ADAM SMITH. Laissez-faire thinking condemned any interference with industry by the government. This principle became very popular and strengthened the demand for FREE TRADE.

At the time of the INDUSTRIAL REVOLUTION in the 18th century the doctrine was moving from theory to practical application. As a philosophy it was a check to factory legislation which, if passed, could have improved conditions for factory workers, particularly children. In the 19th century the growth of industry and the industrial towns brought many problems which only the government could effectively handle. There was also a growth in social responsibility, and during the 1830s and 1840s government bills such as the FACTORY ACTS and the PUBLIC HEALTH ACT became law.

The government also regulated the railways by the RAILWAY ACTS, 1839 AND 1844. Inspectors were appointed with the power to prosecute if the companies failed to conform with the law. In foreign trade the government was prepared to intervene too. The British Navy took action to force the Chinese to admit British merchants on British government terms in 1842. Local government began to assume greater powers as well. Acts of Parliament promoted by cities such as LIVERPOOL, MANCHESTER and LONDON gave them powers to impose standards of housing and sanitation and, in the case of Liverpool, to build houses out of corporation funds.

In social matters laissez-faire ideas had been defeated, but in economic affairs laissez-faire triumphed with free trade legislation which brought an end to protection by 1860.

A.J.P. Taylor, *Laissez-faire and State Intervention in Nineteenth Century Britain* (Macmillan 1972).

Lancaster, Joseph (1778–1838)

A QUAKER educationalist who opened a school for poor children in Borough Road, LONDON, in 1798 and was one of the founders of the MONITORIAL SYSTEM of teaching. He lectured widely about his method and even impressed GEORGE III in 1805. The Royal Lancasterian Society was formed in 1808 by his supporters to develop his ideas. In 1814 it became the BRITISH AND FOREIGN SCHOOLS SOCIETY, a name change which offended Joseph Lancaster. He left the Society and in 1818 emigrated to North America, where he opened a number of schools.

Land Drainage

Joseph Elkington, a Warwickshire farmer, first used a boring iron to drain land in 1764. The iron penetrated vertically into the earth or horizontally into a hillside to tap water. The mole plough was invented about 1797 by Adam Scott, an Essex farmer, and a subsoil plough was invented during the 1820s by James Smith, a Scotsman, to break up packed subsoil and improve poorly drained land. Drainage became important in the 1840s and 1850s as the result of a number of INVENTIONS, including a MACHINE for making cylindrical clay pipes. The price of pipe-laying fell when, in 1846, the government gave cheap drainage loans to farmers. The loans were a great success and pipe-laying was improved by JOHN FOWLER, who developed a mole plough which made pipe-laying automatic.

Latch Needle

A needle used on a knitting machine and invented about 1850 by Matthew Townsend of Leicester. It had a pivoted lever to open and close the hook and did away with the need for a presser (a device for closing the hook) for knitting coarse fabrics.

Visit Leicester Museum of Technology – knitting machinery. **M***

Law Enforcement

In the 1750s Henry Fielding (1707–54), novelist, dramatist and magistrate, started the Bow Street Runners as a law enforcement squad in London. The METROPOLITAN POLICE ACT, 1829 passed by ROBERT PEEL, set up the first paid and uniformed police force in Britain. Its territory was limited but it was under the control of the Home Secretary. The MUNICIPAL CORPORATIONS ACT, 1835, required all corporate towns to establish Watch Committees, which were to appoint sufficient constables to keep the peace. In 1839 the County Police Act permitted counties to establish paid police forces, but there was no compulsion and a number ignored the Act. The COUNTY AND BOROUGH POLICE ACT, 1856, compelled all counties and boroughs to establish and maintain a police force. Three inspectors of constabulary were appointed and forces deemed to be efficient qualified for a government grant of one-quarter of the cost of the pay and clothing of the force.

V. Bailey (ed.), *Policing and Punishment in Nineteenth Century Britain* (Croom Helm 1981).

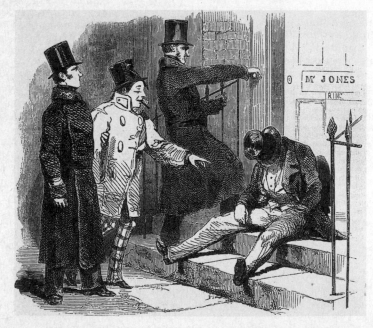

Peelers dealing with two wealthy but inebriated men. While Home Secretary between 1828 and 1830, Sir Robert Peel founded the Metropolitan Police, members of which became known as 'Peelers'. They wore a distinctive uniform which included a top hat. (*Mary Evans*)

Lawes, Sir John Bennett (1814–1900)

With Joseph Henry Gilbert he experimented with phosphatic fertilizers in 1835. In 1841 he patented his process for producing superphosphates from bones, and established a works at Deptford, LONDON, three years later. He was the first person to manufacture superphosphate fertilizer on a large scale. In 1842 he extended his scope to mineral phosphates – coprolitic deposits – and in 1857 used apatite, a mineral phosphate he imported from Norway. In 1872 he sold his interest in the Lawes Chemical Manure Company and did experimental work on his estate at Rothamsted, where he founded a research establishment which has gained a world-wide reputation.

Lawn Mower

A machine invented in 1830 by EDWIN BEARD BUDDING of Stroud, Gloucestershire, who is said to have been inspired by the use of a machine to shear the nap off cloth in the textile factory in which he worked. He came to an agreement with John Ferrabee of the Phoenix Ironworks near Stroud, who developed and patented the idea. The first licence to manufacture the machine was taken by RANSOME's, the Ipswich AGRICULTURAL ENGINEERING firm, in 1832. The machine was very difficult to push and a horsedrawn version was developed. The horses wore pads to avoid marking the turf, and demand increased during the second half of the 19th century from MIDDLE- and UPPER-CLASS families who played croquet, and later on tennis. The first steam mower was introduced in 1892 and a few years later petrol-driven models were built.

Laxey

The location of a large waterwheel, the Isabella wheel, on the Isle of Man. Built in 1854 to drain local zinc mines, it was designed as a spectacle and remains one of the major tourist attractions on the island. The wheel has a diameter of 72 feet (21.8 m) and castings for it were made at the Vauxhall Foundry, LIVERPOOL.

Visit Laxey, Isle of Man – waterwheel and mine trail with cottages, turbine house and washing floors. **M***

Lead-free Glaze

Fired pottery in 1760 was coated with a lead or salt glaze. Both materials were available in or near THE POTTERIES but the use of lead could result in lead poisoning. The Medical Officers of MANCHESTER and LIVERPOOL opposed the use of lead and specifically attacked JOSIAH WEDGWOOD's Queen's Ware (see CREAMWARE). Wedgwood tried to make a glaze without lead; in time other materials were used and the amount of flint was increased to make a leadless glaze.

Lead Mining

In the late 18th century Britain was probably Europe's chief source of lead, mainly used for making pewter, in building, for shot and in printers' type, but also in making paint and glass.

In Scotland the main mines in the 19th century were in Argyllshire, Perthshire and (of more importance) at Leadhills and Wanlockhead on the Dumfries and Lanarkshire borders. In England lead mines were to be found in the north Pennines, where the QUAKERS owning the London Lead Company built houses and made social provision for their workers. In Yorkshire there were mines in Swaledale and Wharfedale, and there was extensive mining in the High and Low Peak districts of Derbyshire. The ores of the lead mines in Devon and Cornwall were rich in silver. There was a group of mines in the upper Teign Valley, south Devon, and many mines in north and east Cornwall as well as in the Helston and Falmouth areas to the south.

Lead ore in North Wales had been worked since Roman times, around Holywell and at Minera in Denbighshire. In mid-Wales there were over 100 mines in some of the most remote areas of North Cardiganshire and West Montgomeryshire, including the

Cwmsymlog, Cwmsebon, Cwmerfin and Frongoch mines.

Visit The Pavilion, Matlock Baths, Derbyshire – Peak District Mining Museum with details of lead mining. **M***
Mid-Wales Mining Museum, Llywernog – silver-lead mine, Ponterwyd.
Aberystwyth – underground and surface mining museum. **M***
Museum of Scottish Lead Mining, Wanlockhead, Dumfries and Galloway, Scotland – period cottages and a history trail. **M***

L. Willies, *Lead and Leadmining* (Shire Publications 1984).

Lead Smelting

In the 18th century lead was smelted successfully, using a furnace first introduced by Edward Wright in North Wales in 1701. It was a relatively easy metal to smelt using an open furnace heated by coal.

Nearly all lead contains some silver and the ore is a profitable source of that metal. By 1704 silver was being separated from the lead by the cupellation process. The lead was refined in a specially designed REVERBERATORY FURNACE called a cupola, at a temperature which melted the lead but left the silver as a small cake at the bottom of the furnace. This process was developed at Ryton-on-Tyne Smelt Mill, new NEWCASTLE, owned by the Quaker Lead Company.

In 1829 HUGH PATTINSON discovered a method for extracting a greater quantity of silver from lead. He found that when molten lead cooled, the first crystals to separate are of pure lead. He patented a process in 1833 which included skimming the molten lead, using a perforated ladle, to remove the crystals. The process was repeated and the lead rich with silver separated, to be purified by cupellation in a reverberatory furnace.

Alexander Parkes (1813–90) used a process after 1850 based on the fact that when zinc and lead are melted together and allowed to cool, any silver becomes concentrated in the zinc. This method of extraction was more efficient than Pattinson's and eventually superseded it.

Lea Mills

Cotton mills near CROMFORD in Derbyshire, started in 1784 by Peter Nightingale and Thomas Smedley. John Smedley and other members of the Smedley family built churches and a hospital in nearby Matlock for the treatment of rheumatism. The factory is still producing knitted and other textile garments.

Visit John Smedley Ltd, Matlock, Derbyshire – tour of mill. **M***

Leather, George (1787–1870)

An engineer and son of the man who constructed the SURREY IRON RAILWAY in 1804. He was the consulting engineer for the Pocklington CANAL, completed in 1818, and from 1820 for the Aire and Calder Navigation Authority. He constructed bridges across the rivers Aire and Trent and his greatest iron bridge (see BRIDGES – IRON), the Stanley Ferry AQUEDUCT, was completed in 1839 to carry the Aire and Calder Canal over the River Calder. In 1838 he took responsibility for making a number of reservoirs for the LEEDS water supply. The first to be built, the BILBERRY RESERVOIR, partly collapsed in 1852 and the flood water killed 81 people and caused much destruction. Among the properties destroyed were 4 mills and 10 dyeworks, with 17 mills and 5 dyehouses badly damaged. The reservoir commissioners were found guilty of gross negligence and George Leather's reputation suffered. He retired three years later.

G.M. Binnie, *Early Victorian Water Engineers* (Thomas Telford 1981).

Leather, John Wignall (1810–87)

A water engineer, eldest son of GEORGE LEATHER and adviser to the BRADFORD Waterworks Company, which was set up in 1838. As the city grew new demands were made on its water supply, and Leather's task in the 1850s was to add considerably to the sources of supply. He produced a far-sighted proposal for taking water from the upper Wharfe valley in Yorkshire. An AQUEDUCT was built together with five main dams along the route between 1856 and 1861. In 1864 his employment was terminated and responsibility for the project was given to another engineer.

Leeds

A woollen town in Yorkshire, linked with Hull and the Humber by navigable rivers in the 18th century. It was a market centre for the woollen textile industry and was connected to collieries at Middleton by a WAGONWAY. Between 1782 and 1793 the town centre was redeveloped with streets, squares and 'places'. At the end of the 18th century houses were built along the main roads, leaving fields between. Fields to the north- east and south of Leeds were filled with new streets and alleys with rows of houses, nearly all of which were BACK-TO-BACK. The western part of Leeds, held in larger estates than in the rest of the town, was developed for better-class housing in the 1780s and 1790s.

This west end of the city contrasted sharply with the east end where, towards the end of the 18th century, new housing was built by infilling the long, narrow crofts behind the streets of houses, shops and inns. These new houses were built by lining the interior walls of an inn or a garden with cottages. These were the forerunners of back-to-back housing.

After 1780 new streets of WORKING-CLASS housing were built adjacent to the infill development. These streets were planned with back-to-back houses, many with separate cellar dwellings underneath. The houses were not built by speculative developers but by a building club. Between 1787 and 1815 streets of back-to-back houses invaded fields to the north, east and south of Leeds. The growth of these back-to-backs continued into areas where land values were low, probably due to the zeal for maximizing rents per square yard on the part of the landowners. The houses also fitted neatly into vacant spaces available as 'building ground'.

The typical working man's cottage of this period was no more than 15 feet (4.6 m) square, with one ground floor room and one bedroom above. What made them squalid and disease-ridden was lack of ventilation – they had only one window at the front of the house, giving poor ventilation and an absence of light. A sanitary map of 1842 showed the high incidence of CHOLERA and contagious diseases of the period 1834–9 in the poor housing areas. Death, disease, moral squalor, poverty and high crime rates made up the east end of the city.

Back-to-backs were built in Leeds right up to 1937, even though at that time the 150-year old back-to-backs were being cleared as SLUMS. In other aspects of urban living the town was more progressive. In 1837 a joint-stock company, the Leeds Waterworks Company, was set up. The source of water for the town was the River Aire, which was very polluted, so the company build the large Ecup Reservoir for storage. Between 1842 and 1852 the number of houses supplied with piped water increased from 3,000 to 22,732.

In 1861 the population was 207,000, making Leeds the largest town in Yorkshire.

Visit Middleton Colliery Railway, Tunstall Road, Hunslet, Leeds – steam railway. **M*** .
Armley Hall and Leeds Industrial Museum, Leeds – textile machinery. **M***

S.D. Chapman (ed.), *The History of Working Class Housing* (David and Charles 1971).

Leeds–Liverpool Canal

Work began in 1770 on a CANAL to make navigation possible between the North Sea and the Irish Sea. The route was a difficult one and the 127 miles (204 km) were not completed until 1816. Transport costs between Lancashire and Yorkshire were then cut by four-fifths and there was an enormous increase in the volume of trade. The canal had 91 LOCKS and suffered from winter shortages of water at the summit. There was little trade carried over the summit between Lancashire and Yorkshire; most was confined within each of those two counties. Passenger services started at the LIVERPOOL end in 1774 and in 1808 there was a daily service to Wigan. Railway competition (see RAILWAYS –

IMPACT ON THE ECONOMY) took away much business in the 1840s, but the last regular coal traffic to power stations did not cease until 1972.

Visit The Wharfmaster's House, Burnley, Lancashire – visitors' centre, canal and relics of the cotton industry. **M***
Leeds, West Yorkshire – locks and canal basin.

Leeds Pottery

A pottery established in the 1750s and extended in 1770. It was close to the WAGONWAY built in 1758 from the Middleton Colliery to a coal STAITHE, where the coal could be collected for sale in LEEDS. Partners in the pottery were Richard Humble, William Hartley and others. There were local sources of white clay and a windmill for grinding flints, which came by sea and river from Sussex. The works made white, SALT-GLAZED stoneware, red stoneware and Delftware, but it achieved its greatest fame for plain and decorated CREAMWARE. TRANSFER PRINTING was introduced about 1775, and from 1815 underglazed printing took place. The original company went bankrupt in 1820 but production continued until 1878.

D. Towner, *The Leeds Pottery* (Cory, Adams and Mackay 1963).

Legging

A method of human propulsion used for moving boats through low tunnels on the CANALS. It involved placing planks at the fore-end of the boat on which two boatmen lay flat on their backs and pushed with their feet against the tunnel wall. At some tunnels men were registered as 'leggers' and employed for this unpleasant task. Traffic through the Standedge Tunnel in the Pennines, constructed in 1811, was still moved in this fashion in 1928.

Visit Stoke Bruerne, Northamptonshire – Waterways Museum, close to entrance to Blisworth Tunnel; open-air exhibits and museum. **M***.

Leslie, James (1801–89)

An engineer who was consultant to the DUNDEE Water Company in 1844. In 1846 he was appointed engineer to the Edinburgh Water Company and in the years that followed he built a series of dams in the Pentland Hills, to store water in reservoirs so that the city could be supplied continuously with water.

Liberal Party

One of the two major political groups in Britain during the 19th century, although as an organized political party it was not unified until the 1860s.

For most of the 18th century the Whigs, who provided the core of the Liberals, were a power, although they were not an organized party but consisted mainly of personal groupings. The term 'Liberal' was first used in the second decade of the 19th century by Tories (see CONSERVATIVE PARTY) who despised the reforming ideas of liberal groups in Spain and France. The Liberals supported the abolition of slavery, CATHOLIC EMANCIPATION and the REFORM ACT, 1832.

The Parliamentary Liberals, supported in the country mainly by groups of MIDDLE-CLASS businessmen and nonconformists (see DISSENTERS) were unified by Lord Palmerston and became a powerful force between 1846 and 1866. They stood for a minimum of government interference in business and for the rights of the individual. The Parliamentary party was helped to become a national party in the 1860s by: the reform agitation of that decade; the creation of a predominantly Liberal, cheap, daily press outside London; links forged with organized labour and with militant nonconformists; and the national stature of GLADSTONE. The party developed a central organization based on the Liberal Registration Office, founded in LONDON in 1860, which carried out much of the normal work of a party headquarters.

During this period a number of provincial, WORKING-CLASS Liberal clubs were formed. After 1865 the Liberals came to represent great and dynamic social forces in the country because of the connections which had been built up within the rank and file. Gladstone dominated the party and headed the administration between 1868 and 1874. Support came mainly from the middle-class urban vote and business interests.

J. Vincent, *The Formation of the British Liberal Party 1857–1868* (Harvester Press 1976).

Lime Kilns

Kilns were built to burn lime for agricultural use as a fertilizer, and for making lime cement. They were often built into hillsides near chalk and limestone quarries, and some still exist dating from the first half of the 19th century. They are usually made of local stone or brick.

Visit Black Country Museum, Dudley, West Midlands – lime kilns built in 1842. **M***

R. Williams, *Limekilns and Limeburning* (Shire Publications, 1989).

Limelight

A form of lighting invented in 1826 by THOMAS DRUMMOND, an army officer. A block of lime was made incandescent by heating it with a very hot oxyhydrogen flame. This form of lighting was used to illuminate theatre stages and the term 'limelight' became associated with acting and the theatre.

Limited Liability Act, 1855

In the 18th and early 19th centuries the only companies with limited liability were those set up by Act of Parliament, such as the CANAL companies. Joint-stock companies suffered from unlimited liability, making an individual liable to lose all his property if a company failed in which he had an interest. As the MIDDLE CLASSES became politically stronger there was a demand for limited liability. In 1855 the recommendations of a select committee were incorporated into a Limited Liability Act. In the next year the Joint Stock Companies Act was passed, followed by a Consolidation Act in 1862 to remove anomalies. This legislation

safeguarded individual investors, whose loss was limited when a company failed. Investment of CAPITAL by the Victorian middle classes expanded quickly after the introduction of the Act.

Linen

In the 18th century hemp and flax were grown throughout the country and the linen industry was widespread. Near the coast coarse linen was made into ships' sails, but the industry received its greatest demand from the cotton industry, because linen was used as the WARP thread in FUSTIAN cloth. RICHARD ARKWRIGHT's WATER FRAME made it possible to make cotton cloth with a cotton warp and linen was then no longer needed for this. It was still used, however, for sails, sacking, furnishing, thread and coarse material. Darlington in County Durham was an important centre in 1790, but the biggest spinner was JOHN MARSHALL of LEEDS. In Scotland linen was a domestic industry until the POWER LOOMS were introduced in 1810, but progress was slow even then, partly because the MACHINES did not work very well and partly because the low wages paid to HAND LOOM WEAVERS discouraged manufacturers from buying expensive power looms. Hand looms did not disappear until about 1870. DUNDEE, Arbroath, Forfar, Kincardine, Perth and Aberdeen were important centres.

In the early linen industry the weaver depended for most of his work on commissions from local families to weave up their yarn. This was known as custom or customary weaving. It was prevalent in much of the country, but died out in the first decades of the 19th century, because it was superseded by the products sold through shopkeepers. Weavers lost their independence and became dependent on yarn given out by local manufacturers or agents.

W. English, *The Textile Industry* (Longman 1969).
P. Baines, *Flax and Linen* (Shire Publications 1985).

Linoleum

An industry founded in KIRKCALDY in

Scotland in 1847, using locally spun jute as the backing material. Kirkcaldy became an important centre of the jute-spinning industry in the 1840s, having been previously a major centre for the spinning and weaving of fine LINEN cloth.

Liquid Manure Drill

A drill developed by Thomas Chandler in 1847 for a firm of AGRICULTURAL ENGINEERS in Wiltshire. A water container was mounted beneath the seed box and distributed manure in solution, as well as seeds. In 1851 Thomas Chandler designed a liquid manure distributor using revolving buckets. Further improved models of the drill were made and sold throughout the country.

Lister, Joseph (1827–1912)

Professor of surgery at GLASGOW, he proved the value of antiseptic surgery. He used a weak solution of carbolic acid to spray the air while an operation was being performed and he also insisted on the scrupulous cleanliness of his assistants and the surgeon's instruments.

R.B. Fisher, *Joseph Lister, 1827–1912* (Macdonald and Janes 1977).

Lister, Samuel (1815–1906)

The owner of the Mannington WORSTED mill near BRADFORD, Yorkshire. He built up a silk spinning and weaving business using waste silk to weave velvets and plushes. His high-quality products became known in many parts of the world and the mill was extended in 1873.

Literacy

The level of attainment in a society of the dual skills of reading and writing. The definition of the minimum standard required to make a person literate varies from country to country, and for the historian no statistics are available to provide accurate information about the literacy rate during the INDUSTRIAL REVOLUTION. Marriage registers, however, which required signatures and were marked with an X by those unable to sign

their names, provide some evidence of the large numbers who could not write, and the statistics that follow are based on these registers.

Whereas, in 1760, literacy was almost universal among the gentry, professional classes and retailers, WORKING-CLASS people had no incentive to become literate – there were no material benefits and EDUCATION did not provide SOCIAL MOBILITY. In towns the literacy rate was higher than in the countryside – between 1754 and 1762 it was 61 per cent for adult males in NOTTINGHAM and 66 per cent in BRISTOL.

Overall, literacy increased in the 18th century, although the rise was not spectacular. From the 1780s an increasing number of working men were able to gain access to books, and by the 1830s the percentage able to sign the marriage register had risen by some 7 per cent to 10 per cent. By 1840 about two-thirds of the male population and half the females could sign their names. In 1850 the position had not improved to any great degree, although reading material was more accessible. There were also regional differences in the literacy rate which are not fully explained.

The root cause of illiteracy was inadequate elementary education, with an assortment of schools catering for a minority of the population.

Liverpool

A seaport in Lancashire which had built its fortunes on the slave trade and then turned to cotton in the second half of the 18th century. The first sale of raw cotton was in 1757, and imports increased considerably in the first half of the 19th century, so that Liverpool replaced LONDON as the principal import port for cotton. Eight new docks were built between 1815 and 1835, and in 1838 the transatlantic steamer (see STEAM BOATS) service was started, increasing the town's importance still more.

A further series of docks was built, including the Albert and Stanley Docks in the 1840s. Large warehouses were also erected and the dock area eventually spread for 7 miles (11.3 km) along the Mersey Estuary. Liverpool had the important function during the 19th century of being a major port, and this gave the city close contact with shipping services, marine INSURANCE and commerce. In addition there were a number of industries based on the port, such as marine engineering, clothing manufacture and food processing. By 1861 the population had reached 444,000, having increased from the 22,000 of 100 years earlier.

Visit Merseyside Maritime Museum, Albert Dock, Liverpool. **M***

Llanelly

A COPPER SMELTING works was established in 1805 by the BIRMINGHAM merchant JOHN GUEST, the Cornish merchant Robert Daniel and the LONDON merchant William Savill. Other copper smelting works were built because Llanelly had the advantage of being, like Swansea, close to the coal required for smelting. Copper ore could be carried by sea from Cornwall or PARYS MOUNTAIN on Anglesey. The pure copper was sent to the industrial towns of the Midlands.

Locke, Joseph (1805–68)

Joined GEORGE STEPHENSON at the age of 18 and learned a great deal about railway engineering and construction. His first major work was a railway line in the North East, from the Black Fell colliery to the River Tyne. This was successful and he emerged as one of the foremost engineers of the railway era, surveying lines between MANCHESTER and Bolton, Canterbury and Whitstable, and LEEDS and Hull. In 1840 the line from LONDON to Southampton, which he had surveyed, was opened. He built as straight as possible and avoided RAILWAY TUNNELS to reduce costs. He went on to construct lines in France before returning to build lines for the Lancaster and Carlisle Railway and the Caledonian Railway.

Locks

Devices for raising or lowering boats from one water level to another by using a chamber large enough to take a boat, which can be flooded or emptied. Locks were also used to check the flow of water from one water system to another; for example, between a CANAL and a tidal river or the sea. On the early river navigations the passage of weirs was achieved by a flash lock. This was a small, movable section of the weir formed of wooden flats (known as 'rimers' and 'paddles') on a framework. Later a single gate or pair of gates called watergates were introduced. Flash locks and watergates were slow to operate and wasteful of water, and flash locks could be dangerous to navigate.

These problems were solved by the pound lock, which consisted of a chamber controlled by gates at either end. They were quick and safe to work, for only the chambers needed to be filled and emptied, and the use of water was limited to the capacity of the lock chamber. The gates were, at first, designed to rise vertically but in the 15th century mitred pairs of horizontally swinging lock gates were introduced in Europe. In 1577 they were used at Waltham Abbey Lock on the River Lee.

River locks were used to join canals with the various levels of a river, while waterways with access to the sea or an estuary had sea locks fitted to counteract the tidal movement, impounding water at high tide. Two or more locks so close together that the chambers have common gates is called a staircase, the top gate of one acting as the bottom of the next. The staircase overcame steep slopes and saved costs. Scotland has the greatest assembly of staircases, on the CALEDONIAN CANAL.

Stop locks were normally designed like a pound lock at the junction of two canals, to prevent loss of water from one canal to the other. They were also called regulatory locks since they controlled the water flows from one canal to the other. There is a stop lock on the Stratford-upon-Avon Canal at King's Norton, at the junction with the Worcester and BIRMINGHAM Canal.

Lifts or balance locks were often associated with INCLINED PLANES, using water-filled CAISSONS. At Anderton near Northwich, a hydraulic lift was completed in 1875 to link the Weaver Canal with the TRENT AND MERSEY CANAL 50 feet (15.2 m) above it.

Visit Anderton, Cheshire – hydraulic lift.
Devizes, Wiltshire – flight of 21 locks.
Waterway Museums, Stoke Bruerne,
Northamptonshire – cast-iron lock gates.
M*
King's Norton, Warwickshire – stop locks
at the junction of the Stratford-upon-Avon
and Worcester and Birmingham Canals.

Locomotion

An engine ordered by the STOCKTON AND
DARLINGTON RAILWAY from ROBERT
STEPHENSON and Company. The engine,
which had its wheels coupled with rods
instead of chains, was delivered in 1825.
In the same year GEORGE STEPHENSON
drove it at the opening of the Stockton
and Darlington Railway. It pulled a
passenger coach and 21 wagons fitted
with seats and crammed with
passengers. The engine made speeds of
between 4 and 15 mph (6 and 24 kph). It
was found that pulling coal by
locomotive was cheaper than using
horses, but less reliable.

Visit Darlington Railway Centre and
Museum, Darlington, County Durham –
original *Locomotion* and painting of
opening of Stockton and Darlington
Railway. **M***

Lombe, Sir Thomas (1685–1739)

A silk merchant who, with his half-
brother John Lombe (1693?–1722), built a
silk mill at Derby *c*.1718, a year after
Thomas had taken out a patent for
machines to throw or twist silk. The
building was a five-storey throwing mill
able to accommodate 300 workers.
Because of the nature of the silk thread
the mill was circular in design and very
large, with three MACHINES; one to wind,
another to twist a thread and a third to
twist two or more threads together. A
large waterwheel operated these. It was
the first large textile factory or TEXTILE
MILL, as the early works were called.
When the Lombe patent expired in 1732
factories copying the Derby mill were
built in Lancashire, SHEFFIELD and
Watford. The Derby works was used for
silk production until 1891.

Visit Industrial Museum, The Silk Mill,

Derby – railway engineering and other
local industries. **M***

London

With no coal deposits nearby and very
little water power, today's London was
not a product of the INDUSTRIAL
REVOLUTION although it has always been
Britain's premier centre of manufacturing.
It was the administrative, commercial and
financial capital of the country and had
developed a range of consumer
industries, based mainly in small
workshops in the East End. These
included the silk trade at Spitalfields set
up by Huguenot refugees, brewing, flour
milling, printing and furniture-making. In
the 18th century there were also a number
of machine tool shops and engineering
works. Many of these, like the PORCELAIN
manufactories, moved to the industrial
regions during the Industrial Revolution.
   In 1800 London had two wet docks and
a population of just under a million,
making it by far the largest urban centre
in the country. In the first decades of the
19th century docks were built
downstream and its importance as a port
grew. The RAILWAY DEVELOPMENTS of the
1830s to 1850s made the city the centre of
the network and a number of major
terminals were built, including Euston
(1838) and King's Cross (1852). By 1861
over 11,000 people were employed by the
railways in London, a figure which had
more than doubled by 1881. The
population rose to nearly two million in
1841 and 2.8 million in 1861.

Visit Kew Bridge Steam Museum,
Brentford – steam-powered steam
engines, narrow gauge railway. **M***
Brunel's Engine House, Tunnel Road,
Rotherhithe – pumping engine. **M***

London Corresponding Society

A popular movement for reform set up by
Thomas Hardy, a shoemaker, among the
ARTISANS of LONDON in 1792. The
movement wanted lower taxes, food and
goods cheaper, young people educated,
prisons less crowded and old age better
provided for. Similar societies were set
up in other towns and Hardy organized a
meeting in 1795 to demand universal

suffrage and an annual Parliament. The meeting ended in a riot and Parliament quickly passed the Treasonable Practices and Seditious Meetings Act, which resulted in the Society's collapse.

Longwall System

A method of COAL MINING in which the working moves forward along the seam in a continuous line, rock and other non-coal material being packed behind to support the roof. Timber was also used to support the roof, which was allowed to collapse when the timber was moved forward. This type of mining originated in Shropshire in the 17th century.

The longwall system allowed all the coal in a seam to be removed but it required large numbers of underground workers. Settlement could take place, which could result in surface subsidence with damage to buildings. It also allowed overlying coal seams to break and release dangerous gas. The system was, nevertheless, increasingly used in the 19th century because of its merits.

Loom Houses

In the 1780s and 1790s yarn spun on CROMPTON's MULE was in great demand and there was a boom in the weaving industry. To keep pace with the demand barns and other buildings were converted into WEAVING SHEDS, and loom houses were added to cottages. The HAND LOOM WEAVERS who worked in these houses prospered, but their prosperity waned in the first half of the 19th century when MACHINES were introduced driven by steam or water power.

Visit Milnrow, near Rochdale, Lancashire – a concentration of loom houses.

Lovett, William (1800–77)

A Cornish Chartist (see CHARTISM) who was associated with Parliamentary reform and the CO-OPERATIVE MOVEMENT. He drew up the PEOPLE's CHARTER, which formed the basis of Chartism. After the failure of the Chartist movement he became a teacher and wrote science textbooks.

Lucifers

The name given to matches of a modern type, first sold by John Walker of Stockton-on-Tees in 1827. The name was first used by a LONDON manufacturer, Samuel Jones, in 1829. Wooden splinters were dipped in a mixture of chemicals, gum and starch. The match ignited when struck against a rough surface or sandpaper. Later, white phosphorus was used as one of the chemicals. Workers using phosphorus were poisoned by the vapour and contracted 'phossy jaw' (necrosis), with the jaw gradually rotting away. Britain banned the use of white phosphorus by signing the Treaty of Berne in 1908.

Luddites

Combinations of workers formed during a period of economic distress in 1811 to destroy the newly introduced textile MACHINES, which they regarded as the cause of their troubles.

During the first 20 years of the 19th century there was a great deal of industrial unrest, notably in 1811 and 1812. The cause was economic; INDUSTRIAL WAGES were low and many people, particularly craftsmen, faced insecurity and redundancy. They were suffering from the abnormal conditions of the prolonged war with France; the Continental blockade (see CONTINENTAL SYSTEM); restricted trade and raw materials, all of which resulted in a continuous rise in the price of food.

Fearing for their future, workers turned on the new machines which were increasing productivity enormously, and destroyed them. The rioters were believed to be organized by a leader known as King Ludd, and letters opposing the introduction of machines bore his name. The main areas of unrest were Lancashire, Yorkshire, Nottinghamshire and Chesh- ire. In Yorkshire the introduction of mechanical shearing frames threatened the employment of CROPPERS. Some mills were burned down and soldiers fired on the attacking mobs. In the East Midlands, however, the stocking knitters vented their anger against their employers by breaking up their frames, which were not new introductions to the mills. The FRAMEWORK KNITTERS were particularly incensed at the making of low-quality goods, bad workmanship and the dishonesty of some employers.

The government reacted with harsh measures and frame breaking was made punishable by death. Nothing was done to alleviate the misery which caused the unrest, and within a few years of the unrest some of the trades, such as those of the croppers, framework knitters and HAND LOOM WEAVERS, were on the point of extinction.

The causes of the Luddite riots are complex. The ARTISANS felt themselves robbed of their constitutional rights, established over many generations. Workers in the DOMESTIC SYSTEM saw the spread of factories as the death warrant to their own livelihood, and saw the capitalist (see CAPITAL) as intent on destroying the custom of APPRENTICESHIPS, beating down wages, undercutting his competitors and undermining standards of craftsmanship.

E.P. Thompson, *The Making of the English Working Class* (Penguin 1971).

P. Liversidge, *The Luddites* (Franklin Watts 1972).

Lunacy Act, 1845

An Act which set up a Board of Commissioners to inspect lunatic asylums, WORKHOUSES and institutions where the mentally ill were detained. It resulted in some improvements in living conditions for the inmates of those institutions.

Lunar Society

A society formed by MATTHEW BOULTON and others in BIRMINGHAM about 1766. Meetings took place at the full moon at members' homes, to make the journey through country lanes better lit and so more convenient. JOSIAH WEDGWOOD and others attended and scientific questions were frequently on the agenda. Other members included Sir Joseph Banks, president of the Royal Society, the astronomer Sir William Herschel, the chemist DR JOSEPH PRIESTLEY, JAMES WATT and ERASMUS DARWIN. The Society was at its peak in the 1780s and then declined, to disappear by about 1800.

M

Machines

Mechanisms which carry out the movements of a technical operation previously performed by one or more persons. Machines were in use long before the INDUSTRIAL REVOLUTION; for example, waterwheels operated quite intricate machinery for grinding corn or lifting forge hammers. Nevertheless, it was the development of machines on a large scale and of an intricate design, made of metal and not of wood, that gave the Industrial Revolution its distinctive character.

Machine Breakers

Damaging or smashing machinery was practised long before the LUDDITE movement of the early 19th century. JAMES HARGREAVES experienced some of the earliest machine breaking when his home was attacked in 1768 and 20 SPINNING JENNIES were smashed. The first Act of Parliament against machine breakers was passed in 1769. It made the destruction of an agricultural building containing machinery, by a single person or a mob, punishable by death. There were disturbances in Lancashire in 1779 against the installation of machinery in the COTTON INDUSTRY. Several thousand workers destroyed MULES near Chorley and in other localities. Troops were sent from LIVERPOOL and dispersed the rioters without difficulty.

Some MIDDLE-CLASS people were also hostile to the machines which, by increasing unemployment, could bring about an increase in the poor rates – the local taxes levied under the POOR LAW.

J. Stevenson, *Popular Disturbances in England, 1700–1870* (Longman 1979).

Machine Gears

In wind- and watermills, gears were made of hard wood and so rotated fairly slowly with little noise. Iron gears were noisy and quickly wore out because they were not designed with sufficient precision. In the Albion flour mills the gears were filed and chipped to shape by craftsmen, but the results were still inaccurate and inefficient. Gear-cutting MACHINES were operating by 1820, based on the machines used by clock-makers, but it needed mathematical skills, interpreted into terms understandable in engineering workshops, for gears to reach the degree of precision required by the machines of the period and the ever increasing speeds at which they could be operated.

John Hawkins, the translator of the works of the French mathematician Louis Camus, and JOSEPH CLEMENT carried out experiments in 1837 which changed people's ideas on the shape and design of gears. A gear-cutting machine was perfected by JOSEPH WHITWORTH in 1844, and another machine was designed by Joseph Saxton in 1842. He was an American, from Philadelphia, and it was in America that the most efficient gears were to be made in the last decade of the 19th century.

Macintosh, Charles (1766–1843)

A Scottish chemist who patented a rubberized waterproof fabric in 1823. His business was to supply woollen manufacturers with chemicals, and from the surplus chemicals came his INVENTION. He went into partnership in the late 1820s with the Birley family, who owned cotton mills in MANCHESTER, and a large order came from the War Office despite the fact that the material was unsuitable as clothes. Experiments by THOMAS HANCOCK led to an improved waterproof material at a lower cost, and the two men built up a large business together. Thomas Hancock patented a vulcanization method using sulphur in 1844, but CHARLES GOODYEAR had taken out a similar patent in the USA in 1841. Law suits against Hancock were lost, and it is possible the two men had reached similar conclusions on either side of the Atlantic.

Macintosh, George (1739–1807)

A dyemaster and the father of CHARLES MACINTOSH. In 1777 he established the manufacture of cudbear (a vegetable dye obtained from lichen). In 1785 he invited a French dyer, M. Papillon, to come over and help establish turkey red dyeing. With DAVID DALE's co-operation he built a large works near Dalmarnock in Scotland in the 1790s.

Mackay, John (?–1783)

A Scot who emigrated to LONDON, where in 1761 he took out a patent for a new method of making salt. His interest in salt took him to ST HELENS, where there were saltworks; he sank a pit near Ravenhead in St Helens and opened up coal mines in 1770 and 1771. With partners he raised enough CAPITAL to start the British Plate Glass Manufacturers and opened a large works at Ravenhead in 1776. The site on the St Helens Canal was ideal for obtaining raw materials by water and coal from local mines. PICKFORDS' boats moved the firm's glass to warehouses in London and LIVERPOOL, from where the glass was exported to the United States.

John Mackay provided cottages for his employees and the works became one of the industrial wonders of its age. In 1788 a BOULTON AND WATT STEAM ENGINE was installed to drive the machinery for polishing glass, and in 1792 the firm began manufacturing cast PLATE GLASS.

Madocks, William Alexander (1773–1828)

A landowner who purchased land to the south of the Snowdon range in North Wales. He built a new town in 1803–4 called Tremadoc, with a water-powered woollen factory. A CANAL linked the town with the River Glaslyn and the sea. In 1807 he received permission to reclaim and improve the Traeth Mawr, the estuary of the River Glaslyn, which had quicksands and marshes blocking communications with northwest Wales. A large embankment called the Cobb was completed in 1811 and a new harbour called Portmadoc was built. The harbour was used to ship out slate from inland quarries at Ffestiniog, and a railway was built after his death in 1836.

Visit Porthmadog, Gwynedd – harbour and maritime museum. **M***
Ffestiniog Railway, Gwynedd, North Wales, with route along Cobb and a road over Traeth Mawr. **M***

E. Beazley, *Madocks and the Wonder of Wales* (P and Q 1967).

Mail Axle

Patented by John Besant, a coach builder and designer, in 1795 and used on MAIL COACHES. The axle was designed with long bolts and washers to prevent the wheel coming off accidentally. The firm of Besant and Vidler held a monopoly granted by the Post Office for the supply of mail coaches, hence John Besant's interest in their safety.

Mail Coach

The first mail coach left BRISTOL for LONDON in 1784 and the service was extended to other routes. Carrying mail was a monopoly of the Post Office, but JOHN PALMER, a theatrical manager, was able through contacts to persuade the prime minister, WILLIAM PITT, of the speed and efficiency of such a service compared with the time taken by post boys.

Mail coaches carried passengers as well as mail and within a few years the service covered most of the main roads in Britain. In 1836 there were 27 services from London and a further 82 in other parts of the country. Some 700 coaches were needed for this service. In charge of the coach was a mail guard, complete with blunderbuss and pistols. He blew a horn to warn other traffic to give way and to alert TURNPIKE keepers.

A monopoly for the supply of mail coaches was held by Besant and Vidler, later Vidler and Co., using a coach designed by John Besant. The coaches were hired by the Post Office on a maintenance and mileage-hire contract. The monopoly expired in 1836.

Visit Science Museum, London – 1827 mail coach. **M***
Museum of Transport, Glasgow – mail coach. **M***

T. DeQuincey, *The English Mail Coach* (Macdonald 1956).

Malthouse

A building used for the storage and germination of barley and the drying and dressing of the malt. They were to be found in every market town in the early 19th century. Some malthouses dating from this period had a distinctive shape: the barley was spread out on large germination floors which were at or below ground level, with floors above. CAST-IRON frames were used throughout these big buildings, and the kiln had a furnace with a floor above laid with perforated tiles, so that the grains of green barley would not fall through, but the heat could pass upwards.

The barley moved progressively through the building. The first process was to steep the grain for a few days to allow it to swell. It was then drained, spread out to a depth of several centimetres and left to germinate for a week to turn the starch it contained into sugar. After that, it was placed on the kiln floors for water to evaporate. When dry it was dressed (that is cleaned, polished and the rootlets removed) before going to the brewery.

In the second half of the 19th century industrial-scale maltings developed.

Visit Mistley, Essex – maltings.
Upper St John Street, Lichfield, Staffordshire – malthouse (1858).

Malthus, Thomas Robert (1766–1834)

A parson and later professor of history and political economy. He is best known for his *Essay on the Principle of Population as it Affects the Future Improvement of Society*, published in 1798. The book appeared after the factory system had begun and factory workers were increasing in numbers. It was a time of social unrest, with bad harvests and high food prices leading to an increase in poverty. Malthus attempted to prove that the rapid growth of the population was the cause of the acute distress. Population, he said, grew faster than resources with the result that there would be a reduction in the STANDARD OF LIVING. The first CENSUS OF POPULATION in 1801 confirmed Malthus' fears about population growth. He advocated restraints on the size of the family and considered that population balance was maintained by the natural disasters of war, pestilence and famine.

Malthus' philosophy was pessimistic and aroused fears of social unrest and revolution. The UPPER CLASSES interpreted his theories to mean that the WORKING CLASSES could not increase their share in the national wealth. That share must always remain somewhere about the subsistence level. Poverty was therefore inevitable and unless population increase

was checked, disasters would prevent population and food adjusting to one another. Malthus' theory provided a natural justification of the poverty in which most people lived and therefore absolved the propertied classes from responsibility for it.

Manchester

The most important cotton centre in Britain and sometimes known as 'Cottonopolis' as a result. With neighbouring Salford it had about 25,000 inhabitants in 1772, 181,000 in 1821 and 455,000 in 1851. In the last decades of the 18th century MANUFACTURERS found it necessary to have a warehouse or stock-room in Manchester. Cotton spinners were maintaining stocks for sale in the town, and LONDON warehouses found it advantageous to have an agent based at the centre of manufacturing. In 1772 there were 120 warehouses in the town, 726 in 1820 and 955 in 1829. Overseas merchants joined the provincial manufacturers and London warehouse-men based in Manchester. The delays in

Throwing what appears to be a candlestick holder at an early pottery. The girl on the left is turning the large wheel by hand to provide the power for the potter's wheel which is being used to shape the clay. In the centre the clay is being weighed out before it is given to the potter to throw. (*Wayland Publishers Ltd*)

improving textile technology in Europe which resulted from the NAPOLEONIC WARS brought an increase in the number of continental merchants in Manchester.

The town grew up with SLUM areas like Little Ireland, which horrified FRIEDRICH ENGELS and other visitors. Some of the mills and warehouses were magnificent buildings but their surroundings were often appalling, overcrowded and a magnet to the rural poor and IRISH IMMIGRANTS. There were also better-style houses for the WORKING CLASSES in districts such as Hulme, reflecting the prosperity of the city and a considerable degree of domestic comfort for many of the workpeople.

Visit Manchester Museum of Science and Technology – Richard Arkwright's throstle frame, slubbing mills and textile machinery. M*

Manchester School

The term used for members of the FREE TRADE movement. A group of cotton MANUFACTURERS, many of whom were connected with MANCHESTER and strongly advocated free trade, formed the core of the movement. Their leaders were RICHARD COBDEN and John Bright, and they believed that free trade would not only bring prosperity, it would also remove economic grievances between countries and result in peace. The repeal of the CORN LAWS and the final reduction in tariffs in 1860 resulted in the demise of the Manchester School and their MIDDLE-CLASS, RADICAL philosophy.

Manufactory

The term used to describe a pottery from about 1780 onwards. Previously the industry had been based in 'potworks', and the term 'manufactory' was first used in the report of a government enquiry into the employment of children in manufactories (1816). By 1833, however, government documents classed the pottery establishments as 'factories'.

Manufacturers

The manufacturers were a new CLASS of capitalist (see CAPITAL) whose main interest was with industrial development. They acted as ENTREPRENEURS organizing the factors of production to maximize profits. With some exceptions, manufacturers were not the inventors of the MACHINES which made their fortunes. The manufacturing class was new and an addition to the landowners, merchants and bankers. Nevertheless, manufacturers such as RICHARD ARKWRIGHT recognized that to gain acceptance in society they had to own land, live in large houses and be surrounded by their wealth. This was the accepted basis for UPPER-CLASS distinction and recognition.

Marshall, John (1765–1846)

A LINEN manufacturer who, in 1793, perfected a series of processes for producing linen thread and yarn. In 1796–7 he was making linen at a FIREPROOF MILL in Shrewsbury, and in 1789 he leased a mill just north of LEEDS, before establishing a linen industry in Leeds in 1791. In 1838–40 he had the Temple Mill in Leeds built, designed by Ignatious Bonomi, who based it on the temple of Karnak in Upper Egypt. It was a single-storey building, the roof supported by CAST-IRON columns which also act as drainpipes. It was as a flax spinner that John Marshall gained his reputation and he, with others, dominated the social and political life of Leeds. After his death the business declined, and it closed in 1886.

W.G. Rimmer, *Marshall of Leeds: Flax Spinners 1788–1886* (Cambridge University Press 1960).

Marx, Karl (1818–83)

Born in Trier, Germany, the son of a MIDDLE-CLASS family who were christianized Jews. He wrote the *Communist Manifesto* in 1848 and was forced to flee to Britain in 1849, where he lived for the remainder of his life. He was a close friend of FRIEDRICH ENGELS, who gave him and his family financial support.

Marx spent most of his time in Britain carrying out research in the library of the British Museum, where he developed his theories on the formation of an urban proletariat (the wage-earning class with no CAPITAL, who lived in the rapidly growing industrial towns), the CLASS struggle and the economic laws of capitalist society. He was greatly influenced by the CLASSICAL ECONOMISTS, especially DAVID RICARDO. With Engels as his guide he was able to observe at first hand the social and economic problems of the INDUSTRIAL REVOLUTION which Engels described in his writings.

For Marx, capitalism was a stage in the process of evolution from a primitive agricultural economy, which would eventually lead to the elimination of the class structure, to the abolition of private property and to communism. He published the first volume of *Capital* in 1867 and two further volumes, edited by Engels, were published posthumously. Karl Marx regarded Britain as the workshop of the world and LONDON as the headquarters of international capitalism. He helped found the International Workingmen's Association in London in 1864 to co-ordinate attempts to achieve socialism in various countries. After internal disputes the Association was dissolved in 1876.

D. McLellan, *Karl Marx: The Legacy* (British Broadcasting Company 1983).

Mason, Charles James (1791–1856)

The founder of the Ironstone Pottery factory at Fenton in THE POTTERIES *c*.1813. He produced ironstone china wares, which were made by adding glassy ironstone slag to PORCELAIN constituents. In 1813 a patent was taken out which lasted for 14 years. The ironstone was suitable for table ware and large objects including vases and chimney pieces. Until 1829 he was in partnership with his brother George Miles Mason (1789–1859). He had a bad reputation as an employer, particularly for introducing flatware machinery which the workers did not like. During riots in 1842, his house was burned down and the firm went bankrupt in 1848.

Matrimonial Causes Act, 1857

An Act that set up courts to grant divorces. Previously divorces had been obtainable only by men and a special Act of Parliament was required for each one. The Act did not make divorce easy. A man had to prove his wife's adultery, while a woman had not only to prove her husband's adultery, but also to have other causes for seeking a divorce.

Maudslay, Henry (1771–1831)

A machine tool maker who became head foreman at JOSEPH BRAMAH's Pimlico engineering works. He started his own workshop and invented a number of machine tools, including the slide rest used in lathe work. In 1802 he set up MACHINES in Portsmouth Dockyard for the manufacture of wooden pulley blocks. The machinery cut the labour force from 110 skilled men to 10 unskilled men. On the profits from this contract he set up a works in Lambeth, LONDON, for the manufacture of STEAM ENGINES. Marine engines were his speciality but he also made saw mills and printing machines.

His main contribution to engineering was the improvement of screws by means of his lathes. He introduced interchangeable bolts and nuts which required new standards of accuracy, and also invented a MICROMETER to produce highly accurate engine parts. He liked uncomplicated machinery and was the founder of the British machine tool industry. His workshop was the training ground for a number of brilliant toolmakers including JOSEPH CLEMENT, RICHARD ROBERTS and JOSEPH WHITWORTH.

Visit Science Museum, London – screw cutting lathe (1800) and pulley-block machine. **M***

K.R. Gilbert, *Henry Maudslay* (HMSO 1971).

McAdam, John Loudon (1756–1836)

A Scotsman who travelled extensively and wrote a book, *Remarks on the Present System of Road Making*. In 1816 he became surveyor-general to the BRISTOL Turnpike Trust. He believed that stones about 1–2 inches (25–50 mm) across, laid without clay or binding material on a well-drained foundation, to a depth of 1 foot (30 cm), would compact into a strong surface. His roads were successful as well as cheap to construct, and turnpike trusts sought his advice.

Much of John McAdam's fame was based on the economy of his system. Work was precisely allocated, with the light stone breaking done by women, children and old men. He carefully analysed and costed his work and was the first person to persuade the trustees of TURNPIKE ROADS to improve them extensively. Roads built using his methods were said to be 'macadamized'. In 1826 he was appointed surveyor-general of the Metropolitan Turnpike Roads.

McNaught, William (1813–81)

A Scottish engineer who, in 1845, invented the compound STEAM ENGINE which made the BOULTON AND WATT engine more efficient, extracting the maximum amount of energy from the hot steam. This was done by using the steam twice, once in high-pressure cylinders. The technique was known as 'McNaughting' and a number of other technical improvements followed. With his brother he set up the firm of J. and W. McNaught in Rochdale, Lancashire, in 1862, where they made steam engines until 1914. Many of the engines he made, which numbered just under a hundred, were used in Lancashire and Yorkshire textile mills.

Visit Glasgow Art Gallery and Museum, Kelvingrove, Glasgow – McNaught engine. M*

Mechanics' Institute

An educational institution founded by George Birkbeck in GLASGOW in 1799, by getting together a group of adults to learn about the new MACHINES that industry was using. It became the Glasgow Mechanics' Institute in 1824 and a LONDON Mechanics' Institute was set up in the same year. Other institutes appeared and by 1844 there were 200, with over 50,000 members. Many had

their own buildings, paid for by MANUFACTURERS and subscriptions from members, and they were self-financing. A number of institutes were sponsored by Utilitarians (see UTILITARIANISM) and UNITARIANS and were looked on with great suspicion by the CHURCH OF ENGLAND and WESLEYAN clergy. The institutes trained the literate artisans who aspired to become foremen or master-fitters; they were not the forerunners of technical universities, because they operated at a lower technical level. The movement withered away after 1850.

Mellor

A cotton mill was built by SAMUEL OLDKNOW in the village of Mellor, Derbyshire, about 6 miles (9.7 km) east of Stockport in 1793. The mill used water power by diverting the course of the River Goyt. Nearby Oldknow built himself a house, employing some of the men whose wives and children worked at the mill. Parish apprentices from Clerkenwell in LONDON and elsewhere were also employed and houses were built in the village of Marple, near Mellor, for the workers. In 1809 a Methodist (see METHODISM) chapel was built for the local community and in 1812 there were 345 workers at the mill. On Samuel Oldknow's death the mill became the property of RICHARD ARKWRIGHT. Scarcely anything now remains of the buildings erected at Mellor.

Menai

The first bridge over the Menai Straits joining North Wales and Anglesey was designed by THOMAS TELFORD to carry the Holyhead Road, and was opened in 1826. Thomas Telford had designed a SUSPENSION BRIDGE with a main span of 579 feet (176.5 m). Sixteen chains were used as supports and the roadway consisted of two parallel roads 12 feet (3.6 m) wide, separated by a footpath 4 feet (1.2 m) wide. The road surface was of fir planks with oak timbering as wheel guides. The bridge was widened in the 1960s.

A railway bridge over the Menai Straits known as the Britannia Bridge was built by ROBERT STEPHENSON and opened in 1850. The bridge was made up of two huge, rectangular, WROUGHT-IRON tubes, which had to be floated out on pontoons before being placed in position by hydraulic jacks installed near the tops of the towers built to support the tubes. The bridge was destroyed by fire in 1970 but the piers remain, and it has been adapted to carry both a new road and the railway.

Visit Menai suspension bridge, Gwynedd, North Wales.

Mercantile System

The regulation of trade by the government through Acts of Parliament that protected home industries and checked the natural expansion of trade. The term was first used by ADAM SMITH, who attacked it as a system contrived by merchants for merchants' ends. He advocated FREE TRADE without restrictions, in order to allow trade to expand naturally. The age of the mercantile system was from the 1650s to the 1780s, a time of great economic expansion. The government hoped to earn a great deal from the tariffs imposed. Mercantilism encouraged smuggling, which was extensive until free trade repealed or reduced tariffs in the 19th century.

Merthyr Tydfil

In 1750, an insignificant village; it became the largest town in Wales in the first half of the 19th century. In 1801 there were 7,000 inhabitants, by 1831 the number had risen to 30,000 and in 1861 it was 55,000. Merthyr Tydfil developed the greatest concentration of ironworks in Britain. The lower coal beds or measures outcropped (reached the surface) around the village, and within these measures were bands of iron ore. Limestone beds outcropped a short distance to the north, giving the region the three essential ingredients for the iron industry. Furnaces were built on the banks of the river Taff and its tributaries and feeder ponds were constructed on the hill slopes, from which water was channelled down to the works. The TURNPIKE ROAD to the coast was built in 1797 and the

GLAMORGAN CANAL in the following year. The main railway, the Taff Vale Railway, was completed in 1841. The large ironmasters built houses for themselves and for their workers in and around Merthyr. Among them was SIR JOHN GUEST, owner of the DOWLAIS IRONWORKS. He became MP for Merthyr Tydfil in 1832.

The speed with which the town grew made it densely populated, lacking in sanitation and with few underground SEWERS in 1848. People moved in from the neighbouring rural areas and from Ireland and other parts of Britain. In 1851 the numbers employed mining for coal, iron and other minerals were more than double the numbers employed in the ironworks.

Visit Ynysfach Engine House Museum, Merthyr Tydfil – exhibition on the iron industry in Merthyr. **M***

Metcalf, John (1717–1810) (Also known as Blind Jack of Knaresborough; he lost his sight as a child)

A surveyor who improved roads by using a firm foundation covered with road stone which formed a cambered surface to drain rainwater into ditches on either side. His technique was first used on TURNPIKE ROADS in Yorkshire in 1765. Roads in the Peak District of Derbyshire were also improved by John Metcalf. When he retired in 1792 he had improved some 180 miles (289.7 km) of roads for turnpike trusts in the West Riding of Yorkshire, south Lancashire and north Derbyshire. He was the first real pioneer of modern road-building in Britain.

A. Bird, *Roads and Vehicles* (Longman 1969).

Methodism

While a young man at Oxford, JOHN WESLEY joined a group of friends calling themselves 'Methodists'. They were members of the ESTABLISHED CHURCH who sought to regulate their lives according to strict standards of discipline, in contrast to the slackness and indifference of society as they found it at Oxford. John

Wesley took his closely organized religion to Georgia, one of the American colonies, in 1736, where he adhered strictly to the letter of the Prayer Book of the CHURCH OF ENGLAND and tried to convert some of the natives. In 1738 he returned to England, where he underwent a spiritual conversion that turned his previous concern for his own spiritual well-being into a concern for bringing spiritual salvation to others. He joined his friend GEORGE WHITEFIELD and others, who had begun walking about the country preaching their Methodist beliefs to all and sundry.

Despite opposition from the clergy, groups of supporters began to form in the towns and John Wesley organized these groups into Methodist Societies. The Societies prayed together, helped one another and acquired premises where they could hold meetings. In 1744 an Annual Conference was founded to appoint men to lead the meetings, not as rivals to the established church but to supplement what the clergy were so inadequately doing. The Wesleyan movement spread to America and made rapid progress among the settlers. At John Wesley's death in 1791 there were said to be 70,000 Methodists in the British Isles and a further 60,000 in America. Although he hoped that his movement would remain within the Church of England, the Methodist Conference broke away in 1795 and a new dissenting sect (see DISSENTERS) had been formed.

Early Methodism had a direct appeal to ordinary working people which the Church of England lacked. Many chapels were built in the industrial areas and became the focus of community life. This early missionary fervour of Methodism was less evident by the 1840s and it was no longer a religion of the proletariat (see KARL MARX). The Report on the RELIGIOUS WORSHIP CENSUS, 1851, noted that in the industrial districts new chapels had been built for the MIDDLE CLASSES and a distinction had arisen between 'respectable' and common people, those who could dress for chapel on Sundays and those who could not. Wesley's principle of no distinction between rich and poor was overturned in many chapels, where the poor sat apart from the wealthy, who had the best seats screened off by curtains. A gulf developed between the poor and many Methodists who became prosperous through their own hard work, and as a result Methodism tended to take the standard set by middle-class society of the time rather than give a standard of its own.

Visit Carharrack, Redruth, Cornwall – Museum of Cornish Methodism. **M***

S. Andrews, *Methodism and Society* (Longman 1970).

Metropolitan Police Act, 1829

Introduced by the Home Secretary, SIR ROBERT PEEL, the Act made provision for the appointment of constables for LONDON with their headquarters in Whitehall Place, overlooking Scotland Yard. The constables were to be civilians armed with truncheons and wearing a distinctive uniform of a metal-framed top hat and frock coat with brass buttons. They were unpopular at first but London's crime rate fell. In 1830 they patrolled an area extending 7 miles (11.3 km) outwards from Charing Cross in all directions, except for the City of London. At that time the force consisted of 3,300 men. They became known as 'Peelers' and 'Bobbies'.

Metropolitan Water Supply Act, 1852

An Act which obliged water companies drawing water from the River Thames to take water only from above Teddington Lock, the upper tidal limit. Reservoirs had to be covered in and water for domestic services filtered. Within five years a constant supply had to be laid on by every company. Sources such as the Surrey springs were ignored, however, and supplies continued to be fouled by refuse from towns along the river. In 1866, during a CHOLERA epidemic, it was revealed that the East London Water Company was distributing water which was not filtered and its supplies were unreliable. The Act was strengthened by the Metropolitan Water Act of 1871, but the position was not satisfactory until the end of the century.

Micrometer

A measuring device invented by HENRY MAUDSLAY in 1805 and called by him the 'Lord Chancellor', because any disputes over accuracy were referred to it. The essential part of this instrument consisted of a screw with 100 threads to the inch and an index wheel with 100 divisions around its edge. Each division therefore represented 0.0001 of an inch of movement between two measuring faces. It was a superlative piece of craftsmanship.

Visit Science Museum, London – original micrometer. **M***

Middlesbrough

A town in North Yorkshire founded in 1829 by a group of QUAKERS associated with the STOCKTON AND DARLINGTON RAILWAY. They intended the town to be a coal-shipping port and laid it out in a grid-iron pattern with a church, chapels, schools and a MECHANICS' INSTITUTE. In 1831 the population was less than 200. This grew in 1841 to 5,000 and in 1850 the exploitation of iron ore in the Cleveland Hills brought blast furnaces to the town. By 1861 there were 40 furnaces in the area and the population had jumped to 20,000.

A. Briggs, *Victorian Cities* (Odhams 1963; Pelican 1968).

Migration

The internal migration of workers which accompanied the INDUSTRIAL REVOLUTION largely took the form of short-distance travel to the nearest industrial town. The Lancashire cotton towns became the homes of people from Lancashire, Cheshire or Ireland. Migration into LONDON came from the home counties of Kent, Essex, Hertfordshire, Middlesex, Surrey and Berkshire. Migration into the Midlands came from other parts of Warwickshire, Staffordshire or Worcestershire. Similar patterns prevailed in South Wales and the industrial towns of central Scotland, with the addition of considerable numbers of IRISH IMMIGRANTS. The folk tradition of a static, immobile rural population is not correct. Nor did the POOR LAW, which only allowed assistance from inside the home parish, prevent people from moving. The majority of the workers in the new industrial centres were from within 20 miles (32 km) to 30 miles (48 km), but a small number of workers travelled much further. SHEFFIELD attracted only 8 per cent of its cutlery apprentices between 1775 and 1799 from over 40 miles (64.4 km) away.

Mild Steel

Chemically closely akin to WROUGHT IRON because it is iron with the minimum quantity of other elements, such as carbon. It can be forged, rolled and worked like wrought iron but is not very good for corrosion resistance. It is used for numerous types of engineering and constructional work where special qualities such as hardness, corrosion resistance and great strength are not required. It was first made by Henry Bessemer in 1856 by what became known as the BESSEMER PROCESS.

Mileposts

TURNPIKE trusts were responsible for erecting mileposts along their routes and many trusts had distinctive designs. Many mileposts were made of CAST IRON, often V-shaped to make for ease of reading. THOMAS TELFORD designed a tapering post with a cast-iron plate for the Holyhead Road.

Visit Road from Leek to Buxton, Derbyshire – early mileposts.
Road from East Grinstead to Hailsham, East Sussex – mileposts with Bow bells design.

Mill, John Stuart (1806–73)

Economist and philosopher, the son of a Utilitarian (see UTILITARIANISM), he published three important books, *A System of Logic* (1843), *Principles of Political Economy* (1848) and *On Liberty* (1859). He believed that some state interference was necessary to prevent the abuse of LAISSEZ-FAIRE principles. In 1867 he introduced a motion in Parliament to give women the vote, but it was defeated.

Mines Act, 1842

A report on mining conditions published in 1842 made Parliament and the general public aware of the appalling conditions in the mines, especially as it included some sketches of life underground. Parliament passed the Mines Act in the same year and it prohibited the employment of women and boys below the age of 10 under ground. The Act was not enforced until 1850, when inspectors were appointed.

Minton, Thomas (1765–1836)

A PORCELAIN transfer engraver who founded the Minton porcelain factory at Stoke-on-Trent in 1793. After 1796 he started to produce BONE CHINA, mainly tableware decorated with blue transfers in imitation of imported Nanking porcelain. He formed a CHINA CLAY company in Cornwall in 1799 which operated until the 1850s.

His son, Herbert Minton made the firm one of the leading porcelain works in the 1820s and 1830s. He succeeded in cutting production costs so that formerly expensive table services became everyday commercial wares. By 1858, when he died, 1,500 workers were employed.

B. Hillier, *Master Potters of the Industrial Revolution* (Cory, Adams and Mackay 1965).

Model Villages

A number of mill owners and factory masters built settlements for their workers which were considered 'model' villages at the time. Some MANUFACTURERS built settlements to attract workers to remote mills, while for others it was a philanthropic gesture, aimed at the social well-being of the workers.

RICHARD ARKWRIGHT built a village at CROMFORD, Derbyshire, 1771–91. As well as homes for his employees, a corn mill, a market square, an inn and a church were erected. His partner, JEDEDIAH STRUTT, also created houses for his workpeople at BELPER. SAMUEL OLDKNOW built a village at MELLOR at the end of the 18th and

beginning of the 19th centuries. In Cheshire, SAMUEL GREG built houses, a school, a MECHANICS' INSTITUTE, a chapel and a shop near his QUARRY BANK MILL at Styal. Additions and improvements were made to the buildings in the 1830s.

In Scotland, DAVID DALE founded a village in the 1780s, which, with the mill at NEW LANARK, attracted much attention. ROBERT OWEN added a community school to the village.

Edmund and HENRY ASHWORTH built villages near their cotton mills in Lancashire at Turton, Egerton and Bank Top in the 1830s and 1840s. From 1835, the cottages had water boilers and ovens with piped water. Communal buildings included schools, a library, a newsroom and chapels, but no public houses. In the mid-19th century SIR TITUS SALT built SALTAIRE near BRADFORD, and near Halifax Colonel Edward Akroyd gave his name to his model settlement and called it AKROYDON.

Social and political factors motivated FEARGUS O'CONNOR to set up the CHARTIST LAND COMPANY in 1845. The company laid out a number of model villages which were planned as settlements for rural smallholders. Estates were built in Hertfordshire, Oxfordshire, Gloucestershire and Worcestershire, but the scheme was shortlived, the company collapsing in 1851. The villages still remain as a contrast to the industrial SLUMS of the same period. Other model villages include Ironville (1834–60), built by the BUTTERLEY COMPANY and Bournville, built at the end of the 19th century by George Cadbury (see JOHN CADBURY).

Visit Cromford Mill, near Matlock, Derbyshire – industrial housing. **M***
Styal, near Wilmslow, Cheshire – industrial housing. **M***
New Lanark Mills, New Lanark, Scotland – New Lanark Conservation Village. **M***
Turton, Egerton, Bank Top, near Bolton, Lancashire – industrial villages.
Saltaire, near Bradford – industrial houses.
Akroydon, near Halifax – industrial housing.
Heronsgate, near Rickmansworth, Hertfordshire; Charterville, near Minster Lovell, Oxfordshire; Dodford, near

Bromsgrove, Hereford and Worcester; and Snigs End and Lowbands, near Tewkesbury, Gloucestershire – Chartist Land Company estates.

Monitorial System

A method of teaching which introduced into schools the mechanical and repetitious atmosphere of the factory. It was commonly in use in the first half of the 19th century. A small group of senior boys (monitors) were taught a lesson by the teacher. They then taught groups of other boys who were then tested orally. The system encouraged mechanical learning by memory and did not encourage the pupils to think or to understand what they were taught. The two founders of the system were REVEREND ANDREW BELL and JOSEPH LANCASTER. They were hailed as inventors of a piece of social machinery that was both simple and economical. It therefore appealed to JEREMY BENTHAM and the utilitarians. The monitorial system dominated education for half a century and ROBERT OWEN introduced a modified form at NEW LANARK, whereby the teacher had a limited number of pupils and there were no rewards or punishments.

Monkland Canal

The high cost of coal in GLASGOW led to the building of a CANAL from Coatbridge to the city of Glasgow, a distance of 9 miles (14.5 km). The canal was opened in 1790 and provided a waterway from the collieries to Port Dundas on the north side of Glasgow, where it joined a branch of the FORTH AND CLYDE CANAL. One result was the exploitation of new mines in the Coatbridge area. There was a boom in coal mining and in the first decade of the 19th century many new pits were opened.

Monorail

A railway with a single rail which was first proposed by Henry Palmer in 1823. He was an engineer and principal founder of the INSTITUTION OF CIVIL ENGINEERS. He advocated the use of sails on a railway in East Anglia with a monorail system. Two monorail lines were built, one in Deptford, near LONDON, and one at Cheshunt in Hertfordshire. Horses were used to pull the wagons instead of using sails.

Monteith, James (?–1802)

A cambric weaver and yarn importer of GLASGOW who became a partner with DAVID DALE in a cotton mill at Blantyre in 1787. His son, James, became the owner in 1792 and on the elder James's death in 1802 another son, Henry, took over management of the mill. Henry established a works at Barrowfield for bandana handkerchiefs in the same year. A third son, John, experimented with power-looms at his Pollokshaws factory.

More, Hannah (1745–1833)

A philanthropist and educator who wrote influential books and pamphlets. As an EVANGELICAL she stressed self-discipline and personal responsibility. She influenced wealthy people and was referred to by WILLIAM COBBETT as 'the old bishop in petticoats'. The campaign against the slave trade attracted her and she became involved in reforming the manners and customs of the poor, as well as of the influential people in society. In 1788 she published *Thoughts on the Importance of the Manners of the Great to General Society*, in which she stressed the need for the 'higher orders' to set the moral tone of society. What JOHN WESLEY had done for the poor, she attempted to do for the rich.

M.G. Jones, *Hannah More* (Cambridge University Press 1952).

Muffle Kiln

A furnace used for some processes in the manufacture of PORCELAIN, such as enamelling on glaze, delicate colouring and the production of some lustres. It was designed in 1812 by SAMUEL WALKER at the WORCESTER PORCELAIN COMPANY and made enamel painting on porcelain more reliable, producing a finer result. It was a small, circular-topped kiln, about 54 inches (1.37 m) high and 78 inches

(1.98 m) long, heated by coal with flues to draw the flames beneath and around it, protecting the contents from direct contact with the smoke and flames. A considerable amount could be stacked in the kiln, with each firing taking between six and seven hours for BONE CHINA.

Muirkirk Company

An ironworks set up in Ayrshire in 1789, close to coal, ironstone and limestone. One of the partners was Thomas Edington, who had helped found the CLYDE IRONWORKS three years earlier. By 1796 there were three furnaces operating making PIG IRON.

Mule

A cotton-spinning machine invented in 1779 by SAMUEL CROMPTON. It was called a mule because it was a hybrid, combining some of the features of the SPINNING JENNY and some of RICHARD ARKWRIGHT's WATER FRAME. The machine was first made of wood and then, in 1783, with metal rollers and wheels. In 1790 William Kelly made an automatic version which was worked by a waterwheel. By 1812 the mule was in use in hundreds of factories. It was responsible for two-thirds of the output of the industry and produced a fine thread which made it possible to manufacture MUSLINS of a high quality. (See also MULE SPINNERS.)

Visit Textile Machinery Museum, Moor Road, Bolton, Lancashire – mule, water frames and other machinery. **M***
Higher Mill, Helmshore, Lancashire – mule. **M***
Welsh Folk Museum, St Fagans, South Glamorgan – mule. **M***

Mule Spinners

In the 1780s cotton MULES were introduced at many mills, and by 1800 CROMPTON's mule could spin 300 hanks in the pound (454 g), a hank measuring 840 yards (768 m). The degree of fineness was unequalled; a hand spinner, by comparison, could spin only 16 to 20 hanks in the pound, while RICHARD ARKWRIGHT's WATER FRAME attained only 60. As a result some owners, such as SAMUEL OLDKNOW, started making MUSLIN, which requires very fine threads, and other MANUFACTURERS diverted CAPITAL to buy mules. Mule spinning superseded WARP spinning using Arkwright's water frame.

Mule spinning depended on the sensitive touch of the mule spinners and they were the best paid ARTISANS in the COTTON INDUSTRY. In the mill they enjoyed semi-independent status, were paid on piece rates, employed their own 'assistants' and were responsible only to the spinning room overlooker. Mule spinners maintained their own TRADE UNIONS and outside the mill their status was recognized by the community. Public houses had rooms set aside for mule spinners only. Even in the 1830s, when the mules became automatic, the spinners retained their quasi-independent status.

Mungo

Wool recovered from 'hard' rags, such as thickly woven or heavily milled cloth. The spinning properties of the wool were reduced but, blended with other fibres, mungo was of importance for blankets, overcoats and uniform cloths. In the mid-1830s machinery was developed for grinding the harder rags by Benjamin Parr of Batley. He is reputed to have given the name to the new material, saying that it 'mun go' through the carding machine. (See also SHODDY.)

Municipal Corporations Act, 1835

The MIGRATION of population to the industrial regions and the decline of some rural areas resulted in the stagnation of many of the boroughs, coupled with their inefficiency and corruption. The 1835 Act dissolved nearly 200 borough corporations and replaced them with councillors elected by the ratepayers. The councillors were elected for a period of three years, and to give continuity they could elect aldermen for six years. The councils were given powers to carry out public works such as lighting and paving the streets. The Act gave a uniform pattern of government for 178 boroughs and cities, although it did not apply to the City of LONDON. It marked the beginning of local government reform, with the municipal corporations taking on the power of improvement commissioners, and over time many other functions were given to them including those affecting public health. These powers, both compulsory and adoptive, were consolidated in the Municipal Corporations Act of 1882.

Murdock, William (1754–1839)

An engine erector who worked for BOULTON AND WATT. He designed and built a model STEAM COACH but did not go on to build a full-size version. He also invented a valve for STEAM ENGINES and lighting by coal gas (see GAS LIGHTING). In 1792 he lit his Cornish home by gas produced by coking coal. In 1798 he became manager of the SOHO WORKS and used part of the plant to manufacture gas equipment. By 1803 part of the works was lit by gas. He failed to patent his gas-making process and others used his ideas. Boulton and Watt received orders for gas-making equipment (the first customer owned a Salford cotton mill) and in 1806–7 over 900 gas lights were installed to illuminate the Soho Works. Murdock remained at the Soho Works until 1830 but the firm abandoned its interest in gas appliances in 1814.

Murray, Matthew (1765–1826)

An engineer who, with the help of partners, established a firm at LEEDS called Fenton, Murray and Wood in 1797 to repair engines and MACHINES. Using RICHARD TREVITHICK's patent, the works built a STEAM BOAT called the *Experiment* which went into passenger service in Norfolk. The factory became famous for machine tools, particularly textile machinery. In 1814 Matthew Murray patented a cloth baling press for compacting woollen goods. He also designed locomotives using the rack and pinion system invented by JOHN BLENKINSOP. The firm built the locomotives and Murray improved them by providing two double-acting cylinders, making for a smoother action. The rack-rail enabled these light locomotives to draw heavy weights up

hill, and they were used at the Middleton Colliery, Leeds. He was probably the first man to manufacture machine tools for sale, but unfortunately the firm's records were destroyed in a fire in 1872.

Mushet, David (1772–1847)

A Scot who joined the CLYDE IRONWORKS in 1801, and discovered the blackband ironstone of Scotland which led to the expansion of the Scottish iron-making industry. It was viewed by the ironmasters with suspicion until 1825 and its use was increased by using HOT BLAST after 1828. David Mushet moved to the Forest of Dean, Gloucestershire, in 1810 and continued to experiment. In 1840 a volume of his scientific papers was published as *Papers on Iron and Steel*. He was the father of ROBERT FORESTER MUSHET.

Mushet, Robert Forester (1811–91)

Steelmaker in the Forest of Dean and pioneer of modern alloy steels such as tungsten, manganese and high carbon steels. He improved the BESSEMER PROCESS by adding a manganese compound, spiegeleisen, to remove the excess oxygen which had previously made Bessemer steel difficult to work. Robert Mushet had been using the compound since 1848 and solved a problem that Bessemer had been unable to solve.

Muslin

A fine cotton cloth imported from India in the 18th century. The first attempts to weave it in Britain were made by JAMES MONTEITH of GLASGOW. However, the product was not as fine as that from India and it was not until CROMPTON's MULE was brought into use about 1785 that both WEFT and WARP could be produced sufficiently fine for muslins.

Muspratt, James (1793–1886)

An Irishman who emigrated to LIVERPOOL in 1822 and started up in the town making Prussian blue dye for textile printing. In partnership with Josias Gamble he established a large works in ST

HELENS in 1828 to make soda for the soap industry, using the Leblanc process. In 1838 he visited the USA to explore the potential chemical market, and two years later shipped the first cargoes of soda alkali (sodium carbonate) across the Atlantic. By 1860 nearly three-fifths of the British production of soda crossed the Atlantic. In 1851 the firm he had started became James Muspratt and Sons Ltd, and in 1890 it became part of the United Alkali Co. Ltd.

Mylne, Robert (1734–1811)

An architect and engineer who prepared the winning design for Blackfriars Bridge, LONDON, in 1759. Before the bridge was finished he was appointed surveyor to St Paul's and Canterbury cathedrals. In 1767 he was made engineer to the New River Company and became an expert in river and CANAL navigation. He worked on the Ouse above King's Lynn and designed harbours at Yarmouth and Wells in Norfolk. He became engineer of the Gloucester and Berkeley Canal in 1793, but quarrelled with the resident engineer and was dismissed in 1797. He was one of the last notable architects who was at the same time an eminent engineer.

N

Nail Making

Nailers were present in different parts of the West Midlands long before the INDUSTRIAL REVOLUTION. It was a poorly paid branch of the iron industry and many nailers sought different employment. It was a village industry mainly to the west and southwest of BIRMINGHAM with Dudley, West Bromwich and Stourbridge as large centres. Nail makers were often employed by ENTREPRENEURS who bought their nails and sold them to the nail ironmongers. They supplied the nailer with money for nails at short notice or in hard times. The system was called fogging, and the men who employed the nailers were known as foggers. They were associated with long hours, low wages and the TRUCK SYSTEM. The conditions of the nailing population were bad, particularly during the NAPOLEONIC WARS and the ANGLO-AMERICAN WAR.

From 1830 the making of nails by hand gave way to production of machined nails. In the United States MACHINES were being used for this as early as 1800. The battle with the machine-cut nail was socially disastrous, with deprivation for the nailers similar to that of the HAND LOOM WEAVERS. The decline accelerated during the 1870s.

Visit Avoncroft Museum of Building, Bromsgrove, Worcestershire – 18th-century forge and nailshop. **M***

D. Bythell, *The Sweated Trades* (Batsford 1978).
H. Bodey, *Nailmaking* (Shire Publications 1982).

Nailsea Glass House

A glassworks founded in 1788 at Nailsea, Somerset, 7 miles (11.3 km) from BRISTOL, by John Robert Lucas (1754–1828) with a partner, William Chance, who sent his son ROBERT LUCAS CHANCE to the works to gain experience. A second glassworks was founded nearby in 1790 by William Chance and others. In 1810 the works came under the management of his son, Robert, who went on to own the Spon Lane Glassworks, BIRMINGHAM, in 1824. Originally the factory made mainly CROWN GLASS for windows and later SHEET GLASS, bottles and household ware including flasks. The glass ware was copied by other firms and attributed to Nailsea. The works closed in the 1870s.

Napier, David (1790–1869)

A marine engineer and steamship (see STEAM BOATS) owner who built the boiler of the COMET. In 1818 he designed a steamship to replace the sailing ships on the route between England, Scotland and Ireland. He designed a sharp bow to weather the rough seas and named the vessel *Rob Roy*. This steamship was the first to provide a service between GLASGOW and Belfast, and in 1821 moved to the Dover–Calais route as the first cross-Channel steamer service. David Napier built other steamships which started service as steam packets, carrying cargoes, passengers and mail.

D. Bell and D. Napier, *David Napier, Engineer* (J. Maclehose and Sons 1912).

Napier, Robert (1791–1876)

A marine engineer and the cousin of DAVID NAPIER, he started an engineering business in GLASGOW in 1815. In 1823 he designed the engines for the *Leven*, a Dumbarton-built boat. In 1841 he founded SHIPBUILDING yards at Govan, and in 1850 he began building iron ships for the Cunard and P & O Companies as well as for the Royal Navy and foreign governments.

Napoleonic Wars

The war between Britain and its allies and France, which continued from 1793 to 1815 except for one short break. Napoleon Bonaparte was a French army commander during the war until 1799, when he seized power. From then on the conduct of the war was under his personal command.

In Britain, the war brought a demand from the government for large quantities of arms and clothing, while the metal and IRON INDUSTRIES were boosted by the demand for armaments. The flow of overseas trade was disrupted by French warships and in 1806 the mainland of Europe was blockaded as a countermeasure. Restrictions on British imports and exports brought much suffering to some groups of the manufacturing population, with 32 cotton mills idle in MANCHESTER alone in 1809.

At the end of the war demand fell away drastically and hopes of large-scale sales to Europe were dashed because the continental countries were too poor to buy. In 1815 the iron industry had a productive capacity in excess of peacetime needs and many ironworks shut down some or all of their furnaces. Rioting took place at MERTHYR TYDFIL and improvements did not show themselves until 1823. Furthermore, the end of the war flooded the labour market with returning soldiers and sailors, causing more disorganization in the labour market. There was an increased burden of taxation and a rise in the COST OF LIVING. The economic cost of the war is difficult to measure, but if there had been no war the international trade in textiles would have developed more smoothly, although Britain might have suffered from European competition.

Narrow Boat

A CANAL boat designed for the narrow LOCKS and canals of the Midlands, but which could also be used on the Lancashire canals and on the HUDDERSFIELD Canal. In Scotland the only narrow canal with similar boats was the Glasgow, Paisley and Johnstone.

A typical narrow boat was 70 feet (21.3 m) long and 7 feet (2.1 m) wide. It had a capacity of about 15–30 tonnes (16.8–22.4 US tons) and carried coal and general cargoes but not timber or bulky goods. PICKFORDS used narrow boats for their cargo services. Some narrow boats were lived in and had cabins which, although small, were the homes of the BOAT PEOPLE. Narrow boats which undertook short-haul work carrying bulk goods needing no weather protection were called day boats and were not lived in. They operated on the BLACK COUNTRY system, in South East Lancashire and THE POTTERIES.

Coal was the basic traffic, but narrow boats also carried bricks, PIG IRON, foundry materials, slates, timber, rubbish, dung, limestone, forgings and castings.

Visit Ellesmere Port, Cheshire – boat museum. **M***
Stoke Bruerne, Northamptonshire –

Waterways Museum with cabin of narrow boat. **M***
Dudley, West Midlands – Black Country Museum with canal boat exhibits. **M***

T.A. Chaplin, *A Short History of the Narrow Boat* (Hugh McKnight Publications 1974).
P.L. Smith, *Canal Barges and Narrow Boats* (Shire Publications 1986).

Narrow Boat – Castles and Roses Decorations

Canal boats were frequently painted with bright decorations which followed a set of conventions, often including landscapes containing castles or bunches of stylized flowers, mostly roses. The origins of this traditional form of decoration are unknown and they are unique to the BOAT PEOPLE community. The colours used are simple – greens, reds and yellows – with decorations extending to buckets and other household items.

Visit Stoke Bruerne, Northamptonshire – Waterways Museum with decorated exhibits. **M***

A.J. Lewery, *Narrow Boat Painting* (David and Charles 1974).

Nasmyth, James (1808–90)

A machine tool maker who worked with HENRY MAUDSLAY. He set up a factory in MANCHESTER in 1836, known as the Bridgewater Foundry, making locomotives and machine tools. He built a vertical CYLINDER BORING MACHINE and a shaping machine (1836) which, relatively unchanged, is still an essential item of equipment in an engineer's workshop. He is best known for his steam hammer (1839) which was driven upwards by steam and then fell with gravity. Large forgings such as the shaft for ISAMBARD BRUNEL'S *GREAT BRITAIN* could not have been made without this hammer. It considerably reduced the cost of making marine engines and heavy calibre guns. In 1845 he adapted the principle of the steam hammer for a steam-powered pile driver.

National Association for the Promotion of Social Science

A society founded in 1857 with HENRY BROUGHAM as its first president. It concerned itself mainly with discussion and propaganda on law reform, penal organization, education, local government and public health. It published its transactions and women were prominent among its members.

National Association for the Protection of Labour

Set up by JOHN DOHERTY in 1830, it aimed to unite all TRADE UNIONS. It had ambitious ideas for the organization of the WORKING-CLASS movement, and a number of societies connected with the textile trades, mechanics and coal miners joined. The main strength of the movement was in Lancashire, Cheshire, NOTTINGHAM and Leicester. It produced a newspaper called *The Voice of the People* and aimed to support strikers' financial needs, but the scheme was too ambitious. It did not have the money, the organization or the discipline required and the Association came to an end, although individual unions flourished.

National Society

The full title was 'National Society for Promoting the Education of the Poor in the Principles of the Established Church'. It was formed in 1811 by the Anglican church (see CHURCH OF ENGLAND) to provide schools for poor children. By 1830 there were 3,670 schools and 30,000 pupils, but few attended regularly and the teaching was inadequate. The MONITORIAL SYSTEM was used and teachers were trained to operate it. In 1833 the National Society, together with the BRITISH AND FOREIGN SCHOOLS SOCIETY, was given a government grant for EDUCATION, which was renewed annually. The National Society was much larger than the British Society and attracted the largest proportion of the government's grant.

Navigation Acts

Acts passed in 1651 and 1660 requiring British trade to be carried in British ships. The Acts aimed to strengthen the merchant fleet, partly because the navy was never large enough and the merchant fleet was a source of sailors. The Navigation Acts encouraged the Americans to trade in goods, transporting them illegally to foreign ports without going through British ports. The Acts were modified by WILLIAM PITT and then by WILLIAM HUSKISSON in 1825. They were finally repealed in 1849.

Navvy

A workman employed to build the CANALS and later the railways (see RAILWAY DEVELOPMENT) during the INDUSTRIAL REVOLUTION. Agricultural work was poorly paid and large reserves of labourers from all parts of Britain were available for the unskilled but hard work of shifting the rocks and earth to form a routeway for these new forms of transport. The word came from 'navigator' and refers to the 'navigations', as the first canals were sometimes called.

The men lived in shanty towns in the countryside, and moved on from site to site as the work progressed. Their accommodation was basic; they slept in tiers of bunks, 20 or 30 to a hut. They ran sick clubs and had to use the TRUCK SYSTEM when they were a long way from shops. They had a reputation for hard drinking and hard living as well as for hard work, and their presence was disliked by local landowners and other residents. They were supplemented by local casual labour en route and were employed for a specified job, which was often dangerous. A navvy was expected to shovel about 20 tonnes (22.4 US tons) per day. When blasting was done the dangers increased. For example, while building the Woodhead Tunnel between SHEFFIELD and MANCHESTER between 1839 and 1845 there were 32 killed, 140 seriously hurt and 400 lesser casualties.

The navvies were employed by engineers, the greatest of whom was Thomas Brassey. He laid over 2,000 miles (3,200 km) of track in Britain and was said to be like the commander of a private army, since he was in charge of up to 100,000 men at a time.

T. Coleman, *The Railway Navvies* (Pelican 1968).

Need, Samuel (1718–81)

A wealthy NOTTINGHAM hosier, a DISSENTER and supporter of JEDEDIAH STRUTT with whom he was associated for 20 years, for part of the time as a partner in a hosiery business. At his death the cotton partnership between RICHARD ARKWRIGHT and Jedediah Strutt was dissolved and these MANUFACTURERS went their separate ways.

Neilson, James Beaumont (1792–1865)

An ENGINEWRIGHT who became the manager of GLASGOW gasworks in 1817. In 1828 he invented HOT BLAST for the BLAST FURNACES of the IRON INDUSTRY, disproving the common belief that cold air was essential for the making of iron. His inventions gave immediate economies to blast furnace operations as considerably less fuel was needed. The first establishment to use the hot blast was the CLYDE IRONWORKS. The method tended to melt the tuyere or orifice through which the hot air entered the furnace, but this problem was solved when John Condie invented the spiral tuyere cooled by water passing through. The invention of hot blast resulted in an expansion of the iron foundry in Scotland, with a period of boom from 1835 to 1870.

Newcastle-upon-Tyne

The most important town in the North East, before, during and after the INDUSTRIAL REVOLUTION. It was the lowest point downstream at which the River Tyne could be bridged and its growth in the 18th century was based mainly on its coal trade. Nearby coal deposits encouraged the development of a GLASS INDUSTRY in the 17th century and the town became the centre for the manufacture of window glass, distributing the fragile glass by coastal vessels (see COASTAL TRADE). Local salt deposits were also worked and an alkali works was built in 1778 using the salt and local coal. The associated industry of soap-making also developed before the end of the century and iron foundries grew up nearby.

The period 1770 to 1840 saw major building developments in the centre of the town, but at the beginning of the 19th century the built-up area was still largely confined within the line of the town walls, with the densest population and some of the poorest housing behind the waterfront. The coming of the railway (see RAILWAY DEVELOPMENT) in the 1830s further increased the town's importance. ROBERT STEPHENSON built the High Level Bridge over the river between Newcastle-upon-Tyne and Gateshead in 1849. It carried the railway and a roadway suspended from the arches. In 1876 a swing bridge replaced the ancient low-level Tyne Bridge and the two bridges form one of the world's most breathtaking industrial landscapes.

Newcastle-upon-Tyne was a commercial as well as an industrial centre and was a focus for a number of learned societies, including the Literary and Philosophical (1793) and the North of England Institute of Mining and Mechanical Engineering (1852). The population climbed from 33,000 in 1801 to 109,000 in 1861.

Visit Robert Stephenson's High Level Bridge, Newcastle-upon-Tyne.
Museum of Science and Technology, Blandford Square, Newcastle-upon-Tyne – Tyneside's industrial history. **M***

Newcomen, Thomas (1663–1729)

A Devon blacksmith by trade, who experimented to improve a steam pump (see STEAM ENGINE – PUMPING) in 1712 to pump water more efficiently from mines. The engine used a piston which operated at one end of a long beam and was pulled down by the pressure of the atmosphere, so it was called an atmospheric engine. At the other end of the beam was a red pump rod which removed water at the rate of 120 imperial gallons (545 litres, 96 US gallons) a minute. Many of Newcomen's engines were used in

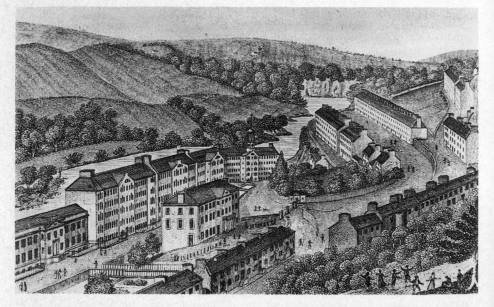

A view of New Lanark in 1818 by John Winning. In the centre is Robert Owen's Institute for the Formation of Character with children in the playground. Along the riverside are the tall buildings of the cotton mills with a bell-tower on one of them. The workers' tenements can be seen in the foreground forming part of the 'model' community developed by Robert Owen having been started by David Dale. (*New Lanark Conservation Trust*)

Cornish COPPER MINING and there were about 100 in use by 1733. The steam pump was also used at collieries in the Midlands and then in the North East. These atmospheric engines, or fire engines, as they were often called, were also widely used in Europe.

A considerable number of engines were working in the second half of the 19th century, making it possible to work coal and mineral seams below water layers, so increasing output. The engine provided a workable prime mover for mines and manufactures throughout the 18th century and by 1800 just over 1,000 had been built, 90 per cent of which were used for pumping.

Royal Avenue Gardens, Dartmouth, Devon – Newcomen engine, the oldest steam engine in existence. **M***
Black Country Museum, Dudley, West Midlands – replica engine. **M***
Elsecar, South Yorkshire – Newcomen steam pumping engine. **M***

L.T.C. Rolt and J.S. Allen, *The Steam Engine of Thomas Newcomen* (Moorland Publishing 1977).

New Hall China

A mansion in THE POTTERIES called the New Hall, converted into a pottery by a group of businessmen in 1782. They used the patents and manufacturing plant bought from RICHARD CHAMPION at BRISTOL and the pottery's HARD-PASTE PORCELAIN became well known as tough and serviceable. The firm became celebrated for its tea and coffee sets and about 1810 it began making BONE CHINA. The works was closed in 1830 because it was unable to meet competition from SPODE, MINTON and COALPORT.

New Lanark

While touring Scotland in 1783–4 to expand the COTTON INDUSTRY outside Lancashire, RICHARD ARKWRIGHT visited the Falls of Clyde at Lanark. With DAVID DALE as a partner, he leased the ground for a mill and homes for the workers. A tunnel was driven through the hillside to tap the waters of the River Clyde and a weir was built to raise the water level through the lade (channel) to the mill wheels. Local stone was quarried for the mill, which was in operation by 1786. Two years later it was destroyed by fire and another built. In all, four mills were built on the site as well as houses for more than 200 families.

The New Lanark Mill and village were bought by ROBERT OWEN and his partners in 1798, and the next year he married David Dale's daughter, becoming manager of the mill in 1800. He reorganized and modernized the mill, which he controlled for 30 years. By 1815 New Lanark was spinning the finest yarn in the world and had a workforce of 1,600. As a social reformer, Robert Owen applied his ideas to the living and working conditions at New Lanark. He built an Institution for the Formation of Character in 1816, and one room of the building was used as an infant school where the children followed a timetable based on singing, dancing and an appreciation of natural objects. For children over 10 (the minimum working age at New Lanark) there were evening schools with reading, writing, accounting and sewing, as well as dances and concerts in the hall of the Institution. After 1825 Robert Owen lost his influence at the Institution and the curriculum became more orthodox. The New Lanark Mill became a showplace visited by tourists from many European countries.

Visit New Lanark Conservation Village, New Lanark Mills, Lanark, Scotland – original mill and accommodation. **M***

Newman, John Henry (1801–90)

A leader of the OXFORD MOVEMENT and vicar of St Mary the Virgin, Oxford, in 1829. A tract he wrote in 1841 roused a fear of Popery in England. He became a Roman Catholic in 1845 (see ROMAN CATHOLICISM) and was created a cardinal in 1879.

News of the World

A Sunday newspaper first published in 1843, at a time when there were seven other newspapers published on a Sunday. The difference was that, whereas the other newspapers were read by the UPPER and MIDDLE CLASSES, the *News of the World* was designed to attract the WORKING CLASS and it built up a large working-class reading public with its RADICAL politics and sensational journalistic style. It was owned by John Browne Bell until 1855 and then by other members of the family.

Northampton

A market town in the 18th century with a domestic boot and shoe industry which was stimulated by orders from the army and navy during the AMERICAN WAR OF INDEPENDENCE and the NAPOLEONIC WARS. In 1801 the population was 7,000 and the town grew slowly, with its own CANAL link after 1815. By 1831 one-third of the men living in the town were shoemakers, and 40 years later the proportion had risen to over two-fifths. WORKING-CLASS terraced houses developed in the west and north of the town with MIDDLE-CLASS housing to the east. MACHINES were not developed for the shoe industry until the 1850s and it was only then that factories began to appear, gradually displacing the journeyman shoemakers (see ARTISANS) who worked at home or in a small workshop. By 1861 the population had reached 33,000.

Visit Central Museum and Art Gallery, Guildhall Road, Northampton – boot and shoe exhibition. **M***

Nottingham

An industrial town in the East Midlands which was an important centre for the lace and hosiery industry. The town began to grow in the 1780s with the boom in cotton spinning and the increased demand for domestic hosiery products. At that time the FRAMEWORK KNITTERS were prosperous wage-earners and the relatively high wages attracted many newcomers. Houses were built to meet the growing demand. They consisted of three boxes on top of one another, used respectively for living, sleeping and working. Often there was a cellar underneath. They were built blind-back (without windows or doors at the back)

as infillings for yards, or as BACK-TO-BACKS. The more wealthy merchants and independent weavers lived in brick and slate homes, three storeys high with enough room on the top storey for eight to ten stocking frames.

A boom period after 1817 brought a flood of immigrants and greedy speculators erected houses, usually infills or back-to-backs. The decline in the fortunes of the framework knitters in the 1830s and 1840s was evident from the squalid SLUMS in which they lived, being too poor to buy or rent the ARTISANS' houses going up in the suburbs. The Second Report of the HEALTH OF TOWNS COMMISSION in 1845 stated that the slums and overcrowding in Nottingham were worse than those of any other industrial town. By that time the population had reached 52,000 and the town was growing rapidly, employing large numbers in the lace and hosiery factories. The evils of poor housing were cured only slowly.

The town had other problems as a result of its industrial structure. In 1842 the Factory Commissioners reported that many tasks connected with the lace trade were being performed in warehouses by women and children. Warehouses had been built for operations such as clipping, scalloping and drawing, which were performed in high temperatures and a humid atmosphere. Often 500 or 600 people would be employed in one warehouse for more than 12 hours a day. The significance of the use of warehouses by the MANUFACTURERS was that they were not regulated by the FACTORY ACTS and working conditions were therefore poor. In 1862 the Commissioners recommended the extension of the Factory Acts to cover warehouses, and conditions were improved by the Workshops Act of 1864, which was extended to private houses and home workers in the Workshops' Regulation Act of 1867.

Visit Industrial Museum, Nottingham – lace display. **M***
Waterways Museum, Nottingham – canal warehouses and exhibition centre. **M***

O

Oastler, Richard (1789–1861)

A factory reformer who campaigned against child labour in Yorkshire mills and urged resistance against the POOR LAW AMENDMENT ACT, 1834. He left the Methodist Church (see METHODISM) to join the CHURCH OF ENGLAND, and with JOHN FIELDEN promoted the TEN HOURS MOVEMENT.

O'Connor, Feargus (1794–1855)

An Irish barrister and RADICAL reformer who became a Chartist leader (see CHARTISM) and founded the National Charter Association in 1840. He owned and edited the Chartist periodical *Northern Star*. After defeat of a petition to Parliament in 1842, O'Connor became interested in settling families on the land as smallholders. A CHARTIST LAND COMPANY was set up in 1845, but he had no clear ideas on the sort of economy and society he wanted, and the Company collapsed in 1851 following the demise of Chartism after 1848.

Oil Exploitation

One of the earliest commercial supplies of oil came from the IRONBRIDGE GORGE in Shropshire, where, in 1787, a tunnel struck quantities of natural bitumen. This Tar Tunnel was exploited into the 19th century. Exploitation in Scotland began in 1851 when James Young (1811–83), who had worked with MICHAEL FARADAY, started mining oil shale in West Lothian. He refined paraffin and paraffin wax from the shale, but the industry's growth was restricted by his patent, which ran out in 1864. After that date a number of firms were founded but many failed.

Visit Ironbridge Gorge Museum, Shropshire – Tar Tunnel at Coalport. **M*** Torbane, near Bathgate, West Lothian – waste tips from oil shale workings.

Old Hall

An ancient moated manor which became

the centre of the JAPANNING industry in Wolverhampton in the last decade of the 18th century. It was leased by two brothers, William and Obadiah Ryton, who were PAPER WARE and TINPLATE workers. Part of the house was used as their home; the rest became a factory employing about 600 women and girls. After about 1810, when one of the brothers died, the firm became known as Ryton and Walton.

Oldham

A Lancashire town which, in 1778, had six small cotton mills and one or two collieries. A branch of the Ashton Canal was completed in 1796 and the local coal provided cheap fuel for the introduction of STEAM ENGINES at cotton mills such as Lees Hall (1796) and Greenbank Mill (1816). The town became a centre for cotton spinning, and an engineering industry also developed, making spinning and weaving machines for the local market. In 1842 the Oldham branch of the Lancashire and Yorkshire Railway was completed (see RAILWAY DEVELOPMENT), and by 1861 the town had a population of 72,000.

The town gradually recovered after the loss of trade during the American Civil War (1861–5), and there was a building boom which included the construction of large cotton spinning mills. These huge buildings, completed between 1880 and 1920, were often built of red brick with yellow brick details. They were sometimes capped at one end by a tower complete with a clock. Their solid rectangular shapes still dominate the skyline in Oldham.

Oldknow, Samuel II (1756–1828)

After an APPRENTICESHIP in his uncle's drapery shop in NOTTINGHAM, he set up in 1782 as a MANUFACTURER of cotton goods in Anderton, southwest of MANCHESTER. The MULE had made it possible to produce MUSLIN, and this was the material he specialized in. Some of the products were sent for sale in the Nottingham shop and then a market developed in LONDON.

In 1785 he started a business in Stockport, near Manchester, with over 300 trained outwork weavers supplying cloth to his specifications. In 1790 he built a spinning mill in the town, using a BOULTON AND WATT engine for power. In 1793 he built another mill at MELLOR, and two years later he concentrated his work there, leasing the Stockport premises and abandoning the making of muslin. He was a leading promoter of the Peak Forest Canal, which was opened in 1800. In the depression of 1797–8 his business suffered and RICHARD ARKWRIGHT entered into partnership with him, probably paying off his debts. Samuel Oldknow became manager of the Mellor Mill, which passed to Arkwright at his death.

G. Unwin, *Samuel Oldknow and the Arkwrights* (Manchester University Press 1968).

Oliver, William

A pseudonym used by William Richards, a government spy and agent provocateur who was instrumental in undermining the reform movement and in the rounding up of JEREMIAH BRANDRETH and his followers in 1817. William Oliver was helped out of a debtor's goal by a RADICAL shoemaker, Charles Pendrill, and showed eagerness to join political associations. He met leading reformers in the Midlands and the North and reported their names to Lord SIDMOUTH. Oliver was sent to NOTTINGHAM, where he joined the revolutionary group led by Jeremiah Brandreth and reported the plans of the group to his masters in London.

He was exposed by the *Leeds Mercury*, much to the horror and amazement of many ordinary people who had no idea such things could take place. The exposures had a bad effect on the government and several trials for high treason and seditious libel resulted in acquittals. The use of Oliver as an informer put the WORKING-CLASS reform movement on the alert, and his name was often used by speakers to silence critics.

J.L. and B. Hammond, *The Skilled Labourer* (Longman 1979).

Omnibus

A vehicle for carrying passengers on regular services, drawn by horses before the advent of the internal combustion engine. The omnibus had been in service in France since 1662 and an Englishman resident in France, GEORGE SHILLIBEER, brought the omnibus to England. He started a service in London in 1829. The first 'shillibeers', as they were called, were drawn by three horses abreast and carried 22 passengers inside. The fare was one-third of that paid on the COACH SERVICES and the buses were an immediate success, partly because they were clean and reasonably comfortable. In 1833 a scheduled service was started in London by a steam-driven bus. After a few years restrictions on their use led to the service being abandoned. In 1850 seats for five passengers were placed on the roof.

The omnibus services spread rapidly throughout the country and in 1854 there were nearly a thousand buses in London alone. In 1857 the London General Omnibus Company was started as a joint-stock limited company.

Orders in Council

Government measures passed in 1806 during the NAPOLEONIC WARS which declared France to be in a state of blockade and banned French overseas trade. Neutral ships trading with France and her allies had to call at British ports, unload and reload their cargoes and pay a duty. Those selling British goods were exempt.

British MANUFACTURERS and merchants disliked the trade restrictions and were alarmed when the United States, a neutral country, closed its ports to British and French ships. Economic depression in 1810 and 1811 led to demands for the Orders in Council to be repealed and they were abandoned in 1812, the same year in which Napoleon abandoned the CONTINENTAL SYSTEM.

Ornamental Ware

Pottery produced for decorative purposes

rather than its usefulness as tableware. Much of the demand for ornamental ware pottery came from the BIRMINGHAM and SHEFFIELD cutlery and TOY TRADE manufacturers. They ordered pottery buttons, knife handles, tiepins, brooches and other pieces for mounting, and then sold them to retailers. Ornamental ware commanded a higher price than table ware and JOSIAH WEDGWOOD was one of the first potters to exploit the demand. He also mounted seals and cameos at his works without sending them to setters or wholesale jewellers.

Visit Barlaston, Stoke-on-Trent – Wedgwood Museum. **M***

Outram, Benjamin (1764–1805)

An engineer who used L-shaped section plate rails placed on blocks of stone for making a horse tramroad. He surveyed the CROMFORD canal for WILLIAM JESSOP and became a partner in the BUTTERLEY COMPANY, which owned mines and quarries near the canal and were also iron founders and engineers. He designed a small iron AQUEDUCT for the Derby Canal, for which he was engineer in 1795. He was also engineer to the Peak Forest Canal.

Owen, Robert (1771–1858)

The son of a Welsh tradesman, he was a shop assistant from the age of 10 to that of 18. He then set up business with a partner as a MANUFACTURER of textile machinery, using £100 ($170) which he borrowed. He was manager of a cotton mill in MANCHESTER at the age of 20 and then, with partners, became the owner of the NEW LANARK Mills in 1798 and manager in 1800. He introduced humanitarian working and living conditions with good houses, a school and other amenities for his employees.

His school reflected his advanced thinking on education, since he believed that the first business of EDUCATION was to develop character and that the environment helped to shape this character. Education, he held, was the common right of children and had the power to right the world's wrongs. In 1813 he published *A New View of Society*, in which he emphasized the importance of education. By 1833 he was established as the leader of the TRADE UNION movement and the next year he set up the GRAND NATIONAL CONSOLI- DATED TRADES UNION, which he saw as the inclusion within one union of all the 'productive classes'. Internal dissension and the antagonism of the government and the employers rapidly led to the demise of the GNCTU, which was never a practical proposition at that time.

He advocated 'Villages of Co-operation' in which workers would produce enough for their own needs on a profit-sharing basis, and in 1839 he was active in setting up a model village of co-operation in Hampshire. He spent a great deal of money on making the centre, Queenwood, a show place, but the enterprise failed in 1845. He also set up a community at New Harmony in Indiana, USA, but this also failed.

Owen was idealistic and never fully understood the WORKING-CLASS people whose needs he wanted to champion. His influence in advocating community activities helped to establish co-operative societies for trading purposes.

G.D.H. Cole, *The Life of Robert Owen* (Cass 1965).

Oxford Movement

A movement to increase the rituals and ceremonials of the CHURCH OF ENGLAND, started in 1833 by a group of clergymen who were fellows of Oxford colleges. Among its advocates were Edward Pusey and JOHN HENRY NEWMAN, who urged a return to greater ceremonial and beauty in church services. The use of elaborate rituals aroused a great deal of hostility, as it appeared to identify Anglicanism with ROMAN CATHOLICISM, and congregations were often bitterly divided. Newman and some other members became Roman Catholics and in 1879 he became a cardinal. The Oxford Movement resulted in parishioners in some parishes making their churches more beautiful and money was raised to restore existing churches and build new ones.

N. Yates, *The Oxford Movement and Anglican Ritualism* (Historical Association 1983).

P

Paine, Thomas (1737–1809)

A RADICAL who was dismissed from the Excise service in 1772 for agitating for more pay. He went to America and in 1776 published *Common Sense*, a work on the causes of the American War of Independence. He returned to England in the next year and published *The Rights of Man*, a work which advocated provision for the aged and the limitation of armaments. The authorities disliked the book and Paine fled to France, where he became a member of the Convention (the French House of Representatives). In 1793 he published *The Age of Reason*, which raised more antagonism in England and some in France. He returned to the United States in 1800 and died in New York.

A. Williamson, *Thomas Paine* (Allen and Unwin 1973).

Paisley Shawls

Paisley was the centre of the COTTON INDUSTRY in Scotland, and in 1802 attempts were made there to make shawls in imitation of the richly designed and coloured Indian products. There was a small production which expanded very quickly after the depression of 1818. At first the shawls were made of cotton but later, imitating the real cashmere shawls, they were made of spun silk. As articles of fashion the demand for them and other Paisley goods made by skilled weavers was liable to fluctuations, and the weaving of the shawls ceased between 1870 and 1880 because they had gone out of fashion.

Palmer, John (1742–1818)

Surveyor and comptroller general of the Post Office, 1786–92. His appointment was in recognition of his helping to introduce MAIL COACHES.

Paper-making

In the 18th century, paper was made from LINEN and cotton rags which were shredded and beaten in a vat until the fibres were reduced to a fine pulp. A flat strainer or mould was used to lift a layer of the fibres from the vat and deposit it in a felt blanket. The wet sheet of paper was then pressed, to remove water, and dried. Before it could be used for writing it had to be coated with gelatine size and dried. Paper-making was done in water mills, whose power was used to pulp the rags using wooden hammers. By the end of the century JAMES WHATMAN and his son had improved the quality of their paper with WOVE PAPER. BLEACHING using a chlorine dye was introduced by William Simpson in 1791 and patented the next year by Clement and George Taylor.

The first machine for making paper was promoted by the FOURDRINIER BROTHERS and set up by BRYAN DONKIN at FROGMORE MILL, Hertfordshire, in 1803. In 1809 JOHN DICKINSON introduced a cylinder mould machine, and later steam-heated cylinders were used to help dry the paper. In 1825, John and Christopher Phipps, papermakers at Dover, patented the DANDY ROLL to provide paper with a watermark and improve the sheet formation.

As the demand for paper increased in the 19th century rags became scarce, and attempts were made to use straw and other fibres. The problem was solved in 1857 when ground wood pulp was used in Germany. Seven years later a process for using wood and breaking down the fibres with chemicals was introduced by Watt and Burgess.

Visit Greater Manchester Museum of Science and Industry, Castlefield, Manchester – paper-making exhibition. **M***

A.H. Shorter, *Paper Making in the British Isles* (David and Charles 1971).
D.C. Coleman, *The British Paper Industry* (Clarendon 1958).

Paper Mills – Location

Early paper mills were located near rivers because water was needed for power and to make the pulp used for PAPER-MAKING. A waterwheel operated a beater, consisting of a heavy roller with bars attached rotating in a ridged iron trough. This action pulped the rags, teasing out the fibres. Mills also needed large supplies of suitable rags and this made proximity to large urban centres essential. Towns could also supply a market for the finished product and many mills were located close to LONDON, BRISTOL, Edinburgh and MANCHESTER. There were about 400 mills in 1785 and some mills from that time still exist as paper-making centres. The use of steam power did not change the location pattern greatly, mainly because water was still needed in large quantities in the paper-making processes. When wood pulp replaced rags as the raw material in the 1860s mills grew up near tide-water, where timber could be imported easily and paper exported.

Visit Dalmore Mill, Milton Bridge, Midlothian – paper mill, 1837.
Wookey Hole Mill, near Wells, Somerset – paper mill.

Paper Ware

A form of papier mâché made by pasting stout sheets of paper over a core which was later removed. It was patented by Henry Clay, a japanner (see JAPANNING) in 1772. He employed 300 people at his BIRMINGHAM factory turning out these goods, which in time were called papier mâché. The material was ideal for japanning and made a serviceable basis for tea trays and many small household articles. Henry Clay was for many years the most important Birmingham japanner; at the same time he was also a button maker, and he remained in business until 1802.

Paper – Wove

A smooth paper of high quality, first introduced by JAMES WHATMAN about 1754. He made a cover for the mould in which the pulp was placed. This was of woven wire cloth – hence the name 'wove' paper. His wire cloth eliminated the laid and chain lines caused by the wire mesh from which the cover of the mould was previously made.

Papier Mâché   See Japanning and Paper Ware

Parish Apprentices

Children and young people without parents or whose parents were too poor to look after them were the responsibility of the parish, and these pauper children were an expense which the parishes were always anxious to reduce, since the money came out of the rates (local taxes). One means of removing the expense was to make them the responsibility of the factory masters who took them on as apprentices. The children were given contracts for one to eight years depending on the age they entered the mill. Apprentices for the Midland and Lancashire cotton mills came from LONDON, BIRMINGHAM, Hereford and other towns.

At the Cuckney Mill, Nottinghamshire, between 1786 and 1805, 15 per cent of the apprentices ran away, 8 per cent died and 12 per cent had to be returned to overseers or other senders. The number who died were probably unhealthy before they were taken into the mill, where living conditions were known to be good. Maintaining pauper apprentices was expensive and few were eventually taken on as adult workers. RICHARD ARKWRIGHT never employed pauper apprentices and by the beginning of the 19th century other mills followed his example. However, evidence provided for the FACTORY ACT, 1834 showed that the system was still in operation in a number of centres.

Parkes, Alexander (1813–90)

A chemist and inventor who patented a process in 1841 for waterproofing fabrics by the use of a solution of india rubber. The patent was later sold to CHARLES MACINTOSH. In 1850 Parkes patented a process for recovering gold and silver from lead bullion. The method was improved the next year and by 1870 had superseded HUGH PATTINSON's process. In 1858 he took out a patent for seamless metal tubes and cylinders for CALICO printing.

Parys Mountain

A copper-working site on the island of Anglesey, North Wales. It was started in the 1760s as a small series of mines and developed into a large open-cast quarry. In 1790 some 1,500 men worked at the site at a town which had grown up at Amlwch. Ore was shipped from the port to LIVERPOOL and Swansea for smelting. The mine was a tourist attraction with its spectacular steep sides and different levels worked by hundreds of men. Mining ceased for a time after 1815 and then continued at intervals until 1883.

Visit Parys Mountain, Anglesey – Copper mine, with town of Amlwch nearby.

Patent Laws

Applications for patents had to follow a devious and expensive procedure until 1852. A declaration had to be made before a commissioner and an application made at the Home Office. Other applications had to go to the monarch, the attorney general, the Lord Privy Seal, the Lord High Chancellor, the Lord High Chancellor's Porter and the Patent Office. To these officials the applicant had to submit a petition with provisional specifications. A royal grant made by letters patent or 'open letters' (they were not sealed and therefore open to be seen) was granted for a maximum of 14 years, and the patent owner had the sole and exclusive right to work or make the patent. Until 1835 the term of a patent could be extended only by a special Act of Parliament. For ordinary people obtaining a patent was costly; for example, a patent for a WATER CLOSET in 1773 cost £120 ($204). An application to extend a patent was even more costly because of the need to draw up an Act of Parliament.

In 1852 the Patent Law Amendment Act was passed. This set up one Patent Office, with all procedures confined to one office under a new body, the Commissioners of Patents.

Charles Dickens, 'A Poor Man's Tale of a Patent', essay from *Household Words* reprinted in *Reprinted Pieces* (Chapman and Hills 1858) and in B.W. Matz (ed.), *National Edition of Dickens' Work* (Chapman and Hall 1905).

Pattinson, Hugh Lee (1796–1858)

Inventor who took out a patent in 1833 to separate silver from lead by a method which was an improvement on the cupellation process used since Biblical times. Molten lead was slowly cooled, allowing lead crystals to form, leaving a silver-rich liquid. By repeating the process several times the silver was concentrated. It was known as the Pattinson process. (See also LEAD SMELTING.)

Paul, Lewis (?–1759)

With John Wyatt he patented a roller spinning machine in 1738. This machine used several pairs of rollers, each pair revolving faster than the pair before it, drawing out a sliver of wool and spinning it. About 1741 a machine powered by donkeys was installed in a building in BIRMINGHAM. A second mill in NORTHAMPTON had five machines and was driven by water power. The machines were moderately successful and a second patent for an improved machine was taken out in 1758. RICHARD ARKWRIGHT improved on Lewis Paul's idea to produce his WATER FRAME.

In 1748 Lewis Paul took out patents for a carding machine, which had a card covered with slips of wire placed round a cylinder. Underneath was a concave fixed card in contact with the cylinder. The cylinder was driven by hand and the idea was later developed by SAMUEL CROMPTON and others. Paul's ideas were therefore the forerunners of some of the machinery developed later for the textile industry.

Pawnshops

Pawnbrokers' shops were common in all the large industrial towns; MANCHESTER had over 60 in 1844. The unemployed and irregularly employed workers were usually in debt to the shopkeepers, and most working-class families needed loans from time to time to pay for essential foods or medicines. Loans were obtained from the pawnshops and it was common to pawn clothing on Monday and take it out after being paid on Saturday. This pattern of life was familiar to the working classes and debt was continuous, since the pawnbroker's interest rates were high and shopkeepers were ready to supply goods on credit, forcing the customers to take over-priced or inferior, adulterated goods.

Paxton, Sir Joseph (1803–68)

The agent to the Duke of Devonshire and a director of the Midland Railway. He designed Birkenhead Park in Cheshire in 1844. When the park was opened in 1847 it was a success financially as well as socially, peripheral land being sold as house plots at over eleven times the original purchasing price. His greatest work was to design the Crystal Palace which housed the GREAT EXHIBITION, 1851. The design was an enlarged version of conservatories he had built at Chatsworth, The Duke of Devonshire's seat in Derbyshire. The building was made of wood, iron and glass and over 2,000 men were employed to assemble it. It was completed in 22 weeks.

J. Anthony, *Joseph Paxton* (Shire Publications 1976).

Peelers

The nickname for policemen set up by SIR ROBERT PEEL's METROPOLITAN POLICE ACT, 1829. They were also known as 'bobbies' (from his first name, Robert). One of their first tasks was to control political demonstrations during the movement for the first REFORM ACT, 1832.

Peelites

Supporters of SIR ROBERT PEEL who represented the intellectuals of the CONSERVATIVE PARTY, the administrators and businessmen who had supported him for the repeal of the CORN LAWS in 1846. They formed a minor political party with opinions of the centre ground, which overlapped those of moderate liberals. Over 200 of Peel's former supporters deserted him after the Corn Laws were repealed, and in the 1847 election only Peelite candidates were supported by party funds and 89 were elected. Peel made no efforts to organize them into an effective opposition group, but by 1852 they were in a position to join a coalition government under a Peelite prime minister, Lord Aberdeen. They held half the Cabinet posts between 1852 and 1855.

Peel, Sir Robert (1788–1850)

The son of SIR ROBERT PEEL, SENIOR, he became an MP at the age of 21 and was home secretary from 1828 to 1830. He formed the Metropolitan Police (see METROPOLITAN POLICE ACT) and was responsible for the CATHOLIC EMANCIPATION ACT, 1829. As prime minister from 1841 to 1845 he abolished the CORN LAWS, having pledged to maintain them. In doing so he split the CONSERVATIVE PARTY. He also passed a number of financial reforms including the BANK CHARTER ACT.

D. Read, *Peel and the Victorians* (Blackwell 1987).

Peel, Sir Robert, Senior (1750–1830)

The son of the Robert Peel who had started up as a CALICO printer in 1764, he took over the firm in the 1770s and expanded with branches at Tamworth and Burton-on-Trent. In 1795 the firm owned 23 mills in Lancashire and the Midlands and employed over 15,000 people. For some time the Blackburn mills employed nearly all the workpeople of the town. He became an MP and supported WILLIAM PITT. In 1802 he was responsible for the FACTORY ACT known as the Health and Morals of Apprentices Act.

Pellatt, Apsley (1791–1863)

The son of a father with the same name who acquired the Falcon Glassworks at Southwark, LONDON, about 1790. He introduced sulphides from France and produced cameos set in glass. He took out a patent in 1819 and called the product encrusted cameos. He also made paperweights, decanters and candlesticks, as well as writing books about glass-making in the first half of the 19th century.

Pennant, Richard (1737?–1808)

The son of a LIVERPOOL merchant who married the heiress to what became the slate quarrying area at Penrhyn in North Wales. His agent, William Williams, directed the opening up of the quarry in the 1780s and the town of Bethesda grew up for the workers. By 1790 a harbour was being built, called Port Penrhyn, for the export of the slate which reached the harbour by a newly constructed road, and by 1798 a slate 'factory' had been established where writing slates, gravestones and chimney pieces were manufactured. In 1801 a railway was completed between the quarry and Port Penrhyn which included three INCLINED PLANES. By the early 19th century the whole area had been transformed and supported a thriving community of several thousand people. In 1783 Richard Pennant was created Baron Penrhyn. The slate quarry is still being worked and at present employs 400 people.

Penny Post

A uniform charge for sending letters, introduced in 1840 by SIR ROWLAND HILL. Previously there had been a charge of 8 pence (5.6 US cents) for sending a letter. The cheap post was welcomed by businessmen and reformers since it made it much cheaper to communicate. Penny stamps were black and were adhesive but unperforated. The number of letters posted increased dramatically from 75 million in 1838 to 642 million in 1864.

Pentridge Rising, 1817

An insurrection planned by JEREMIAH BRANDRETH and others, who gathered at Pentridge in Derbyshire. The recruits were quarrymen, iron workers, textile machine operators and labourers, and their object was to march to NOTTINGHAM,

where more recruits were expected, and to gather enough support to overthrow the government. Near Nottingham the men were confronted by a force of Hussars and were captured. Plans for the uprising had been given to the government by a spy, WILLIAM OLIVER. Brandreth and three others were convicted and hanged.

The Pentridge rising was one of the first attempts in history to mount a wholly proletarian insurrection (see KARL MARX), without MIDDLE-CLASS support; but in 1817 a WORKING-CLASS insurrection had no hope of success. It lacked organization and experienced leadership.

Penydarren Ironworks

An ironworks near MERTHYR TYDFIL in South Wales, founded in 1784 by the HOMFRAY BROTHERS. It used the PUDDLING process developed by HENRY CORT from 1787, and built RICHARD TREVITHICK's STEAM ENGINE in 1804. The ironmaster, SAMUEL HOMFRAY, made a bet of 500 guineas (£525 – $892.5) that the locomotive could haul a load of 10 tonnes (11.2 US tons) down the tramroad to Abercynon, a distance of 9 miles (14.5 km). In fact the engine showed that it could haul 25 tonnes (28 US tons) and Homfray won his bet.

Visit Welsh Industrial and Maritime Museum, Cardiff – full-size working model of the locomotive. **M***

People's Charter

The six points made by the Chartists in 1838. See CHARTISM.

Perkin, Sir William Henry (1838–1907)

A chemist who worked on the synthesizing of coal tar in 1856. He discovered the first coal-tar dye, but work on the dye in a cloth factory at Perth in Scotland was not successful. Consequently he set up his own dye factory in north LONDON, and by the 1860s had created a number of synthetic dyes which were used in fabrics and on postage stamps. Later he started the artificial perfume and flavouring industries with his discoveries.

Peterloo Massacre

The killing of 11 people and wounding of over 400, of whom 100 were women or girls, by yeomanry cavalry at St Peter's Fields, MANCHESTER, in 1819. A crowd of some 80,000 had gathered to demand universal suffrage, vote by ballot, annual Parliaments and the repeal of the CORN LAWS. The area most of them came from was unrepresented in Parliament, being a new industrial region.

Reports of the massacre brought protests from many parts of the country but the magistrates who had given orders to the yeomanry, and the soldiers who had fired the shots, were thanked by the government. The workers called the action Peterloo, mocking Wellington's victory over the French at Waterloo four years earlier. The massacre remained as a symbol of WORKING-CLASS resistance to oppression. Political antagonism hardened but the reformers had conflicting views and their unity was short-lived. Any hints of rioting were suppressed by the SIX ACTS.

J. Marlow, *The Peterloo Massacre* (Rapp and Whiting 1969).

Physiocrats

The name given to a group of 18th-century French economists and philosophers who, among other things, advocated LAISSEZ-FAIRE policies.

Pickfords

A road carrying firm in MANCHESTER set up by James Pickford in the mid-18th century. His two sons Matthew and Thomas became interested in CANAL transport, and in 1794 Matthew opened a depot in Manchester. His brother Thomas looked after the LONDON end of the business. When the Grand Junction Canal was fully open in 1805, Pickfords ran a canal service to London with their depot in Paddington Basin.

Matthew died in 1799, Thomas in 1811, and their four sons took over the partnership in 1801, opening up canal traffic to Leicester and the use of FLY VANS on the Manchester to London route. On the canals they operated narrow FLY BOATS carrying a variety of goods.

In 1816 new partners had to be brought in to rescue the firm, which passed into the hands of the Baxendale family. By 1838 the firm owned a thousand boat horses, but it transferred traffic to the railways in the late 1830s and 1840s, especially lighter goods. In 1847 they became goods agents for the London and North Western Railway, and gradually they transferred all their business to rail and road, running down their canal fleet.

Piece Halls (Also known as cloth halls)

Large buildings in the towns of the West Riding of Yorkshire where individual weavers and clothiers could meet merchants to sell their products. The only significant survivor is the Halifax Piece Hall, opened in 1779. It contained 315 rooms where selling took place. Later it became a wholesale vegetable market and is now a museum.

Visit Halifax, Yorkshire – piece hall, visitors' centre and museum. **M***

Pig Iron

Impure iron that is an alloy of other elements, chiefly carbon, together with phosphorus, silicon and manganese.

Molten iron from a BLAST FURNACE was run into a channel formed in a sand bed in front of the furnace. From this channel, side channels were made at right angles, with a set of dead-ended channels going off from the side ones. This resulted in a series of comb-like moulds for the molten iron to run into. When the iron cooled it could be broken into pieces of a useful size for handling. The first channel from the furnace was called the runner, the side channels the sows and the dead-ended channels the pigs. The sand bed containing the channels was called the pig bed. The terms runner and pig iron or pigs are still in use.

Pilkington, William (1800–72)

A businessman who became a partner in a glass manufacturing company at ST HELENS in 1826. In the 1820s there was a building boom and an increase in the demand for glass. The partnership

William Pilkington joined was formed to start the ST HELENS CROWN GLASS COMPANY, with John Bell as another of the partners. Land next to Bell's plant formed the site for the factory and in 1829 William Pilkington began to take an active part in the management, backed by his brother Richard (1795–1869).

The failure of some competitors in the 1830s gave the firm more business and new buildings were added, and production increased seven-fold between 1828 and 1836. The firm started making SHEET GLASS about 1835, and took over and adapted a cotton mill to smooth and polish the glass. There was a big increase in the demand for window glass in the 1840s, particularly after the excise duty on glass was lifted in 1845, halving the price. In 1845 the St Helens Works employed about 500 men, a schoolteacher was employed to teach young apprentices until they were 17, and recreational facilities were provided.

The Eccleston Crown Glass Works was bought in 1852 and the firm began exporting glass. A colliery was sunk and the chemicals required came from a works purchased a 1865. In 1869 William Pilkington retired from the firm and the second generation began to expand the business.

Visit Prescot Road, St Helens, Lancashire – Pilkington Glass Museum. **M***

T.C. Barker, *Pilkington Brothers and the Glass Industry* (Allen and Unwin 1960).

Pillar and Stall System (Sometimes known as the bord and pillar system)

A means of extracting coal in which coal was taken from passages (stalls or bords) between pillars many metres square. The system was used throughout the North East and in many other coalfields. The deeper the mine the thicker the pillars to support the greater weight of the roof. Soft underlying material could result in 'creep', reducing the height of the passageways, and larger pillars were needed to prevent this happening. Pillar and stall working was very wasteful of coal. Less than half the coal available was extracted from some pits and even where the pillars were small only about two-thirds of the coal could be removed.

Pitt, William (1759–1806) (Also known as Pitt the Younger)

The son of Lord Chatham, he entered the House of Commons when he was 22, became chancellor of the exchequer the next year and prime minister a year later. He was prime minister until 1801 and again in 1804–6. He was influenced by ADAM SMITH's *Wealth of Nations*, and encouraged trade by simplifying the collection of customs duties. He negotiated the Eden trade treaty (see ANGLO-FRENCH TREATY) in 1786 and introduced a number of tax reforms. He feared revolution spreading across the Channel from France (see FRENCH REVOLUTION) and passed the COMBINATION ACTS in 1799–1800. He brought about the ACT OF UNION and resigned in 1801 because of GEORGE III's unwillingness to grant Catholic emancipation (see CATHOLIC EMANCIPATION ACT).

D. Jarrett, *Pitt the Younger* (Weidenfeld and Nicolson 1974).

Place, Francis (1771–1854)

A RADICAL activist who fought for the abolition of the COMBINATION ACTS. He was a friend of JEREMY BENTHAM and his ally in Parliament was Joseph Hume (1777–1855), a radical critic. By skilful manoeuvring, the arguments against the Combination Acts were strongly put and the Acts were repealed. Place helped formulate the demands for Parliamentary reform (see REFORM ACT, 1832) and helped draft the PEOPLE'S CHARTER.

Plate Rails

Rails with a vertical flange (L-shaped) to guide the wheel. They were first introduced about 1777 by JOHN CURR and used underground at a SHEFFIELD colliery. The flange was on the inside of the rail and the plate rail was laid on stone blocks or sleepers made of wood or iron. They were made popular by BENJAMIN OUTRAM, and the majority of early 19th-century lines were laid with plate rails.

Plateways   See Wagonways

Ploughs

In 1770 John Brand of Lawford, Essex, designed and made his first iron ploughs, which became known as the Suffolk iron plough. In Norfolk a lighter plough had an iron mouldboard and WROUGHT-IRON shoe. Iron ploughshares had been made in Rotherham about 1730; in 1785 ROBERT RANSOME successfully tempered CAST-IRON ploughshares, and went on to develop the self-sharpening chilled share in 1803. By cooling the under-surface of the cast share more quickly than the upper side, it became harder and wore away at a slower rate, thus providing a sharp edge.

In 1808 Ransome made a major contribution to agricultural implement manufacture by introducing interchangeable components. A basic range of plough bodies was produced and a variety of components made in cast or wrought iron which could be bolted to the frame. Ploughs could be made up which suited the regional variations in use throughout the country. By 1840 the Ransome factory at Ipswich was making 86 different types of plough to suit the needs of local farmers. In 1843 the firm made its first cast-iron plough, which replaced the old wooden and metal implements. The implement was a standardized version of John Brand's iron plough.

Plug Plot Riots

Action taken by workmen after the rejection of the second Chartist (see CHARTISM) petition in 1842. Gangs of striking workers in the North and Midlands knocked out boiler-plugs to render boilers useless and prevent steam being raised to work MACHINES. It was one of the ways anger was expressed by the workers; the government responded by sending troops into the areas of greatest unrest, and the violence was squashed.

Pontcysyllte Aqueduct

Built between 1795 and 1805 by THOMAS TELFORD to carry the Ellesmere Canal over the valley of the River Dee. The aqueduct is supported by 19 CAST-IRON arches mounted on stone piers, and the water is carried in an iron trough built of wedge-shaped plates, flanged and bolted together. The aqueduct has a maximum height of 126 feet (38.4 m).

Visit Llangollen, Clwyd, North Wales – Pontcysyllte Aqueduct.

Poor Law – Act of Settlement, 1662

A law giving magistrates the power to return people not legally 'settled' in a parish to the parish where they were legally settled. The Act safeguarded the interests of the parishioners since they were responsible for the relief only of poor people in their parish. It deprived the WORKING CLASS of the right to move freely to find work (although many still did) and it remained in force until 1795. The concept lingered on even after that, and had an important influence on rural communities. In the 18th century new industries had been able to develop because the Act had in fact been broken and large numbers of country people had moved to other parishes to work.

Poor Law – Amendment Act, 1834

This Act reorganized the Poor Law arrangements by changing the role of the WORKHOUSES. Parishes were grouped into unions to finance the building of workhouses where these did not exist already. Relief for poor families was given only in the workhouse, and to discourage lazy claimants conditions were made less pleasant in the workhouse than those endured by the poorest people outside. The workhouse regime was strict, families were separated and workhouses became a symbol of the oppression of the working class.

Local boards of GUARDIANS were to be elected to administer the Poor Law and these guardians were responsible to the Poor Law Commissioners. The new Poor Law was welcomed by landowners and those who wished to see the rates (local taxes) reduced. The law was not an attempt to deal with the fundamental causes of poverty, only with its symptoms as expressed in the demand for relief. In the industrial northern towns it had only limited success, since factory operatives required short-term relief to tide them over periods of temporary unemployment, and in some areas outdoor relief was continued. It was an assumption of the new Poor Law that pauperism was due largely to personal weakness, and improvement could be effected by individual effort. SELF HELP was the Victorian answer to working-class problems.

A. Digby, *The Poor Law in Nineteenth Century England and Wales* (Historical Association 1982).

Poor Law – Gilbert's Act, 1782

A poor law Act promoted by Thomas Gilbert (1720–98), brother of JOHN GILBERT, which allowed parishes to combine into unions for more efficient administration of the poor law. Each union was to provide its own WORKHOUSE (previously each parish had that responsibility). The system was made less severe by limiting workhouses to the old, the sick and children. Paid GUARDIANS of the poor were appointed by JUSTICES OF THE PEACE to provide work for the able-bodied and grant outdoor relief if no work was available. The Act also abolished the contracting of workhouses to local businessmen. Of the 15,000 parishes in England and Wales, 1,000 joined to form unions.

M.E. Rose, *The English Poor Law 1780–1930* (David and Charles 1971).

Poor Law – Speenhamland System, 1795

A system drawn up by magistrates in Berkshire in 1795 to remedy unrest among the poor. The magistrates agreed that a worker had the right to a subsistence living and if he could not earn part of it then society owed him the difference. They adopted a system of assistance based on the price of a loaf of bread. Support to poor families rose and fell with the price of bread. The system spread to a number of other counties but was never adopted in Scotland and Ireland. Where it operated it was very popular, reducing the

danger of riots and opposition to MACHINES, since money provided by the parish made up for any loss of earnings by people in cottage industries. The effect of the payment of allowances out of rates (local taxes) was to keep wages down to the lowest level, the MANUFACTURER relying on the parish to make up the difference. As prices rose the system became very expensive, and disturbances in the 1830s led to an examination of the system and to its abolition in 1834.

Population Growth

The reasons for the increase in population which took place during the INDUSTRIAL REVOLUTION are extremely complex. Earlier in this century it was thought that the major cause was the fall in the DEATH RATE, but today some historians regard the BIRTH RATE as the major factor. At the time population was increasing all over Europe, where there was no Industrial Revolution, so the arguments that increasing employment lessened restraints against marriage and children are not sound.

There is evidence of a decline in epidemics and diseases in the mid-18th century. Inoculation against smallpox was a medical improvement which was widespread. Resistance to disease may have been strengthened by improved and regular food supplies.

Probably a number of factors combined to account for the population increase. There is evidence of different rates of marriage and fertility in the industrial communities, and the birth rate may have risen as a response to the expanding economy. The growth of population continued throughout the period of industrialization, and the CENSUS OF POPULATION records the totals for the UK as:

Year	Population (millions)	Rate of growth (%)
1801	15.9	–
1811	18.1	13.8
1821	21.0	16.1
1831	24.1	14.9
1841	26.6	10.8
1851	27.4	2.4
1861	29.0	5.8

Josiah Wedgwood studied sketches of classical Greek and Roman art and had copies made of antique vases and similar objects. These superb pieces of craftmanship became very popular ornaments in upper-class homes and Wedgwood's designers were encouraged to create original pieces based on classical examples. Many of these ornaments had a background of black Jasper, as in this first-edition copy of the Portland Vase. The original of this was in cameo glass, and Josiah I emulated its form. It took over three years of experimentation before the first good copy in black-and-white Jasper was produced in 1789. (*Trustees of the Wedgwood Museum, Barlaston, Staffordshire*)

Porcelain – Hard-Paste

A porcelain made from silicate of alumina, known as petuntse, china stone or feldspar and kaolin (CHINA CLAY). The kaolin gives the paste its plastic quality and the ingredients, blended together and fired at great heat, produce a vitreous, white substance which is extremely hard.

Hard-paste porcelain was imported from China until suitable deposits of kaolin were found in Europe in the early 18th century. It was first made at Meissen in 1709 and then manufactured at Sèvres in France in 1768. In the same year WILLIAM COOKWORTHY took out a patent for hard-paste porcelain using Cornish china clay. He started a factory in BRISTOL in 1770, but the process was restricted until 1796 when the patent expired.

Porcelain – Soft-Paste

To find suitable substitutes for Chinese HARD-PASTE PORCELAIN, experiments took place in Europe using a mixture of white sand, gypsum, soda, alum, salt, clay and lime. When fired at low temperatures a translucent, creamy or ivory white porcelain was obtained. It had a texture similar to glass and consequently broke or cracked if boiled water was poured on it. It was, therefore, used only for making ornamental pieces until it was found that adding soapstone strengthened it.

Porcelain Manufacture

Porcelain is a translucent ware, while earthenware is opaque. English porcelain is of two types, HARD-PASTE and SOFT-PASTE. Until the middle of the 18th century porcelain was imported from China, and attempts to reproduce oriental porcelain in England in 1506 had resulted in failure. The method of making the hard, translucent porcelain was unknown in Europe until the beginning of the 18th century, when it was produced at a factory at Meissen near Dresden. A less suitable material, soft-paste porcelain, was used in France and introduced to England. This was improved by adding soapstone and in the 1790s by the addition of bone ash. A number of porcelain factories were built in the 1740–1800 period, including CHELSEA (1743), DERBY (1749), WORCESTER (1751), Lowestoft (1757), NEW HALL (1781) and MINTON (1796). Others set up in the first decades of the 19th century include Nantgarw (1813) and Madeley (1825).

There was an increasing demand for porcelain table ware and the introduction of TRANFER PRINTING, BONE CHINA and more efficient kilns improved both the quality and quantity of the porcelain. Hard-paste porcelain was first made by WILLIAM COOKWORTHY using Cornish CHINA CLAY or kaolin in 1768. By 1815 French Sèvres porcelain, with its rich colours and translucency, was almost unobtainable, and the demand in England was met by factories such as Madeley being set up to copy the old Sèvres style. By 1840, however, the demand for this type of porcelain had fallen away.

Porter

A type of beer first brewed in 1722 by

Ralph Harwood. It was a black, thick beer, stronger and more bitter than existing ales, and was matured in casks for a year or more. Technically it was suited to mass production and exploited more efficiently the raw materials, malt and hops. The new beer was adopted by brewers in the 1740s and a number of large-scale breweries were established by the end of the century.

Portland Cement

Patented in 1824 by a LEEDS bricklayer, Joseph Aspdin (1799–1855). He found that a very strong cement was made when a mixture of chalk and clay was calcined at a temperature which caused it to coalesce without melting. It took its name from Portland stone but its grey colour meant it was not a suitable substitute for that material. The first Portland cement works was set up on the Medway in Kent in 1851, and from the 1850s Portland cement was increasingly used instead of the lime cements because it was stronger and set more rapidly. Mixed with stones it formed concrete.

Ports

Until the railway network (see RAILWAY DEVELOPMENT) had been built there were over 500 small ports around the coast which catered for local fishermen and the COASTAL TRADE. Overseas trade was handled by a few larger ports and concentrated heavily on LONDON, which dealt with three-quarters of the imports and exports. In the 18th century BRISTOL was the second port, but it quickly lost ground after 1800 to LIVERPOOL and then GLASGOW.

During the period 1760–1860 trade increased enormously and existing ports expanded by building new docks, dredging the entrances and increasing the land area available for warehouses, cranes and later railway sidings. Improvements were made on the Clyde at Glasgow between 1773 and 1781, and in London the West India Docks were opened in 1802, the London Docks in 1805, the East India Docks in 1806 and St Katherine's Dock in 1829. At Liverpool the Albert Dock opened in 1845 and Stanley Dock in 1848. Many of these docks, particularly the Albert Dock and its adjacent warehouses, are impressive monuments of 19th-century engineering.

The CANAL engineers of the time, including JOHN SMEATON, WILLIAM JESSOP, THOMAS TELFORD, JOHN RENNIE, ISAMBARD BRUNEL and JESSE HARTLEY, had to excavate basins and provide massive dock walls, LOCK gates and warehouses to meet the needs of the growing number of trading vessels. These included steamships (see STEAM BOATS) after about 1820. Smaller ports dealing with coastal or cross-Channel trade were also improved and enlarged and a few new coastal and continental trading ports were built, including Seaham in County Durham, Shoreham in Sussex (1760s) and Goole at the Humber end of the Aire and Calder Canal in 1826. Many small schemes and the large dock basins can be seen today.

Visit Albert Dock, Liverpool – Merseyside Maritime Museum. **M***
Industrial Museum, Bristol – 19th-century warehouses, floating dock, transit sheds and SS *Great Britain*. **M***
Ramsgate Harbour, Kent – built by John Rennie (1806).

N. Ritchie-Noakes, *Old Docks* (Shire Publications 1986).
P. MacDougall, *Royal Dockyards* (Shire Publications 1989).

Potbank

The early name given to a works producing pottery. The works were usually small and limited to making plain, glazed and earthenware pots. Clay and other materials might be bought from a larger pottery and on average the small works employed perhaps 20 people in 1769. In that year Arthur Young estimated there were 300 houses in the potteries engaged as potbanks. From about 1780 potbanks were called MANUFACTORIES.

Potteries, The

A region of North Staffordshire which became the centre of the pottery industry during the INDUSTRIAL REVOLUTION.

It is believed that JOHN ASTBURY of Shelton, Stoke-on-Trent, developed a SALT-GLAZED WARE, called stoneware, that was white throughout, using white-burning clay and calcined flint. There was a large market for stoneware since it was much cheaper than imported PORCELAIN. About 1750 Enoch Booth of Tunstall introduced double firing – before and after applying the glaze. He also dipped the products, after the first firing, into a slip of liquid glaze containing lead oxide. This gave the Staffordshire earthenware a cream colour, later improved by JOSIAH WEDGWOOD, who set up a pottery at Burslem in 1759 and 10 years later built his works and housing about 3 miles (5 km) away at ETRURIA on the TRENT AND MERSEY CANAL.

The region became important after the building of this canal in 1777 and improvements to the roads. Close by were plentiful supplies of cheap coal and a wide variety of clays, and there was a tradition of pottery-making in the villages of the region. By 1787 there were 200 master potters in the district and some 20,000 workers.

D. Sekkers, *The Potteries* (Shire Publications).

Power Loom Weaving

The first power loom was patented by EDMUND CARTWRIGHT in 1787. Some of his looms were powered by waterwheels but as early as 1789 he was using steam power in his BIRMINGHAM factory. In the last decade of the 18th century the power loom was very unpopular with the HAND LOOM WEAVERS. Weavers burnt down factories and destroyed looms, including a large mill near MANCHESTER partly owned by Edmund Cartwright. The power loom was, however, a valuable MACHINE because advances in spinning machinery had not been matched by more efficient weaving machines and weaving was still largely done by hand.

At the beginning of the 19th century there were only a few hundred power looms, but an unskilled boy could weave three and a half pieces of material on a power loom in the time a skilled weaver using the fly shuttle wove only one. The hand loom weavers were forced into poverty as their wages dropped, and it became cheaper to use hand loom weavers than buy power looms. Nevertheless, by the 1830s power looms dominated the industry in England, but they were more slowly introduced in Scotland – in 1834 there were no power looms in Paisley, but by 1838 there were 112. By the late 1840s power looms for cotton weaving were commonplace, but the hand loom weavers held on, and in 1872 there were still 10,000 in Lanarkshire, Renfrewshire and Ayrshire, mainly making PAISLEY SHAWLS. This trade collapsed between 1870 and 1880.

Pratt ware

Lead-glazed earthenware made at Lane Delph in THE POTTERIES, at a factory started about 1775 by William Pratt (1753–99) and taken over by his son Felix in 1800. The ware had a cream-coloured body to which colours were added. It usually took the form of jugs, oval plaques and figurines. Pratt ware became very popular and was copied by other potters. In the mid-19th century pot lids and other wares were made with polychrome TRANSFER PRINTS.

G. and J. Lewis, *Prattware 1760–1840* (Antique Collectors' Club 1984).

Press Gang

A group of men who were active in coastal regions in forcing men to join the army or navy, particularly in times of war. Between 1793 and 1800 no less than 2,781 seamen were impressed for the navy at the ports of NEWCASTLE and Sunderland in the North East. A further 1,597 'volunteered' for service and in 1790, even though there was no war, colliers operating between Hartley and Blyth in Northumberland could not sail because so many men had been taken. As a result prices rose in LONDON. In 1803 the North East trade was almost halted by a press gang which took some keelmen and prevented others from working for fear of being taken.

Impressment into the army ceased in 1815 and into the navy in the 1830s, when improvements in pay and conditions of service led to suitable volunteers enlisting.

Price Changes

Research suggests that the price of a typical basket of consumers' goods showed no increase between 1730 and 1760. A rise of nearly 40 per cent was shown between 1760 and 1792, and a doubling of prices between 1793 and 1813, the period of the NAPOLEONIC WARS.

Bad harvests in 1795 and 1796 caused a rapid rise in the price of wheat, and after further fluctuations the price rose again, until by 1801 it was nearly three times the 1792 price. This was a famine price and Parliament passed laws closing distilleries and starch factories to save grain. The return to peace in 1802 resulted in a fall in the price of wheat, but the price rose once more when hostilities were resumed during the next year. The prices of other foodstuffs, such as meat, cheese and potatoes, also rose, and the average WORKING-CLASS family was forced by high prices to eat a monotonous diet of bread, cheese, porridge and skimmed milk.

Priestley, Dr Joseph (1773–1804)

A theologian, philosopher and chemist who discovered the properties of oxygen. He was a DISSENTER, strong supporter the cause of the FRENCH REVOLUTION and an active member of the LUNAR SOCIETY. He kept in close contact with JOSIAH WEDGWOOD and received from him an annual gift of 25 guineas (£26. 5s. 0d – $44.6) towards the cost of his experiments. In 1783 he was elected a Fellow of the Royal Society. During the BIRMINGHAM RIOTS in 1791 his laboratory and home were destroyed. In 1793 his three sons emigrated to America and Joseph Priestley followed the next year, living there until his death.

A.D. Orange, *Joseph Priestley* (Shire Publications 1974).

Prince Albert of Saxe-Coburg and Gotha (1819–61) (Also known as the Prince Consort)

The husband of QUEEN VICTORIA, whom

he married in 1840. He was willing to work long hours with Germanic thoroughness and championed serious causes such as the abolition of slavery. He strongly encouraged scientific research and took an active interest in industry and in the Society for Improving the Condition of the Labouring Classes, founded in 1844. He also played an important part in organizing the GREAT EXHIBITION, 1851. He cared little for rank or the aristocracy and was condemned by members of the UPPER CLASSES with entrenched views.

R. Pound, *Albert – A Biography of the Prince Consort* (Michael Joseph 1973).

Printing Press

The Times was, in 1814, the first newspaper to be printed on a press driven by steam and using horizontal cylinders. The press was designed by a German immigrant, Friedrich Koenig – previously printing had been done on a hand press at a quarter of the speed. Improvements were made to Koenig's machine by a press manufacturer, DAVID NAPIER. In 1857 a machine reached England from the United States, having been invented by Richard Hoe, the son of a Leicestershire man who had emigrated. The machine was large and was installed by *The Times* and other newspapers. It could provide 20,000 impressions an hour, but it needed 25 people to operate it.

Visit Whitefriars, Norwich, Norfolk – John Jarrold Printing Museum; printing machines from 1825. **M***

Professional Institutions

Local clubs of men in well-established professions such as medicine and law evolved into professional institutions, including the Law Society (1825) and the British Medical Association (1856). New or greatly expanded professions also set up institutions which exercised control over recruitment, competence and conduct within the profession. They included the Civil Engineers (1818), Architects (1848) and Ships' Masters and Navigators (1857). Others followed in the second half of the 19th century. By Act of Parliament these institutions were granted self-governing status, which made them independent of pressure from government departments.

Prostitution

In the 19th century prostitution was extensive in the cities and larger towns, although accurate statistics on it do not exist. The root causes of the evil were the appalling economic and social conditions of some groups within the WORKING CLASSES and the attitudes to prostitutes displayed by the MIDDLE CLASS.

Large numbers of women were forced onto the streets by poverty – the result of low wages, unemployment or in some cases improvidence. For many respectable working women existence was drab, hours of work were long and pay low, with no opportunities for financial independence. In the squalor of the time prostitution was accepted as unavoidable by members of the working classes.

Late marriage was common among the middle class and the medical profession warned against the possibility of untold horrors, leading to insanity and death, which could result from masturbation. To the married middle-class man in an age when contraception was little used, prostitutes were a useful source of release, an acceptable form of birth control. The sexual attitudes of many members of the male-dominated society encouraged prostitution and limited legal sanctions. The idealistic view held by middle-class society of feminine purity and the need for chastity among middle-class girls did not extend to those who were considered socially inferior.

Various attempts were made throughout the century to suppress prostitution. In 1812 the Guardian Society formed a committee to discover the best means of driving prostitutes from the streets and supplying a refuge for those who wished to reform, and in 1815 prostitutes in London were being vigorously prosecuted. In 1842 the Committee of the London Society for the Protection of Young Females presented a bill which would have given the police

more power over brothels. The Bill was withdrawn, but 40 years later a similar attempt was made through the Criminal Law Amendment Bill. This was talked out in the Commons.

By the 1850s prostitutes were being mentioned in literature and were to be seen in public places at all hours of the day. The middle class, however, had a talent for not seeing the unpleasantly obvious, hiding behind their own veneer of respectability. In 1864 the Contagious Diseases Act was passed to control venereal disease in the prostitute population. It allowed police doctors to examine medically any woman they thought to be a prostitute. No action was taken to give men who had been with prostitutes a similar examination. Women registered as prostitutes had to undergo regular examination or face penal servitude with hard labour. A campaign against the Act was started by JOSEPHINE BUTLER, assisted by her husband George, and after a long campaign the Act was abolished in 1883.

Public Health Act, 1848

Early attempts to improve health included Acts of Parliament, requested by some towns for such things as lighting, cleaning and water supply. The 1848 Act followed a CHOLERA epidemic and the revelations made in EDWIN CHADWICK's Sanitary Report of 1842, as well as the reports of the HEALTH OF TOWNS COMMISSION of 1844 and 1845. The Act established a Central Board of Health of three members, with powers to initiate sanitary measures. In districts with municipal institutions the town council was to be the public health authority. Other districts were to have local boards of health. Medical officers of health could be appointed, although this was not obligatory. The local board had powers to provide a water supply and no new houses were to be built without some form of lavatory.

Such strength and purpose as the Act had, it owed to Edwin Chadwick. It improved conditions in those towns where it was introduced. The Act had enabled the Central Board to force the hand of a reluctant local authority, but not to compel the authority to take any effective action. The Central Board had no powers of inspection and a local authority that chose to neglect its duty could defy the Board. The Board was dissolved in 1854 after mounting criticism of its interference with local self-government.

F.B. Smith, *The People's Health, 1830–1910* (Croom Helm 1979).

Public Libraries Act, 1850

An Act making it possible for authorities to levy a rate to subsidize the provision of libraries. It was a permissive Act, which meant it could be obstructed or delayed locally. By 1869 only 35 towns had adopted the Act and opened public libraries. Where they were opened they were patronized by WORKING-CLASS people.

Puddler

A worker in the IRON INDUSTRY who had the task of stirring the molten iron in the furnace with a slurry-bar during PUDDLING. The work was extremely hard and took place at high temperatures. It was considered by some to be the toughest regular work in any industry. The puddler also needed to develop a feel for the process, to learn how to read the colour of the flames in the furnace and to know the texture of the molten metal when the carbon and other impurities had been sufficiently removed from the PIG IRON.

Puddling

A process patented by HENRY CORT in 1783–4. It was a method for refining WROUGHT IRON from CAST IRON, which was normally PIG IRON or scrap. The fuel did not come into contact with the metal because the fire's heat was reflected off the ceiling of the REVERBERATORY FURNACE down to the metal. The molten pig iron formed a pool or puddle in the furnace, giving the process its name. When molten, the pig iron was stirred by a PUDDLER, bringing impurities to the surface to be burned off. Puddling was also linked to rolling, with reheated metal being shaped between rollers to form bars.

Puddling spread after about 1790 when technical problems had been solved. The high profits made in the NAPOLEONIC WARS encouraged the rapid adoption of puddling and an increase in output. About 1830 WET PUDDLING or pig boiling was developed by JOSEPH HALL. He lined the puddling furnace with roasted slag instead of cast iron. When pig iron was placed in the furnace the oxygen in the lining combined with the carbon in the iron in a violent manner, making the pig iron 'boil'. This process speeded up refining and reduced pig iron wastage.

Puffing Billy

An early locomotive, built by WILLIAM HEDLEY in 1813 at the same time as another locomotive, the *WYLAM DILLY*. They both operated on the Wylam Colliery TRAMWAY near NEWCASTLE.

Visit Science Museum, London – original engine. **M***

Pupil-Teacher System

A system of teacher training introduced by SIR JAMES KAY-SHUTTLEWORTH in 1846, to provide more teachers and as an improvement to the MONITORIAL SYSTEM. Classroom monitors were replaced by pupil apprentices. These pupil-teachers, who were paid, had to be at least 13 years of age and had to pass an annual examination conducted by the school inspectors. At the end of the APPRENTICESHIP, at age 18, they were eligible to compete for Queen's scholarships. The scholarships were tenable at the teachers' training colleges which were opened in the 1840s and 1850s.

The system was designed to provide the opportunity for elementary school children to be trained as teachers and then to teach in elementary schools themselves. It remained as the basis for teacher training until the 20th century.

Pyrometer

An instrument for measuring high temperatures which was invented by JOSIAH WEDGWOOD to measure heat in pottery ovens. He carried out careful experiments over a long period of time and noted that the amount of shrinkage in clays increased with the degree of heat. The results of his experiments were read as a paper to the Royal Society in 1782, and the next year he was elected a fellow of the Royal Society. His pyrometer greatly reduced the number of failures in fired wares and increased the proportion of successes.

Quakers

The name given to members of the Society of Friends, founded by George Fox (1624–91), who began preaching in 1647 and continued at home and overseas until his death. In the 1660s organized groups of Quakers emigrated to Massachusetts in America and established their own businesses. Quakers founded Pennsylvania in 1681 and spread to other areas of the 13 American colonies. At first rigid Puritans, they gained respect for their sincerity and activities in humanitarian and philanthropic enterprises.

Many industrialists were Quakers; they formed a successful and progressive group who were well known for their honesty and philanthropy. The DARBYS of COALBROOKDALE were Quakers as were other ironmasters including William Rowlinson of Backbarrow, Isaac Spooner of BIRMINGHAM and the HUNTSMANS of SHEFFIELD. Intermarriage between Quaker families was common. It brought about links between the Crowleys of CROWLEY IRONWORKS and the Lloyds (Birmingham ironmasters), and between the Lloyds and the Pembertons (Birmingham ironmongers and bankers), and there are many other similar examples which help to explain the relative ease with which trading agreements were effected.

Quaker other-worldliness led to the reinvestment of wealth in the business and the refusal to sacrifice principles, such as the shutting down of the furnaces on Sundays, by the Derbys at Coalbrookdale, even though this created many technical difficulties.

A. Raistrick, *Quakers in Science and Industry* (Bannisdale Press 1968).

Quarry Bank Mill

A spinning mill built at Styal in Cheshire by SAMUEL GREG in 1784. People from the neighbouring counties of Lancashire, Cheshire and Staffordshire worked at the mill, as well as PAUPER APPRENTICES from the WORKHOUSES of LONDON and LIVERPOOL. Housing was provided, with large gardens and a dormitory for the apprentices. At first there were 150 operatives spinning coarse yarn on WATER FRAMES. In 1801 a weir was built to provide water for two new wheels. In 1816 there were 252 operatives, and after further expansion over 2,000 were employed by 1833. A school, a chapel, a shop and a MECHANICS' INSTITUTE were added to the village.

The mill was recognized as an archetype of the rural factory *c.*1840, and put forward as exemplifying everything that was good about the FACTORY SYSTEM. It closed in 1959 with descendants of Samuel Greg still playing an active part.

Visit Styal, Cheshire – Quarry Bank Mill; mill now a working museum. **M***

Queen's College   See Governess

R

Radcliffe, William (1760–1841)

A cotton MANUFACTURER and inventor. The family moved from farming into weaving, and William learned carding and spinning in the family workshop. After marrying in 1785 he set up business on his own, and by 1789 was well-established employing both spinners and weavers at MELLOR, near Stockport in Lancashire. By 1801 he was giving work to over 1,000 weavers.

To speed up the weaving process an adhesive size was applied to the yarn by hand. In 1803 Radcliffe invented a MACHINE in which the yarn passed through the size on rollers. A fan speeded the drying process, which could be used with POWER LOOMS. About 1804 he invented a ratchet wheel connected to the loom, which moved the cloth forward automatically. Hand looms equipped with this action were called dandy looms.

Radicals

The name given to groups and individuals who desired thoroughgoing reforms. Some radicals sought reforms by argument and persuasion, others were prepared to take more militant action. In this period radicals were particularly active in attacking the COMBINATION ACTS and supporting the movement for the REFORM ACT, 1832, the ANTI-CORN LAW LEAGUE and CHARTISM.

Raikes, Robert (1735–1811)

A SUNDAY SCHOOL organizer and owner of a newspaper, the *Gloucester Journal*. He opened three Sunday schools in Gloucester in 1780, and carried on a campaign for more Sunday schools through his newspaper. Many more were opened for adults and children in different parts of the country; they provided the first opportunity for many people to learn to read.

Railway Acts, 1839, 1844

Lord Seymour was responsible for the 1839 Act, which set up a railway department at the Board of Trade in 1840. This department, through its inspectors, supervised the railway companies and particularly their safety standards. WILLIAM GLADSTONE promoted the 1844 Act, which made it possible for the state to take over a private railway company which had not complied with the Board of Trade regulations by 1865. This threat encouraged the railway companies to obey the regulations. The Act also required each company to run one passenger train a day along the length of their lines at the cheap rate of one penny (2 US cents) a mile (1.6 km). The carriages on this train had to be provided with seats and protected from the weather.

Railway – Bridges and Viaducts

Whereas railway bridges either had a single arch or were supported by a small number of pillars, the viaducts consisted of multiple arches and were extensions of embankments, a means of traversing the ground using minimum land surface.

In the early days of railways many bridges and viaducts were made of timber. ISAMBARD BRUNEL, for example, used timber trusses between 1845 and 1860. A number of laminated bridges and viaducts were also built by gluing individual pieces of timber together. Timber structures were prone to fire and decay and none has survived. A few of the earliest bridges were in CAST IRON, including the girder bridge of the Cromford and High Peak Railway. Most of the oldest metal bridges that have survived are of WROUGHT IRON. Brunel used a wrought-iron girder form at Chepstow, and ROBERT STEPHENSON's Britannia Bridge over the MENAI Straits consisted of wrought-iron tubes raised into place with hydraulic lifting tackle. The first British bridge to use MILD STEEL was the Forth Railway Bridge in 1890.

Viaducts were frequently used in towns to enable stations to be placed in central positions with little disruption to existing buildings, roads and CANALS. The heights of the viaducts varied considerably, as did the number of supporting arches. The Stockport, Lancashire, viaduct consists of 22 arches 110 feet (33.5 m) high, and has an overall length of 1,800 feet (548 m).

Viaducts were also constructed to cross deep inland valleys. If stone was available it was considered the best building material; if not, brick was the best substitute. A number were built by Robert Stephenson and the form he developed with high, stone-faced piers on pier bases, continued to be used into the 20th century. The Settle–Carlisle railway line included 20 viaducts along its 72-mile (116-km) route.

Visit Saltash, Devon – Prince Albert Bridge (1859).
Balcombe Viaduct – London–Brighton Line (1839).

Railway – Canterbury and Whitstable

Opened in 1830, this was the first railway (five months before the LIVERPOOL AND MANCHESTER RAILWAY), to provide a regular passenger service. Trains were hauled by a stationary engine for 4 miles (6.4 km) over the steepest part of the route and for the other 2 miles (3.2 km) by GEORGE STEPHENSON's locomotive *Invicta*. The journey took 35–40 minutes and there were 10 trains a day. Passengers rode in open wagons.

Visit Dane John Gardens, Canterbury – locomotive *Invicta*. **M***

R.L. Ratcliffe, *The Canterbury and Whitstable Railway* (Locomotive Club of Great Britain 1980).

Railway Coaches

Important passengers on the STOCKTON AND DARLINGTON RAILWAY in 1825 were carried in a coach specially made for the opening ceremony. It had a 'door at each end, glass panes to the windows, a table and seats for inside, top seat and steps, cushioned and carpeted' and was called the *Experiment*.

By the 1830s first class coaches consisted of three compartments built together, with luggage and a brakesman riding on the roof. Similar accommodation was provided for second class passengers but the seats were hard. Third class passengers sat in uncomfortable open trucks.

During the period from 1840 to 1870 a typical first class passenger coach had three compartments placed on an underframe with four wheels. Second class passengers could normally expect a roof, walls and windows but no padded upholstery. Third class passengers were given a wall to waist level, and no more shelter until the RAILWAYS ACT 1844, insisted on seats protected from the weather. Companies complied with the basic requirements and the Midland Railway provided three compartment coaches for third class passengers by 1845.

All coaches were low until the 1860s and passengers had to sit down and take off their hats. There was no lavatory provision or refreshment facilities but stops were lengthy at suitably equipped stations. First class accommodation had crude sleeping facilities by the 1840s and oil lighting a few years later. The first gas lamps were used on the Metropolitan Railway in 1863 and experiments with electric lights started in the 1880s. Heating was more difficult and ordinary travellers had to use hot-water bottles supplied at the stations. Passenger facilities remained basic until the end of the 19th century, except for those who travelled first class.

Railway Development

Between 1800 and 1820 iron railway construction was limited to small-scale, localized railways, most being attached to a coal mine or ironworks and using horses or stationary engines to pull wagons. Some 300 miles (483 km) were open to the public by 1830 and the steam railway age had begun.

Between 1830 and 1855 nearly all the main railway lines from LONDON had been either built or planned for much of their length, and by 1855 over 8,000 miles (13,000 km) of track had been laid. The peak building period was reached in 1847 when nearly 6,500 miles (10,460 km) were under construction. There was opposition from some landowners to the railways. Farmers near towns feared food would be brought in more cheaply from outlying districts and a number of towns, including the five towns of THE POTTERIES, refused to give permission for the railways to pass through them. Eton College forced ISAMBARD BRUNEL to make a detour when laying the GREAT WESTERN RAILWAY track, and Oxford UNIVERSITY held back the railway for many years, not allowing it any nearer than Didcot. No natural network was planned and development was piecemeal, with two different gauges (see RAILWAY GAUGES). Parliament wanted to uphold the principle of competition but was forced to recognize that monopolies were bound to take place. THE RAILWAYS ACT 1844, made the offering of cheap travel obligatory, although the compulsory train per day was often notoriously slow and inconvenient. The Gauge Act, 1846, provided for a uniform gauge in due course.

Railway shares were a popular form of investment for the MIDDLE CLASSES and there were a series of booms or manias when speculators rushed to buy shares in the hope of quick profits. The first mania was in 1824–5, the next in 1835–7 and the third in 1844–6. Each boom was followed by a lull, with the promotion mania giving way to several years of construction. Many of the proposals were dubious financially and some were corrupt. In 1846 the financial bubble burst and many speculators, including the 'Railway King', GEORGE HUDSON, were ruined.

After 1855 much of the new railway growth was in suburban and branch lines. Railway development made profound changes to social life. The growth of towns was largely due to railways and new towns were created by them. Associated industries such as coal, iron and engineering expanded to meet the demands of the railway age.

Visit Wylam, Northumberland – Railway Museum. **M**[*]
National Railway Museum, York. **M**[*]

Railway Gauges

The railway network developed in the 1830s and early 1840s with two gauges, the standard gauge of 4 feet 8½ inches (1.55 m) and the broad gauge of 7 feet 0¼ inches (2.2 m). Passengers had to transfer trains at places such as Gloucester where the two gauges met. In 1845 a Royal Commission heard evidence and held trials to recommend the most suitable gauge. The fact that only 10 per cent of the lines were in the broad gauge resulted in the Gauge Act 1846, which made the standard gauge compulsory for new railways. The GREAT WESTERN RAILWAY retained its wider gauge until 1892, when it was converted to the standard gauge.

The origin of the standard gauge is obscure. It probably derived from the TRAMWAYS of northern England where cart wheels had to be far enough apart to be drawn by a horse without overturning.

Railway – Great Western

Promoted in 1832 as a line from LONDON to BRISTOL. ISAMBARD BRUNEL was chosen as the engineer to survey the route in the following year. The first section was opened in 1838, but the line was not completed until 1841 because of difficulties in boring the 1¾-miles (2.8-km) Box Tunnel through the Cotswolds. The line was designed as broad gauge (see RAILWAY GAUGES), and an ornate gothic terminus was built at Bristol Temple Meads. The line is an example of the brilliance of Brunel's civil engineering work. His attention to detail was thorough, extending to the smallest wayside station, the bridges and the signals.

Visit Exploratory Museum, The Old Station, Temple Meads, Bristol. **M**[*]
Swindon, Wiltshire – Great Western Railway Museum. **M**[*]
Great Western Society Ltd – Didcot Railway Station.

F. Booker, *The Great Western Railway* (David and Charles 1985).

Railway – Impact on the Economy

The railway building programme had an enormous impact on the economy. Between 1846 and 1848 railway investment was absorbing 5–7 per cent of the national income, about half of the CAPITAL investment, with a quarter of a million men constructing the lines. The railway building programme also had a considerable effect on other industries. The IRON INDUSTRY grew enormously and coal production was stimulated by a demand for one million tonnes (1.12 million US tons) for the railways. The brick industry expanded to meet the increased demand and the railways brought about increased URBAN GROWTH. Long-distance COACH SERVICES had virtually ceased to run by 1850 and the CANAL network stagnated. Road conditions also deteriorated with the winding up of TURNPIKE trusts.

Railway – Liverpool and Manchester

In 1824 GEORGE STEPHENSON was appointed as engineer and carried out a survey for a railway between the port of LIVERPOOL and the manufacturing town of MANCHESTER. An Act of Parliament giving consent to the line was strongly contested by landowners and coach proprietors, and Stephenson's survey was shown to be inaccurate. The Bill was defeated in 1825.

A new surveyor, Charles Vignoles, resurveyed the line and an Act setting up the Liverpool–Manchester Railway Company was passed in 1826. George Stephenson was brought back as engineer and the physical difficulties were overcome brilliantly by building RAILWAY TUNNELS and a viaduct (see RAILWAY BRIDGES AND VIADUCTS) and by the use of brushwood as foundations across the peat bog of CHAT MOSS. The type of locomotive was decided by the RAINHILL TRIALS in 1829, which George Stephenson's *Rocket* won. The opening of the line in 1830 was marred by the death of WILLIAM HUSKISSON, an MP who had supported the railway but was run down by the *Rocket* and died later.

R.H.G. Thomas, *The Liverpool and Manchester Railway* (Batsford 1980).

Railway Mail Coaches

The Grand Junction Railway provided MAIL COACHES on its trains from about 1840. The coach was first class and carried four passengers per compartment instead of six, and in one compartment the seats could be converted into a bed. Mail bags were carried in a large box on the roof, guarded by a Post Office mail guard high up on an external seat. Spectacles were provided to prevent sparks from the boiler getting into the guard's eyes. Mail coaches had, by law, to carry the Royal Arms painted on the outside. By 1842 there were 20 Post Office mail guards employed on railway routes, and as the railway network developed mail was transferred to trains. In some cases road coaches were transferred to rails. The *Quicksilver* coach, for example, was carried by train from LONDON to Basingstoke and then continued its journey by road. Connections were also arranged between road mail coaches and railway mail coach services, but many long-distance road deliveries could not compete with the railways.

Railway Stations

One of the most striking architectural developments of the mid-19th century was the building of railway termini and large city stations. In scale the buildings came close to the cathedrals of the Middle Ages.

In all railway stations the distinction must be made between the operational parts, that is the tracks and platforms, and the ancillary parts including booking offices, waiting rooms and administrative offices. These ancillary facilities are usually located in forebuildings which, in the case of termini, face the ends of the tracks and platforms. Through stations have their forebuildings to one side.

Once the tracks were laid at larger stations there was the problem of overall roofing. This resulted in some spectacular architectural engineering, providing covered areas and train sheds with iron arched roofs. This form of roof construction was first used at NEWCASTLE

Central in 1848, and the style was repeated in many major cities including York (1874), BIRMINGHAM New Street (now replaced), MIDDLESBROUGH (destroyed during the Second World War 1939–45), and LONDON Bridge (1866).

The earliest great London terminus still intact is King's Cross, which was completed in 1852 by Joseph and SIR WILLIAM CUBITT. Paddington was completed two years later, to the design of ISAMBARD BRUNEL assisted by Digby Wyatt, with a magnificent train shed supported by CAST-IRON columns. Other London termini include St Pancras (1865–76), with a train shed manufactured by the BUTTERLEY COMPANY, and Liverpool Street, 1875. Outside London, Brunel's terminus train shed at BRISTOL Temple Meads (1841) has survived with a Tudor gothic forecourt building. Newcastle Central (1848–65) and York are also proof of the brilliance of the railway engineers.

Large hotels were sometimes added to the city stations. The Great Northern Hotel at King's Cross was built in 1854 and the Charing Cross Hotel opened in 1864.

Smaller town and country stations did not have overall roofing but the forebuildings were often designed for the railway companies with distinctive house styles. The Jacobean manor-house style was a favourite with early station architects and was used in 1850 at Stoke-on-Trent, the most important station of the North Staffordshire Railway. Opposite the station is the North Stafford Hotel, just like a Jacobean mansion on the outside. Smaller Tudor stations built by this company include Rushton and Cheddleton.

The opening of the Stockton and Darlington Railway on 27 September 1825. This painting by John Dobbins shows many facets of transport in addition to the railway. The variety of vehicles on the road, which is the Darlington to Durham turnpike, includes a stagewagon and a stagecoach as well as various private carriages. The little boy has a toy steamboat with wheels on a piece of string. Ahead of the train is a horseman carrying a flag. The engine is the *Locomotion* driven by George Stephenson. The railway company's passenger coach is attached to 21 open wagons fitted with seats and crowded with passengers. At times the train reached a speed of 15 mph (24 km) and the journey ended with a banquet at Stockton Town Hall. (*The Borough of Darlington Museum*)

The Newcastle and Berwick Railway built a collection of Tudor stations including Chathill and Acklington. While most of the flamboyant architecture was reserved to gain prestige, many minor stations have great architectural merit. The list is very long and must include Stone, Staffordshire (gabled Jacobean), Gobowen, Shropshire (Italianate), Monkwearmouth, Tyne and Wear (Greek Revival) and Battle, East Sussex (Victorian gothic).

M. Binnie and D. Pearce (eds), *Railway Architecture* (Bloomsbury Press 1979). F.G. Cockman, *Railway Architecture* (Shire Publications 1988).

Railway – Stockton and Darlington

This was built as a transport route in the North East between the collieries of southwest Durham and their markets at Darlington and Stockton. A line was surveyed by George Overton from the collieries to both towns, a distance of 26 miles (42 km), and an Act forming the Stockton and Darlington Railway Company was passed in 1821. Overton's idea of a horse-drawn railway was rejected in favour of GEORGE STEPHENSON's steam locomotives. Stephenson became the railway's engineer and used T-section WROUGHT-IRON rails. The work on the line started in 1822 and it was opened in 1825 using the engine *Locomotion*, driven by George Stephenson and pulling a passenger coach as well as coal wagons.

Visit North Road, Darlington – Darlington Railway Centre and Museum; locomotives and other relics of the line. **M***

Railway – Surrey Iron

The first public railway, opened in 1804 between Croydon and the River Thames at Wandsworth. It provided a railroad for goods wagons and carts, which paid tolls as on a TURNPIKE. Like a CANAL it had a towpath, because the wagons were pulled by horses. It was 9 miles (14 km) long and was intended to be the first section of a line between LONDON and Portsmouth.

Visit Purley, Surrey – Surrey Iron Railway track at Rotary Field. **M***

Railway Towns

There are two main types of railway town. The first group consists of towns developed by the railways for their own purposes, either from nothing or as an addition to an existing village or market town, so that the town was dominated by the railway, with any existing settlement completely submerged by the new RAILWAY DEVELOPMENT. Crewe, Eastleigh, Wolverton, Swindon, Horwich and Shildon are the main towns of this type.

Another group of towns became the focus for railway works and the railway became the most powerful local employer. Ashford, Darlington, Dorchester, Gateshead, Oswestry and Derby come in this category, together with the very important railway junctions of York, Carlisle and Peterborough. Some very much smaller country towns, and even some villages, became important engineering centres with locomotive sheds and other railway installations. These included Wellingborough, Grantham, Boston, Didcot, Bletchley, Tebay (Cumbria), Hellafield (Lancashire) and Melton Mowbray in Leicestershire. The oldest of these smaller centres is Earlestown, Lancashire.

At Newton-le-Willows a factory to produce parts required in railway engineering was set up in 1830–2. This factory grew in 1847 and made locomotives for the overseas market. In 1853 the London and North Western Company decided to make railway wagons nearby, and a collection of cottages built for the men was given the name Earlestown, after Sir Hardman Earle, a member of the North Western Railway Board. Later Earlestown became part of the urban district of Newton-le-Willows and never became a separate town.

Of the towns completely dominated by the railway works, the oldest was Shildon, where the STOCKTON AND DARLINGTON RAILWAY began to establish works to maintain its locomotives in 1826.

Although the land on which the town grew belonged to the railway company the erection of houses and streets was unplanned. Like many other railway towns the sequence of events was the construction of railways buildings, which attracted skilled workers from other areas, followed by the building of estates for these workers, to which were often added a church, schools and other public buildings. At Wolverton in North Buckinghamshire, at roughly the midway point, the London and Birmingham Railway established a settlement, which by 1844 had streets, a church, schools, a market and about 200 houses, all provided by the railway. About 180 locomotives were made at Wolverton between 1845 and 1863.

The Great Junction Railway moved its works from Edge Hill to Crewe, which was to become a very important junction. Houses were built in the mid-1840s, and the locomotive works expanded until by 1848 the works turned out a locomotive a week and employed 1,000 men. In the 1860s at Crewe a BESSEMER PROCESS steel-making plant was built and open-hearth furnaces were also installed. The town more than doubled its population in the 1860s to reach 19,000 in 1871. The railway company, which had originally planned the developments carefully, took less interest and private companies built new estates of a poorer quality. Nevertheless, the railway company gave the town a cottage hospital, schools, a church, a MECHANICS' INSTITUTE and the Queen's Park.

The GREAT WESTERN COMPANY decided to establish its works close to the small town of Swindon in Wiltshire in 1840. On the south side of the railway line contractors built 300 cottages, carefully planned to make an attractive settlement, to which were added a church and school. On the north side of the line workshops were built in 1843 and a ROLLING MILL for rails in 1861. The works steadily grew but the new town was deliberately kept apart from the old by the railway company. The settlements were fully linked by buildings about 1890 and a single borough of Swindon was created in 1900.

Not one railway town was comprehensively planned, although in some cases the first stages of the town proceeded according to a plan. This may be because the railways were joint-stock companies and accountable to the shareholders, whereas the factory masters like SIR TITUS SALT owned their mills and could plan their MODEL VILLAGES as they wished. Few of the railway towns were centres for competition between companies. In only three, Peterborough, Carlisle and Derby, were rural railway companies competing with one another to attract labour. In each of the others one railway company was the sole employer of railwaymen in the town. The companies did pay, in part, for mechanics' institutes, churches, baths, schools and sports grounds, and in so doing evolved towns that suited their own industry and its management.

Visit Great Western Railway Museum, Swindon – railway exhibits, terraces of workmen's houses, church and mechanics' institute. **M***

J. Simmons, *The Railway in Town and Country 1830–1914* (David and Charles 1986).

Railway Tunnels

Tunnels are numerous in towns as well as upland regions, mainly because of high land costs. One of the earliest tunnels was that on the LIVERPOOL AND MANCHESTER RAILWAY in LIVERPOOL, called the Wapping Tunnel. It was started in 1826 using 20 men in each of 10 gangs. The men could work for only a limited period in the darkness and cramped conditions. The work went on night and day with two shifts employed. The method was based on working in both directions from the bottom of shafts which were sunk along the line of the tunnel. Men and rock were hauled up and down in buckets using a HORSE GIN. The tunnel was lined with bricks and when the work was finished in 1828 it had a length of 2250 yards (2,057 m). It was the first to run under the city, was whitewashed throughout and had GAS LIGHTING at the Wapping end, where it emerged. At Edge Hill an area was excavated for locomotive sheds and several lines of rails to accommodate the trains.

ISAMBARD BRUNEL built the Box Tunnel on the GREAT WESTERN RAILWAY route to BRISTOL between 1838 and 1841. The tunnel is 3,212 yards (2,937 m) long. As at the Wapping Tunnel, shafts were dug as a means of removing material from the tunnel and for ventilation. A horse gin provided the lifting power and at times a tonne (1.1 US tons) of gunpowder was used each week. Construction involved round-the-clock working and progress was hindered by the ingress of water. During the final six months it is said that 4,000 men and 300 horses were at work on the project. The west portal of the Box Tunnel was visible from the TURNPIKE ROAD and it was given an impressive façade of Bath stone.

Isambard Brunel built shorter tunnels on the same route and directed the building of tunnels on the Bristol and Exeter, the Cheltenham and the GREAT WESTERN railways. The largest tunnel built was the Severn tunnel (1886) which was 4 miles 628 yards (7 km 11 m) long. Many tunnels were given elaborate portals; that at Red Hill between Leicester and Derby has a fortified appearance, while at Shugborough, Staffordshire, there are castellations.

In the churchyard of Otley Parish Church in West Yorkshire there is an elaborate gothic memorial to the men who died building the Bramhope Tunnel.

Visit Box Hill Tunnel – 5 miles (8 km) east of Bath.
Bramhope, West Yorkshire, on the Harrogate line – castellated north portal to tunnel.
Shugborough, Staffordshire – castellations and ornamentations.

Rainhill Trials

A competition held near LIVERPOOL in 1829 on a section of the LIVERPOOL TO MANCHESTER RAILWAY, to decide whether wagons on the railway should be hauled by cables attached to a stationary engine, or by a locomotive. The prize of £500 ($850) was won by GEORGE STEPHENSON's *Rocket*, which exceeded the required 10 mph (16 kph), reaching at times 30 mph (48 kph). The trials proved the value of locomotives and their ability to carry passengers much faster than could road coaches (see COACH SERVICES) or STEAM BOATS.

Visit Science Museum, London – *Sans Pareil* and *Rocket*, two of the locomotives taking part in the trials. **M***

Ramsden, Jesse (1735–1800)

An instrument maker who made the first satisfactory SCREW-CUTTING LATHE in 1778. The cutting tool was propelled along the workpiece by means of gear wheels, and the number of threads per inch depended on the gearing. The machine was needed to make long, fine-thread screws of high accuracy in order to scribe linear scales on to the mathematical and astronomical instruments which he also made.

Ransome, James (1782–1849)

The son of ROBERT RANSOME, he entered his father's business in 1795, and with his brother James Allen took out patents for improvements to PLOUGHS, THRESHING MACHINES and other farm implements. In the 1840s the firm became the largest MANUFACTURER of railway chairs for the railway industry, for which they had a patent. Patents were also taken out for keys and treenails for securing the chairs and rails. In 1849 the firm moved into new premises beside the River Orwell in Ipswich, with their own quay.

Ransome, Robert (1753–1830)

A QUAKER born in Norfolk, the son of a Wells schoolmaster. He opened a small iron foundry in Norwich in the 1780s and in 1785 he obtained a patent for tempering CAST-IRON ploughshares (see PLOUGHS). In 1789 he moved to Ipswich and developed his ploughshare business. In 1808 he introduced standardization of parts, making spares available so that delays were reduced. He retired in 1825 and his two sons JAMES and James Allen carried on the business.

Rastrick, John Urpeth (1780–1856)

An engineer who in 1827 invented a waste-heat boiler, which used the waste heat from iron furnaces to generate steam. He was the partner of a foundry at Bridgnorth, Shropshire, and the firm built a number of RICHARD TREVITHICK's stationary engines, as well as his locomotive CATCH ME WHO CAN in 1808. Under GEORGE STEPHENSON Rastrick surveyed the southern section of the Liverpool to Birmingham Railway route in 1829, and he was one of the three judges at the RAINHILL TRIALS in the same year. Later in his life he was employed to lay out a railway by the Thames and Medway Canal Company, beside the CANAL from Gravesend to Strood in Kent, and the railway was opened to passengers in 1845.

Visit National Railway Museum, York – locomotive *Agenoria*, built by John Rastrick. **M***

Rattle Chain

A winding chain used in colliery winding gear. The chains were introduced in Shropshire in the last decade of the 18th century, but the miners did not like the single-link chains, which could break suddenly. Flat chains were developed in the BLACK COUNTRY about 1800, using the idea of JOHN CURR's flat rope.

Rawlinson, Sir Robert (1810–98)

An assistant to JESSE HARTLEY, he went on to work for ROBERT STEPHENSON on a section of the London and Birmingham Railway. From 1843 to 1847 he was chief engineer to LIVERPOOL Corporation. After the passing of the PUBLIC HEALTH ACT 1848, he was chosen by EDWIN CHADWICK and began a long career as a government engineering inspector. In 1852 he advocated the use of piped SEWERS with manholes. He served on several goverment commissions and was consultant to the Swansea Waterworks Company. He became engineer-in-chief in the building of the Lliw Reservoir in Wales in 1862.

Reaping Machine

A simple MACHINE was introduced in Scotland in 1828 by REVEREND PATRICK BELL. The cutter was a series of scissors worked with a clipping action, the grain being bent over by sails. American models made by Cyrus McCormick and Obadiah Hussey were exhibited at the GREAT EXHIBITION, 1851. These machines attracted much interest and were one of the century's important developments in agriculture. The Bell machine, which had sold in small numbers, received a new lease of life after 1851 and by 1860 there were many hundreds of reaping machines in use, some developed from the American machines.

Reciprocity of Duties Act, 1823

An Act permitting government ministers to make tariff treaties with any country willing to accept a mutual tariff reduction. In the next few years several trade agreements were made with European countries and the new South American states, whose independence from Spain had been recognized in 1823.

Reform Act, 1832

Before 1832 representation in the House of Commons was based on the distribution of the population in Tudor times, and the changes in the population distribution pattern brought about by the INDUSTRIAL REVOLUTION were ignored, with the result that large numbers of people were not represented in Parliament. Towns like MANCHESTER and BIRMINGHAM had no member of Parliament, whereas some small villages and almost empty rural areas returned two members. These inequalities and the restrictive measures taken by the government in the years following 1815 resulted in social unrest, intensified by a slump in the economy in 1830.

The 1832 Reform Act was an attempt to correct some, but not all, of the inequalities. There was a redistribution of seats and new ones were formed, although the same overall number of 658 was retained. Anomalies still remained; the South of England was still over-represented, and Scotland, with three times the population of Wales, had less than twice as many seats. Seats were given to the northern industrial towns but county representation was also increased, strengthening the landed interests. Men of moderate means were given the vote, based on property ownership or tenancy, but such groups as paupers, Post Office workers, policemen, magistrates and women were still disqualified from voting. Approximately one in seven adult males had the right to vote.

The reformed electoral system brought about only slow changes in the composition of the House of Commons. Parliament still consisted mainly of aristocrats and country gentlemen. Even in industrial constituencies there was a tendency to elect 'gentlemen' and social superiors. Some of the abuses of the old system remained, including bribery at elections and the purchasing of seats in certain towns, such as Lewes, Ipswich and St Albans. Despite these deficiencies, however, the Act was a tentative step towards democratic government.

E.J. Evans, *The Great Reform Act of 1832* (Methuen 1983).

Religious Tract Society

Founded in 1799, by DISSENTERS and members of the CHURCH OF ENGLAND for the publication and dissemination of Christian literature as part of the EVANGELICAL MOVEMENT.

Religious Worship Census, 1851

The government carried out a unique census of religious worship in 1851. The findings were published as the *Report on the 1851 Census of Religious Worship*, and related only to England and Wales. A separate census and report were produced for Scotland. Horace Mann, who compiled the English and Welsh report, estimated that nearly one-third of the people stayed away from church or chapel on Sundays. The CHURCH OF ENGLAND had the largest number of places of worship, followed by the Wesleyans (see JOHN WESLEY), Congregationalists, Primitive Methodists and Baptists, in that order.

Rennie, John (1761–1821)

A millwright and engineer from a prosperous Scottish farming family. In 1784 he joined BOULTON AND WATT and

was put in charge of the planning of the mill machinery at the steam-driven Albion flour mills in London. This work brought him many commissions, including CANAL surveying. In 1790 he was involved with the Kennet and Avon Canal scheme and four years later he became engineer of the work. He also worked on other canals including the Glasgow, Paisley and Johnstone Canal in 1800. He designed a new Royal Mint in 1798 and built two bridges across the Thames in LONDON, Waterloo Bridge (1817) and Southwark Bridge (1819). He constructed a breakwater at Plymouth in deep water, consisting of a 1-mile (1.6-km) wall in the Sound with over 3 million tonnes (3.36 million US tons) of rough stone. It was started in 1811 and finished by his son, Sir John Rennie (1794–1874). Both Sir John Rennie and his brother George Rennie (1791–1866), were also distinguished engineers, particularly involved with the building of the railways.

Reverberatory Furnace

A furnace in which fuel and the ore were effectively separated and the heat of the coal fire was reflected, or reverberated, down from the roof of the furnace, so as to smelt the ore directly. These furnaces were successful for LEAD SMELTING from 1690, having been perfected by Dr Edward Wright, a QUAKER metallurgist. HENRY CORT used this type of furnace to make WROUGHT IRON, and he patented his PUDDLING process in 1783 and 1784. A type of reverberatory furnace was also used in the GLASS INDUSTRY and in some processes in PORCELAIN MANUFACTURE.

Reynolds, Richard (1735–1816)

A QUAKER who was manager of the COALBROOKDALE works from 1756 to 1772. He married ABRAHAM DARBY II's daughter Hannah in 1757 and became a partner in the company. He was responsible for re-laying the wooden WAGONWAYS with CAST-IRON rails in 1767, and continued to influence the company after ABRAHAM DARBY III took over in 1769. In 1788 he took a leading part in obtaining an Act of Parliament to allow a CANAL to be cut from the ironworks to the River Severn, and he helped the firm with loans in 1789 when it was in financial difficulties.

As a Quaker he followed the traditions of the sect by looking after the welfare of the company's employees. He laid out walks in Madeley, near Coalbrookdale, and used his own money to house workpeople there and at nearby Ketley and to help charitable institutions in BRISTOL.

Reynolds, William (1758–1803)

The son of RICHARD REYNOLDS, he took over the management of the firm's Ketley Works, Shropshire, in 1777. He brought a scientific mind to iron-founding and improved the transport links. With ABRAHAM DARBY III he built several BOULTON AND WATT engines for the works. In 1788 he built the SHROPSHIRE CANAL, for which he acted as engineer. He was also concerned with the Shrewsbury Canal, providing the design and ironwork for the AQUEDUCT of the River Tern at Longdon.

Ricardo, David (1772–1823)

An economist who propounded a theory of wages stating that the price of labour depended on the price of the food, necessaries and conveniences required to support the labourer and his dependents. The market price, according to the theory, was fixed by supply and demand and there was a tendency for this price to gravitate towards subsistence. Ricardo was a political reformer who, with THOMAS MALTHUS, helped get rid of the COMBINATION ACTS. In 1817 he wrote *Principles of Political Economy and Taxation*, a work that greatly influenced economic thought for 40 years. He advocated the labour theory of values, which said that

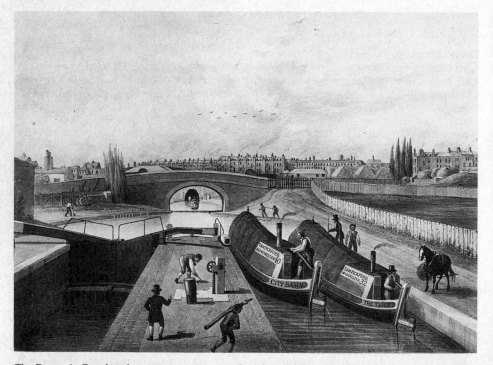

The Regent's Canal at the eastern entrance to the Islington Tunnel. Although the building of the canal was approved by an Act of Parliament in 1812, it was not completed until 1820. It soon became a busy waterway as this painting by T.H. Shepherd shows. The boats are Pickford's fly boats used to carry general merchandise on regular fast services. The fly boat on the right is being gauged by the gentleman in a top hat. He is measuring how low the boat floats to ascertain the toll to be paid based on the weight of the cargo. (*British Waterways Archives*)

the value of goods and services was proportional to the labour expended on them. He also advocated FREE TRADE and followed the theories of Malthus.

Richards, William   See William Oliver.

Rising Star

The first steamer (see STEAM BOAT to cross the Atlantic from east to west. The voyage took place in 1821 with an engine made by MAUDSLAY, Son and Field. As with other ocean-going steamers of that time the voyage was not made entirely under power; sails were used when the winds were suitable, and steam when they were not. The boilers used huge quantities of coal, and insufficient could be carried to make the crossing entirely by steam.

River Navigation

In 1760, before the CANAL building era began, Britain had about 1,000 miles (1,609 km) of navigable rivers. Many rivers had been improved in the early 18th century and small rivers and streams had been made navigable by dredging, using pound LOCKS and the building of weirs which created a greater depth of water. Only upland parts of Britain were more than 15 miles (24 km) from a navigable river or the sea. The Severn was navigable from the sea to Pool Quay, near Welshpool, a distance of 140 miles (225 km). The main ports were Bewdley and Bridgnorth. Navigation on the Great Ouse in eastern England gave access from the North Sea to towns and villages in Cambridgeshire, Bedfordshire and Huntingdonshire. The Thames could carry small vessels as far as Lechlade, while its tributary the Kennet was navigable to Newbury. NEWCASTLE could be reached on the River Tyne, Norwich by the River Yare and Peterborough by the River Nene. In the North West the Mersey was navigable to Winsford and MANCHESTER, while the rivers draining to the Humber gave access to York, Leeds, Halifax, Burton-upon-Trent and Derby.

The boats used were usually barges between 20 and 80 tonnes (22.4 and 89.6 US tons) in size. They carried sails, although horses or manpower were sometimes used. Delays occurred on river navigation because of seasonally low water or the slowness of millers to open their weirs. Water transport coped best with long-distance transfer of bulky and non-perishable goods. River traffic increased when the canals were built, since canals linked navigable rivers or were feeders for them. There was often a need for the trans-shipment of cargoes between canal and river craft, and where this happened settlements grew up, such as Stourport in Worcestershire.

Roads

By 1650 there was a well-organized transport system in Britain, with pack-horse services and coaches (see COACH SERVICES) providing a carrying network which was well integrated. The networks were country-wide, with many smaller settlements as well as large towns having carriers. Kendal in Cumberland, for example, had links all over the North and weekly services to Norwich and LONDON. Most goods were carried by pack trains consisting of a gang of pack-horses and their riders. Carriers normally operated from inns, which were convenient collecting centres and meeting points with other carriers. Pack-horses were more in evidence than wagons for carrying goods, but in addition there were coaches, horsemen and droves of animals to be seen on the roads. Many roads had medieval or earlier origins.

In the latter half of the 18th century the TURNPIKE trusts improved the roads and provided a limited network of routeways. Coach journey times on these roads were reduced. In 1754 the journey from Edinburgh to London took 10 days; 20 years later it could be done in 4 days. By 1777 Matthew PICKFORD was advertising a journey of 4½ days for carrying goods from MANCHESTER to London. Those roads in country areas not controlled by a turnpike trust could become impassable in wet weather and dusty tracks in summer, but the improvements made by JOHN METCALF and THOMAS TELFORD were to make communications considerably better than in the first half of the 18th century.

In the Highlands of Scotland some 920 miles (1,480 km) of road were built in the first two decades of the 19th century. Road surfaces were further improved by JOHN MCADAM after 1816, and there was also a boom in turnpike trusts in the 1820s. Road engineering continued to develop with the construction of bridges, such as Thomas Telford's MENAI Straits bridge. Coach travel became better organized and faster, averaging about 10 mph (16 kph) in the 1820s. In addition, by 1828 some 600 long-distance services were based on London. Improved road services also brought benefits for freight traffic, with the stage wagon pulled by four or six horses as the main form of road freight transport.

The railways (see RAILWAY – IMPACT ON THE ECONOMY) resulted in a decline in long-distance road traffic, and schemes to improve these roads were shelved. In contrast roads to and from RAILWAY STATIONS and in towns were improved. The turnpike trusts were disbanded and road maintenance was reduced or abandoned, as roads reverted to being the responsibility of groups of parishes called highway districts.

E. Pawson, *Transport and Economy. The Turnpike Roads of Eighteenth Century Britain* (Academic Press 1977).
J. Copeland, *Roads and their Traffic, 1750–1850* (David and Charles 1968).

Road Tarring

As early as 1838 part of Oxford Street in LONDON was paved with wooden blocks, which were made waterproof by a thick covering of hot pitch. This method became popular, especially in fashionable districts, since it produced less traffic noise. Coal-tar was becoming cheaper as a byproduct of the growing gas industry, but the practice of surfacing minor roads with tar, or an amalgam of tar and road metal, did not become extensive until after the end of the century.

Roberts, Richard (1789–1864)

A tool-maker and inventor who worked for a time at an ironworks in Shropshire and then with HENRY MAUDSLAY in 1814, before setting up on his own. In 1816 he

invented a machine tool for correctly sizing wheels and an improved screw lathe. He originally built his MACHINES to enable improved machinery to be made for the textile trade, and his first customers were MANCHESTER cotton mill owners. He designed an automatic MULE for spinning, which made it possible for less skilled people to be employed. He also made precision parts for steam locomotives. In 1848 he designed a jacquard multiple punching machine, working on the same principle as the JACQUARD LOOM, which punched holes with great accuracy in metal and was used on iron plates for the tubular bridges, including those at Conway and over the MENAI Straits. He has been described as the greatest mechanical inventor of the 19th century, but unfortunately he had no business sense, and he died a pauper.

Rob Roy

The first successful steamship (see STEAM BOATS) to operate on the open sea. It was made at Dumbarton in Scotland in 1818, with engines by DAVID NAPIER, and took mail and passengers between GLASGOW and Belfast. In 1821 it was the first cross-Channel steamship on the Dover–Calais route – the crossing took 2 hours 45 minutes. The boat remained in service for two years, until purchased by the French government.

Rochdale Pioneers

A group of workers in Rochdale, Lancashire who opened a CO-OPERATIVE store in Toad Lane, Rochdale, in 1844, having formed the Rochdale Society of Equitable Pioneers. The workers saved weekly until they could afford to open a small shop and stock it with goods. They traded fairly, unlike the TOMMY SHOPS, and did not adulterate their products (see ADULTERATION OF FOOD). They cut out the middleman, and members received a dividend on the amount they had purchased over a period of time, so their goods were bought more cheaply than the retail market price.

Rocket

GEORGE STEPHENSON's locomotive, which took the prize at the RAINHILL TRIALS in 1829. The engine had a multi-tube boiler and was built at the works of ROBERT STEPHENSON, who had helped to design it.

Visit Science Museum, London – original *Rocket*. **M***

Rockingham Pottery

A pottery works set up by Joseph Flint at Swinton, South Yorkshire, in 1745, on the estate of the First Marquis of Rockingham. The works produced brown domestic earthenware until 1778 when, under Thomas Bingley, it was enlarged and white earthenware called Rockingham china was produced. In 1806 John Brameld acquired the works, which was managed by members of the Brameld family until it closed. The factory produced lavish PORCELAIN which was very costly to make, and this resulted in the firm becoming bankrupt in 1842. The buildings were used for making pottery until about 1865.

A. and A. Cox, *Rockingham Pottery and Porcelain 1745–1842* (Faber 1983).

Roebuck, John (1718–94)

A physician in BIRMINGHAM who applied his chemical knowledge to improving the method of refining gold and silver used by the Birmingham TOY TRADE. He set up a laboratory for the assay and refining of the precious metals and also improved the manufacture of SULPHURIC ACID, using lead chambers instead of glass retorts. The chambers were less fragile and could hold large volumes of acid. His partner in Birmingham was SAMUEL GARBETT, but the partnership was dissolved in 1766.

Roebuck founded the CARRON IRONWORKS, near Falkirk in Scotland, in 1760 and bought coal mines nearby to supply coal to the works, but the mines suffered from severe flooding. He asked JAMES WATT to build an engine to pump water from the mines, with parts to be supplied by the Carron Ironworks. Watt found that the ironworks could not produce the parts with sufficient accuracy, and eventually moved to Birmingham to work at the SOHO WORKS. In 1768 John Roebuck went into partnership with James Watt, but he was hit by the commercial depression of 1772–3 and became bankrupt in 1773.

Rolling Mill

A MACHINE in which metal bars are passed between rotating iron rolls, which can be grooved so that the metal is shaped as it passes through the rollers. Because rolling needed a great deal of power it took place at a mill where water power was available, before the advent of the STEAM ENGINE. Rolling mills were used in conjunction with SLITTING MILLS to flatten iron into a sheet before slitting it into narrow strips from which nails could be made (see NAIL MAKING). In 1720 John Hanbury used plain rolls for making sheet iron for tinplate (thin sheet iron).

HENRY CORT used rolls that were different – instead of being plain they were grooved around their circumference. By using two rolls, one placed above the other, and cutting a semi-circular groove in each, round iron bars could be made. Henry Cort patented his successful grooved rolls in 1784 and it was realized that grooves with different designs could produce a variety of shaped iron sections. At first there were two-high mills (one roller above another), and then three-high mills (three horizontal rollers above one another) were introduced to speed up the process. Three-high mills were not widespread until the 1860s. In the 1860s George Bedson of MANCHESTER developed the continuous rolling mill consisting of a series of two-high stands placed one behind the other.

Roman Catholicism

The Roman Catholics in England, Wales and Scotland were a small and sometimes persecuted group, whereas in Ireland they formed a majority of the population. IRISH IMMIGRATION into Great Britain resulted in increased membership of the Roman Catholic Church, and the added responsibility of the church to cater for the needs of this WORKING-CLASS congregation. Roman Catholics were excluded from Parliament and executive posts by the Test and Corporations Act of 1763. This Act was repealed in 1828 and the next year a CATHOLIC EMANCIPATION ACT was passed, which permitted Roman Catholics to become MPs and hold public office, provided they took an oath denying the Pope's right to interfere in British domestic affairs. They were unable to take degrees at Oxford, Cambridge and Durham UNIVERSITIES until the University Religious Tests Act was abolished in 1871.

Roman Cement

A natural hydraulic cement consisting of about two-thirds chalk, one-quarter clay and some iron oxide. It was patented by J. Parker in 1796, and termed 'Roman cement' in the belief that it was used by the Romans. It was much used for underwater work until it was superseded in the 1820s by PORTLAND CEMENT, which is two or three times as strong.

Rose, John (1762–1828) See
Coalport

Royal Agricultural Society

in 1838 the English Agricultural Society was founded and two years later it received royal patronage and became the Royal Agricultural Society of England. It was the showpiece for agricultural improvements and displayed new pieces of agricultural machinery, as well as carrying out tests to judge the quality of the MACHINES for different localities and soils. There was a competitive flavour to the implement trials and the Society's annual exhibition became a shop window for the industry.

Royal Albert Bridge

the railway bridge over the River Tamar at Saltash linking Devon with Cornwall. It was built by ISAMBARD BRUNEL and opened by PRINCE ALBERT in 1859. Brunel, who was very ill, managed to attend the ceremony, but died a few weeks later, and as a memorial his name was placed in large letters on the bridge.

Visit Saltash, Devon – Royal Albert Bridge.

Russell, John Scott (1808–82)

A CANAL engineer, SHIPBUILDER and naval architect. He became shipyard manager at Greenock in 1836 and joint secretary of the GREAT EXHIBITION, 1851. He constructed the *GREAT EASTERN* in 1858 and founded the Institution of Naval Architecture in 1860.

Russell, Lord John (1792–1878)

(Created Earl Russell, 1861). A WHIG who championed Parliamentary reform and was largely responsible for the REFORM ACT, 1832, and the MUNICIPAL CORPORATIONS ACT, 1835, passing through Parliament. He became prime minister briefly on the fall of SIR ROBERT PEEL in 1846 and after 1852 held other Cabinet posts, with a further short spell as premier in 1865–6.

S

Sadler, Michael Thomas (1780–1835)

A banker and TORY MP who supported factory reform, together with JOHN FIELDEN. He introduced a Bill in Parliament in 1831 limiting hours in all mills to 10 for persons under the age of 18. Before the Bill could be passed there was a general election and he lost his seat. His cause was taken up by Lord Ashley (later EARL OF SHAFTESBURY), but the TEN HOURS Bill was not passed until 1847.

Safety Lamp

A lamp with a shielded flame, used in mines to prevent explosions and fire due to FIREDAMP. A number of people were responsible for the development of the safety lamp. The credit is usually given to SIR HUMPHRY DAVY, but Dr William Clanny and GEORGE STEPHENSON also invented safety lamps and others improved their ideas.

The Davy lamp was based on the principle that fine wire gauze around the flame would prevent an explosion. It was tested in 1816 and was completely successful. Early safety lamps were imperfect, however, ventilation systems were inefficient and COAL MINING continued to be a highly dangerous occupation. The lamps gave a very poor light and were not used in all mines in the first half of the 19th century. Many mines kept only one safety lamp, and that was used for testing for gas; a blue 'gas cap' formed over the flame when firedamp was present.

The main consequences of the adoption of the safety lamp was to increase the size and depth of pits and produce more coal. Miners saw the lamp as an evil which allowed workers to be put in more dangerous situations than previously. There was, however, a sharp decline in the number of deaths underground after 1820.

Visit Museum of Mining, Buile Hill Park,

Salford – collection of safety lamps. **M***

Sailing Ships

In 1800 sailing ships were small, with a breadth which was proportionately greater than we see today. A 32-gun frigate measured slightly less than 170 feet (51.8 m) long and 40 feet (12.2 m) wide. When full rigged a ship of this size would carry some 37 sails. Few of these wooden ships survive, although they were in operation well into the 19th century as merchant ships, warships and pleasure craft. The *Cutty Sark*, a tea clipper, can still be visited. This sailing ship was built at Dumbarton in Scotland in 1869 and was the fastest tea clipper of her day, carrying wool from Australia as well as tea from China. She has an iron frame and a wooden hull.

Visit Portsmouth Dockyard, Hampshire – HMS *Victory*, built 1765; Nelson's flagship at the Battle of Trafalgar, 1805. **M***
Greenwich, London – *Cutty Sark*, tea clipper. **M***

Saint Monday

This expression was used to describe the ARTISANS' habit of absenting themselves from work on Monday to recover from the excesses of the weekend. This habit conflicted with the discipline required in the factories to keep the MACHINES operating regularly and efficiently, and the term was used by mill owners with some disparagement.

Saltaire

A model industrial town built by TITUS SALT in the 1850s and 1860s for workers at his new mill outside BRADFORD. In 1863 a wash-house was built, with machines powered by three STEAM ENGINES, enabling washing to be done in an hour. By the mid-1870s there were some 800 cottages arranged in streets on a simple grid pattern. There were many communal buildings, a Congregational church, a school, almshouses, a hospital and a park. The town was dominated by the mill, opened in 1853.

Visit Saltaire, near Shipley, West Yorkshire – original settlement and buildings.

Salt-Glazed Ware

Pottery made from the end of the 17th century in England after John Dwight (1637–1703) took out a patent in 1672. Salt-glazed stoneware was made by firing pottery at a high temperature until it was hard. It was glazed by throwing salt into the kiln when the fire was very hot.

Salt Industry

In the 17th century salt was imported from the west coast of France and Portugal, but the development of the Cheshire fields after 1690 made salt a steady element in the commerce of LIVERPOOL and played a vital part in the expansion of the port in the 18th century, with shipments to northern and western Europe. Salt was an important key raw material of the chemical industry during the INDUSTRIAL REVOLUTION, and there was considerable trade in the commodity. The extraction of salt from the sea by evaporation was practised at a number of sites in medieval times and continued at Lymington in Hampshire until 1865. In the summer brine was evaporated by solar energy and in the winter coal from NEWCASTLE was used to provide the heat necessary. The salt was largely used by the Royal Navy at Portsmouth to preserve meat.

The northeast coast of England was also a centre for manufacture, using sea-water and local coal, but the area declined in the 18th century because of the exploitation of the large salt deposits at Droitwich in Worcestershire and around Northwich and Middlewich in Cheshire. CANAL barges took salt to Liverpool from the Cheshire fields and returned with Lancashire coal, which was needed to evaporate the water from brine. Large quantities of coal were needed, about 12 cwt (610 kg – 0.6 US tons) to make 1 tonne (1.12 US tons) of salt. By 1830 the River Weaver, which flows through the salt region to the Mersey estuary, was a busy waterway with 600 boats engaged in the trade. Brine was reduced to salt crystals by boiling in open pans inside buildings made of timber to limit corrosion.

Visit The Salt Museum, London Road, Northwich, Cheshire – exhibition of salt-making. **M***
Maldon, Essex – salt works.

Salt, Sir Titus (1803–76)

A Congregationalist wool MANUFACTURER in BRADFORD who experimented with fibres which MACHINES at the time could not handle. He was able to modify machinery so that alpaca could be spun. As a result of his success he built a new factory in 1853 outside Bradford. The factory provided very good working conditions and the town of SALTAIRE was built nearby to house the workers.

Sankey Brooke Navigation (Later called the ST HELENS Canal)

England's first CANAL built in 1757, four years before the BRIDGEWATER CANAL. It was sponsored by LIVERPOOL Common Council, salt refiners and merchants, and the surveyor was Henry Berry. The Sankey Brook was too small to be used as a waterway, so a lateral canal was cut, which was connected to the brook only in order to obtain a supply of water. The navigation ran from the St Helens coalfield in South Lancashire to the River Mersey, and drastically cut the price of coal in Liverpool.

Savannah

The first steamer (see STEAM BOAT) to cross the Atlantic from the United States to Britain in 1819. She was a sailing vessel with auxiliary steam propulsion, and the engine was used for only a short period during the voyage.

Savery, Thomas (c.1650–1715)

An engineer who made an 'engine to raise water by fire' in 1698. This engine, called the Miner's Friend, was the first steam pump (see STEAM ENGINES – PUMPING). Its lift was, however, inadequate for mine drainage and it was used to pump water from large buildings. Only one is known to have been used for the drainage of a coal mine, and that was at Willingworth Colliery in Staffordshire in 1706. It has been estimated that some 33 Savery engines were built in the 18th century. The engine never entered into widespread use and none has survived.

Scab

The expression used by TRADE UNION members about another member who has broken their rules or does not adhere to their principles. The term is known to have been in use as early as 1802, when correspondence between unions in different parts of the country included this definition of a scab: 'He is to his trade what a traitor is to his country.'

Schools – Charity

Schools founded in the 18th century in many parishes, usually by the CHURCH OF ENGLAND. They taught the Anglican catechism, reading, writing and arithmetic. Girls were admitted, although they often took needlework instead of arithmetic. Attendance was voluntary and the teachers of poor quality, but the schools gave the poor some EDUCATION, which they would otherwise not have had, and the schools were attacked for educating children above their station. Some charity schools were well endowed, gave the schoolmaster a salary and provided the children with clothing. The movement after 1698 was co-ordinated by the SOCIETY FOR THE PROMOTION OF CHRISTIAN KNOWLEDGE, and was based on the idea that the poor could be reformed and kept in their place in society by instruction in the Bible and catechism. By 1754 over 2,000 charity schools had been established.

J. Lawson and H. Silver, *A Social History of Education in England* (Methuen 1973).

Schools – Circulating

Started about 1730 by GRIFFITH JONES, rector of Llanddowror in Carmarthen-shire, Wales, and inspired by the schools sponsored by the SOCIETY FOR THE PROMOTION OF CHRISTIAN KNOWLEDGE. He gathered together a band of unpaid teachers, who travelled round the countryside taking day- and night-schools in Welsh for young and old, in chapels, churches and other buildings, during the winter period when outside work was limited. Religious instruction was the basis of the curriculum and reading was taught so that the Bible could be read aloud. In the 1760s there were 279 circulating schools throughout Wales, but the movement faded away after the founder's successor died in 1779.

Schools – Dame

Small schools run by a private person, often a man, although many were run by widows or spinsters. These schools existed as early as the 16th century, and for a few pence per week children were taught to read and, in the case of girls, to sew. Standards varied but many were run by people with little education, who might supplement their earnings as teachers by sewing, washing or shopkeeping. The schools were often held in the home of the teacher and conditions varied. At their worst the children in them learned little and were kept in small crowded rooms. In 1851 there were 14,000 dame schools, although their numbers had been higher in the previous decades.

Schools – Endowed

Schools that received money from individuals and organizations for their formation and maintenance. Many were established as GRAMMAR SCHOOLS between the 16th and 18th centuries. Their curriculum was out of date and inappropriate for the industrial age, and only when a vigorous and enlightened head was appointed did the schools prosper. Some enhanced their status, such as Eton and Rugby, to become top-ranking PUBLIC SCHOOLS. Others saw their endowments reduced by the COST OF LIVING and withered away.

Schools – Girls'

The majority of girls educated in the 18th and 19th centuries came from wealthy families. Sometimes they were sent to boarding school or educated at home, and it was not until the 1840s that schools were started for girls to attend on a daily basis. In 1847 Elizabeth Reid started classes for girls at her home, which in 1860 became Bedford College, the first college to provide higher education courses for women. Other schools started at this time included Queen's College (see GOVERNESS) and, in 1858, Cheltenham Ladies' College.

M.C. Borer, *Willingly to School* (Lutterworth, 1976).

Schools – Grammar

Founded in some towns in Tudor times for the purpose of teaching poor boys and sometimes girls. These schools existed on endowments, and by the late 18th century many were very poor, the endowments having run out or suffered from inflation. There were some 500 endowed grammar schools in England and Wales, and every large Scottish burgh had its own. Greek, Latin and some Hebrew were taught, with occasionally English and arithmetic. Not until the Grammar Schools Act of 1840 could other subjects be taught. There were some good grammar schools, including those at MANCHESTER, BRADFORD and LEEDS, where the standards were high.

Schools – Industrial

The 1723 General Workhouse Act made provision for parishes to provide schools for children in their care, with APPRENTICESHIPS as soon as the children were old enough. They provided semi-skilled industrial training in spinning, weaving and knitting, as well as giving some time to literacy. Industrial schools were also established by charitable foundations. In 1791 there was a Day School of Industry at St Marylebone, London, where the boys were taught shoe-making and pin-heading, while girls were taught wool-spinning, reeling, knitting and needlework.

Industrial schools developed in the period 1830–70 as schools to which children under 14 could be committed as vagrants (see VAGRANCY). In 1861 these schools were placed under Home Office inspection.

Schools – Public

The definition of those schools which could be called public was not clear until the 1870s. The larger schools for boys from rich families, such as Harrow and Eton, formed an elite group whose membership was based on the concept of interaction – mainly who played whom at games – and apparently similar schools such as Mill Hill were not part of this elite group. Some of the endowed GRAMMAR SCHOOLS, which sent boys to Oxford and Cambridge UNIVERSITIES, were being improved in the first half of the 19th century by good headmasters such as Dr Thomas Arnold, who reformed Rugby between 1828 and 1842.

The rise of the MIDDLE CLASSES increased the demand for good schools, and by the 1840s social distinctions had sharpened between the old public schools and a new generation of them, such as Radley, Wellington and Marlborough. The matter came to a head when the government set up the Clarendon Commission (1861) to enquire into the nine great public schools, Eton, Harrow, Rugby, Westminster, Winchester, Charterhouse, St Paul's, Merchant Taylors and Shrewsbury. In 1868 the Taunton Commission, also set up by the government, reported on the grammar schools. The distinction between the two reports caused resentment among the headmasters, especially Edward Thring at Uppingham, and the result was the establishment of the Headmasters' Conference in 1869, membership of which became recognized as the stamp of a public school.

Public schools had a reputation as grim places. Bullying was commonplace, the teaching was confined to grammar, Greek and Latin, and discipline was left to the older boys, with little interference from the masters. Those public schools patronized by royalty or the aristocracy were very elitist, and places like Eton became the training ground for Parliament and the state services.

T.W. Bamford, *The Rise of the Public Schools* (Nelson 1967).

Schools – Ragged

The ragged school movement began in the 1840s, promoted by John Pounds, a Portsmouth cobbler who collected ragged children together and tried to give them training 'in virtue and knowledge'. LORD SHAFTESBURY helped to form the Ragged School Union in 1844. Voluntary funds were raised with the motive of giving a level of care to the most deprived children. Some schools lodged the children, some fed them and some children were helped to find work or to emigrate (see EMIGRATION). In 1870 the Ragged School Union had 132 schools and there were also ragged schools outside the Union. After the 1870 Education Act (see EDUCATION), the Union concentrated on ragged SUNDAY SCHOOLS.

Schools – Sunday

A national movement started in 1780 by ROBERT RAIKES, a Gloucester printer and newspaper owner. He decided to keep children off the streets and out of mischief on Sundays, and arranged for them to be taught the catechism, with money paid from public subscriptions. In 1783 he published his activities in his newspaper and papers in other areas reported the article. Schools began to spring up all over the country and a Sunday School Union was founded in 1785. Children were taught to read from books of a religious and improving nature. The system was cheap, and MANCHESTER could boast 36 schools by 1785. Educationally they were a poor substitute for day-schools, but they created a point of social contact between the CLASSES and encouraged the spirit of voluntary service.

Sunday schools were more vigorous in the North of England and Methodist (see METHODISM) visitor teachers were common. Various religious sects,

including the ROMAN CATHOLICS and nonconformists (see DISSENTERS), set up their own Sunday schools. In Wales the collapse of the CIRCULATING SCHOOLS was followed by a CHARITY SCHOOL movement, begun by Thomas Charles in North Wales in the 1780s. This included Sunday schools which were open to adults as well as children.

Sunday schools helped to bring about a marked change in the attitude towards EDUCATION. They were a civilizing influence on society, but opposition came from sources outside the CHURCH OF ENGLAND and from extreme EVANGELICALS, who considered that teaching on Sunday broke the fourth commandment.

Scott Archer, Frederik (1813–57)

The inventor in 1848 of the wet collodian method used in photography until the 1880s. This method replaced the daguerreotype and calotype methods previously used and gave a clear, fine grain. It was also an easy method which brought photography within reach of amateurs.

Screen

Machinery used in COAL MINING to separate the large lumps of coal from the small ones. Early screens were made of wood but CAST-IRON gratings were introduced about 1760. The gratings were set at intervals on sloping platforms, with bars spaced according to the size of coal required to pass through them. From the gratings the coal passed down wooden chutes to waiting wagons. By the middle of the 19th century mechanical tippers were used to tip the coal tubs over the top of the screens. In the Midlands screens were not introduced until the second half of the 19th century, before which any screening was done by the collier at the coal face with a fork or a riddle.

Screw-Cutting Lathe

A lathe invented by HENRY MAUDSLAY in 1798 which was the prototype of the modern lathe. Maudslay was at great pains to perfect an accurate screw thread and produced an inclined knife, shaped to fit the cylinder to be cut. The cut made by the knife was carried along the cylinder as the lathe revolved and in this way threads were obtained. These could be altered by adjusting the angle of the knife. Once the thread had been obtained and finished by hand, the machine was designed to be fitted with the prototype and then reproduce it. An improved lathe was produced in 1800.

Visit Science Museum, London – original Maudslay lathe. **M***

Scribbling

The first part of the carding operation in the WOOLLEN INDUSTRY. A scribbling MACHINE was designed to disentangle the fibres and deliver the wool in the form of a continuous web. The wool was then passed to the carding machine, which removed any small knots of tangled fibre which had passed through the scribbler. By the end of the 18th century scribbling was mainly done by machines in scribbling mills which, in Yorkshire, were sometimes separate buildings. These small factories were set up on a co-operative basis by a group of domestic clothiers, and preceded the larger TEXTILE MILLS.

Seaward, Samuel (1800–42)

A marine engineer who joined his older brother John (1786–1858) and built engines for boats which ran between Gravesend in Kent and London. They later built 24 STEAM BOATS for the government and adapted their engines for a number of ships. Samuel Seaward also designed swing bridges, cranes and dock apparatus, boilers and MACHINES for sugar mills.

Seed Drills

Jethro Tull (1679–1741) demonstrated a seed drill in 1733, but it was used on very few farms because it was expensive and not designed for heavy soils. About 1800 a drill was developed by James Smyth and his brother, of Peasenhall in Suffolk. They devised a method of making seed drill coulters (the blades or discs that cut into the soil) individually adjustable, so that they could be set at different distances apart. They provided swing steerage for the drill, which allowed the driver to keep the seed line straight. The Smyth brothers also designed and marketed a corn and manure drill, probably the first combined commercial drill on the market. By 1850 Smyth's seed drill, called the Suffolk drill, was used throughout Britain. The works continued to make drills until the 1960s, when it closed.

Self Help

Self Help was the title of a book published in 1859 by Samuel Smiles (1812–1904), a LEEDS physician. The book consisted of a series of lectures given by the author to a group of young men in Leeds, who taught themselves reading, writing, grammar and arithmetic. There were other manuals designed to be 'instructive' and 'improving'. They included the *Penny Magazine*, the *Family Economist* and the *Family Friend*. They all based their advice on the need to work hard and the doctrine of self help. This doctrine was seen as a means whereby WORKING-CLASS people could obtain personal and social advance. It also took a collective form as, for example, a mutual improvement society, co-operative store or friendly benefit group.

P.H.J.H. Gosden, *Self Help* (Batsford 1973).

Settlement, Act of, 1662   See Poor Law – Act of Settlement, 1662

Seven Years War, 1756–63

A war in which Britain and Russia fought against France, Austria and Russia. The French were attacked by Britain in North America and India. The war brought increased demand for guns and other weapons and in 1756 the price of iron moved suddenly upwards. New iron foundries were established near COALBROOKDALE, in South Wales at Hirwaun (1756) and DOWLAIS (1759), and at Seaton in Cumberland (1762). In 1763 there were a few months of prosperity after the end of the war, and then a slump.

Sewers

The first underground sewers used for the discharge of waste were bricked-over water-courses. It was then decided to build special brick sewers flushed by a regular supply of water. In LONDON this task was undertaken in 1855 by SIR JOSEPH BAZALGETTE, an engineer to the Metropolitan Board of Works. He built five main sewers running parallel to the River Thames, three on the north side and two on the south. The sewers discharged some 12 miles (19 km) downstream from London Bridge. Pumping stations were built and the main sewers were fed by a network of smaller ones. Later in the century outfall works were built to treat the sewage.

Sexual Relationships

Before and during the INDUSTRIAL REVOLUTION pre-marital sexual intercourse between WORKING-CLASS courting couples was not considered to be promiscuous, but an anticipation of the marriage, which would hasten the wedding day if pregnancy resulted. The FACTORY SYSTEM probably had little effect on sexual immorality and sexual abuse, although there is some evidence of abuse in the TEXTILE MILLS when families were split up.

In MIDDLE-CLASS society the wife was expected to be submissive to her husband, sexually as well as socially. She was not expected to desire any pleasure from sex but to perform it as a duty to her husband and the need for procreation. Sex was unmentionable in the middle-class home and female chastity was an ideal for all single women.

There were double standards of sexual morality in a society that was male dominated. For young men the chastity of middle-class wives and daughters prohibited pre- or extramarital intercourse, although more latitude was possible with female domestic servants, who were considered of a lower CLASS. This was a form of exploitation on the part of the middle-class màn, aided by the deference and temptations arising from poverty on the part of the servant girl. The other alternative available without any stigma to the middle-class male was recourse to prostitutes. The middle classes pretended that PROSTITUTION did not exist, although it was tacitly allowed to continue as a safety valve.

Shaftesbury, Anthony Ashley-Cooper, Seventh Earl of (1801–85)

Elected to Parliament as a TORY in 1826, he became the champion of measures to improve factory conditions and promoted a number of FACTORY ACTS and the MINES ACT, 1842. He was a philanthropist who supported the EVANGELICAL MOVEMENT, as well as Bible societies at home and overseas.

Shafting

A method of propelling a coal boat through a tunnel. The boatman pushed against the sides, roof or bottom using a length of timber – the shaft. It was a method preferred to LEGGING because it was easier. Some CANALS banned shafting because of damage to the brickwork. On the Grand Junction Canal, wooden rails were fitted below water level with chocks fixed at intervals for the shafts to push against.

Shearman   See Cropper

Sheffield

A steel manufacturing town in Yorkshire. By the mid-18th century the town was the centre of a region in which the people depended for their livelihood on COAL MINING, the production of iron and steel and the manufacture of cutlery, scythes, files, saws and other types of edged tools. The work was done in houses and workshops on a small scale with some degree of specialization; for example, grinding was done separately, using wheels turned by local streams. Nailers (see NAIL MAKING) were also at work in the locality, obtaining rods from the iron forges. BENJAMIN HUNTSMAN developed his crucible steel process in the town about 1742, and it was copied by others because it was not patented. By 1787 there were between seven and eleven steel-makers using his method in the area.

Steel was required for the cutlery trade, which consisted of many processes carried out in small workshops. MACHINERY were not much used until the end of the 19th century, although by then some factories had been built. The development of MILD STEEL using the BESSEMER PROCESS took place from about 1860, with the demand coming mainly from the transport industry – boilers and rails for the railways and plates for ships' hulls.

Old Sheffield Plate was made in the town after the invention of the process by Thomas Boulsover in 1742. It helped to make Sheffield famous for the quality of its silver-plated articles, such as candlesticks, tea urns and tankards. During the second half of the 18th century industrial development and population growth increased the demand for houses, and stone was superseded by brick as the main building material. East of Sheffield the Don Valley was an area of industrial and residential expansion after 1800 as the steel and engineering industries expanded on the low-lying land as far as Rotherham.

By 1850 social stratification was evident in the town, with larger houses on the higher, south-facing slopes of the ridges and small ARTISANS' terraces on the colder, northern slopes. In 1861 the population reached 185,000, having nearly trebled in the previous 40 years.

Visit Abbeydale Industrial Village, Sheffield – scythe works with forges, exhibitions and workers' cottages. **M***

Shillibeer, George (1797–1866)

A coachbuilder who set up business for a few years in Paris before returning to LONDON in 1829 to start an OMNIBUS service. The word 'omnibus' was already in use in Paris and he introduced it to describe the horse-drawn passenger vehicle he built. His first service ran from Paddington to the Bank of England and used two omnibuses. They were each drawn by three horses, harnessed abreast, they carried 22 passengers, and were known as 'Shillibeers'. By 1830 he had 12 omnibuses operating in London and in 1834 he started running buses from London to nearby Greenwich and Woolwich.

The introduction of the railways helped to ruin his business (see RAILWAY – IMPACT ON THE ECONOMY), and in later years he became an undertaker and invested in a patent funeral coach. In 1854, the London General Omnibus Company was formed and buses became a popular form of transport in London and other large towns.

Shipbuilding

The wooden SAILING SHIPS of the 18th century were built to designs which changed very little, in shipyards which used traditional constructional techniques. The increase in overseas and COASTAL TRADE during the century kept the shipbuilding ports busy building new ships, with a total tonnage in 1788 three times what it had been in 1700. Shipbuilding took place at a number of ports including LONDON, GLASGOW, NEWCASTLE, Hull, Sunderland and BRISTOL. At these ports ancillary trades such as rope- and sailcloth-making could be found. The largest employers were the naval dockyards at Rosyth, Portsmouth, Chatham, Sheerness and Plymouth. These ports were particularly busy during times of war, especially the NAPOLEONIC WARS. Towards the end of the century copper sheathing was added to the wooden hulls to prevent attack by the Teredo ship worm, and improvements were made in the dockyards, including the introduction of MACHINES designed by SIR MARC ISAMBARD BRUNEL to mass produce wooden pulley blocks.

The 19th century brought considerable changes to the shipbuilding industry. Steam ships (see STEAM BOATS) for the coastal trade and passenger services were built in increasing numbers after 1812, but timber remained the traditional building material, strengthened with iron struts and bolts. The first large iron-hulled ship was the *GREAT BRITAIN*, launched at Bristol in 1843. Its success resulted in the introduction of iron hulls for both naval and merchant ships, and in the concentration of the industry at ports where the raw materials were available and there was sufficient space and depth of water to develop shipyards. Ships were still being built at Blackwall on the River Thames in the 1860s but the yards were later closed, as Tyneside, Glasgow, Birkenhead and the iron and steel town of BARROW-IN-FURNESS became the main centres. At these ports marine engineering became an important source of employment. The naval ports contain much evidence of their past importance and tours of some of the yards are now possible.

Visit Industrial Museum, Bristol – *Great Britain* and museum. **M***
Museum of Dockyard Apprentice, Portsmouth – ship models, engines and trades. **M***
Chatham Dockyard, Kent – tours and visitors' centre. **M***

Shoddy

Originally wool reclaimed from soft rags, particularly knitted goods such as stockings. Later the word was confined to torn-up WORSTED cloth. Special machinery was invented in 1801 to reduce fabrics to a loose, fibrous state before being spun into yarn, and by 1830 the use of shoddy was increasing. In 1859 Charles Garnett invented a method for tearing up stronger fabrics; the machine was known as a garnetting machine. This and other developments led to the introduction of cheap, all-wool clothing. (See also MUNGO.)

Shoe Industry

An industry dependent on outworkers until the second half of the 19th century. The main centres were in Staffordshire, Northamptonshire, Somerset and Norwich, but many smaller centres existed throughout the country. The industry required abundant manual skilled labour until the 1850s, and could be readily carried out in the home. The uppers were distributed for stitching and then the soles were attached in a separate operation by shoemakers. Firms such as

CLARKS of Street, Somerset, were essentially distribution and collection centres, co-ordinating the work done with material supplied by them. In Norwich, 1,700 people were employed in the industry in 1841. Numbers grew rapidly after machines were introduced in the 1850s, and in 1861 5,300 people were employed in the town making boots and shoes.

In 1810 David Mead Randolph invented a machine for riveting boots, and in the next year MARC BRUNEL produced a machine for the nailing of army and navy boots. Neither machine was widely adopted and the first machine to be used on a large scale was the Singer sewing machine of America, operated by a treadle and available in Britain in the 1850s. The machine was used for stitching uppers and upper workers were made redundant, resulting in demonstrations and strikes in Stafford and Northampton between 1858 and 1860. Other machines were introduced, including the Blake sewer from America in 1859.

J. Swann, *Shoemaking* (Shire Publications 1986).

Shropshire Canal

A TUB-BOAT CANAL from industrial east Shropshire to the banks of the River Severn, where goods could be trans-shipped, was built between 1788 and 1792. It was financed by local industrialists led by WILLIAM REYNOLD, and reached the Severn at COALPORT, with a branch to Horsehay and COALBROOKDALE. The hilly country through which it passed made it necessary to build three INCLINED PLANES to take the 5-tonne (5.6 US tons) tub boats.

The Shrewsbury Canal was built in 1795 to supply the county town with coal from Donnington Wood. It crossed the River Tern by a CAST-IRON AQUEDUCT at Longdon and joined the short Wombridge Canal, which connects with the Shropshire near Donnington Wood. The main traffic on the canal consisted of iron and coal and it was busy until the 1850s. The canal was troubled by mining subsidence, and after it was bought by the London and North Western Railway in 1857 it was gradually closed.

Visit Ironbridge Gorge Museum, Shropshire – Hay inclined plane and part of canal restored. **M***

Sickness Benefits

The risk of injury at work was high, with unfenced machinery in the mills and dangerous working conditions in the mines and construction industries. Some employers made token payments or charitable gestures when workers were 'laid up' for long periods. If the wife and children of a sick workers could not find work, the family became paupers and had to apply for assistance to the GUARDIANS of the WORKHOUSE. Some of the skilled ARTISANS had support for sickness and unemployment benefits from their trade societies; other groups were not so fortunate. Workers were often worn out by the age of 50 and there was no provision for old age except from within the family. The only alternative was to go to the workhouse.

Sidmouth, Addington Henry, First Viscount (1757–1844)

A TORY of the old school who became an MP in 1784 and was a friend of WILLIAM PITT. He became speaker of the House of Commons 1789–1800 and was prime minister 1801–4. Between 1812 and 1822 he was home secretary, and it was in this position that he proved to be a severe opponent of the LUDDITES and other WORKING-CLASS groups. He employed SPIES extensively, a practice which reduced his popularity with some members of the UPPER CLASSES. The PETERLOO MASSACRE resulted in further oppressive measures including the SIX ACTS. He opposed CATHOLIC EMANCIPATION in 1829 and voted against the REFORM BILL, 1832.

Silk Industry

The FACTORY SYSTEM which developed in the textile industry towards the end of the 18th century had its origins in the silk industry at the beginning of the century. A three-storey spinning mill was erected at Derby in 1702 by Thomas Cotchett. His enterprise attracted the LONDON silk merchants John and THOMAS LOMBE and in 1719 they built a silk spinning mill at Derby six storeys high, with accommodation for over 300 workers. At that time silk was very expensive, and high-quality, cheaper silks were kept out of Britain only by high tariffs. Derby was a suitable centre for the industry; it was close to the FRAMEWORK KNITTING industry of the East Midlands and the River Derwent provided the water power that was needed. The main centre of the industry was, however, Spitalfields in London, where refugee Huguenot weavers had settled after fleeing religious persecution in France in the 17th century.

The industry developed slowly in the first half of the 18th century because of the shortage of raw silk and because of competition abroad from Italian, French and oriental silk firms, limiting any possible export markets. Factories were established in Macclesfield, Chesterfield and Stockport. By the end of the century mills were also operating in MANCHESTER, Salford and Pebmarsh in Essex. The Essex firm, which started production in 1799, was founded by GEORGE COURTAULD and was to become an important silk-producing firm throughout the 19th century, and world famous for artificial silk in the first decades of the 20th century.

The JACQUARD LOOM was introduced in the 1820s, making large and attractive designs possible, and the silk HAND LOOM WEAVERS suffered from competition from POWER LOOMS, which were introduced at Macclesfield and Congleton in Cheshire, with a tendency for the industry to concentrate in that area. The industry became more mechanized after the invention in 1836 of a spinning machine which could deal with the short fibres from the cocoon of a type of silkworm which cannot be unreeled. In 1851, the CENSUS OF POPULATION showed that 133,000 people were employed in the silk industry, 60 per cent of whom were female.

In France the silk industry had also introduced powered machinery and the British industry suffered a setback in 1860 when a Franco-British commercial treaty, the Cobden Treaty, permitted imports of silk from France.

Visit King's Street, Leek, Staffordshire – silk workers' houses.
Heritage Centre, Macclesfield – Paradise Silk Museum with jacquard looms. **M***
Fournier Street, London – silk weavers' houses with attic workshops.

'Silver Cross' Canals

'Silver Cross' was a contemporary expression describing the pattern of canals linking the four main estuary navigations of southern Britain – the Mersey, Severn, Humber and Thames. The project was completed by 1790 when the four estuaries were linked by inland waterways. The TRENT AND MERSEY CANAL was completed in 1777 and was joined by the Stafford and Worcestershire Canal (1772). The Coventry canal was joined to the Trent and Mersey at Lichfield, and these were joined to the Oxford Canal in 1790. Most of these canals could take only NARROW BOATS with a 7-foot (2.1-m) beam, while most river navigations could take boats which were much broader – 14 feet (4.3 m).

Simpson, James (1799–1869)

A water engineer who, in 1828, constructed for the Chelsea Water Company a slow sand filter bed, the design of which is still in use with few modifications. He also improved a Cornish engine (see STEAM ENGINES – CORNISH) in 1845, reducing the coal consumption by about two-thirds. He constructed waterworks for the supply to the royal residence of Windsor Castle, and went on to design or provide water supplies for sanitary work in other royal palaces. In 1848 he advised the Lambeth Water Company, and new intakes were made from the Thames, 3 miles (5 km) above Teddington Lock. He improved the water supply of BRISTOL as engineer to the Bristol Water Company in 1845, and was also involved with water projects in Aberdeen, Newport and Stockport. In 1854 and 1855 he was president of the INSTITUTION OF CIVIL ENGINEERS.

G.M. Binnie, *Early Victorian Water*

Engineers (Thomas Telford 1981).

Simpson, Sir James (1811–70)

A doctor who, in 1847, used ether as an anaesthetic during childbirth, and later introduced chloroform. He is regarded as the founder of the use of anaesthetics in British medicine.

Sirius

During the 1830s there was fierce rivalry among STEAMSHIP COMPANIES to provide the first steamship passenger service east–west across the Atlantic, using steam power all the way. To meet the challenge the GREAT WESTERN RAILWAY directors formed the Great Western Steamship Company, and in 1837 the *GREAT WESTERN* was launched, built to ISAMBARD BRUNEL's design with the objective of starting a steamship service across the Atlantic. Other companies were provoked to act and the British and American Steam Packet Company chartered the *Sirius*, which sailed from Cork in 1838, four days before the *Great Western* left BRISTOL. The *Sirius* docked in New York a few hours before the *Great Western*, but had only 15 tonnes (16.8 US tons) of coal to spare, whereas the *Great Western* had 200 tonnes (224 US tons). The *Sirius* had taken 19 days to make the crossing whereas the *Great Western* had taken 15 days. *Sirius* made one more Atlantic crossing before resuming passenger services on the Irish Sea.

Six Acts

Acts passed after the PETERLOO MASSACRE in 1819. Drilling and military exercises were prohibited; the right to hold public meetings was limited, with six days' notice to be given of any meeting of more than 50 people; the freedom of the press was restricted; and magistrates were empowered to search for, and to seize, arms. There were severe punishments for seditious libel and a stamp duty was placed on newspapers in an effort to put them beyond the reach of working people. The Acts were known as the Gag Acts.

Slate Quarrying

Several parts of North Wales were once important slate-quarrying centres. With the development of the CANAL network and the railways (see RAILWAY DEVELOPMENT), slate became the cheapest available roofing material over much of Britain. Slate was easy to quarry and dress and could be provided in uniform quality, accurately cut. It was an ideal material for roofing the workers' houses in the industrial towns, and a number of slate centres grew up in North Wales. They include Blaenau Ffestiniog, which had underground mines, and Dinorwic Quarry near Llanberis, which was first worked in 1809 and enjoyed its greatest prosperity towards the end of the 19th century.

Visit Llanberis, Gwynedd – Welsh Slate Museum. **M***
Blaenau Ffestiniog, Gwynedd – slate caverns, museum and furnished cottages. **M***

J. Lindsay, *A History of the North Wales Slate Industry* (David and Charles 1974).

Slitting Mill

A piece of machinery which was used to cut iron sheet into a number of narrow strips for conversion into nails and other products. The first strip mill in Britain was in use at Dartford in Kent *c*.1590. In order to obtain iron which was thin enough for the slitting mill a bar was hammered flat and then passed between metal rolls, which squeezed it and flattened it still further. These rolls were the forerunner of the ROLLING MILL. The strip of iron was then passed through the slitting mill, which was worked by a waterwheel. Discs or rotary cutters slit the iron into a number of narrow strips suitable for the nailer, blacksmith or other craftworker to use.

Slums in Manchester. The interior of 12 Southern Street, Liverpool Road, *c*.1840. It was scenes like this which shocked Friederich Engels into writing *The Condition of the Working Class in England* in 1845. (*Mary Evans*)

Slubbing Billy

Sometimes known as the 'billy', a MACHINE invented by John Swindells in 1782. It was a combination of a MULE and a SPINNING JENNY. It made the carded cotton into rovings which were suitable for the jenny, mule or WATER FRAME and could be made to any degree of fineness and at greatly reduced cost. The invention of the billy prolonged the usefulness of the jenny, with the smaller jennies and mules continuing to be used by cottage spinners.

Slums

Towns and cities contained areas of low-quality housing with few facilities and much overcrowding. Cellar dwelling was common in some cities in the 1830s, with more than 40,000 people in Greater MANCHESTER living in them. Lighting was provided only by a grating and the cellar was the cheapest and most undesirable room to be let. Older and larger houses were often broken down into single-room dwellings with courts and alleys between the buildings. Lodging houses were noisy and notoriously overcrowded and insanitary, and a survey of lodgings in LEEDS in 1851 calculated that there was an average of 2½ persons to each bed and 4½ persons to each room. The pattern of slum houses varied from town to town, with tenements in GLASGOW, BACK-TO-BACK in Leeds and cellar dwellings in LIVERPOOL. They shared the common lack of sanitation and privacy but were no worse than some rural slums, which could be just as squalid, although in a pastoral setting away from the smoke and deprivation of the urban environment.

J.N. Tarn, *Working Class Housing in Nineteenth Century Britain* (Lund Humphries 1971).

Smalley, John (?–1782)

A Preston merchant who was persuaded by RICHARD ARKWRIGHT to become his partner in 1768 and provide CAPITAL for a small cotton mill at NOTTINGHAM. In Nottingham, Arkwright found another partner, JEDEDIAH STRUTT, and John Smalley was retained as a manager. In 1777 Smalley moved to Holywell, North Wales, and set up a cotton mill in the Greenfield Valley. The mill was built on the site of an old corn mill, was three storeys high and had a large waterwheel. Part of the mill was constructed of stones from a medieval abbey and, because of the colour of the stones, was known as the Yellow Mill.

After John Smalley's death an obituary appeared in a local paper referring to him as 'the patron and founder of the fortunes of Sir Richard Arkwright'. His son Christopher built new mills in 1783 and 1785 which were six storeys high. A fourth mill was added in 1790 and 1,225 people were employed by the firm, which was known as the Cotton Twist Company and flourished in the first half of the 19th century.

Smeaton, John (1724–92)

A LONDON instrument-maker who became Britain's first professional civil engineer. He carried out experiments from 1769 onwards to improve the efficiency of NEWCOMEN's engine, and had some success, but the more important developments were to be made by JAMES WATT. John Smeaton is probably best remembered for his construction of the EDDYSTONE LIGHTHOUSE off Plymouth in 1759. Two previous lighthouses had been destroyed by gales and fire respectively, but Smeaton's building was a success, and he was consulted on many other projects for harbours, bridges and drainage schemes. In 1791 he was commissioned to build a harbour near St Austell in Cornwall, which was to be called CHARLESTOWN. He designed much of the machinery for the CARRON IRONWORKS, and was responsible for building Scotland's first important CANAL, the FORTH AND CLYDE, as well as canals in the Black Country and Yorkshire. He gathered around him a group of engineers, nicknamed the 'Smeatonians', who formed the nucleus from which the INSTITUTION OF CIVIL ENGINEERS later developed.

Visit Charlestown, near St Austell, Cornwall – harbour built by Smeaton.

Smiles, Samuel (1812–1904)   See
Self Help

Smith, Adam (1723–90)

An extremely influential economist and writer, whose main book, *An Inquiry into the Nature and Causes of the Wealth of Nations*, in 1776 established political economy as a social science and influenced political thought for many decades. He attacked the mercantilist theories (see MERCANTILE SYSTEM) of the day, arguing that they restricted the natural expansion of wealth. He advocated the removal of artificial barriers to trade and propounded the philosophical arguments for FREE TRADE and a LAISSEZ-FAIRE policy. He believed that the government should limit itself to a minimum of tasks, such as defending the country from invasion and keeping law and order. He promoted the doctrine that trade was hampered by governments and by anyone who interfered with 'the obvious and simple system of natural liberty'. Disadvantages resulting from uncontrolled competition would eventually be eliminated by the natural operation of economic forces. He was opposed to the COMBINATION ACTS, which punished workmen for combining when their masters could combine and go unpunished.

Adam Smith's views about labour were totally disregarded by the UPPER CLASSES as was his suggestion of a tax on ground rents. His arguments against protection, whereby tariffs or quotas were imposed to restrict the inflow of imports, were also ignored. He was very much an advocate for the new and rising capitalist (see CAPITAL) CLASS and believed the main mechanism through which the laws of human values worked was the 'division of labour', whereby productive processes were divided up into many parts so that each worker specialized and the total output was greater if many workers were employed.

D. Raphael, *Adam Smith* (Oxford University Press 1985).

Smith, Sir Francis Pettit (1808–74)

The designer in 1836 of a successful screw propeller for STEAM BOATS. He received financial backing and constructed a small boat with a wooden screw. The Admiralty became interested and a company was formed to produce a large boat, the ARCHIMEDES. In 1841 orders were given for the *Rattler*, the first screw steamer in the British navy. Sir Francis acted as adviser to the Admiralty until 1850.

Soap Industry

Soap-making was essential to the early WOOLLEN INDUSTRY for cleaning fleeces and cloth, and it was manufactured by boiling together soda and potash. BRISTOL became an important centre in the Middle Ages, because of local coal and local demand from the West Country woollen industry.

Until the Leblanc process for making soda was developed (see SODA MANUFACTURE), soap could only be made in small quantities. Once the Leblanc process was established near NEWCASTLE-UPON-TYNE and LIVERPOOL it was natural that the soap industry should develop nearby, since soap manufacture needed not only soda but supplies of cheap coal. The soap industry developed at Widnes, Warrington and Liverpool on Merseyside, on Tyneside, and to a lesser extent in east LONDON. William Hesketh Lever (1851–1925) founded Port Sunlight on the Cheshire side of the Mersey Estuary in 1888, and developed a factory and MODEL VILLAGE for the workpeople.

Visit Port Sunlight, Cheshire – model village and art gallery. **M***
Museum of the Chemical Industry, Mersey Road, Widnes, Lancashire – includes a history of chemicals. **M***

W.A. Campbell, *The Chemical Industry* (Longman 1971).

Social Mobility

The movement of individuals within a society, which can be considered in four different ways.

(a) Geographical mobility. The movement of population from one part of the country to another, for example, MIGRATION from the countryside to industrial towns.

(b) Occupational change. This was possible as the result of EDUCATION and SELF HELP. For the manual labouring CLASSES it was relatively unknown, and there were barriers between manual and non-manual jobs as well as between the skilled and unskilled ARTISANS.

(c) Acquirement of property. Industrialists bought landed estates and the MIDDLE CLASSES owned their homes. For the WORKING CLASSES who could never save enough to buy their homes the possession of personal property was important and enhanced social status – hence the Victorian clutter of household goods in the parlour.

(d) Cultural and religious mobility. By adopting new cultural habits, people were able to help their upward social movement. The MECHANICS' INSTITUTES offered popular lectures, and upward mobility was assisted by a change in religious conviction – for example, from METHODIST to CHURCH OF ENGLAND, from chapel to church.

Society for Superseding Climbing Boys

A society set up by William Tooke in 1803 to improve the conditions of child chimney sweeps (see CHILD LABOUR – CHIMNEY SWEEPS). Societies were formed in a number of towns and a reward was offered for a sweeping MACHINE. A satisfactory machine was made by a Mr Smart, and was promoted in different parts of the country. The master sweeps disliked the machines and tried to prove them inferior to the boys. The machines were not adopted and boy chimney sweeps were to remain for the first half of the 19th century.

Society for the Diffusion of Useful Knowledge

A society formed in 1827 uniting WHIGS and RADICALS, it was nicknamed 'The Steam Intellect Society'. Chaired by HENRY BROUGHAM, the society published two books, *The Results of Machinery* and *The Rights of Industry*. They were intended to explain economic law to the WORKING CLASS, and labourers were reminded that it was in their interest to protect the rights of property. The society also published a journal, the *Penny Cyclopaedia*.

Society for the Encouragement of Arts, Manufactures and Commerce

A society founded by William Shipley in 1754 to promote INVENTIONS. It offered two prizes in 1761 for the best invention of a MACHINE that would spin six threads of wool, flax, cotton or silk at one time. It presented ABRAHAM DARBY III with its gold medal in 1788, and in the 1840s started the movement which resulted in the GREAT EXHIBITION, 1851. The first president of the society was Thomas Yeoman, who had spent many years draining the Fens.

Society for Promoting Christian Knowledge (The SPCK)

Started in 1698 with the purpose of spreading CHARITY SCHOOLS throughout the land, in order to spread Christianity among the godless poor. Its primary objective was to promote Anglicanism (see CHURCH OF ENGLAND) at home and in the colonies. It advised on the setting up of local societies to raise funds by subscription and manage schools under the direction of the Society. Most of the schools were set up in LONDON and the larger towns; some town corporations gave generous support and church collections were also made. The schools were intended for the poorest children and the curriculum, which centred on moral and religious discipline and social subordination, also included reading, writing and number for the boys, with sewing for the girls.

By 1730 the fashion had passed, and there were fears of the social and economic risks which could come from over-educating the poor. The SPCK had established the tradition of a central body which encouraged local effort to educate poor children, and this tradition helped to determine the form that state intervention in EDUCATION was eventually to take.

Society for the Suppression of Vice and Encouragement of Religion

A society started by William Wilberforce and Dr John Bowdler, members of the EVANGELICAL MOVEMENT in the 1790s. In 1801 and 1802 the Society made 623 successful prosecutions for breaking the Sabbath Laws. It then extended its interests to 'twopenny hops' (dances with a 2d entry charge), gingerbread fairs and obscene pictures. Nude sea-bathers were prosecuted, but attempts to pass legislation requiring imprisonment as the punishment for adultery were rejected. The pressures towards discipline among the lower CLASSES were strengthened by the evangelical extremists, but the TORY government disliked this form of nonconformist (see DISSENTER) 'fanaticism' and modified their demands.

Society of Civil Engineers

An organization set up by JOHN SMEATON in 1771. Members met at the King's Head in LONDON, and MATTHEW BOULTON and JOSIAH WEDGWOOD were both members. The Society paved the way for the formation of the INSTITUTION OF CIVIL ENGINEERS in 1818.

Soda Manufacture

Soda is an alkali (sodium carbonate) and can be obtained from common salt.

In the 18th century soda and also potash were obtained from the ashes of wood and seaweed, but supplies were limited and demand from the GLASS and SOAP INDUSTRIES increased. In 1791, a French chemist, Nicholas Leblanc (1746–1806), succeeded in developing a process in which salt was heated with coal and limestone or chalk. The first works in England to use the process was at Walker, east of NEWCASTLE-UPON-TYNE, in 1823, with brine from the Walker Colliery spring. In the same year JAMES MUSPRATT established a works in LIVERPOOL, where salt was available from the Cheshire salt fields (see SALT INDUSTRY) and coal from the Lancashire field. In 1828, Muspratt, in partnership with Josiah Gamble, set up another works at ST HELENS. Meanwhile, in Scotland, CHARLES TENNANT began to make soda at his ST ROLLOX WORKS in

GLASGOW, which by the 1830s was the largest chemical works in Europe.

The Leblanc process resulted in the release of large quantities of hydrochloric acid gas into the atmosphere, causing heavy local pollution, and as the result of public indignation the Alkali Works Act was passed in 1863, requiring 95 per cent of the gas to be condensed. The Leblanc process was not superseded until the Solvay process of the 1870s.

Soho Works

A MANUFACTORY founded in 1766 on Handsworth Heath, to the north of BIRMINGHAM by MATTHEW BOULTON. In the 1780s a visitor noted, 'The building consists of four quadrangles with work shops, warehouses etc. for 1,000 workmen.' The barren heath 'now contains many houses and wears the appearance of a populous town'. A reservoir at the top of a nearby hill provided water for a large waterwheel, which was joined by a STEAM ENGINE in 1775. The works made TOY TRADE ware, vases, chandeliers and plated goods.

Matthew Boulton would undertake work only of the highest quality and used the best materials and most skilled workmen. JAMES WATT transferred his steam-engine business to the works after the bankruptcy of JOHN ROEBUCK in 1773, when Matthew Boulton became Watt's partner. The works did not make the entire steam engine. Some parts were made by foundries, with the Soho factory providing the skilled labour and parts of the mechanism which required special care and precision in manufacture. Soho also became famous for coining money automatically, making forgery more difficult.

Sough

A wide ditch dug to drain a COAL MINE or CANAL workings when a canal was being built through a tunnel. The term 'sough' was used in the Midlands, while 'water gate' was used in the North East and 'adit' in southern England. Many soughs were driven in the coal seams themselves, and there were many legal tangles because mine owners drained their water into soughs which had been made at considerable expense by others. In the Forest of Dean it was illegal for one miner to sink a pit within 300 yards (274.3 m) of a sough made by someone else unless he had permission.

Soughs were narrow channels, often no more than 18 inches (437 mm) wide at the base. They were expensive to cut through rock and small-mine owners used buckets instead to wind up water from a mine. In the 19th century, soughs were lined with bricks, but earlier ones were unsupported or supported with wooden props. The sough from the Worsley Mine (see BRIDGEWATER, FRANCIS EGERTON) was extended and widened by JAMES BRINDLEY to provide a feeder for the BRIDGEWATER CANAL, allowing barges to be loaded at the coal face.

Spa Fields Meeting

A radical demonstration in LONDON in 1816 to demand reforms. Two meetings led and addressed by HENRY HUNT resulted in a section of the crowd marching to the Tower of London and other parts of the city and looting gunsmiths' shops. They were dispersed by troops and a third meeting was held on Spa Fields, but further attempts to hold meetings were unsuccessful. The year 1816 was one of extreme misery and unemployment after the NAPOLEONIC WARS, and London was thronged with discharged soldiers and sailors without work.

Speenhamland System   See Poor Law – Speenhamland System.

Spence, Thomas (1750–1814)

A NEWCASTLE schoolmaster who became a JACOBIN propagandist. He arrived in LONDON in 1792 to advocate the appropriation of aristocrats' land and the nationalization of land. He wrote and distributed broadsheets and a periodical, *Pig's Meat*, between 1793 and 1796. He was imprisoned in 1794 and 1801, but built up around him a group of converts, the Spenceans. He championed the rights of women and the right of common people to divorce. Even after his death

his followers were active, particularly in 1816 after the NAPOLEONIC WARS, when a small group formed a Spencean Society which included Arthur Thistlewood and Thomas Preston. They gained support among discharged soldiers and sailors as well as among mechanics and MANUFACTURERS. In 1820 the government's harsh measures reduced their numbers, but their views continued to be aired.

Spies

The government and local magistrates frequently used spies to obtain information and identify trouble-makers during periods of unrest or suspected combinations of workers. The system was in force in the industrial districts before the LUDDITE riots. Men with bad reputations were often recruited as spies, and their uncorroborated statements were usually sufficient to result in TRANSPORTATION for the accused.

The government represented informers and *agents provocateurs* as 'detectives', performing a dangerous but important task. The recruits fall into two groups; those who had fallen foul of authority in some way and bought their freedom by being spies, and active reformers who became spies to save their own skins, or for money. Spies who appeared in court were in some danger afterwards and were given careers in the army, sent to the colonies or given the opportunity to live in another part of the country. Some spies were arrested by magistrates by mistake, but the authorities were often shrewd, employing more than one informer to corroborate the evidence. A government spy called WILLIAM OLIVER was believed to be responsible for the collapse of the PENTRIDGE RISING in 1817, as a result of which four men were hanged and 11 transported to Botany Bay, Australia.

Spinning Jenny

A machine invented by JAMES HARGREAVES about 1764, which enabled a worker to spin a number of threads at the same time. The word 'jenny' is probably derived from 'engine', the name commonly used for all new MACHINES at that time. The yarn spun on the jenny was soft and suitable for the WEFT yarn in cotton–LINEN fabrics. It was also suitable for spinning the soft, full yarns used in the WOOLLEN INDUSTRY.

The jenny was simple to construct and cheap enough for cottagers and small MANUFACTURERS to buy. Other inventors improved the jenny and it was widely used, especially in Lancashire. It was estimated in 1788 that there were at least 20,000 jennies in England, the smallest of which could do the work of six to eight hand spinners and could be operated by children. The effect of the jenny was to multiply many times the amount of yarn that could be spun by a single operator. It survived in some parts of Derbyshire and Staffordshire until the close of the NAPOLEONIC WARS.

Visit Higher Mill, Helmshore, Lancashire – spinning jenny. **M***
Tonge Moore Textile Museum, Bolton – multiple spinning jenny and other textile machinery. **M***

Spode, Josiah I (1733–97)

A master potter, appointed manager of a pottery at Stoke-on-Trent in 1762. He bought the business eight years later and experimented to find a solution to the problem of making PORCELAIN. He was unable to develop his ideas because of the patent prohibiting the use of Cornish clay, taken out by WILLIAM COOKWORTHY, which did not expire until 1796. Josiah Spode added bone ash to china stone and CHINA CLAY and fired the mix in new kilns and ovens which he built in 1796, producing the first BONE CHINA, as it was later called. His pioneer work revolutionized the pottery industry.

L. Whiter, *Spode: A History of the Family, Factory and Wares, 1733–1833* (Barrie and Jenkins 1978).

Spode, Josiah II (1754–1827)

He directed the Spode works, after the death of his father, JOSIAH SPODE I, with his partner William Copeland taking responsibility for the commercial side of the business. Josiah Spode II introduced a STEAM-DRIVEN BEAM ENGINE by JAMES WATT

in 1802, to replace one of TREVITHICK's installed in the late 1770s. The engine was used to drive the grinding mills and also operated the throwers' and turners' lathes. He introduced feldspar into the paste, making it harder and more translucent. He also pioneered the making of STONE CHINA, a hard earthenware which resembled china.

After his death the pottery was managed for a time by his son, but he took little interest in the works, and in 1833 it was acquired by the son of William Copeland. In 1867 Copeland took his four sons into partnership and the firm became W.T. Copeland and Sons Ltd.

Visit Spode Ltd, Church Street, Stoke-on-Trent – factory tour and museum. **M***

Stage Coach   See Coach Services

Stage Wagon

A horse-drawn wagon which carried freight by road before the railway network (see RAILWAY DEVELOPMENT) was built. Stage wagons carried a few passengers and served the major towns throughout the country. Their service was slow and organized by local carriers or by large firms such as PICKFORDS.

Staithe

A waterside depot for coal brought from nearby collieries to be loaded onto ships. Staithes were heavy wooden structures, generally with a roof and built to accommodate up to six KEELS at a time. They were common along the banks of the Rivers Tyne and Wear in North East England, or at coastal ports on the Northumberland and Durham coalfield. Piers were also used to enable the coal to be poured down wooden chutes called spouts, into the keels. In 1812 staithes were built out into deep water on the River Wear so that coal could be loaded into sea-going vessels instead of into keels. Staithes were also to be found on other rivers and at some other ports.

Visit Blyth, Northumberland – coal staithes.

Stamping and Potting

A process for removing the carbon, sulphur and silica from coke-smelted PIG IRON, patented in the 1760s by Charles and William Wood. Pig iron with silica removed in a refinery was broken up by heavy stampers and placed with lime in covered pots or crucibles. These pots were heated in a furnace, and the lime absorbed the sulphur in the iron. The high temperature also oxidized the carbon in the metal and removed it.

Because the process was popular in Shropshire it was sometimes called the Shropshire process. It was adopted at the CYFARTHFA IRONWORKS by Charles Wood in 1766, and was in use in many other areas by 1780. It was an important agent in the elimination of charcoal forges (see BLAST FURNACES – CHARCOAL BURNING) because it was a cheaper process and undercut their prices. The adoption of the potting process and coke smelting (see BLAST FURNACES – COKE-FIRED) enabled the IRON INDUSTRY to increase output significantly. Further patents were taken out by G. Cockshutt and by the West Bromwich ironmasters Wright and Jesson in the 1770s. The PUDDLING process resulted in a gradual reduction in stamping and potting.

Standard of Living

It has been suggested, although not all historians agree, that the years leading up to the NAPOLEONIC WARS saw a rise in the standard of living of WORKING-CLASS people. During the war there were shortages due to the blockade of Europe and dislocations in the supply of food and raw materials, which resulted in a lowering of living standards and periods of widespread distress. This situation continued after the war until about 1820.

Between 1820 and 1840 there was some progress in living standards, but the experiences of different groups of workers varied and an assessment of general trends is difficult. Skilled workers improved their standard of living, whereas the CROPPERS and other domestic industrial workers suffered a sharp decline in standards. After 1840 there was a steady increase in living standards, for which there were a number of reasons. These included more regular employment opportunities, an increase in the proportion of better-paid jobs and cheaper consumer goods, placing a wider selection within the reach of working people. However, there were still large groups of workers for whom the standard of living remained at the point of subsistence, including those whose skills were no longer needed, such as the HAND LOOM WEAVERS.

H.J. Taylor, *The Standard of Living in Britain in the Industrial Revolution* (Methuen 1975).

Stanhope, Charles, Third Earl (1753–1816)

A scientist and inventor who was also a RADICAL and supported reform at home and the FRENCH REVOLUTION. He built a STEAM BOAT to be driven by a propeller in 1792–3, but the vessel had a very limited success. He also planned a CANAL from Bude in North Devon to the interior of Devon and Cornwall to carry sea-sand as a fertilizer. The canal was planned as a TUB-BOAT CANAL with an INCLINED PLANE. It was dug between 1819 and 1823 after his death, having been delayed by the NAPOLEONIC WARS.

Starvationer

The nickname given to the first CANAL boats which were used on the BRIDGEWATER CANAL. The boats were very narrow and had a length of up to 48 feet (14.6 m). The nickname may have been derived from the ribs of the boat, which were exposed. The NARROW BOATS used on the canal system at the end of the 18th century were descended from those used to carry coal from the Duke's mine at Worsley.

Visit National Mining Museum, Retford, Nottinghamshire – starvationer on display. **M***

Statute of Artificers, 1563

An Act of Parliament stating that no one could operate a trade in Great Britain unless he had first served a seven years'

APPRENTICESHIP, under an indenture which set out the regulations to be observed by both the master and the apprentice. The skills the master must teach the apprentice were listed, as well as the living conditions, clothing and other essentials the master had to supply to the apprentice. The apprentice was usually required to live with the master, serve him and not play unlawful games, visit ale houses or get married during the years of the apprenticeship.

The INDUSTRIAL REVOLUTION struck a fatal blow at the Statute. A long technical training became less necessary, and the large number of apprentices in the mills were nothing more than young workers or children whose age was an excuse for low wages and strict discipline. Some groups of workers, such as the CALICO printers and wool weavers, attempted in 1803–4 and 1811–14 to have the Statute restored. Parliament appointed a committee to investigate, but it failed to reach a conclusion. The MANUFACTURERS wanted a greater degree of economic freedom and the Statute was repealed in 1814.

Steam Boats

A boat powered by a STEAM ENGINE. The first to go into commercial service carrying cargo and passengers was the *COMET*, which started sailing from GLASGOW to Greenock in 1812. Other steam boats quickly followed and services spread to other estuaries, including the Firth of Forth, Mersey and Thames. By 1817 British steam boats were also operating on the Seine in France and the Rhine and the Elbe in Germany. By 1830 there were extensive steam boat services around the coast of mainland Britain, as well as to the Hebrides, Ireland and the Continent. Coastal steam boats competed with STAGE COACHES and offered cheaper fares. Steamer services sometimes linked up with fast overland coaches, shortening journey times. For example, passengers could travel from Glasgow to LIVERPOOL by steamer and then by coach to LONDON. Piers were built at a number of coastal towns between 1800 and 1840 for the steam boat trade.

The coastal, river and estuary steam boat services declined after the 1830s, unable to compete with the rapidly expanding railway networks (see RAILWAY DEVELOPMENT). The railways could not compete with ferry crossings, but were responsible for increasing traffic on the routes by providing connecting trains. Train services linked with the cross-Channel steamers at Folkestone started in 1843. Paddle steam boats continued to operate in the summer months and eventually became popular attractions for holiday makers. Some remained in service on short routes such as London to Margate until the start of the Second World war in 1939.

M.K. Stammers, *Steamboats* (Shire Publications 1986).

Steam Coaches

Steam coaches were introduced in the 1820s, and in the 1830s operated between LONDON and Brighton on the south coast, and between Cheltenham and Gloucester in Gloucestershire. Services never became widespread and any possible developments were overtaken by the growth of the railway network (see RAILWAY DEVELOPMENT).

A company called the Steam Carriage Company of Scotland operated a steam carriage passenger service between GLASGOW and Paisley for seven months in 1834. The Company used six 26-seater steam coaches designed by JOHN SCOTT RUSSELL. On one journey a heap of loose stones placed on the road by order of the trustees of the TURNPIKE trust caused a wheel to collapse; the boiler burst and five people were killed. Probably this was the first fatal motor accident in Great Britain. The Court of Session stopped the steam carriages from running and the coaches were dismantled. The turnpike trust agreed to pay damages out of court.

Steam Digging

The first major digging machine was James Usher's rotary STEAM PLOUGH of 1849. It was a portable STEAM ENGINE with the boiler mounted on rollers instead of wheels. The soil was broken up by rotating shares. It weighed 5 tonnes (5.6

US tons) and worked at an average rate of 2 mph (3.2 kph). Other inventions followed, but it was found that steam-powered cable ploughing was more successful than rotary cultivation, particularly since the steam engine used for rotary work was extremely heavy.

Steam Engine

The steam engine, or fire engine as it was called at first, was used originally as a pump. A simple engine was made by THOMAS SAVERY at the end of the 17th century, followed a few years later by NEWCOMEN's engine. It was JAMES WATT who improved on this engine, reducing the loss of energy by condensing the steam in a separate condenser. He also invented other improvements and successfully developed the engine at the SOHO WORKS.

Watt's steam engine was first used for pumping water from mines. His invention in 1781 of a rotative steam engine made it possible to drive MACHINES directly from the engine. The first cotton mill to use a rotative steam engine was at Bulwell in Nottinghamshire in 1788. In the decade which followed mills in Derbyshire began to decline because of lack of coal nearby, and the coalfields of Lancashire and Yorkshire attracted mills which were built several storeys high. Tall chimneys led away the smoke from the boilers while water was obtained from nearby streams. Each mill had an engine house where the 'engineer' cleaned and prepared the engine. Estimates suggest that approximately 2,100 steam engines were manufactured in the 18th century, with about half the number pumping water from mines and about 460 in use in textile mills.

By the beginning of the 19th century James Watt's steam engine was rapidly taking over as the main source of power. After 1830 it proved itself as power for the railways and this brought

The reconstructed pit head at the North of England Open Air Museum, Beamish, County Durham. The tall stone-built engine house contains a steam vertical winding engine built in 1855 by J. and G. Joicey of Newcastle-upon-Tyne. (*Beamish, North of England Open Air Museum*)

about a revolution in communications.

Visit Steam Museum, Atlas No. 3 Mill, Bolton – various engines. **M***
Science Museum, London – early steam engines. **M***
Kew Bridge Steam Museum, Brentford, Middlesex – steam-powered beam engines. **M***
Summerlee Heritage Trust, West Canal Street, Coatbridge, Strathclyde – steam engines and other industrial machinery. **M***

H.W. Dickinson, *A Short History of the Steam Engine* (Cass 1963).
G.N. Von Tunzelmann, *Steam Power and British Industrialization to 1860* (Clarendon 1978).
G. Hayes, *Industrial Steam Locomotives* (Shire Publications 1989).
A.E. Musson, *James Watt and the Steam Revolution* (Adams and Dart 1969).

Steam Engines – Beam

An early engine powered by steam, in which the movement was regulated by a large wooden or CAST-IRON beam. This originally operated a mine pump and then later, when the crank was introduced, was used to provide rotary action and turn wheels. It enjoyed its greatest popularity for driving machinery between 1800 and 1880 and was in use in both its rotative and non-rotative forms until the early 1900s.

Visit Papplewick, Nottinghamshire – beam engine (1884). **M***
Stretham, Cambridgeshire – beam engine (1831) used for Fen drainage.

Steam Engines – Colliery Winding

A NEWCOMEN engine was used at a colliery on the Northumberland coast in 1763 for winding coal in CORVES. The rotary motion did not work well and the miners would not use the engine for descending and ascending. JAMES WATT's SUN AND PLANET rotary motion gear, which was patented in 1782, provided a more suitable action for winding with steam power, and the first Watt engine was erected at the Walker Colliery on Tyneside in 1784. In the 1790s BOULTON AND WATT engines were introduced at a

number of collieries. Those used for winding were called WHIMSEYS, and were very common in the early 19th century, working at a speed of 250 feet (76 m) per minute.

Visit North of England Open Air Museum, Beamish, County Durham – vertical colliery winding engine. **M***
Washington, Tyne and Wear – colliery winding engine.

Steam Engines – Cornish

A STEAM ENGINE developed from JAMES WATT's engine after the expiry of his patent in 1800. It was more efficient and economical of fuel than the earlier engines and designed for pumping water from mines. It was installed in a number of deep mines with serious drainage problems in the first half of the 19th century. The first one was erected by RICHARD TREVITHICK at the Wheal Prosper tin mine, Cornwall, in 1811. It was highly efficient and was installed in other mining areas of Britain as well as overseas, where fuel was scarce. The engine required a stronger boiler than those in use because of the high pressure of the generated steam, and Richard Trevithick developed a cylindrical boiler, which became known as the Cornish boiler and was widely adopted as high-pressure steam engines became more popular.

The Cornish engine was installed in a rectangular house with a·round chimney at one corner and a strong wall at the opposite end on which the beam rocked (see STEAM ENGINES – BEAM). These engine houses can be found in a number of mining districts in the West of England and at isolated mining areas elsewhere. Five engines are preserved by the Cornish Engines Preservation Society and are in the care of the National Trust.

Visit Holman's Museum, Camborne, Cornwall – model of Cornish engine and boiler house. **M***
Taylor's Shaft, East Pool, Camborne, Cornwall – winding engine (1892).
Levant Mine, near Land's End, Cornwall – rotative engine (1840).
Scottish Mining Museum, Prestongrange,

East Lothian – restored Cornish engine (1874). **M***

Science Museum, London – Cornish boiler. **M***

D.B. Barton, *The Cornish Beam Engine* (Truro 1969).

Steam Engines – Cotton Industry

JAMES WATT's rotary STEAM ENGINE was introduced into cotton mills to drive carding and spinning MACHINES in the 1780s and 1790s. The early machines were expensive, frequently broke down and had running costs far in excess of those of a waterwheel. About a quarter of the 2,000 or more steam engines produced in the 18th century were used in the textile industry. By 1835 the engine had been improved to the point where it was the predominant source of power in the industry, providing 75 per cent of the power required. Water power still survived at a few Pennine centres such as Halifax and Glossop. It was still as expensive to use steam as to use water, but the increasing concentration of the cotton industry on the Lancashire coalfield reduced fuel costs.

Economies in power costs did not come in the 1830s, but cotton prices fell and MANUFACTURERS adopted the more efficient CORNISH ENGINE to cut fuel costs. High costs and low profit margins checked the expansion of steam power and extended the life of water power until the middle of the century.

By the end of the 19th century the large textile mills of Lancashire and Yorkshire required a more powerful engine to drive their vast number of machines, and a mill engine was specially designed to meet their needs. These engines were horizontal, with high- and low-pressure cylinders mounted either one behind the other or side by side.

Visit Steam Museum, Atlas No. 3 Mill, Bolton, Lancashire – stationary steam engines from textile mills and factories. **M***

Trencherfield Mill, Wigan, Lancashire – large steam engine (1907). **M***

Science Museum, London – Mill engines. **M***

Birmingham Museum of Science and Industry – mill engines. **M***

Steam Engines – Land Drainage

The first STEAM PUMPING ENGINE on the Cambridgeshire Fens was built in 1821, and at least 14 others were in use by 1850. Rotative BEAM ENGINES were used and their use was extended to the Vale of York and the Hull valley.

Stretham, Cambridgeshire – Beam engine used for Fen drainage. **M***

Steam Engines – Ploughing

The earliest patent for a steam haulage system where a plough was dragged along on the end of a rope was taken out in 1810 by a Major Pratt, but the idea was not developed on a practical basis until the 1850s. JOHN HEATHCOAT took out a patent in 1832 for a STEAM ENGINE to drive huge drums, with a rope wound in and paid out alternately so that the plough could go to and fro. It was designed for the reclamation of marshland, and was not taken up by farmers who wanted a MACHINE to plough ordinary land.

This came in 1854 with a machine invented by JOHN FOWLER. It was made by RANSOME's at Ipswich and used a fixed steam engine to wind the rope while an anchor was placed at the other end of the field. Unfortunately the cost of the machine was quite beyond the ordinary farmer's pocket, but 33 complete sets were ordered by 1860, mainly for contractors who hired them out. By 1862 two engines were being used, moving down opposite sides of the field and winding the plough to and fro between them. Small fields, narrow lanes and restrictions on the movement of engines on roads in daylight limited the use of the steam engine for ploughing.

Steam Engines – Pumping

STEAM ENGINES performed two important pumping functions: removing water from mines and recirculating water at factories, ironworks and waterworks as well as on CANALS.

The NEWCOMEN engine had been designed and was used for pumping water from mines, and it was in use over a long period. At Elsecar in South Yorkshire a Newcomen-type engine pumped out mine water from 1787 until 1923. JAMES WATT's engine was also designed for use at mines and was invaluable. Both of these engines were BEAM ENGINES, and in its rotative and non-rotative forms the beam engine was used for water and sewage pumping until the early 1900s. It was very strong and reliable and by the last decades of the 19th century reached a high degree of development. A number of beam engines used by water and a sewage companies have been preserved, together with the decorated interiors of the engine houses.

Pumping engines were also needed on some canals to lift water to higher levels where supplies were inadequate. At Crofton in Wiltshire, on the Kennet and Avon Canal, a BOULTON AND WATT engine was installed in 1812 to supply a 35-mile (56-km) section of the canal. It has been restored, and is the oldest engine in the world which can still be seen in steam (at selected weekends).

Visit The British Engineerium, Hove, East Sussex – beam pumping engine; one with steam on Sundays (1876). **M***
Papplewick, Nottinghamshire – pumping engines (1884). **M***
Eastney, Portsmouth – two sewage pumping engines (1887). **M***
Ryhope, near Sunderland, Tyne and Wear – two pumping engines (1868).

Steam Engines – Threshing and Barn Use

Portable STEAM ENGINES for farm use were first made in the 1830s. In 1840 Robert Willis designed the 'Farmer's Engine', but unfortunately it was not strong enough for the tasks on a farm. RANSOME's made a self-propelling portable engine and thresher in 1842. Self-propelling portable engines were cheaper than the heavier traction engines, and by 1860 the engines used on farms were likely to be either common portable engines moved about by horses, or self-propelled engines, still steered by a horse in shafts but propelled by their own machinery and usually capable of hauling the threshing machine as well.

Very large farms might have a fixed engine set in a brick-built engine house and used for threshing, root pulping, cake crushing, chaff cutting or sawing wood. Steam from the boiler could be used to heat drying-rooms and for steaming chaff.

Visit Bressingham, Diss, Norfolk – Steam Museum with farm steam engines. **M***
Strumpshaw, Norwich, Norfolk – Strumpshaw Hall Steam Museum, traction, ploughing and other steam engines. **M***

Steam-Heated Cylinders

Cylinders through which steam was passed to heat them were first used in the drying process for PAPER-MAKING in 1817, by JOHN DICKINSON. Each cylinder had its own felt surface; the paper passed around the cylinders so that when it came off the final cylinder it was dry. A number of these cylinders were added to FOURDRINIER machines to improve the drying facilities.

Steamship Companies

The first companies to run regular steamships (see STEAM BOATS) were formed between 1810 and 1820. They ran services on the Clyde between GLASGOW and Greenock, on the Mersey, on the Firth of Forth and on the Thames estuary. These steamship companies were small and operated with only one or two ships. Cross-Channel and Irish services using steam followed in the 1820s together with coastal services, such as that between Glasgow and LIVERPOOL. To meet the threat of competition from the railways (see RAILWAY DEVELOPMENT), some CANAL companies introduced steam boat services in the 1830s, but the goal for a number of investors was a service across the Atlantic. More capital was needed for this route and it was provided by the GREAT WESTERN RAILWAY COMPANY, which formed a separate steamship company in 1836. The decision by this company to build the *GREAT WESTERN* provoked the formation of other transatlantic steamship companies. These included the Transatlantic Steamship Company and the British and American Steam Navigation Company.

Companies already operating SAILING SHIP services also introduced steam services and became steamship companies. In 1840 Samuel Cunard and ROBERT NAPIER founded the Bristol and North American Royal Mail Steam Packet Company (later called Cunard). Samuel Cunard had won a government contract to carry the mail between England and North America, and the first steamer, the *Britannia*, which had wooden paddles, sailed from Liverpool in 1840. It was built by Clyde shipbuilders, as were later vessels. By 1848 the fleet consisted of 12 ships operating a service between Liverpool in Britain and Halifax in Canada and Boston in the USA.

In 1822 Brodie Willcox (?–1862) and Arthur Anderson (1792–1868) became partners in a business as traders running sailing vessels to Spanish and Portuguese ports – the Iberian peninsula. Later, steam vessels were used, and in 1837 the firm obtained contracts to carry the mail to the Iberian peninsula. In 1840 the Peninsular and Oriental Steam Navigation Company was formed, with services between Suez and the Indian ports and through the Mediterranean to Alexandria in Egypt. Mail was carried overland through Egypt to Suez to link up with the Company's ships sailing to Bombay and, from 1852, to Singapore and Australia. The Company started its first tourist service to Egypt and Palestine in 1844.

B. Cable, *A Hundred Years of the P. and O., 1837–1937* (Ivor Nicholson and Watson 1937).

F.E. Hyde, *Cunard and the North Atlantic, 1840–1973* (Macmillan 1973).

Steam Tugs

The first CANAL steam tug was designed by ROBERT FULTON and used a NEWCOMEN engine to tow eight boats, carrying a total of 200 tonnes (224 US tons) of coal, from Worsley to MANCHESTER on the BRIDGEWATER CANAL. The FORTH AND CLYDE CANAL refused to use the *CHARLOTTE DUNDAS* in 1802 for the same task because of damage to the banks, but in 1827 the *Cupid* was used to tow scows

(the Scottish name for canal boats). River tugs were being used between Hull and Gainsborough in 1818, and on the Humber between Hull and Goole from 1826. In 1830 steam tugs operated between Runcorn and LIVERPOOL.

Canals were slow to accept canal tugs because of damage to the banks and the hindrance they could cause if there were many LOCKS. Some of the first tugs were used for tunnel navigation and more were used on stretches of canals without locks in the 1840s, particularly on the Ellesmere and Chester, Birmingham and Liverpool, and Macclesfield Canals.

All these early tugs had paddles, which gave them an advantage in shallow water. Some paddle tugs were still operated on the Mersey in the 1920s.

Steel Industry

Steel is difficult to define since there are many types with widely differing characteristics. There are, however, three basic types: carbon steel, MILD STEEL and alloy steel.

Carbon steel was in use long before mild steel was invented. It was made by heating pure WROUGHT IRON in contact with charcoal so that it would absorb carbon. This produced a hard skin on the wrought iron and was used for tools and weapons requiring a sharp edge. Attempts to make steel directly from iron, giving the iron a consistent hardness, were made by BENJAMIN HUNTSMAN, who improved on earlier cementation furnaces to develop the crucible technique at SHEFFIELD in 1742. CRUCIBLE STEEL was superior in hardness to other steels and was first used for chains, watch springs and files for the use of clock-makers.

Although Huntsman tried to keep the process secret, at least seven Sheffield firms were using his method in 1787. Steel was supplied in rods, as wire, or as tools and cutlery, and in the first half of the 19th century small-scale firms specializing in the converting and refining of steel developed in Sheffield. There was a rapid expansion of steel-making, with an estimated production of 14,200 tonnes (15,600 US tons) in 1835, and production boomed between 1851 and 1861 as a result of improved techniques, particularly in casting from the crucibles. There were 135 steel firms in Sheffield in 1856, with an output of some 50,000 tonnes (56,000 US tons).

The next major breakthrough was in 1856, when mild steel was produced by the BESSEMER PROCESS. This made it possible to produce steel in sufficient quantities, and at prices cheap enough, to replace wrought iron for structural purposes. In the 1860s Bessemer steel began to be used extensively for railway rails, and later for boiler plates and SHIPBUILDING. The next big development occurred in the 1860s when C.W. Siemens introduced the open hearth furnace, which was adopted for converting PIG IRON into steel.

Alloy steels were introduced in 1887 when Robert Hadfield (1858–1940) invented manganese steel – manganese alloyed with carbon steel to give it new properties such as hardness.

Visit Abbeydale Industrial Hamlet, Sheffield – steel furnace, scythe works, workmen's cottages and manager's house. **M***
Kelham Island Industrial Museum, Sheffield – Sheffield's industrial history. **M***

W.K.V. Gale, *The British Iron and Steel Industry* (David and Charles 1967).

Stephenson, George (1781–1848)

An engineer who developed the experiments undertaken by RICHARD TREVITHICK on locomotives. He was born in a one-roomed cottage near NEWCASTLE, and became an ENGINEWRIGHT before building locomotives for hauling coal wagons along the Killingworth WAGONWAY between 1814 and 1817. In 1814 he built the *BLUCHER* for this work. He built the Hetton Colliery Railway in County Durham between 1820 and 1822, taking it 8 miles (13 km) to the River Wear at Sunderland. Between 1822 and 1825 he supervised the engineering work on the STOCKTON AND DARLINGTON RAILWAY, and in 1829 his locomotive *ROCKET* won the RAINHILL TRIALS, held on the LIVERPOOL AND MANCHESTER RAILWAY. The *Rocket* reached a speed of 35 mph (56 kph) and

proved that passengers as well as coal could be transported quickly and safely.

In addition to building locomotives he also invented the Geordie SAFETY LAMP in 1815 for use in mines. His invention was almost simultaneous with a similar development by SIR HUMPHRY DAVY.

Visit Camden, London – roundhouse locomotive shed (now a theatre) designed by George Stephenson.
Wylam, Northumberland – birthplace of George Stephenson, with railway museum. **M***

L.T.C. Rolt, *George and Robert Stephenson* (Longman 1960).

Stephenson, Robert (1803–59)

An engineer who was educated by his father GEORGE STEPHENSON to complement his own expertise as a steam rail engineer. In 1823, in conjunction with his father and others, he formed Robert Stephenson and Company in NEWCASTLE. The works built *LOCOMOTION* which ran on the STOCKTON AND DARLINGTON RAILWAY. Later the *ROCKET* was also built at the works. Robert Stephenson helped WILLIAM JAMES survey the LIVERPOOL AND MANCHESTER RAILWAY, and then joined a mining company in South America. He returned in 1827, took charge of his locomotive works and improved the design of locomotives. After surveying a route for the London and Birmingham Railway in 1830, he was appointed engineer-in-chief in 1833. In 1850 he built the Britannia tubular bridge in WROUGHT IRON over the MENAI Straits, completing the rail route from LONDON to Holyhead.

D.J. Smith, *Robert Stephenson* (Shire Publications 1976).

St Helens

A Lancashire industrial town that owed its development mainly to its coal field and the ease of transporting the coal by means of the SANKEY BROOK NAVIGATION. This, the first British CANAL, linked St Helens with the Weaver Navigation and LIVERPOOL, making it possible to move coal cheaply to Liverpool and to Northwich in Cheshire, where it was used to boil brine and make SALT. Coal also attracted the COPPER SMELTING industry to the town, with ore brought in by sea from PARYS MOUNTAIN and smelted at the Ravenhead Works built in 1779. Engineering was established at the St Helens Foundry in 1798 and glass-making was a major industry by 1820, with flint, bottle, PLATE and CROWN GLASS all being made at glass houses in the town. The alkali trade, making soft soap, was established in the 1820s and the population grew from 4,000 in 1821 to 11,800 in 1845 and 25,000 by 1870.

Visit St Helens Museum and Art Gallery, College Street, St Helens – mining life. **M***

T.C. Barker and J.R. Harris, *A Merseyside Town in the Industrial Revolution. St Helens 1750–1900* (1959).

St Helens Crown Glass Company

A glass works started in ST HELENS, Lancashire, by John William Bell and partners, including WILLIAM PILKINGTON, in 1826. It was renamed Greenall and Pilkington in 1829 and Pilkington Brothers Ltd in 1849. The importance of the site for the import of raw materials and the neighbouring Lancashire coalfield made it a centre for the development of the manufacture of glass, which is still carried on by Pilkington's today.

Visit St Helens, Lancashire – Pilkington Glass Museum. **M***

Stock Exchange

Dealings in company shares were first carried out by brokers, many of whom met for business in coffee houses in LONDON. By 1773 the Stock Exchange had its own premises and in 1803 it issued a list of companies in whose shares it was prepared to deal. Virtually all the stocks sold and traded were government securities. Shares in incorporated concerns such as the East India Company were not usually bought or sold, or even quoted, on the Stock Exchange; dealings were arranged by the company itself. By 1800, however, the Stock Exchange was adding to its list the CANAL enterprise, INSURANCE companies and the few public utilities.

In the 1830s and 1840s railways (see RAILWAY DEVELOPMENT) brought a great deal of business to the Stock Exchange, but few industrialists used its facilities to borrow money until after the Joint Stock Companies Act of 1856 and the Consolidation Act of 1862. (The Joint Stock Companies Act provided for the setting up of limited liability companies with CAPITAL supplied by the public. A committee of directors was to be responsible to the shareholders for company policy, and a shareholder's liability was limited to the value of his or her subscribed shares. The 1862 Consolidation Act codified piecemeal legislation passed between 1856 and 1861.) After 1862 there were investment booms on the Stock Exchange in each decade, with an increasing volume of business.

Stockinger

A worker who made stockings. Until the late 1840s stockingers worked on home knitting frames (see FRAMEWORK KNITTERS) in their own homes or in small workshops belonging to a master stockinger. The industry remained on a domestic basis into the 1850s. After 1815 the stockingers saw their wages steadily fall. Most did not own their own frames, hiring them from hosiers, middlemen or persons not connected with the trade. Frame rents were a subject of grievance, especially since the rent had to be paid even when there was no work. The stockingers' trade was overstocked with labour and there was not enough work to go round. Entry into the trade was easy and the work was semi-skilled. As with the HAND LOOM WEAVERS, the stockingers' status and earnings were reduced and they experienced much hardship as more and more powered frames were introduced.

Stone China

Earthenware which closely resembled china, first produced by JOSIAH SPODE II in 1805. It was an extremely hard earthenware containing feldspar, which produced a clear, ringing note when lightly tapped.

Street Surfacing

Footpaths which were paved and raised with kerb stones and were introduced in Westminster, LONDON, in 1765. THOMAS TELFORD made rectangular granite setts in 1824 to be placed on a foundation of broken stones. These setts were very noisy and created dust. Wood-blocks were used in London in 1838 but stone paving was most commonly used. Concrete roads were first made in England in 1865.

St Rollox Chemical Works

A chemical works in GLASGOW which was started by CHARLES TENNANT in 1797. The plant originally made BLEACHING powder, and in 1803 the first lead chambers were built in which SULPHURIC ACID could be made. The works grew to become the largest chemical works in Europe in the first decades of the 19th century.

Strutt, Jedediah (1726–97)

A DISSENTER who was apprenticed as a millwright and, in 1758, adapted the knitting frame so that ribbed hosiery could be manufactured. With partners he set up a hosiery business in Derby making mainly silk hose, and by 1769 he was well established and prosperous. In that year or shortly afterwards he went into partnership with RICHARD ARKWRIGHT, a partnership that lasted until 1781 when the death of the financier SAMUEL NEED, a close friend of both men, resulted in the partnership being dissolved. Jedediah Strutt in partnership with his sons built three silk mills at BELPER between 1778 and 1793, as well as mills at Milford (1779) and Derby (1793). He provided houses for his workers, many with large gardens, and additional land could be rented as allotments. He was a modest man who believed that wealth also brought responsibility.

R.S. Fitton and A.P. Wadsworth, *The Strutts and the Arkwrights 1758–1830* (Manchester University Press 1958).

Strutt, W., G. and J.

The business carried on by the three sons of JEDEDIAH STRUTT, William, George and Joseph. William (1756–1830) became a Fellow of the Royal Society in 1817 and maintained an interest throughout his life in many aspects of science. He became the outstanding figure of the Midlands textile industry, successfully designing iron-framed FIREPROOF FACTORIES with heating systems. He embarked on MULE spinning in Derby in 1795, building the Calico Mill, later called the Derby Mill.

The Strutts played a distinguished part in the public life of Derby, where they lived. In 1812 a Lancasterian (see JOSEPH LANCASTER) school was built in the town and in 1824 a MECHANICS' INSTITUTE. The town was given an arboretum by Joseph and an infirmary by William. Schools were built at BELPER and Milford, where the Strutts had mills, and in 1811 they built a UNITARIAN chapel at Milford. They also contributed generously towards the cost of an Anglican (see CHURCH OF ENGLAND) church at Belper.

As Unitarians the Strutts were supporters of political freedom, both at home and abroad; they were sympathetic to the Americans during the AMERICAN WAR OF INDEPENDENCE, and to the FRENCH REVOLUTION.

Visit Belper, Derbyshire – Strutt's North Mill.

Stubs, Peter (1756–1806)

A file-maker and innkeeper at Warrington, Lancashire, who built up a successful business based mainly on the DOMESTIC SYSTEM. He was a maker of high-grade files required by clock-makers, machine workers and cotton spinners. There were many processes in converting the bar steel into a file and these were performed by craftsmen in their own homes. Stubs employed many outworkers, giving them the materials and paying them for the finished goods. After about 1800 he began to build up a business employing workers full time, and in 1802 he built workshops in Warrington. Steel was obtained mainly from SHEFFIELD and exchanged for the finished files. Files were sold through ironmongers and factors, and there are records of them being sent to America and the East and West Indies.

In 1788 Peter Stubs was innkeeper of the White Bear Inn, Warrington. The malt dust and barrel dregs were used to make a paste needed in making the files, so he was able to combine his two occupations in a practical manner. As an innkeeper he made beer and malt while successfully conducting his file business.

T.S. Ashton, *An Eighteenth Century Industrialist. Peter Stubs of Warrington 1756–1806* (Manchester University Press 1939).

Sulphuric Acid

Sulphuric acid was an essential chemical in the industrial development and commercial prosperity of Britain in the 19th century, and it was said that the prosperity of a country could be judged by the amount of sulphuric acid consumed. It was available on a very small scale in the 18th century. Josiah Ward began manufacturing it at Richmond in 1737 by burning sulphur and saltpetre (potash nitrate) above a shallow layer of water in a glass bell. In 1746 JOHN ROEBUCK and SAMUEL GARBETT set up a sulphuric acid plant in BIRMINGHAM. They replaced the fragile glass vessels with lead chambers but used the same process as Josiah Ward. The lead chamber process was improved, and large quantities of sulphuric acid could be made cheaply by this method.

After 1845 sulphuric acid was used in the manufacture of phosphate fertilizers (superphosphates – see ARTIFICIAL FERTILIZERS), which brought about a considerable increase in agricultural productivity. It was also used in the manufacture of explosives and BLEACH. By 1870 the industry was established in North East England, LONDON, Lancashire and GLASGOW, and production, which was 10,000 tonnes (11,200 US tons) in 1820

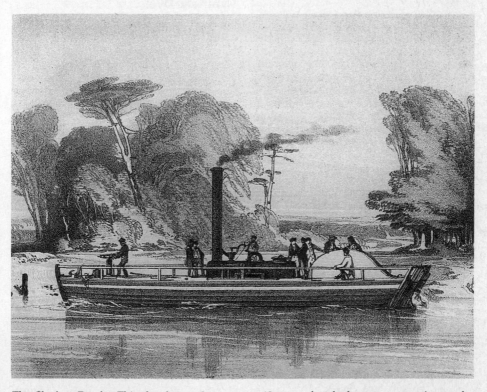

The *Charlotte Dundas*. This sketch was drawn some 40 years after the boat was operating on the Forth and Clyde Canal. It was the first successful British steamboat but it never saw regular service. In 1808 the paddle wheel and steam engine were removed and it was converted into a dredger. (*National Library of Scotland*)

reached 1 million tonnes (1.12m US tons) by 1900.

Sun and Planet Gear

Gearing invented by JAMES WATT in 1781 to enable his STEAM ENGINE to turn wheels and drive MACHINES. It was at the insistence of his partner, MATTHEW BOULTON, that he developed this means of rotative propulsion. The alternative would have been to use the rotary crank developed by James Pickard and pay the patent fees. Watt called his invention 'sun and planet motion' because the 'planet' wheel, fixed rigidly to a connecting rod, moved round the perimeter of a 'sun' wheel. It had mechanical shortcomings which led to its being abandoned in 1802, after BOULTON AND WATT's patent for the steam engine had expired.

Swan, Joseph Wilson (1828–1914)

The inventor of a practical electric lamp. He experimented for many years with carbonized strips in a glass container, but failed to obtain an efficient vacuum in the container. In 1878 he discovered that if a strong current was passed through carbonized material while air was being withdrawn from the glass container, the carbon did not break up and the material glowed. Later he went into partnership with Thomas Edison to find the most suitable filament for the lamp.

Symington, William (1763–1831)

A designer and builder of an atmospheric engine which was less complicated than WATT's STEAM ENGINE. It had been intended to use it to work a pump, but instead it was used to power a boat which had two paddle wheels. In 1802 an improved design using a single paddle wheel at the rear was launched and called the *CHARLOTTE DUNDAS*. An order for eight similar boats for the DUKE OF BRIDGEWATER was cancelled when the Duke died in 1803. William Symington remained a disappointed man for the rest of his life, building no more STEAM BOATS.

W.S. Harvey and G. Downs Rose, *William Symington* (Northgate 1980).

Synthetic Dyes

WILLIAM HENRY PERKIN discovered a synthetic dye using aniline which was bright purple. As a result he set up a factory near Harrow in 1857, and other chemists experimented to find new dyes. On the Continent chemists discovered magenta and other colours in the 1860s.

D.W.F. Hardie and J. Davidson Pratt, *A History of the Modern British Chemical Industry* (Pergamon 1966).

T

Tea Drinking

There was a tremendous increase in tea drinking during the 18th and 19th centuries from 3.7 million lb (1.68 million kg) in 1767 to 31.8 million lb (14.4 million kg) in 1833. The increase in demand was partly caused by a dramatic drop in price because of lower tariffs, tea costing one tenth of the price in 1833 that it cost 100 years earlier. It was also due to a fashion for tea drinking, and was encouraged by a reduction in the tea duty and its removal in the 1850s. As tea drinking increased so did the demand for table ware, and the pottery industry quickly copied the original Chinese tea and table ware which the aristocracy sought from the Far East. With the increased demand for tea pots, cups and saucers, there was also an increase in the demand for dinner ware.

Technical Advances – Major

There were three major technical advances during the period 1760–1860 which changed fundamentally the development of Britain, making it the 'workshop of the world'.

The first was the mechanization of the textile industry. This was most rapid in the COTTON and SILK INDUSTRIES and much slower in the well-established WOOLLEN INDUSTRY. The first factories were the silk and cotton mills of Derbyshire and Lancashire, and the major INVENTIONS were made towards the end of the 18th century.

The second advance was in the production of iron using coal. The technological change in the IRON INDUSTRY was slow until the demand for iron increased rapidly to meet the needs of steam power – the third great advance. Steam power was applied first to pumping water from mines and then, using the rotary engine, to driving MACHINES. The DEVELOPMENT OF THE RAILWAYS after 1830 increased enormously the demand for STEAM ENGINES and iron products, as well as improving communications on a nationwide scale.

Telegraph   See Electric Telegraph

Telegraph Service

In 1843 the GREAT WESTERN RAILWAY agreed that the patentee of the ELECTRIC TELEGRAPH system, William Cooke, should provide the Company with a free telegraph service in return for being able to use the telegraph line as a commercial undertaking. There were offices at Paddington and Slough (the end of the telegraph line) for members of the public who wished to send telegrams to addresses in LONDON or the Slough area. In 1846 William Cooke and J.L. Ricardo, MP, founded the Electric Telegraph Company, and lines were set up linking London with Dover and Southampton and later with MANCHESTER. Cities between Edinburgh and BIRMINGHAM were also linked by a separate line.

Telegraph Stations

The need for speeding communications between French forces during the Continental War at the end of the 18th century resulted in the building of a chain of stations, with semaphore arms and telescopes which could relay messages according to a planned code. The British Admiralty investigated a similar system in the 1790s, using movable shutters instead of semaphore arms, and completed lines of stations on high ground from LONDON to Deal, Yarmouth and Portsmouth. Later, semaphore arms replaced the shutters and a third line was established in 1806 from London to Plymouth. The system worked only in clear weather and required extensive manpower. Ship-to-ship semaphore was also used by varying the combinations of two revolving crosses. After the end of the NAPOLEONIC WARS the system was abandoned, except for the London–Portsmouth link, which was in use until the end of 1847.

Visit Time Ball Tower, Victoria Parade, Deal, Kent – semaphore tower (1821); display of semaphores. **M***
Chatley Heath, Surrey – telegraph station.
Putney Heath, London – The Telegraph inn.

G. Wilson, *The Old Telegraph* (Phillimore 1976).

Telford, Thomas (1757–1834)

The son of a Dumfriesshire shepherd, he became a brilliant engineer and builder of ROADS and CANALS. He was made Surveyor of Public Works for Shropshire in 1787 and was responsible for building 40 bridges in the county between 1790 and 1796. He worked with WILLIAM JESSOP on the Ellesmere Canal, producing the spectacular PONTCYSYLLTE AQUEDUCT, which was completed in 1805. In 1801 the government employed him to survey the Highlands of Scotland and their communications, and he later acted as an engineer on constructions which included the CALEDONIAN CANAL and many Highland roads still in use today.

Thomas Telford's roads consisted of a solid pavement of uniformly sized stones for the foundation and small broken stones of irregular shape for the dressing. The grinding of wheels and horses hooves produced a hard grit which compacted solid. In 1815 he became engineer to the Holyhead Road Commission in North Wales, and in 1826 carried the road over the MENAI Straits on a superb SUSPENSION BRIDGE.

He was also busy in the 1820s building canals, including the Birmingham–Liverpool Canal, known as the SHROPSHIRE CANAL. In 1827 he completed a new tunnel for the Grand Trunk Canal to replace the Harecastle Tunnel, a major bottleneck which could be negotiated by only one boat at a time. He built a new tunnel parallel to the old one, using STEAM ENGINES to pump the tunnel dry and railways to carry away the spoil. He was the first President of the INSTITUTION OF CIVIL ENGINEERS.

L.T.C. Rolt, *Thomas Telford* (Longman 1958).
R. Pearce, *Thomas Telford* (Shire 1978).

Temperance Movement

A MIDDLE-CLASS venture inspired by the BEERHOUSE ACT, 1830, and the excessive drinking of the period. Social reformers were convinced that expenditure on drink reduced the amount of income available for other, socially preferable, activities. To some, drinking was a personal sin from which the WORKING CLASSES had to be rescued. The first temperance society was formed in BRADFORD in 1830, but the first national body was the British and Foreign Temperance Society (1831), which advocated moderation. By comparison the British Temperance Association of 1835 advocated complete abstinence, and nonconformists (see DISSENTERS) were strong in this society.

In 1853 the United Kingdom Alliance was formed and became the leading British temperance organization. Among its proposals was the suggestion that local authorities should be permitted to ban the drink trade from their locality. Parliament was not prepared to legislate for prohibition and the Alliance encouraged people to 'sign the pledge' – to join with others at a Temperance Hall or coffee house and make their children join the Band of Hope. Successive legislation placed restraints on drinking hours and on children in public houses.

Ten Hours Movement

A campaign launched by RICHARD OASTLER and JOHN FIELDEN in 1830 to reduce the hours of women and children to a maximum of ten per day. In the House of Commons their cause was argued by MICHAEL SADLER and Ashley Cooper (later LORD SHAFTESBURY). The MANUFACTURERS said they would be ruined if the costly MACHINES were left idle, and the attempt to get an Act passed failed. The movement continued to agitate and eventually triumphed in 1847, when a FACTORY ACT was passed which limited the working hours to ten in any one day for women and young people.

However the Act applied only to part of the textile industry and not to industry as a whole.

Tennant, Charles (1768–1838)

A LINEN bleacher who set up the ST ROLLOX CHEMICAL WORKS in GLASGOW in 1797. It was the largest in Europe and there was a considerable demand for the chlorine BLEACH it produced in the textile and paper industries. Charles Tennant produced his bleach by a process which was already in use in France and consisted of passing chlorine over lime. The development of bleaching powder was of the utmost importance to the COTTON INDUSTRY, since it speeded up the process and produced a whiter cloth. After consulting French chemists he started the manufacture of synthetic SODA in 1818.

Textile Mills

The first large workshops containing MACHINES for the manufacture of goods were known as mills. This was because they used waterwheels as their source of power, as had grain and other mills for centuries. During the final decades of the 18th century the terms 'mill' and 'factory' were interchangeable. The term 'factory' (from 'MANUFACTORY') became more common, except in the textile industry, where the term 'mill' persisted and is still used today.

Visit Masson Mill, near Matlock, Derbyshire – Arkwright's mill (1783).
Quarry Bank Mill, Styal, Cheshire – mill dating from 1784; museum of the factory system. **M***
Saltaire, near Shipley, Yorkshire – mills and town (1853–70).

Thames Tunnel

A tunnel under the River Thames in east LONDON, built to carry a roadway which was completed by SIR MARC BRUNEL in 1843, having been started in 1825. It was built by using a specially designed shield which made it possible for the men to work at three levels at the same time. The shield was moved forward on jacks and the roof and walls behind were supported by a double arch of stones set in cement. It was the first tunnel in the world to be built in soft clay beneath a river, and was one of the most hazardous civil engineering projects of its time. The tunnel is now used by the Metropolitan Underground line from Wapping to Rotherhithe.

Visit Tunnel Road, Rotherhithe, London – Brunel's Engine House. **M***

Thom, Robert (1774–1847)

A Scottish engineer who designed a combined scheme for Greenock in Scotland for both water power and town WATER SUPPLY, which was completed in 1827. He was in the vanguard of engineers who believed in keeping the water pipes full of water at all times, with the source of supply above the highest houses so that fire engines would have an adequate jet of water to extinguish fires. He also made provision for cleaning the streets, lanes and SEWERS with water, and this helped to limit deaths from CHOLERA OUTBREAKS.

Thomson, Robert William (1822–73)

The inventor of the pneumatic tyre. A Scotsman with a flair for mechanical INVENTIONS, he also designed a fountain pen which was shown at the GREAT EXHIBITION. In 1846 he fitted a brougham (see HENRY BROUGHAM) in LONDON with 'elastic tyre wheels'. The tyres consisted of a tubular rubber ring inside a leather case and inflated with air. The processing of rubber at the time was poor, and pneumatic tyres were never to be popular for horse-drawn vehicles. In the 1860s he made solid rubber tyres for a road steamer (see STEAM COACHES).

Thorncliffe Ironworks

In 1792 the Phoenix Foundry was set up in SHEFFIELD to make stoves, ranges, wheels and MACHINES for cotton mills. In 1794 the partners had sufficient CAPITAL to set up a smelting works with a lease of land, coal and ironstone. The Thorncliffe Ironworks at Chapeltown near Sheffield was started in 1795, and in 1802 the foundry was moved to the same site. The firm specialized in producing iron rails for the WAGONWAYS of local collieries, CAST-IRON pipes for the West Middlesex Water Company, and pipes, lamp posts and other equipment for GAS LIGHTING. The leading partner in the enterprise was George Newton, previously a manufacturer of spades and trowels in Sheffield.

Threshing Machinery

The first successful threshing MACHINE was invented by a Scottish millwright, Andrew Meikle, in 1786. The horse-drawn machine consisted of a rotating drum inside a curved shield. Grain fed in between the drum and the shield had its husks removed. Improvements made it possible to drive the machine by steam, water power, horses or hand. It replaced the flail and resulted in a considerable saving of labour.

Between 1830 and 1832 there were uprisings in the agricultural counties of eastern and southern England which became known as the Swing Riots. Worsening economic conditions resulted in farm labourers, like the LUDDITES, seeking relief from their hardships by smashing farm machinery. Some 387 threshing and 26 other machines were destroyed, and the spread of threshing machines was held up after the riots. The disturbances involved a number of respectable people; subsequently 19 were hanged and some 500 TRANSPORTED for life.

In 1842 RANSOME's, the AGRICULTURAL ENGINEERING firm in Suffolk, won a prize for their use of a portable STEAM ENGINE FOR THRESHING. In 1842 the firm of CHARLES BURRELL at Thetford, Norfolk, combined the grain dressing process with threshing in a portable machine which could be moved from place to place and used with a steam engine. Contract hirers appeared who hired out threshing sets with experienced operators to move from farm to farm. They used self-propelled traction engines which, by the 1860s, were being built in large numbers.

G.E. Fussell, *The Farmer's Tools* (Andrew Melrose 1952).
E.J. Hobsbawm and G. Rudé, *Captain Swing* (Lawrence and Wishart 1969).

Throstle Frame

The name given to RICHARD ARKWRIGHT's WATER FRAME when it had been adapted for steam power. The higher speeds made the machinery give a shrill whistle which workers thought sounded like a throstle (song thrush). The machine was modified in 1788 by Joseph Brookhouse, and was used for the spinning of WORSTED yarns as late as the 1850s.

Tile-Making Machinery

In 1830 Samuel Wright of Shelton in THE POTTERIES obtained a patent for a tile-making MACHINE. The tiles were made in plaster-of-Paris moulds in a metal frame, and then cut to a uniform thickness. The patent was sold to THOMAS MINTON, who produced large quantities of tiles. Richard Prosser patented an invention in 1840 for making tiles by using hydraulic presses. The Minton factory also used this patent, and 90 presses were at work by 1844. In 1852 a firm of iron founders was established in Stoke-on-Trent to manufacture the presses and the STEAM ENGINES to operate them.

Tin Mining

Cornish tin has been mined for over 2,000 years in the mining areas of west Cornwall around Camborne and Redruth and on the Land's End peninsula. The problem of draining tin and COPPER MINES led to work on STEAM PUMPING ENGINES by THOMAS SAVERY and THOMAS NEWCOMEN, with improvements later by JAMES WATT and RICHARD TREVITHICK. The stone pumping houses and tall chimneys are a familiar site on the Cornish landscape. Cheap foreign ores killed the industry in the early 1900s, although mines are reopened from time to time when the price of tin is high.

Visit Wendron, near Helston, Cornwall – Poldark Mine and Heritage Complex. **M***
Pendeen, Penzance, Cornwall – Gevor Tin Mining Museum with Trevithick collection. **M***

Camborne, Cornwall – statue of Richard Trevithick and cottage where he was born.

R.L. Atkinson, *Tin and Tin Mining* (Shire Publications 1985).

Tinplate Industry

Tinplating is a process by which a thin sheet of metal, originally WROUGHT IRON but now steel, is covered by an extremely thin coating of tin. The manufacture of tinplate began in South Wales about 1700 and became firmly established during the 18th century. Wrought iron was rolled into sheet form, cleaned, annealed (toughened), dipped in grease for one hour and then dipped in the molten tin. Surplus tin was brushed off with hemp and the cooling process was carefully controlled to prevent the tin cracking. The tin was then immersed in melted tallow and a bath of molten tin to complete the process.

By 1800 there were 11 works, five in Wales and the others in Monmouthshire and Gloucestershire. The home market was mainly for domestic utensils such as saucepans, lamps and watering cans. At this time the export of tinplate had begun, and between 1796 and 1805 exports more than quadrupled in value. The advance of the STANDARD OF LIVING in the 19th century brought new uses for tinplate. By punching holes in the tinplate colanders could be made, and in large shops and houses tinplate speaking tubes were in use. By 1825 the first attempts had been made to use tinplate for the canning of food.

Visit Kidwelly, Dyfed, Wales – Industrial Museum showing tin plating 1737–1941. M*

Tipton Chemical Works

Founded by JAMES KEIR in 1782 at West Bromwich, near BIRMINGHAM, to make alkali for the SOAP INDUSTRY. The works expanded to make soap, as well as red lead for the glass-makers and white lead for the Staffordshire potters. The factory used 9 tonnes of coal (10.08 US tons) per day, and power was supplied by two STEAM ENGINES and two waterwheels. Skilled labour was not required in large numbers, as most work was done by unskilled workers. The works had high equipment costs and heavy overheads but made considerable profits. It was a large factory at a time when the DOMESTIC SYSTEM predominated in the Midlands.

Toll Charges

The charges made by TURNPIKE trusts for the use of their ROADS, with a toll charge on average every 7 miles (11.3 km). The charges varied considerably. Agricultural produce and livestock being taken or driven to market was generally exempt, as were vehicles taking people to church or to elections, as well as Post Office mail. Some trusts charged double for Sunday travellers. Tolls frequently changed as a result of local pressure and certain types of traffic, such as coal, would be charged one year but not the next.

Toll House

A house set up beside a TURNPIKE ROAD as a home for the keeper who was responsible for collecting TOLLS, which travellers had to pay for the maintenance of the ROAD. Toll houses were usually designed with a window facing along the road and a blank wall where the tolls could be displayed on a board. A padlocked gate across the road was opened only after the toll had been paid. Toll houses can be seen in many parts of the country along roads once the responsibility of turnpike trusts.

Visit Box, Wiltshire – Blue Vein toll house.
Dundee Road, Perth, Scotland – toll house with toll board.
Llanfar P.G., Anglesey – toll house with toll board.
Eynsham, Kent – toll gate and house.

Tolpuddle Martyrs

Six farm labourers from Tolpuddle in Dorset were tried in 1834 for administering oaths as part of the ritual of joining the Friendly Society of Agricultural Labourers. The use of the ritual had been made a crime in 1797 and the men were found guilty. They were TRANSPORTED for 7 years, and ROBERT OWEN and others mounted a national campaign of protest which received widespread support. The men were released after serving 4 years of their sentence.

J. Marlow, *The Tolpuddle Martyrs* (History Book Club 1971).

Tommy Shop

A shop run by the colliery or factory owner, or someone he supplied, where workers had to buy goods under the TRUCK SYSTEM. The workers were given tommy tickets as part or all of their earnings, which they could use for making purchases at the shop. Prices in tommy shops were kept deliberately high, since this was to the advantage of the employer, and workers were compelled to pay 15 per cent to 40 per cent above the market price for their provisions. In remote places the tommy shop often had a virtual monopoly of trade and the workers had no alternative but to use it, even if they received all their earnings as money.

Tools Act, 1785

An Act prohibiting the export of an immense range of tools and engines used in the steel and iron trades. The object was to protect British industry from its tools being copied abroad. BIRMINGHAM MANUFACTURERS were particularly anxious to guard the secrets of tools used in the preparation of raw materials, such as the iron rollers used to prepare sheet copper. The iron manufacturers were against the Act, since they were exporting tools and MACHINES. Their protagonist was RICHARD CRAWSHAY, and the Act was modified in 1786 but not repealed. Tools could be exported with certain exceptions, such as stamps and dies, rollers, lathes, moulds and all other tools necessary for preparing, working and finishing iron and steel products.

Towns Improvement Company

Promoted by EDWIN CHADWICK in 1845, the Company was a grand scheme for a public utility company, not only in Britain but also in other parts of the world. The Company was to be responsible for the interdependent services of WATER SUPPLY, drainage and sewage disposal. It was to have a monopoly and charge a small fee. A number of financial backers were found, but they were lured away by the railway boom (see RAILWAY DEVELOPMENT) and the fear that the company had philanthropic, rather than profit-making, objects. The Company carried out an experiment for using town sewage on farms along the BRIDGEWATER CANAL, but the farmers did not support the scheme. Throughout his life Edwin Chadwick remained convinced of the fortunes to be made from liquid sewage and the idea of a Towns Improvement Company.

Tories   See Conservative Party

Toy Trade

The name given to the manufacture of small metal goods in BIRMINGHAM and the surrounding towns and villages. The workshops produced all kinds of metal goods, such as nails, bolts, screws, buckles, bits, stirrups, pins and tools. In 1759 there were some 20,000 people employed in the toy trade in the Birmingham area and there was a considerable division of labour, with much of the work being done by outworkers. Factories like the SOHO WORKS were the exception, rather than the rule.

Trade Cycles

Rhythmic periods of economic activity followed by recession – that is, boom and slump. The causes of the cycles varied but the length of a cycle averaged only 5 years. In the 1760–1860 period agriculture was the premier British industry and some cycles were related to good and bad harvests. In 1763, at the end of the SEVEN YEARS WAR, there was a boom. The AMERICAN WAR OF INDEPENDENCE brought a trade depression, followed by a boom which collapsed in 1783. The next slump took place in 1793 at the outbreak of the NAPOLEONIC WARS.

One theory is that business cycles between 1790 and 1850 were dependent on the demand for British exports and fluctuations in domestic investment, the factors being interrelated. Six major cycles have been dated: 1797–1803,

1808–11, 1816–19, 1819–26, 1832–7 and 1842–8. An increase in demand for one product, such as cotton cloth, could provide the climate of confidence which resulted in increased investment and output for other industries. In the expansion period of a cycle it was relatively easy to raise money, and that gave businessmen greater confidence. The WORKING CLASSES suffered most from fluctuations in the economic growth because of UNEMPLOYMENT and short-time working. The capitalists (see CAPITAL) and MIDDLE CLASSES had reserves which they could use to cushion themselves against hardship.

Trade Tokens

Small metal discs used in the latter part of the 18th cetury by MANUFACTURERS, in lieu of cash, as pay to their employees. The tokens could be spent only at shops under the master's control and were a form of TRUCK. They were declared illegal by an Act of 1818.

J.R.S. Whiting, *Trade Tokens* (David and Charles 1971).

Trade Unions

Trade societies were first developed long before the INDUSTRIAL REVOLUTION by skilled handicraft workers such as paper-makers, printers, shipwrights and wool-combers. They were an early form of FRIENDLY SOCIETY, insuring the members against sickness and death. Organizations were also formed by the skilled workers in the mills which were being built towards the end of the 18th century. These organizations were concerned to protect their interests and control entry through APPRENTICESHIPS. As industry expanded rapidly, workers with few or no skills were given employment, and periods of economic depression (see TRADE CYCLES) weakened the existing societies. The law was also opposed to combinations of workers; the COMBINATION ACTS drove the trade union movement underground.

After the repeal of the Acts in 1825 attempts were made to create national associations. These schemes were promoted by idealists and were not based among the WORKING CLASSES. The most spectacular scheme, ROBERT OWEN'S GRAND NATIONAL CONSOLIDATED TRADES UNION failed in 1834 and other visionary ideas quickly melted away.

Successful organizations eventually developed from the old-established craft unions, led by the Amalgamated Society of Engineers in 1851. This was a landmark in trade union history and the organization was a model for the other craft unions to follow. In the 1850s and 1860s five craft unions formed trade societies; the engineers, iron founders, boot and shoe operators, bricklayers and carpenters and the joiners. They united all those skilled in a particular craft, charged high union fees and were soon financially strong. They set up central offices, often in LONDON, and paid a general secretary who was usually a man of outstanding ability. Trade unions in their modern form were developed in the 1850s and 1860s.

H. Pelling, *A History of British Trade Unionism* (Penguin 1971).

Tram

1 A metal container, sometimes called a tub, running along rails underground to transport coal or rock from the coal face. Trams were introduced into the SHEFFIELD district in 1790 by JOHN CURR, and replaced the CORF in collieries where there was sufficient headroom. In Yorkshire wheeled trams were in use by 1842. They were dragged by children wearing belts or a harness made of hemp, until the MINES ACT, 1842 made it illegal to employ females or boys under 10 below ground.

2 A service vehicle for carrying passengers. It had metal wheels and ran along sunken rails set into the ROAD surface. The first TRAMWAY was built at Birkenhead in 1860 and there was a boom in horse-drawn trams between 1875 and 1885. Many cities developed electric trams at the end of the 19th and beginning of the 20th century.

Visit National Tramway Museum, Crich, near Wirksworth, Derbyshire – city trams. **M***

Tramways   See Wagonways

Transfer Printed Ceramics

Transfer printing was first introduced at Battersea in LONDON about 1750, as a result of a working partnership between Stephen Janssen, Henry Delamain and John Brooks. Paper suitable for transfer work was obtained by Janssen, a merchant stationer. Brooks, an engraver, is likely to have developed the transfer process, while Delamain, a potter, probably produced the finely ground enamels required, which fused to the surface at high temperatures. The Battersea works operated for only 3 years but the process was taken to Bow about 1756 by ROBERT HANCOCK, one of the engravers. Later the process was used at WORCESTER and DERBY. It was first recorded in use at a Tunstall (Staffordshire) pottery in 1775, and by SPODE in 1781.

PRINTING PRESSES were introduced which were hand operated and later steam powered. Transfer printing cheapened the process of decoration and could be carried out by young girls and women. By 1790 transfer printing presses were widely used in THE POTTERIES, and paper mills at Cheddleton, northeast of Stoke-on-Trent, made the transfer paper.

Transportation

Originally used as a means of providing cheap labour for the plantations in America and the West Indies, but discontinued after the America Declaration of Independence in 1776. It was started to Australia in 1788 and extended to Tasmania in 1803. Transportation was a punishment for a wide range of offences, some very trivial. The sentence was for 7 years, 14 years or life, and very few returned home. In all some 160,000 people were transported to Australia, including 23,500 women, before transportation was stopped. There were no further shipments to New South Wales after 1840, to Tasmania after 1853 or to Western Australia after 1867.

Trapper

A person, usually a young child, who was employed in a coal mine to open and close doors to assist ventilation (see COAL MINING – VENTILATION). The children were aged between five and eight and sat, frequently in darkness, in a small hole made at the side of the door, holding a string in their hands. They normally spent 12 hours underground on each shift.

Travelling Post Office

Special coaches attached to trains equipped for the sorting of mail during the journey. The first travelling post office was introduced in 1838. The coach was a converted horsebox, which was replaced by specially designed coaches fitted internally with pigeon-holes. That same year a Post Office clerk, John Ramsey, invented a frame with a net for catching mail bags from passing trains. He also designed another device to allow mail to be dropped from the travelling post office and prevent it rolling under the wheels.

Visit National Railway Museum, York – replica of a 1938 travelling post office. **M***

P. Johnson, *The British Travelling Post Office* (Ian Allan 1985).

Trent and Mersey Canal (Also known as the Grand Trunk Canal)

Both JAMES BRINDLEY and JOHN SMEATON were interested in building a canal to join the rivers Mersey and Trent. The scheme also interested JOSIAH WEDGWOOD and some of his colleagues, who wanted CHINA CLAY, flint and SALT for THE POTTERIES, and a safe means of transport for their PORCELAIN products. The canal was opened in stages with the full length completed in 1777, having taken 11 years to build. Josiah Wedgwood built a large pottery, at the ETRURIA WORKS, at Stoke-on-Trent beside the canal, and it was linked by a number of smaller canals to other towns in the Potteries. These canals carried the raw materials and coal needed by the pottery firms and took away the products of the region. It was the most successful of all the canals in England and Wales and paid handsome dividends to its shareholders.

Trevithick, Richard (1771–1833)

A skilled engineer who built STEAM ENGINES. He was brought up in the mining region of Cornwall and knew of JAMES WATT's steam engine. He thought of a way to avoid Watt's patent by building an engine to his own design, using high-pressure steam and allowing the used steam exhaust to escape into the air. He first constructed mine winding engines using his idea in 1799, and followed these with a steam carriage (see STEAM COACHES) in 1801. Strictly it was a road locomotive and not a carriage, and it had an inefficient engine. In 1802 he patented a steam carriage which was fitted with a coach body in London and called the 'London Carriage'. It was the first steam carriage and made several journeys at up to 10 mph (16 kph). No one was prepared to finance more vehicles and it was dismantled in 1804.

Richard Trevithick went to COAL-BROOKDALE to experiment with PUMPING ENGINES, and in 1802 he built the first steam railway locomotive at the Coalbrookdale Company works. It is not known whether it operated. An ironmaster at MERTHYR TYDFIL, SAMUEL HOMFRAY, started to build Trevithick's engines at his PENYDARREN IRONWORKS. The engine ran on rails in 1804 but after a time it broke the CAST-IRON plates of the track. Another locomotive, CATCH ME WHO CAN, was built in 1808, and overturned on a circular track when a rail broke.

After that Trevithick's fortune waned and he eventually returned to Cornwall to build engines for agriculture and the mines. He visited Peru to erect pump engines in silver mines and returned in 1827, to die in poverty at Dartford, Kent, in 1833.

Visit Camborne, Cornwall – Richard Trevithick's cottage.
Science Museum, London – Cornish boiler (1812). **M***

H.W. Dickinson and A. Titley, *Trevithick* (Cambridge University Press 1934).

J. Hodge, *Richard Trevithick*, (Shire Publications 1976).

Truck System

A system whereby people received all or part of their wages in goods instead of money, or in truck tickets or TRADE TOKENS which could be used to purchase goods only at a shop run by, or on behalf of, the management. These shops were known as TOMMY SHOPS. In a remote rural area the availability of a store was essential, but obviously open to abuse. The system allowed the masters to charge inflated prices for their goods, which was the equivalent of reducing the wages of the workers. Even when paid in cash the workers were often intimidated into using the tommy shop.

Truck Acts were passed from 1726 onwards prohibiting the payment of wages in kind in specific industries. In 1827 a Truck Act was passed prohibiting the practice in the coal and STEEL INDUSTRIES, but it was never enforced. Further Acts were passed in 1831 and 1841, but the system remained a problem until the 1870s, when rising prosperity, the TRADE UNIONS and the development of CO-OPERATIVE stores put an end to it.

G.W. Hilton, *The Truck System, Including a History of the British Truck Act, 1465–1960* (Heffer 1960).

Tub-Boat Canal

A CANAL which had its origins in the COAL MINES. The first tub-boat canal was the Donnington Wood Canal in the Shropshire coalfield, built in the 1760s by the DUKE OF BRIDGEWATER's brother-in-law, Earl Gower. It linked mines at Donnington Wood with limestone quarries at Lilleshall and a coal wharf on the Newport–Wolverhampton road. Other tub-boat canals were built across the COALBROOKDALE coalfield, linking its ironworks with the River Severn. Boats called tub-boats were designed for use on these canals. Many were rectangular tubs and some were fitted with wheels. On these they could be raised or lowered on the canal's INCLINED PLANES without the need for cradles.

Visit Blist's Hill Open Air Museum, Ironbridge, Shropshire – tub-boats. **M*** Maritime Museum, Exeter, Devon – tub-boats. **M***

P.J.G. Ransom, *The Archaeology of the Transport Revolution 1750–1850* (World's Work Ltd 1984).

Tuke, William (1732–1822)

A QUAKER tea and coffee merchant in York who founded, with the aid of other Quakers, a building in York called the York Retreat. Its purpose was to treat mentally ill patients with kindness and compassion. The Retreat could accommodate 30 mentally ill patients, who were provided with humane treatment in pleasant surroundings. His work attracted interest both at home and in Europe and his methods were copied in other parts of the country.

Turner, John I (1738–87)

A potter who set up business in 1756, in partnership with William Banks, at Stoke-on-Trent in THE POTTERIES. The site was later to become the SPODE-Copeland pottery. Three years later he moved to a new factory at Lane End, near Longton, where he pioneered the use of a NEWCOMEN steam engine to pump water up to a waterwheel. At this works he produced a wide range of pottery, including black basalt and jasper wares, which he developed quite independently of JOSIAH WEDGWOOD. John Turner liked to experiment, and about 1780 he found a vein of fine marl from which he made a variety of stoneware products. About 1780 he began making PORCELAIN at Lane End.

Turner, Thomas (1749–1809)

He took over the management of the Caughley ceramic works in Shropshire in 1774, after working at the WORCESTER works with ROBERT HANCOCK. His factory was known as the Salopian China Works, and production started in 1775. He developed the manufacture of table ware decorated with TRANSFER PRINTING under the glaze. Production increased with the introduction of the willow and other all-over patterns. In 1799 he sold the works to JOHN ROSE of COALPORT, who transferred the plant to Coalport in 1814.

Turner, William (1762–1835) and John II (1766–1824)

The sons of JOHN TURNER who ran the Staffordshire pottery after his death in 1787, in partnership with Andrew Abbott. Like their father they were innovators, and succeeded in making shiny, blue-glazed pottery and a new kind of stoneware, which they patented in 1800. One of the raw materials was found in local COAL MINES and the mix required less heat to fire it, making it less liable to accidents in the kiln. Like other large pottery works the firm had a LONDON showroom, opened in 1783 in Fleet Street. In 1789 the factory was in difficulties because of non-payment of debts by the French, and in 1806 the Turner brothers became bankrupt and the pottery was let, to be sold in 1829.

B. Hillier, *The Turners of Lane End* (Cory, Adams and Mackay 1965).

Turnpike Road

A road which could be used by travellers only after paying a TOLL. The word 'turnpike' refers to swinging bars, tapered like a lance or pike and pivoted at the point of balance, which swung horizontally across the road on an upright post (hence turn-pike). Normal gates soon replaced the swinging pikes, and they remained closed across the road until the traveller had paid the correct toll, which was used for the maintenance of the ROAD.

The appalling condition of the roads in the 17th century led to the setting up of turnpike roads. An Act of Parliament was necessary to levy a road toll, and the first Act was passed in 1663, empowering the justices to levy tolls on a section of the Great North Road in Huntingdonshire, Cambridgeshire and Hertfordshire. No further Acts were passed until 1675–6, when permission was given for the erection of toll gates on sections of two roads in East Anglia.

In 1707, the first turnpike trust was set up. Instead of local JUSTICES OF THE PEACE being given the power to levy a toll, a body, usually made up of local gentry, was set up to act as trustees with permission to borrow money. Throughout the 18th century the powers of trustees were increased. The initiative for a trust had to come from local people, and Parliament made no attempt to make charges and regulations uniform, although in some parts there was general agreement between one trust and another. No tolls, for example, were levied on foot travellers by most trusts. The period 1750–70 saw the greatest expansion of turnpike roads, with 52 per cent of the eventual mileage managed by trusts. The rate of development slowed down in the decades that followed.

By the 1830s over 1,000 turnpike trusts were responsible for 25,000 miles (40,200 km) of road in England and Wales. The DEVELOPMENT OF THE RAILWAY network in the 1840s brought about a steady decline in the income of turnpike trusts, and they could no longer afford to maintain their roads. They lingered on until 1895, when the last toll was levied on the last turnpike road in Anglesey. Then the trusts were dissolved and road maintenance became the responsibility of parishes or highway districts.

W. Albert, *The Turnpike Road System in England 1663–1840* (Cambridge University Press 1972).

Two Acts

Acts of Parliament passed in 1795. By the first it became a treasonable offence to incite the people, by speech or writing, to hatred or contempt of the king, constitution or government. By the second, no meetings of over 50 persons could be held without notifying a magistrate, and magistrates were given wide powers. Defiance of the magistrates' orders were punishable by death, and lecture rooms could be closed as 'disorderly houses'.

The Acts were a response to unrest partly inspired by the FRENCH REVOLUTION, the writings of TOM PAINE, the need for reform, and the unpopularity of GEORGE III – he was hissed and pelted on his way to the state openings.

Typesetting

MACHINES for casting type (the metal characters used for printing) were first used in the United States and reached Britain about 1850. In 1842 HENRY BESSEMER, who later invented the BESSEMER PROCESS for making MILD STEEL, produced a machine known as the pianotype. It had a keyboard like that of a piano, which passed the type to an operator who spread it into lines. A number of new developments improved typesetting enormously by the end of the 19th century.

U

Underwater Telegraphic Cable

A TELEGRAPH cable was laid between Dover and Calais by John and Jacob Watkins Brett in 1851. Attempts were made in 1857 and 1858 to lay a cable between Ireland and the United States, but the cable broke. The link was not made until 1866, when the GREAT EASTERN was used as a cable layer.

Unemployment

Unemployment is essentially a 20th-century concept which gained ground during the mass unemployment of the 1920s and 1930s, when 10 per cent of the insured work force were unemployed in each year, except one, between 1921 and 1938. In the 18th and 19th centuries and the early part of the 20th, the idea persisted that anyone who wanted to could find work, but the concept of *continuous* employment for the WORKING CLASS was quite alien, and periods without work were accepted as inevitable and part of the lot of the lower orders of society.

During trade depressions (see TRADE CYCLES) such as that at the end of the NAPOLEONIC WARS there was cyclical unemployment in a number of industries, including textiles and iron-making, but unemployment was not confined to periods of economic depression. Throughout this period there was underemployment or concealed unemployment. Weather and the seasons not only caused unemployment in agriculture; the docks and the fashion trade suffered as well. The introduction of MACHINES created unemployment to a limited extent (for example, among the HAND LOOM WEAVERS), but it also created opportunities of employment for women, girls and children.

With no unemployment benefits, the unemployed had to depend on POOR LAW relief, or find alternative means of avoiding starvation. In some cases the only alternative means were PROSTITUTION, begging or crime.

Union, Act of, 1801

An Act making Ireland part of the United Kingdom, ruled over from Westminster. It was brought about as a result of unrest in Ireland, which WILLIAM PITT considered could be effectively governed only through a legislative union with Great Britain to form the United Kingdom. The Act maintained the ascendancy of the Protestant minority in the whole of Ireland and trade barriers between the two countries were abolished, except for those on Irish textiles, which were fully protected for 20 years. The Act thus provided a free trade area in the British Isles, contrasting with Germany, where there were over 300 separate states. Concessions, including CATHOLIC EMANCIPATION promised by Pitt, were not granted because of opposition from GEORGE III, and Pitt resigned in the same year. (Catholics had the right to vote but could not become MPs.)

Unitarians

A nonconformist (see DISSENTERS) religious group who rejected the doctrine of the Trinity and the divinity of Christ. They first appeared in the 17th century and grew in numbers in the 18th century, when some nonconformists, especially Presbyterians, joined them. They formed one of the groups within the nonconformist movement.

Universities

Oxford and Cambridge universities were the preserves of the rich, provided they were members of the CHURCH OF ENGLAND. Reformers like HENRY BROUGHAM and Dr Birkbeck formed University College in LONDON in 1828 as a non-sectarian institution. The Anglicans established King's College three years later and the two combined in 1836 to form the University of London. Durham University, with strong ecclesiastical links, was started in 1837 but the majority of non-sectarian universities did not appear until towards the end of the 19th century.

Urban Growth

The rapid growth of towns and cities during the INDUSTRIAL REVOLUTION can be attributed to the FACTORY SYSTEM and to the concentration of industry near to sources of coal, which provided the fuel for steam power. The cotton towns (see COTTON INDUSTRY – LOCATION) showed the earliest and most distinctive development. In 1773 MANCHESTER and Salford had a population of 27,000; by 1790 it had risen to 50,000 and in 1801 it stood at 95,000. In 1760 Oldham was a village of 300 or more people; by 1801 it had a population of 20,000. Population in the woollen towns (see WOOLLEN INDUSTRY) of Yorkshire also showed a sharp increase, but at a later date. LEEDS had 17,000 in 1775 and 53,000 in 1801. Increases also took place in the iron towns (see IRON INDUSTRY), although most of the large ironworks were in the adjacent countryside. Older industrial centres like BIRMINGHAM increased from 30,000 in 1760 to 73,000 in 1801, while SHEFFIELD increased from 20,000 to 45,000 in the same period.

The CENSUS OF POPULATION returns for the period 1801–61 show an acceleration of urban growth, with cities like GLASGOW showing an increase of six times the 1801 number, and LONDON an increase of nearly three times during the same period. Whereas in 1750 less than one-fifth of the population lived in towns of 5,000 or more inhabitants, 100 years later more than three-fifths of a greatly enlarged population lived in such towns. Within a hundred years Britain had moved from being a predominantly rural population to a predominantly urban society.

Living in towns freed people from rural villages and so from close supervision by their social superiors, and for many it liberated them from the Church and the gentry. The segregation by CLASS was the most important social effect of urbanization, with towns developing distinctive zones for the different classes, creating spatial social divisions which had been less obvious in rural societies.

A. Briggs, *Victorian Cities* (Penguin 1968).

Urban Housing

The general standard of housing for working people in the industrial towns was extremely bad. The buildings were not worse than those in rural areas, but the related problems of sanitation and overcrowding made the conditions appalling. The large, high-density urban communities created public health problems which resulted in epidemics and disease.

The pattern of WORKING-CLASS housing varied from town to town, with tenement blocks in GLASGOW, BACK-TO-BACK houses in LEEDS and cellar homes in LIVERPOOL. Sanitation was particularly bad, with outside earth privies shared by a group of houses. WATER SUPPLY was not piped to individual houses – usually a stand-pipe served a group of tenements – and the connection between impure water and disease was not generally recognized until the 1850s. Seepage of impurities into wells, or drawing water from rivers which were also used as SEWERS, was common.

S.D. Chapman (ed.), *The History of Working Class Housing* (David and Charles 1971).

Urban Refuse

The HEALTH OF TOWNS COMMISSION in 1843 found that many towns were paid by scavenging contractors for their refuse. Some refuse was valuable; for example, ashes were used for brick-making, rags for PAPER-MAKING and horse- and cow-dung for manure. Night soil (human excrement) was not used, although EDWIN CHADWICK and others realized its value once treated. Refuse, poor drainage and poor sewage were health hazards in towns, particularly in the crowded WORKING-CLASS districts. There was no co-ordination of services and the interests of different groups often conflicted.

Utilitarianism

A belief promoted by JEREMY BENTHAM that laws should be judged by their usefulness and based on 'the greatest good of the greatest number'. EDWIN CHADWICK, secretary to the Poor Law Commissioners, was a Utilitarian. The Utilitarians played an important part in the passing of the MUNICIPAL CORPORATIONS ACT, 1835.

V

Vagrancy

This was no new problem and vagrants were a common sight. Some were unemployed ARTISANS or labourers who, finding no work, abandoned the search. Many were young people aged between 15 and 25, some of whom were runaway apprentices. Beggars were common on the streets; they were of all ages and both sexes, and some progressed into the lower branches of crime and PROSTITUTION.

Vagrancy Acts were passed which prohibited people from begging or gathering alms. The laws were frequently used against workers who were on strike, sometimes to imprison them. They were also used by the magistrates to put into prison any man or woman of the WORKING CLASS who was collecting money for the families of locked-out workers or distributing literature which the magistrates thought was undesirable.

Victoria (1819–1901)

Queen from 1837 to 1901, she came to the throne at the age of 18 when the monarchy was at a low ebb. Her initial advantages were her youth, her sense of duty and her sex. As the first woman monarch since Queen Anne (1702–14), she followed some unpopular kings (see GEORGE III and GEORGE IV), and the prime minister, William Melbourne, treated her like a young daughter and tutored her politically. She displayed great strength of character and responsibility, was a stern and determined moralist and made the court more restrained and dignified.

In 1840 she married PRINCE ALBERT OF SAXE-COBURG AND GOTHA, and lived a very happy life with him. She did not understand or concern herself with some of his artistic and scientific interests, but was delighted with the GREAT EXHIBITION.

She gave the monarchy a dignity and the age the idea of 'family'. She had strong political prejudices and forcibly expressed her wishes to her ministers, but was not able to influence politics decisively and was forced into a position of neutrality. In later years she led a secluded life and was the focus of much popular affection.

E. Longford, *Victoria R.I.* (1964).

Viewer

An adviser, surveyor and director of a colliery's design, construction and development. The term was most common in the North East and emerged in the middle of the 18th century. Large collieries in the North East had both a resident and a consultant viewer. The former had the responsibility for the day-to-day running of the colliery, while the latter gave orders for long-term or large-scale measures to be implemented and usually held the same position at a number of collieries. Viewers gave estimates of the cost of winning and working (preparing the pit for mining, and extracting the coal) and the amount of coal to be won. John Buddle (1743–1806) and his son, also named JOHN BUDDLE (1773–1843), were important viewers in the North East.

Viewers had a number of assistants

and apprentices attached to them and made reports for overseas mining companies. In 1834 John Buddle made a report on Sydney Colliery, Canada, and in 1839 sent a viewer and miners to restore a colliery in Virginia, America. Viewers spent much time underground, although some avoided this duty by sending down assistants, but the need for underground experience was essential and disasters were often thought to be the responsibility of the viewer. His task was to advise the owner and make recommendations substantiated by facts.

Vulcan

A passenger boat built in 1818 for the

FORTH AND CLYDE CANAL. It was the first iron boat built in Scotland.

H.P. Spratt, *The Birth of the Steamboat* (Griffin 1958).

Vulcanization

A process of heating rubber with sulphur to improve its qualities for a variety of uses. It was discovered by CHARLES GOODYEAR in 1841, and the method used was worked out independently by THOMAS HANCOCK from Goodyear's samples. A British patent was obtained by Hancock in 1843 and rubber production for shoes, waterproof clothing and industrial uses increased rapidly.

W

Wade, General George (1673–1748)

Appointed Commander-in-Chief, North Britain, in 1724, he proposed and carried out schemes to mend the ROADS between garrisons and barracks in Scotland. Fear of a Jacobite uprising made it essential for troops to be able to move swiftly, and repairs and improvements to roads were carried out between 1725 and 1740.

After the 1745 rebellion the network was further expanded by Major William Caulfield. When he died in 1767 over 800 miles (1,300 km) had been constructed, mainly in the Highlands south of the Great Glen. The roads were 16 feet (5 m) wide and were constructed to meet military needs. Bridges were built and several, including one over the river Tay at Aberfeldy, are still in use.

Visit Aberfeldy, Perthshire, Scotland – bridge over the River Tay.

W. Taylor, *The Military Roads in Scotland* (David and Charles 1976).

Wagonway (Also known as a tramway)

A route used by wagons or other forms of

transport carrying coal from mines to markets. Wagonways were built by mine owners and were most common in North East England. A wagonway consisted of ground specially levelled, across which lengths of timber were laid as sleepers. On these sleepers were fixed wooden rails about 4 feet (1.2 m) apart. Horses pulled wagons with flanged wheels along these rails.

These first railways were built in the 17th century, and in 1767 iron rails were cast at COALBROOKDALE. By 1800 it has been estimated there were 290 miles (465 km) of wagonways in use, half of them on Tyneside. A horse could pull four times as much on wagonways as it could on ordinary ROADS, and so they repaid the mine owner for the cost of laying them. Wagonways were also built to feed CANALS because they were less restricted by topography than were canals. The first public wagonway was the SURREY IRON RAILWAY, built in 1803 from Wadsworth to Croydon. It was horse-drawn and had a double track. After 1810 these horse tramroads were often called railways.

Visit National Railway Museum, York – length of wagonway track. **M***

Causey Arch, County Durham – bridge built in 1720 to carry a wagonway.

Cromford and High Peak Railway, Derbyshire – Peak Forest tramway and inclined plane.

C.F. Dendy Marshall, *A History of British Railways down to the year 1830* (Oxford University Press 1971).

M.J.T. Lewis, *Early Wooden Railways* (Routledge 1970)

I. Dean, *Industrial Narrow Gauge Railways* (Shire Publications 1985).

Walker, Samuel (?–1782)

With his two brothers he set up a small forge in 1741 near SHEFFIELD. In 1746 a BLAST FURNACE was built and in 1748 he began to make steel using BENJAMIN HUNTSMAN's method. In 1754 a forge was added and further blast furnaces in 1759. During the AMERICAN WAR OF INDEPENDENCE and the NAPOLEONIC WARS the works produced cannon in large numbers. After Samuel Walker's death his sons carried on the business and their foundries flourished.

Warmley Works

A BRASS works near BRISTOL established about 1740 by William Champion. It was probably the first place in Europe where metallic zinc (spelter) was extracted on a commercial basis. Champion derived spelter from calamine and this led to the manufacture of very fine brass using copper and zinc.

Visit Warmley, Bristol – dam site and Warmley House, home of William Champion.

Warp

The threads which are stretched lengthwise in the weaving loom. Warp threads are fixed to the loom, unlike the WEFT threads, and they need to be carefully prepared before being placed in position. LINEN yarn was used for the warp threads until the invention of the WATER FRAME, which allowed all-cotton cloth to be made – the previously woven mixture of cotton and linen was rather coarse. RICHARD ARKWRIGHT's water frame twisted the thread making it hard and strong enough for the warp, which was therefore known as 'twist' or 'hard yarn'.

Warp Knitting Machine

A MACHINE for introducing the lengthways threads (the WARP) into the knitting process. It was invented about 1775, probably in Nottinghamshire. The resulting fabrics were not as elastic as those made on a stocking frame (see FRAMEWORK KNITTERS), but could be cut into shapes and sewn together as underwear garments.

Water Closets

By 1800 the houses of well-to-do people contained at least one privy, but WORKING-CLASS people had to share a privy with neighbouring houses. Collection was made at intervals, although they were often irregular. By this time, however, primitive water closets had begun to be introduced. The closet was usually in a cupboard and emptied into a cesspool under the house. With no ventilation the closet was a source of infection and evil smells, and there were a number of INVENTIONS to eliminate the foul air. Few water closets were attached to SEWERS, and cesspools in the garden or under the house were common. JOSEPH BRAMAH patented a water closet in 1778 which had its own water supply and a flap which was operated by a cranked arm.

There were no major improvements in water closets and the disposal of sewage until the second half of the 19th century, when towns sewers were developed and a regular WATER SUPPLY was piped to individual houses.

Water-Driven Mills

The earliest mills, such as those at CROMFORD and BELPER, obtained their power from waterwheels until STEAM ENGINES were introduced. Even when steam power was common, a number of mills continued to use their waterwheels. Water-driven mills had a difficulty which the steam-driven mills did not share, that of water shortage when the mill stream was low, or of flooding when there was too much water. The location of water-driven mills was determined by suitable riverside sites, which were usually in remote valleys some way from large settlements. Most mills preferred overshot wheels (with water hitting the blades at the top of the wheel), which became popular after 1751 when JOHN SMEATON had shown to the Royal Society that they were more efficient.

Water Frame

A cotton spinning MACHINE patented by RICHARD ARKWRIGHT and first used at his CROMFORD Mill in 1771. The machine produced cotton yarn strong enough to serve as WARP as well as WEFT, making it possible to produce in Britain for the first time cotton cloth which was not a mixture of cotton and LINEN (previously used for the warp). The water frame was a factory machine designed to be horse operated, but it was initially powered by water (hence the name) and later by steam. When it was first powered by steam it was known as the THROSTLE FRAME. The water frame made large-scale factory industry feasible, and spinning began to be concentrated in factories instead of in the home.

Visit Textile Machinery Museum, Moor Road, Bolton – water frame. **M***

Watermark

A pattern in paper which can be seen when the paper is held up to the light. In about 1760 John Baskerville (1706–75), a printer in BIRMINGHAM, invented the woven mesh made with uniform wires which gave a grid-iron effect. This wire, when pressed into the wet pulp sheet in the PAPER-MAKING process, produced a watermark in the form of horizontal lines in the paper. In 1825 John and Christopher Phipps invented the DANDY ROLL, a roller which was used on a paper-making MACHINE and helped to press out some of the water from the wet pulp and thus improve the sheet formation. In 1839 William Joynson of St Mary Cray, Kent, patented the idea of attaching letters or other shapes to the surface of the dandy roll so that they pressed further into the wet pulp and left watermark patterns. Later, similar wire designs were attached to the cylinders of JOHN DICKINSON's machine, and the watermark to be seen on banknotes is still made on these machines.

Water-pressure Engine

A simple form of hydraulic pump used in mines and quarries during the 18th and 19th centuries. The engine worked by the pressure upon a piston of a head of water, usually from a cistern at a higher level than the engine.

Water Purification

In the last decade of the 18th century the Lancashire dyers and BLEACHERS used gravel and sand beds to purify their WATER SUPPLY. The first slow sand filters in LONDON were built by JAMES SIMPSON in 1827. The Land Water Act of 1852 prohibited companies from distributing water without filtering it or from taking water from the tidal reaches of the Thames. Filter beds of this period worked by gravity, were very slow and took up much space and attention. Better types of sand filter were not patented until 1880.

Water Supply

There had been public water supplies in some towns since Tudor times, but they were inadequate and often polluted. In the 17th century the New River was built to take spring water from Hertfordshire to the City of LONDON. The AQUEDUCT was opened in 1613 and much is still in use. Later a number of private companies took over the supply of water to London, and by 1822 nine separate companies supplied the capital. In most towns water supply was very haphazard, with insufficient street cleaning, SEWER flushing and wash houses. Supplies were intermittent; sometimes the water was turned on for only a few hours each day.

In the early 19th century a number of Acts were passed giving water companies the right to take water from rivers or build reservoirs. In the 1830s the ditch, river and well were the main sources of water, in addition to the main sewers, and in the towns the companies were not always convinced that they could supply each house with water because of technical problems concerning water pressure. The HEALTH OF TOWNS COMMISSION recommended that local administration bodies should be obliged to secure a regular water supply not only for domestic use, but also for street cleaning, extinguishing fires and scouring sewers and drains.

G.M. Binnie, *Early Victorian Water Engineers* (Thomas Telford 1981).

Water Turbine

A rotary motor in which the driving force is water, which turns vanes. The first water turbines were developed in France in the early 19th century, and the first British innovation was patented by James Whitelaw. It was installed near Paisley in 1839, but generated only a few units of HORSEPOWER. Another design, the Vortex type, was developed by James Thompson (1822–94) in 1852. A great number of these turbines were built, together with a centrifugal pump he had designed. Many were installed in traditional water mills to replace waterwheels. The large turbine makers were Gilbert, Gilkes and Gordon, of Kendal in Cumberland. Their first turbine was built in 1856 and many were installed locally. Towards the end of the 19th century turbines were used to generate electrical power.

Watt, James (1736–1819)

One of the outstanding inventors of the INDUSTRIAL REVOLUTION, with his brilliant contribution to the development of the STEAM ENGINE. He was born in Greenock, Scotland, became a scientific instrument maker and settled in GLASGOW, working at the University there. During 1763–4 he was given a model of NEWCOMEN's engine to repair. He diagnosed two main defects in the design, which resulted in a loss of energy and in incomplete condensation. He improved the efficiency of the engine and took out a patent in 1769, using steam as an active motor power. A series of improvements followed and by 1782

Watt had developed the first rotary steam engine.

Two men helped Watt to make his invention a practical success. They were JOHN ROEBUCK of the CARRON IRONWORKS and MATTHEW BOULTON of the SOHO WORKS in BIRMINGHAM. Roebuck became bankrupt, and it was Matthew Boulton who joined with James Watt to apply steam power to MACHINES, making possible the rapid development of large-scale industry in areas where coal could be obtained cheaply.

Watt had a patent for his engine until 1800, and BOULTON AND WATT engines were built for pumping water from mines in different parts of the country as well as to drive machinery. By 1800, when the patent ran out, about 480 engines had been built for customers, one-third of them being used for pumping.

James Watt's brilliance was tempered with caution, and his reluctance to pursue the application of his engine to road carriages or boats was probably due to his concern to improve the engine still further.

Visit Hunterton Museum, Glasgow University – the Newcomen model on which Watt worked. **M***
Science Museum, London – contents of James Watt's workshop. **M***
Museum of Science and Industry, Newhall Street, Birmingham – engine of 1779. **M***

D.W. Dickinson and R. Jenkins, *James Watt and the Steam Engine* (Moorland Publishing 1981).

Weaving Sheds

Workshops in which weaving machinery was operated. They were usually single-storey buildings, the roof supported by CAST-IRON columns. Looms were arranged in lines between the rows of columns and the roof was part glazed for lighting.

Visit Cressbrook Mill, near Bakewell, Derbyshire – weaving shed in front of mill.

Webb Family

A group of glass-makers working in

Stourbridge, Worcestershire, and its surrounding district. John Webb (1774–1835) operated the White House Glassworks in the early 1830s. Thomas Webb (1804–69), his son, took over the Wordsley Glassworks with partners in 1829. In 1837 he operated Platts Glasshouses at Ambleside, Cumberland, and in 1856 built Dennis Glassworks at Ambleside. His sons, Thomas Wilkes Webb II (1837–91) and Charles, succeeded him in 1863.

Wedgwood, Josiah (1730–95)

The founder of the pottery and PORCELAIN firm which is world famous. He was a self-educated man, the son of a potter from Burslem, Staffordshire. In 1759 he started two small potteries in Burslem, and in 1764 took larger premises to produce the cream-coloured ware he had developed. He undertook a commission for an earthenware tea and coffee service with a gold background and flowers raised in green. In 1765 this was presented to Queen Charlotte who was so impressed she allowed Wedgwood to style himself 'Potter to Her Majesty' and to call his newly developed earthenware body Queen's Ware.

As an enthusiastic chemist he was constantly experimenting to improve his products and find new uses for new raw materials. In 1767 he wrote 'Experiments for Porcelain, or at least, a new Earthenware fill up every moment allowed of my time and would take a good deal more if I had it.' Porcelain in this sense refers to Wedgwood's high-fired stoneware body which ultimately became known as Jasper. Bone china (a porcelain-related body) was not produced until 1812 – 17 years after his death. His study of the art of antiquity was transferred to his industrial activities. Sketches in books gave him the idea of making, first, copies of antique ware, and then original creations based on the sketches. He experimented with colours fired in his own furnaces and invented the PYROMETER, used for measuring high temperatures in furnaces.

He keenly supported the building of the Trent and Mersey Canal, which enabled Cornish clay to reach THE POTTERIES by water. Close to the canal he built his factory in 1769, called ETRURIA. He had an open and independent mind and democratic views. The AMERICAN WAR OF INDEPENDENCE and the FRENCH REVOLUTION won his sympathy, and to his workers he was also liberal minded.

His products were made with care and great artistry. Goods were manufactured for the everyday market as well as for expensive table settings. As early as 1763 the bulk of the production of half a million articles was exported, with North America as the largest and most important market. He opened showrooms in LONDON, Bath, and Dublin, and he had representatives abroad including Paris and Amsterdam, and these became fashionable meeting places. Leading artists were employed and public events commemorated with special works. He used travelling salesmen as early as 1777 and clearly had great skills as a salesman himself.

The success of BONE CHINA domestic ware, which was made by SPODE, MINTON and DAVENPORT, forced the firm of Wedgwood to begin bone china production in 1812. The quality was uneven in the works, and production ceased in 1822. The production of STONE CHINA continued, however.

Josiah Wedgwood raised pottery manufacture from a matter of guesswork and rule of thumb to a system of scientific measurement and calculations.

Visit Barlaston, Staffordshire – Wedgwood Museum. **M***

A. Burton, *Josiah Wedgwood: A Biography* (Deutsch 1976).

Weft

The cross-threads which are woven into the WARP to make fabric.

Wesley, John (1703–91)

The founder of the Methodist church (see METHODISM) who brought his own brand of Christianity to parts of the country where industry was developing rapidly and where the ESTABLISHED CHURCH, the CHURCH OF ENGLAND, was not well represented. His message appealed strongly to the poor, disenfranchised workers of the new industrial towns and villages.

John Wesley was originally a Church of England clergyman, who experienced a religious conversion at a meeting in 1738 and was convinced that anyone who turned to God would be saved. He travelled the country preaching in the open because the churches were closed to him. His style was simple, direct and personal in a manner which often aroused members of the congregation to hysteria. He consecrated his own lay preachers, some of whom were sent to the American colonies. He had no interest in altering the existing order of society and preached hard work, avoiding political issues. He believed in equality before God as well as in the 'natural social order', and offered hope of salvation to all who were willing to listen.

Although John Wesley said only three years before his death that he was anxious to 'live and die a member of the Church of England', he had, in fact, created a new sect, closer to the Church of England than other nonconformist sects (see DISSENTERS), although separated from it by social barriers. He retained a strong control of the organization he set up and it was not until four years after his death that the Methodist Conference broke away from the Church of England.

Visit City Road, London – Wesley's House and Museum. **M***

E. Harrison, *Son to Susanna* (Penguin 1976).

Wet Puddling   See Puddling and Joseph Hall

Wet Spinning

A process used in FLAX SPINNING, involving wetting the fibres. A number of people invented MACHINES for wet spinning, including Philippe de Girard, a Frenchman, in 1814 and James Kay of Preston in 1825. When it was found that using hot water speeded up the process, Girard's machine was seen to be more suitable.

Whatman, James (1773–1843)

A paper-maker at the Turkey Mill, near Maidstone in Kent, in the 18th century. In the 1740s he improved the quality of his paper, making it competitive with continental imports. In 1754 he placed a woven wire cloth on top of the mould wires used to lift the pulp from the vat. The paper produced was called WOVE PAPER, and the process was perfected by 1759. His son, also called James, devised larger moulds in 1773 to produce specially commissioned sheets of large paper. It was called ANTIQUARIAN PAPER after the Society of Antiquarians, who had commissioned it. It became a popular paper for maps and navigation charts and was exported to the Continent and the United States. Meanwhile the Whatman wove paper was becoming well known and by 1800 virtually all books were made using this type of paper.

Wheatstone, Sir Charles (1802–75).

A physicist who, with William Cooke (1806–79), invented the five-needle TELEGRAPH system in 1837. Needles were located at the looped ends of five wires, so that electric current passing through could deflect any one of them and a wide variety of signals could be sent, the positions of the needles being identified with letters of the alphabet. The TELEGRAPH SYSTEM was installed along the LONDON to BRISTOL railway, between Paddington and Slough, in 1843. Wheatstone's invention was in use before Samuel Morse had his system in operation in the United States, and Morse was unable to obtain a patent in Britain although his system was superior.

Whieldon, Thomas (1719–95)

A Staffordshire potter who established a factory at Fenton Law in THE POTTERIES in 1740. He made white stone-ware and agate-ware knife and fork handles for the SHEFFIELD cutlers, to compete with the Continental PORCELAIN which had become fashionable. His business expanded and he was soon making a range of pottery. He employed JOSIAH SPODE I as an apprentice in 1749, and was in partnership with JOSIAH WEDGWOOD between 1754 and 1759.

Whigs See Liberal Party

Whimsey

A device, sometimes called a HORSE GIN, used at collieries to wind up coal and rock. It was worked by a horse walking in a circle to turn a cog mechanism connected to a horizontal rope drum. It was invented towards the end of the 17th century and used into the 19th century. STEAM ENGINES used for winding at collieries were also called Whimseys.

Visit Nottingham Industrial Museum, Wollaton Park, Nottingham – reconstructed example. **M***

J. Kenneth Major, *Animal-Powered Machines* (Shire Publications 1985).

Whitefield, George (1714–70)

An EVANGELICAL who founded the Calvinist Methodists (see METHODISM). The son of a Gloucester publican, he became a servant at Pembroke College, Oxford, where he met JOHN WESLEY. They became close friends and he went with Wesley to Georgia, America, in 1738. He returned to England the next year and then sailed again for America in 1740, making an evangelical tour of the eastern states. He had great preaching powers but his Calvinist beliefs led him to clashes with Wesley over the doctrine that salvation for some was fore-ordained by God – predestination, in which Whitefield believed. John Wesley, however, believed in free salvation for all people who turned to God.

George Whitefield was the leader of a group of evangelicals who had as their patron Selina, Countess of Huntingdon (1709–91). She tried to extend the evangelical revival to those of her own CLASS, and gathered in her drawing-room rich, aristocratic and well-known people to hear preachers like George Whitefield. She raised money to build Calvinist chapels and also founded a college at Trevecca in Wales for the training of evangelical ministers. Her Calvinist sect was known as 'Lady Huntingdon's Connexion', and she supported George Whitefield in his clashes with John Wesley. The two men were later reconciled on a personal level, although they held different doctrinal views.

In 1753 George Whitefield restored a church in Moorfields, LONDON, which he called the Tabernacle and where he preached Calvinist Methodism. He travelled extensively, making seven visits in all to the United States, where he died. He is buried at Newburyport, Massachusetts.

A. Dallimore, *George Whitefield* (Banner of Faith Trust 1970).

Whitworth, Robert (?–1799)

A draughtsman who surveyed a number of CANAL routes including the Oxford (1768), the Stockton and Darlington (later built as a railway) and the Andover (1788). His work was under the direction of JAMES BRINDLEY who was responsible for his training. He became engineer for the Thames and Severn Canal and was extremely busy on canal projects in the 1780s. In 1785 he was made engineer of the FORTH AND CLYDE CANAL, leaving his son Robert to complete it. He was a consultant on the Leeds and Liverpool Canal, and as a surveyor in the 1790s worked on, among others, the Dorset and Somerset Canal and the Commercial Canal project in Cheshire.

Whitworth, Sir Joseph (1803–87)

An engineer and tool-maker who went to work for HENRY MAUDSLAY in 1825. Eight years later he set up his own business in MANCHESTER, making machine tools and machinery. He gave his name to the Whitworth screw thread, which he developed in 1841. He produced the MACHINES to give the level of accuracy required to standardize thread, and by 1860 Whitworth standardized screw threads were in general use in Britain. He improved existing tools rather than inventing new ones. His initial improvement was to lathes, and then in 1842 he produced a highly efficient planing machine, based on designs by RICHARD ROBERTS and JOSEPH CLEMENT, and power-driven as well as self-acting.

Wilkinson, Isaac (c.1704–84)

The father of JOHN WILKINSON, he was originally a furnace foreman and then chief caster at iron companies in Cumberland. In about 1748 he moved to Grange-over-Sands and then to Bersham, near Wrexham in North Wales. There he had his own iron furnace and in 1757 he patented a new type of bellows – a kind of blowing engine. He bought shares in the DOWLAIS IRONWORKS and, with JOHN GUEST, founded the Plymouth Ironworks in 1763. He owned the CYFARTHFA IRONWORKS for a short time until 1771. His bellows were never a success, but his own business misfortunes were reversed by his son after his death. He finally settled in BRISTOL as a merchant ironmonger and founder, and had as his son-in-law DR JOSEPH PRIESTLEY.

Wilkinson, John (1728–1808)

The son of ISAAC WILKINSON who, by 1770 and with his brother William, owned three important ironworks in the Midlands – at Bersham in Denbighshire, Bradley in Staffordshire and Borseley in Shropshire. The Bradley Ironworks, which started about 1766, was one of the largest and most complex in Britain. He patented a method for boring cannon accurately in 1774 and in 1776 ordered a BOULTON AND WATT steam pump to pump air for a furnace. Within four years he had four engines at work and was able to supply many of the castings needed for the Watt engines, because he had the skilled workers available to bore the metal cylinders to the accuracy that JAMES WATT demanded.

In 1777 he set up ironworks in France, with BLAST FURNACES, and he also had interests in South Wales foundries and shares in Cornish tin mines (see TIN MINING). With ABRAHAM DARBY III he was responsible for building the IRON BRIDGE near COALBROOKDALE, which was opened in 1779, and a second iron bridge at Sunderland over the River Wear. In 1788 he had 40 miles (64 km) of CAST-IRON pipes made for the WATER SUPPLY of Paris. For his many activities he earned the nickname of 'Iron-mad Wilkinson' and, not surprisingly, was buried in an iron coffin as he had requested.

William IV (1765–1837)

King from 1830 to 1837, he was more astute politically than GEORGE IV and used his influence to secure the passage of the REFORM BILL, 1832 through the House of Lords. He was succeeded by his niece, VICTORIA.

P. Ziegler, *King William IV* (Collins 1971).

Williams, Thomas (1737–1802)

The 'Copper King' of the 18th century. A north Welshman, formerly a solicitor, he controlled two COPPER MINES on Anglesey and by 1785 extended his control to the whole of the copper operations on PARYS MOUNTAIN. He owned smelters in Swansea and South Lancashire and warehouses in LONDON, BIRMINGHAM and LIVERPOOL. His Anglesey mines were worked out in the late 1790s.

J.R. Harris, *The Copper King: A Biography of Thomas Williams of Llanidan* (Liverpool University Press 1964).

Willie Brown's Iron Man

A coal-cutting MACHINE invented in 1768 by William Brown of Northumberland. By turning a crank handle the collier could use a pick mounted in a frame. The machine was less efficient than a man wielding a pick and was not used extensively. Coal cutters using compressed air were not introduced until late in the second half of the 19th century.

Winding Ropes

Th ropes used in colliery shafts were made of hemp or of chain until the 1840s, when they were replaced by iron wire and later by steel. See RATTLE CHAIN.

Visit Glasgow Art Gallery and Museum, Kelvingrove, Glasgow – Newcomen-type winder. **M***
Astley Green Colliery, Tydesley, Greater Manchester – winding drum.

Window Tax

A tax payable according to the number of a house's windows, introduced at the end of the 17th century. After 1766 the tax started with the seventh window and went up on a sliding scale. There were several increases and the tax reached its highest level in 1808. The tax was paid by the occupier, not the landlord. In 1823 the tax was halved and in 1825 the seventh window was exempt. The tax was finally abolished in 1851, increasing the demand for window glass (see GLASS – CROWN and GLASS – SHEET).

Wollstonecroft, Mary (1757–97).

One of the first women to advocate equal rights and opportunities for women. In 1792 she published *A Vindication of the Rights of Women*. This said that women should have the same educational opportunities as men and that MIDDLE-CLASS women should be permitted to earn their own living. She was far in advance of her time and over 50 years passed before any attempt was made to provide higher education for girls.

M. Wollstonecroft, *A Vindication of the Rights of Women* (Penguin 1982).

Women – Economic Conditions

In the INDUSTRIAL REVOLUTION single women at work gained in social and economic independence, but married women, unless they continued to work, became financially dependent upon their husbands. This situation led to the assumption that men's wages should be paid on a family basis and the concept

A girl working in a coal mine. The *Report on Mining Conditions* published in 1842 contained a number of illustrations which emphasized the appalling conditions in which children and women were employed underground. This girl has a harness round her waist attached to a corf on a wooden sledge which is loaded with coal. Many passageways were so low that movement was only possible on all fours. (*Mansell Collection*)

developed of married women acting as home-makers and child rearers.

Some sections of Victorian society were shocked by the new class of women workers in industry. By the 1850s factory women were recognized as an important workforce, and the emancipation of working women had begun. Factory women were better off than those in other occupations, working the shortest hours and receiving the same rates as men employed on the same kind of work. By contrast, women domestic servants, agricultural workers and those employed in domestic industries such as dressmaking were poorly paid and oppressed.

I. Pinchbeck, *Women Workers and the Industrial Revolution 1750–1850* (Cass 1969).

Women in the Coal Mines

About 1780 women and girls ceased to be employed at nearly all the pits in North East England, but in Scotland, until 1799, men and women employed in collieries were literally slaves, unable to work where they wanted and the property of the coal master. At the beginning of the 19th century there were protests at women working underground. In 1830 women made up about 5 per cent of the underground workforce in British COAL MINES, with women in nearly all the mining areas. The Royal Commission set up by LORD SHAFTESBURY to investigate the employment of women and children in mines took evidence in different parts of the country, and issued their *Report on Mines* in 1842.

The report shocked the country by its disclosures. Employment was not widespread, the chief districts being North Lancashire, West Yorkshire, South Wales and the east of Scotland. The labour was shared equally with the men, but women often worked in the worst conditions where the men would not go. In Scotland the women and girls carried baskets of coal up ladders to the surface. In general the owners were in favour of having women and girls in the pits. Some miners did not want women to leave the mines, partly because of the money they earned ad partly from conservatism.

Other colliers objected to their employment because it prevented lads and men from getting proper wages. Women colliers were resentful when they found themselves excluded with no other form of employment available.

The MINES ACT, 1842 caused some suffering, especially in east Scotland, but in many collieries the Act was ignored until 1844, and in some pits in South Wales women and girls were employed as late as 1850.

A.V. John, *By the Sweat of their Brow: Women Workers at Victorian Coal Mines* (Croom Helm 1980).

Women In the Domestic System

The women and children under the DOMESTIC SYSTEM picked clean the cotton wool, carded (straightened the fibres) and spun it. The weaving was mainly done by the men and a good weaver could keep three women spinners active at their wheels, producing the WEFT. If sufficient yarn could not be supplied within the family it was bought from spinsters in the neighbourhood. When JOHN KAY's flying shuttle was introduced the weavers could work faster and had difficulties getting all the yarn they required.

Women In the Metal Trades and Iron Industry

In the ironworks women and children were chiefly engaged in casual work such as breaking limestone, preparing the ore and wheeling it to the furnaces. In 1843 there were 200 adult women working with nearly 5,000 men at the DOWLAIS IRONWORKS in South Wales, as well as a number of girls employed mainly on the tips removing cinders. Girls were also employed in the forges as pilers of the broken PIG IRON, ready for the PUDDLING furnace. In 1864 it was said that the employment of women and girls in ironworks was peculiar to Wales.

In the workshops and homes of the small domestic manufacturers in and around BIRMINGHAM girls were apprenticed in the TOY TRADE until the age of 21 or marriage. As MACHINES were introduced the proportion of women employed increased.

Of all the metal trades, NAIL MAKING employed by far the largest number of women workers. They worked small forges attached to farmhouses and cottages in conditions which were dirty, hot and degrading. Children of 10 or 12 turned out 1,000 nails a day. In chain-making districts the girls often learned both trades, picking up one when the other was slack. Wages were often paid on piece rates (according to the number of items produced), and could be good for the girl or woman who was strong and healthy.

W. Neff, *Victorian Working Women* (Cass 1966).

Women Textile Workers

Women were on an equal footing with men as weavers in the SILK trade, and girls as well as boys were given APPRENTICESHIPS. They had the right to take and train apprentices and were paid the same wages as the journeymen (see ARTISANS). Towards the end of the 18th century the number of women employed in weaving increased rapidly in the cotton and woollen trades. The increase in the demand for labour as industry expanded, the shortage of men during the NAPOLEONIC WARS, together with the loss of spinning as a woman's occupation because of the introduction of MACHINES, increased the number of women employed as weavers.

In the COTTON INDUSTRY, where there was a high proportion of light and uskilled work, women and children were employed in large numbers. By comparison, the LINEN industry employed few women because linen weaving required a great deal of strength.

Ribbon weaving was largely done by women at home, sometimes as a subsidiary occupation. The women HAND LOOM WEAVERS suffered great distress in the 1830s when machines began to dominate the textile industry, wages dropped and they were forced to work the POWER LOOMS sited in factories instead.

In the early WOOLLEN INDUSTRY many tasks were performed by men, but women had the unpleasant job of picking and sorting the wool. Some women were spinners, although there were men spinners as well. Both men and women were employed in finishing the cloth. In the WORSTED mills, spinners were mainly women and girls, and in FLAX mills women were entirely responsible for spinning. However, fewer women were employed spinning cotton on MULES because of the strength and the skill required; many more worked the WATER FRAMES. Women predominated in power loom weaving, partly because they were more easily managed and the level of wages for both sexes was low, making it easier to obtain women than men.

The FACTORY SYSTEM increased tremendously the amount of employment available for women, although women had always worked in large numbers in the textile trades.

M. Hiley, *Victorian Working Women, Portraits from Life* (Gordon Fraser 1979).

Wooden Railways

Wood was used about 1680 near Whitehaven in Cumberland to provide a solid and level surface on which cart wheels could run. There was an early wooden railway at COALBROOKDALE until CAST-IRON rails were used in 1767 or 1768. The flanges or projecting ribs for keeping wagons on the railways, were on the wheels. The introduction of heavy steam locomotives (see STEAM ENGINES) in the early years of the 19th century resulted in wooden rails breaking and iron rails were used as replacements, or WROUGHT-IRON bars were fastened over the wooden rails to strengthen them.

M.J.T. Lewis, *Early Wooden Railways* (Routledge 1970).

Wood Pulp

In 1800 a Dutchman living in London, Matthias Koops, took out patents to use wood, straw and other fibres to make paper. He started on a commercial basis, but went bankrupt because people preferred paper made from the traditional materials, linen and cotton.

The demand for paper increased

rapidly during the first half of the 19th century, and the price of rags doubled between 1848 and 1855 as supplies became scarce. Wood grinding began in Germany in 1857, and in 1864 the chemical method for producing wood pulp was patented by Watt and Burgess. Both the mechanical method (grinding wood to a powder) and the chemical method (dissolving wood in chemicals to break up the fibres), were developed in the 1860s.

Wood Screw Production

This was a laborious process of filing the thread on to a blank piece of iron by hand, until mechanization was achieved early in the INDUSTRIAL REVOLUTION. In 1760 the brothers Job and William Wyatt of Staffordshire took out a patent for cutting screws of iron, known as wood screws since they were made to screw into wood. The machine used two lathes, one to cut the head and the other to cut the thread. A screw factory using water power which they set up was a financial failure, but by 1792 another, larger factory nearby was turning out 170,000 screws per week using 36 lathes turned by one waterwheel. Fifty-nine people were employed, some of whom were children. This is an early example of mass production by means of special-purpose machinery. The method of production remained basically the same until American machinery was introduced by John Sutton Nettlefold in BIRMINGHAM in 1854.

Wool Combers

The skilled workers who combed the wool in the WORSTED industry. They had a strong TRADE UNION organization as early as the 1740s and, retained the national organization into the 19th century despite the COMBINATION ACTS. The APPRENTICESHIP system broke down after the repeal of the STATUTE OF ARTIFICERS in 1814, and thousands were attracted by the high wages of the trade. In 1825, with the weavers in BRADFORD, they went on strike, but after six months were defeated. After the strike the wool combers lost their privileged ARTISAN position and became defenceless outworkers. The threat of introducing combing MACHINES kept wages down. In 1845 there were still 10,000 wool combers in the Bradford area, but their working conditions and STANDARD OF LIVING were extremely low. Combing machines were introduced in the area in the 1850s and 1860s, and wool combers were no longer required.

Woolf, Arthur (1766–1837)

A Cornishman who improved WATT's STEAM ENGINE as used for pumping water from mines. He and his trainees experimented with compound expansion and by 1820 made it possible for the engine to be worked efficiently by high-pressure steam. Woolf's compound engine was also more economical than James Watt's. Woolf set up engines at Cornish TIN MINES in 1814 and 1815, but the complexities of the engine and the high costs of erection outweighed the advantages and no more engines were made, although it was used extensively on the Continent.

Woollen Industry

An industry established in medieval times in rural areas of East Anglia, the Cotswolds, Wales and other regions, using home-grown wool. By 1760 the West of England was manufacturing broadcloths using Spanish merino wool, but elsewhere the pattern continued with the industry organized on a domestic basis. The SPINNING JENNY was in general use in Yorkshire by 1785 and a number of cloth merchants became MANUFACTURERS. New mills were built in the LEEDS area and Calder Valley in the 1790s, but the industry was still mainly based on the DOMESTIC SYSTEM, with only one piece of cloth in 16 being woven in a mill in 1803.

POWER LOOM WEAVING was introduced in the 1820s, and by 1835 about half the mills operating were in West Yorkshire, accounting for 57 per cent of the mill workers in the industry. As steam power became more efficient Yorkshire had locational advantages over many other manufacturing areas, such as the West Country, where steam power was developed much more slowly. In 1835 about two-thirds of the power used in Gloucestershire was produced by water, in Wiltshire the percentage was 59 per cent and in Somerset 32 per cent. In Scotland the woollen centres in the border counties of Roxburghshire, Berwickshire and Selkirkshire, because of their isolation, were slow to adopt steam power, which was also unknown in Wales and Devon.

By 1835 the Devon and Somerset trade was declining fast, whereas in Yorkshire the industry expanded rapidly for the next three decades. In Scotland the Border region increased its output and became more important than the West Country. Australia began to supply most of the wool and the industry began to use waste wool, either reclaimed from the production processes or SHODDY. HAND LOOMS disappeared much more slowly in the woollen industry than they did in the WORSTED industry, and were still in use in Rochdale, Lancashire, in the 1870s, in the West Country in the 1880s, and in Yorkshire in the 1860s and 1870s.

By the 1860s steam power was more important than water in the West Country, but in Scotland 65 per cent of the power was obtained from water, while in Yorkshire only 12 per cent came from waterwheels.

D.T. Jenkins and K.G. Ponting, *The British Wool Textile Industry 1770–1914* (Heinemann 1982).

Woollen Manufacture in England – Report on the State of, 1806

The report of an enquiry commissioned by Parliament. It provided a great deal of information about the WOOLLEN INDUSTRY of that time. It was biased against ARTISAN groups such as the CROPPERS, and did nothing to support their case for the continuation of protective legislation.

Worcester Porcelain Company

Established in 1751 by a group of local businessmen who had taken over the Bristol China Works in 1750, it was at first known as the Worcester Tonquin MANUFACTORY. For 24 years it had as its driving force one of the founder shareholders, Dr John Wall. Like the other PORCELAIN factories of the period, the company had the ambition of being able to produce domestic table ware capable of competing with the oriental porcelain being imported from Nanking, which was hard and translucent. Soapstone was added to SOFT-PASTE PORCELAIN, a material used in France and introduced in England, making it withstand boiling water. About 1797 the firm started to produce BONE CHINA.

About 1812 a new reverberatory-type kiln (operating on the principle of the REVERBERATORY FURNACE) was developed, which made firing less hazardous, and a type of decoration known as bat printing was introduced on cheaper tea-wares at about the same time. The firm expanded considerably in the 1820s, and during the 1840s and 1850s Worcester was responsible for the main part of the bone china produced in England.

Visit Worcester – Dyson Perrins Museum containing Royal Worcester Porcelain. **M***

F.A. Barrett, *Worcester Porcelain and Lund's Bristol* (Faber and Faber 1966).

Work Discipline

People used to working at home or on farms were not adjusted to working conditions in factories, where they had to be turned into human machines. Strict rules replaced the relative freedom of the small workshops, with work starting and stopping at fixed hours. Each person had a particular task to perform, which was usually arduous and monotonous, and a foreman imposed FINES or used other forms of punishment to maintain the standard of discipline required. The introduction of powered MACHINES made strict discipline an absolute necessity. Unfortunately this discipline was often harsh and applied equally to children (see CHILD LABOUR).

Workers' Associations

The first workers' associations were formed between 1700 and 1780 in the WOOLLEN INDUSTRY by WOOL COMBERS, weavers and STOCKINGERS, and the workers in the COTTON INDUSTRY followed suit. In GLASGOW in 1787 MANUFACTURERS of MUSLIN were met by organized resistance when they tried to reduce piece rates (payment according to amount produced). Collective agreements were made between the cotton weavers and the manufacturers of Bolton and Bury in Lancashire in 1792, and by 1797 there was a Society of Cotton Weavers which aimed to lay their grievances before Parliament. In the North of England an Institute of Wool Workers was set up in 1796. The organization was able to threaten and punish workmen who would not leave the workshops that it boycotted. Similar organizations were set up in a variety of industries including the SHEFFIELD cutlers and Kent paper-makers. These agitations made the government uneasy, and the COMBINATION ACTS, 1799 AND 1800, were hastily passed.

Workhouses

In the mid-17th century there was a growing interest in providing places where poor people and children could be taught skills. A UNITARIAN, Thomas Firmin, erected a school in 1676 in Aldersgate, LONDON. It was a type of workhouse for poor children, where they were taught simple manual skills, and similar schools were built in BRISTOL.

In 1723 Parliament passed an Act enabling parishes to erect workhouses for the poor which could be hired out to any MANUFACTURER, who, in return for keeping the inmates alive, obtained cheap labour. Pauper children were at times manacled or ringed by the neck to prevent them from running away from the workhouses, and parishes could refuse relief to anyone who was not willing to enter the workhouse. Within 10 years of the Act being passed there were 100 workhouses in the London area. The inhumanity of the system, particularly the contracting out of the workhouses, resulted in the passing of Gilbert's Act in 1782 (see POOR LAW – GILBERT'S ACT). This abolished the contract system and permitted, but did not require, parishes to continue to form unions and erect workhouses. The POOR LAW AMENDMENT ACT, 1834, extended the system and required parishes to form unions and establish workhouses. By 1838 there were 573 unions, and it was not until 1868 that the Act had been implemented throughout the country.

Poor relief could be obtained only inside these workhouses and families in need of assistance had to live in them. To deter idle families, conditions in the workhouses were made less agreeable than those experienced by labourers outside. One workhouse was built in each union and families were split up when they entered it, females in one section, males in another. Hard and unpleasant work had to be performed, a workhouse uniform had to be worn and overcrowding was common. No segregation of the mentally ill, VAGRANTS, the old or the young was made. In the agricultural counties in southern England the poor rate was reduced and the system was effective if unpleasant, but in the industrial towns of the North the problems were different. Families were often UNEMPLOYED for short periods, work was often on a daily or hourly basis and what was needed was out-of-door relief for short periods. To make matters worse there was a slump from 1838 to 1842 (see TRADE CYCLES), and in some towns there were large numbers of unemployed.

The Poor Law Commissioners often had a hostile reception. They were turned out of HUDDERSFIELD and many towns refused to build workhouses and continued with out-of-door relief. For WORKING-CLASS people the workhouse was seen as a hateful building to be avoided at all costs. It was considered shameful to have to enter it, and its shadow fell over the lives of people throughout Victorian times.

N. Longmate, *The Workhouse* (Temple and Smith 1974).

Working-Class Food

In the 1780s, the basic diet of the rural areas – bread, potatoes, tea and occasionally bacon – was also that of the WORKING CLASSES in the industrial towns. The food was stodgy, monotonous and deficient in nutrients. The poorest town workers, often IRISH IMMIGRANTS, ate potatoes as the staple diet, with weak tea to which sugar and milk were sometimes added.

The dietary habits of workers in the mid-19th century were different from those of the 1780s. By the 1830s, white bread and tea were no longer luxuries and basic food was cheaper and more plentiful. Nevertheless, the diet was lacking in fresh fruit, vegetables, fish (except near the coast) and milk.

J. Burnett, *Plenty and Want* (Penguin 1968).

Worsted

A type of woollen cloth taking its name from the village of Worstead in Norfolk, where it was made in the Middle Ages. The cloth was not fulled (thickened by matting the fibres) and was made from long, combed wool. Combing consists of removing the short fibres from the raw wool, leaving a loose 'sliver' of long fibres for spinning. Worsted fabrics were finer and lighter than the traditional woollen ones.

Combing the wool proved the most difficult process to mechanize. EDMUND CARTWRIGHT in 1792 attempted, unsuccessfully, to solve the problem and the work was done mainly by hand until a MACHINE was patented in 1827. West Yorkshire became the centre of the worsted industry in the INDUSTRIAL REVOLUTION.

Worsted Committees

Committees set up by Acts of Parliament in the 1770s and 1780s to deal with fraud and delays in the returns of work. Inspectors were appointed by the JUSTICES OF THE PEACE to form a kind of industrial police for the detection and punishment of those who embezzled materials. Where the committees were appointed the inspectors could procure a warrant from the justices to search private houses. If suspicious goods, such as wool, were found, the accused were deemed guilty until they proved themselves innocent. Domestic workers were allowed up to eight days to return material given them; if they did not

return it properly worked in that time they could be found guilty of embezzlement. The workers suffered more than their masters since they had no form of compensation available to them.

The Act of 1777 authorized a worsted committee for the West Riding of Yorkshire, Lancashire and Cheshire. Acts of 1784, 1785 and 1790 did the same for Suffolk, the Midland counties and Norfolk. The committees obtained their revenue from a rebate of part of the tax paid on soap – used in large quantities for washing wool. In the 19th century the committees declined because the FACTORY SYSTEM had reduced the number of outworkers. In 1853 the tax on soap was abolished and the worsted committees lost their financial support. They were revived in the 1870s on a voluntary basis but were ineffective.

Worsted Industry

Unlike the fabrics of the WOOLLEN INDUSTRY, worsteds were made of long wools which were combed for spinning and were more easily adapted to MACHINE work. Initial problems with RICHARD ARKWRIGHT'S WATER FRAME checked the growth of worsted manufacture in mills. The first record of a worsted mill is on the Lancashire–Yorkshire border in 1784, to be powered by horses and water. Within a few years mills were set up in LEEDS and the Calder and Worth Valleys. Between 1800 and 1815 the number of mills increased from about 22 to 54. Most expansion was in BRADFORD, Halifax, Bingley and Keighley. Between 1819 and 1835 about 150 new mills started up and the size of mills increased. By the late 1820s the MULE was being used for powered spinning.

The average size in 1835 for the 204 West Riding worsted mills was 52 workers. By that date steam power was more important than water power, with 78 per cent of the power being generated by steam. Norfolk declined as a worsted-producing area in the last decade of the 18th century, because the area had no coal, was technologically backward, lacked ENTREPRENEURIAL connections and lost lucrative markets in France because of the NAPOLEONIC WARS. This decline left Yorkshire with a virtual monopoly of the industry, and there was considerable growth. Bradford became the capital of the worsted industry and merchants moved to that area.

The industry used mainly British wool, and the industry's prosperity increased when a cotton WARP was introduced in 1834. A number of INVENTIONS mechanized the combing operation, and this gave a further impetus to the worsted trade. POWER LOOMS first used steam power in 1824; their number rapidly increased and by the 1850s the hand loom had virtually disappeared.

D.T. Jenkins, *The West Riding Wool Textile Industry 1770–1835* (Pasold Research Fund 1975).

Worstedopolis See Bradford

Wright, Joseph (1734–97)

The first professional painter to express on canvas the spirit of the INDUSTRIAL REVOLUTION. The son of a Derby lawyer, he studied to become a portrait painter and also painted landscapes. His paintings of industrial scenes such as 'An Iron Forge' and a 'Blast Furnace by Moonlight' illustrate the close association of science and industry during the second half of the 18th century. A number of artists were to follow his example in the 19th century, including J.M.W. Turner (1775–1851) and Wilson Lowry (1762–1824).

Wrought Iron

Almost pure iron, containing as little as possible of other elements such as sulphur and phosphorus. For thousands of years it was the only form of iron in use, and it played a very important part in the INDUSTRIAL REVOLUTION. It can be hammered as well as rolled when hot, and welded to another piece when white hot by hammering or squeezing. It melts only at very high temperatures, which were difficult to achieve, so it was always worked by forging or rolling. It has greater resistance to corrosion than MILD STEEL.

Early production was by obtaining CAST IRON from a BLAST FURNACE and then treating it in a separate furnace called a finery to decarburize it (remove the carbon). HENRY CORT succeeded in making wrought iron using a REVERBERATORY FURNACE, stirring the iron by a process known as PUDDLING. This became the standard method of wrought-iron production. An improved method of production was introduced by JOSEPH HALL about 1830, called pig boiling, and wrought iron production remained unchanged until the BESSEMER PROCESS introduced mild steel after 1856.

Wrought iron was used in the early railway bridges, including the Britannia Bridge over the MENAI Straits. ISAMBARD BRUNEL used wrought-iron plates for the *GREAT BRITAIN*, and wrought-iron girders were making their appearance in large buildings by the late 1850s. For construction purposes, wrought iron was widely used until the end of the 19th century, to be superseded by steel.

Visit Sheerness Boat Store, Kent – wrought-iron construction (1858).

Wylam Dilly

A locomotive built using gears designed by WILLIAM HEDLEY in 1814. The name 'Wylam' is taken from a WAGONWAY and colliery on the north bank of the River Tyne. The colliery was the most westerly of the north Tyneside mines and sent its coal to STAITHES on the Tyne at Lemington by a wagonway 5 miles (8 km) long, for which the locomotive was built.

Y

Yeast Drying

Matthew Felton developed a technique in 1796 for drying yeast. He collected the yeast from breweries in barrels, strained off the beer and subjected the yeast to heavy pressure before drying it slowly until it was in the form of a flour.

Yeoman Class

Small-scale farmers who owned the freehold of their land and earned their living by working it. Many of the inventors and MANUFACTURERS of the INDUSTRIAL REVOLUTION were members of this CLASS. Their decline as yeomen had been hastened by the enclosure movement and the increase in the number of large farms. The poverty which resulted forced many to turn to industry as a means of livelihood and as an outlet for their energies. The yeoman class included JEDEDIAH STRUTT, DAVID DALE, ISAAC WILKINSON and RICHARD CRAWSHAY.

Yerbury, Francis (1707–78)

A member of a wool-cloth manufacturing family in Bradford-on-Avon, Wiltshire. He invented CASSIMERE CLOTH in 1766. The cloth was made extensively in the West Country and this helped to maintain the high-class trade of the region, until a decline in demand after 1807.

CHRONOLOGY

	INDUSTRY	TRANSPORT	SOCIETY
1702	Darby's Bristol Brass Mill		
1707	Crowley Ironworks, Newcastle		
1708	Coalbrookdale leased by Darby		
1709	Smelting iron with coke at Coalbrookdale		
1712	Newcomen's steam engine built		
1718	Thomas Lombe's silk mill, Derby		
1720	Japanning tinplate introduced		Royal Exchange and London Assurance Companies received charters
1722	Porter first brewed		
1723			General Workhouse Act
1726			Grand Alliance of Coalowners set up in North East
c.1730			Circulating schools started in Wales
1733	Kay's flying shuttle		
1737	Ward began making sulphuric acid		
1738	Paul Lewis's roller spinning machine		
c.1740	Warmley Brass Works, Bristol		
1742	Process for coating copper with thin silver discovered by Thomas Boulsover		
1742	Benjamin Huntsman's crucible steel process		
1743	Chelsea Porcelain Works		
1745	Rockingham Pottery		Scottish rebellion
1749	Derby Porcelain Works		
c.1750	Leeds Pottery		
1751	Worcester Porcelain Factory	Beginning of turnpike mania	
1754	Wove paper produced		Society for the Encouragement of Arts, Manufactures and Commerce

	INDUSTRY	TRANSPORT	SOCIETY
1756	Hirwaun Ironworks		
1756	Herculaneum Pottery, Liverpool		
1756	Derby Porcelain Factory		Beginning of Seven Years' War
1757	Lowestoft Porcelain Factory	Sankey Brook Navigation	
1759	Wedgwood's Burslem Pottery		
1759	Smeaton's Eddystone Lighthouse		
1759	Dowlais Ironworks		
1760	Carron Ironworks		
1760	Wedgwood's cream-ware		
1760	Wyatt's wood screw patent		
1761		Bridgwater Canal opened	
1762	Bonawe Ironworks		Equitable Life Assurance Society
1763	Plymouth Ironworks		Test and Corporations Act
1763	Newcomen engine used for colliery winding		End of Seven Years War
1764	James Hargreaves invented spinning jenny		
1765	Cyfarthfa Ironworks	John Metcalf's road-building technique first used	
1766	Cranage brothers patent for wrought iron	Highways Act	Huddersfield cloth hall built
1766	Soho Ironworks, Birmingham		
c.1766	Bradley Ironworks		Lunar Society
1766	Yerbury's cassimere cloth		
1767		Passenger traffic started on Bridgewater Canal	Hanway's Act
1767		Iron rails used in Coalbrookdale area	
1768	Cookworthy's hard-paste porcelain patent	Canal basin built at Stourport	
1769	Wedgwood's Etruria Works		
1769	Arkwright's first factory at Nottingham		
1770	First iron plough		
1771	Arkwright's Cromford Mill		Society of Civil Engineers
1772	Paperware used for japanning		
1773	Antiquarian paper produced	Highways Act	Stock Exchange built

	INDUSTRY	TRANSPORT	SOCIETY
1774	Wilkinson's boring machine		
1775	Boulton and Watt partnership		
c.1775	War knitting machine		
1776			American War of Independence started
1776	Plate glass made at St Helens		
1776	Watt's steam engine in use		
1776	Ravenhead Glass Works, St Helens		
1777	Arkwright's Birkacre Mill	Trent and Mersey Canal	Worsted committee set up in Yorkshire
1777	Smalley's cotton mill in Greenfield Valley	Cast-iron rail used in coal mines	
1778	Belper Mill built by Strutt		
1778	Bramah's water closet		
1778	Sirhowy Ironworks		
1778	Ramsden's screw-cutting lathe		
1778	Richard Garrett's Leiston engineering works		
1779	Crompton's mule	Iron Bridge built at Coalbrookdale	Penitentiary Houses Act
1779			Halifax piece hall built
1780	Pickard's crank and flywheel mechanism		Gordon Riots
1780			Sunday school movement
1781	Watt's sun and planet gears		
1782	Tipton Alkali Works		Committee of Manufacturers
1782	New Hall Pottery		Gilbert's Act
1782	Slubbing billy invented		
1783	Cort's puddling process patented		American War of Independence ended
1783	Dale's Barrowfield dye works		
1784	Greg's Quarry Bank Mill built	Mail coach service started	
1784	Penydarren Ironworks		
1784	Cort's grooved rollers patented		
1784	Lea mills started by John Smedley		
1784–	Methodists separate		
1785	from Church of England		
1785	Ransome's patent for ploughshare		Anglo-Irish Treaty
1785			General Chamber of Manufacturers
1785			Tools Act
1786	Albion flour mills, London		Anglo-French Treaty

	INDUSTRY	TRANSPORT	SOCIETY
1786	New Lanark Mills founded		
1786	Clyde Ironworks		
1786	Horrocks's cotton mill, Preston		
1786	Meikle's threshing machine		
1787	Flax spinning machine invented	Cast-iron barge launched	
1787	Cartwright's power loom		
1788	Haigh Ironworks, Lancashire		
1788	Nailsea Glasshouse, Somerset		
1789	Muirkirk Ironworks, Ayrshire		Beginning of French Revolution – storming of the Bastille
1789	Robert Ransome opened Ipswich factory		
1789	Arkwright's water frame patented		
1789	Blaenavon Ironworks		
1789	Higher Mill, Helmshore, Lancashire		
1789	Ebbw Vale Ironworks		
1790	Butterley Ironworks	Forth and Clyde Canal	
1790		Port Penrhyn built	
1791	Bone china	Charlestown Harbour built by Smeaton	Birmingham Riots
1792	Cartwright's wool combing machine	Shropshire Canal	London Corresponding Society
1792	Strutt's first fireproof mill, Derby		
1792	Gott's woollen mill at Leeds		
1792	Phoenix Foundry, Sheffield		
1793	Davenport's porcelain works, Longport		Friendly Societies Act
1793	Marshall's process for linen thread perfected		Beginning of Napoleonic Wars
1793	Oldknow's Mellor cotton mill		
1793	Minton Porcelain Factory, Stoke-on-Trent		
1794	Davenport's porcelain works, Longport	Glamorgan Canal	
1795	Coalport Porcelain Works		Two Acts passed
1795	Thorncliffe Ironworks, Sheffield		Speenhamland System
1795			Methodist Union's break with Church of England
1796	Roman cement patented		Institute of Wool Workers

	INDUSTRY	TRANSPORT	SOCIETY
1796	Spode produced bone china		
1797	Mole plough invented		Norwich Union Insurance Company
1797	Fenton, Murray and Wood, Engineers, Leeds		
1797	St Rollox Chemical Works, Glasgow		
1798			Income tax first imposed
1799	Bleaching powder manufactured		Combination Act
1799	Courtauld's Pebmarsh silk mill		Mechanics' institute formed in Glasgow
1799	Tintern Ironworks		Religious Tract Society
c.1800	Seed drill developed		
1800		Peak Forest Canal	Arbitration Act
1800			Combination Act
1801			First population census
1801			Act of Union
1802	Soho Works partly lit by gas	*Charlotte Dundas* built	Health and Morals of Apprentices Factory Act
1802		Trevithick's steam carriage	
1802–1803			Peace between two parts of Napoleonic Wars
1803	First paper-making machine at Frogmore Mill	London dock opened	Society for superseding climbing boys
1803	Ransome's patent for chilled ploughshare		
1803–1804			Tremadoc new town
1804		Monkland Canal	
1804		Steam dredger and bucket chain	
1804		Highland Commission for Roads	
1804		Surrey Iron Railway	
1805	Llanelly Copper Company	Pontcysyllte Aqueduct	Coal Owners' Association founded in North East
1805	Micrometer invented by Henry Maudslay	London Dock	
1805	Spode introduce stone china	Hackney cab licences issued	
1805		Grand Junction Canal	
1806	Lydbrook Ironworks	West India Dock opened	Orders in Council
1806			Report on State of Woollen Industry
1807	Steam-driven air pump used to ventilate coal mine	*Clermont* built by Robert Fulton	

	INDUSTRY	TRANSPORT	SOCIETY
c.1807	Gilpin's colliery winding chain		
1808		Trevithick's *Catch Me Who Can* exhibition	British and Foreign Schools Society founded
1808			Royal Lancasterian Society
1809	Courtauld's Braintree silk mill		North British Insurance Company, Edinburgh
1809	Dickinson's paper-making machine		
1809	Bobbinet lace-making machine		
1810	Use of tinplate for canning		
1811	Cornish engine erected at Wheal Prosper Mine	Rack and pinion system on railways	National Society formed
1811–1812			Luddite unrest
1812	Gas, Light and Coke Company	*Comet* built	Anglo-American War started
1812	Muffle kiln		Hampden Clubs formed
c.1813	Ironstone Porcelain Factory		
1813	Nantgarw Porcelain Factory	*Puffing Billy* built	
1814	Parish of St Margaret's, Westminster, lit by gas	*Blucher* built	Anglo-American War ended
1814	Steam printing press used to produce *The Times*	*Wylam Dilly* built	British and Foreign Schools Society absorbs Lancasterian Society
1814			Repeal of Statute of Artificers
1815	Steam-heated cylinders in paper-making		Corn Laws
1815	Doulton Pottery, Lambeth		End of Napoleonic Wars
1815	Richard Hornsby set up engineering works at Grantham		
1816	Davy's safety lamp	Leeds and Liverpool Canal	Institution for the Formation of Character, New Lanark Mills
1816		McAdam appointed to Bristol turnpike trust	Spa Fields meeting
1817	Fairbairn and Lillie engineering firm established in Manchester		Blanketeers' march
1817	Jacquard loom patent		Pentridge Rising
1817			Association for the Improvement of Female Prisoners in Newgate

VE

	INDUSTRY	TRANSPORT	SOCIETY
1818	Great Bandana Gallery dye works, Glasgow	*Rob Roy* built	Institution of Civil Engineers
1818		*Vulcan* – first iron boat built, in Scotland	First female reform societies
1818			General Union of Trades
1819	Kaleidoscope invented		Peterloo massacre
1819			Six Acts
1820			Co-operative movement
1821	Clark's shoe factory	*Rising Star* – first steamer to cross Atlantic east–west	
1821	Steam pump used to drain Fens		
1822		Caledonian Canal opened (part)	
1822		*Aaron Manby* (steamboat with an iron hull) launched	
1823	Rubberized waterproof fabric patented		Reciprocity of Duties Act
1823	Soap works at Newcastle		
1824	Portland cement patented	St Katherine's Dock	Friendly Societies recognized legally
1824			Infant School Society
1824–1825		Railway boom	
1825	Dandy roll patented	*Enterprise* sailed to Calcutta	Law Society
1825	Madeley Porcelain Factory	*Locomotion* made	Repeal of Combination Acts
1825		Opening of Stockton to Darlington Railway	
1826	Fly frame patented by Henry Houldsworth	Telford's Menai Straits Bridge	Bank Act
1826	St Helens Crown Glass Company	McAdam appointed to Metropolitan turnpike roads	
1826	Limelight invented		
1827	Modern matches ('lucifers') made	Goldsworthy Gurney patented a steam coach	Society for the Diffusion of Useful Knowledge
1827		Timothy Hackworth built the *Royal George* locomotive	
1828	Bell's reaping machine		University College, London
1828	Hot blast patented by James Neilson		
1828	Alkali factory, St Helens		
1829	Cammel Laird shipbuilding yards, Birkenhead	Omnibus service started in London by George Shillibeer	Catholic Emancipation Act
1829		Rainhill Trials	Metropolitan Police Act
1829			Middlesbrough founded

	INDUSTRY	TRANSPORT	SOCIETY
c.1830	Wet puddling process discovered by Joseph Hall		
1830	Lawn mower invented	Canterbury–Whitstable Railway	Doherty's National Association for the Protection of Labour
1830	Wright's tile-making machine	Liverpool and Manchester Railway	Beerhouse Act
1831	Faraday demonstrated electromagnetic induction	Public steam coach passenger service between Cheltenham and Gloucester	Bristol Riots
1831		*Infant* steam carriage ran from London to Brighton	British and Foreign Temperance Society
1831–1832			Cholera epidemic
1832	Round hearth blast furnace		Reform Act
1832	Improved method for making sheet glass		
1833	Ericsson's Screw Propeller		First government grant for education
1833	Pattinson process to separate silver from lead		Factory Act
1833			Oxford Movement started
1834		Steam carriage service between Glasgow and Paisley	Poor Law Amendment Act
1834			Grand National Consolidated Trades Union
1834			Tolpuddle Martyrs
1835	Fairbairn's shipbuilding firm founded at Millwall	Highways Act	Municipal Corporations Act
1836			Chartist movement started
1836			University of London
1837	Clay Cross Ironworks	*Great Western* launched	University of Durham founded
1837	Electric telegraph developed		
1838		London–Birmingham Railway	
1838		Travelling post office started	
1838		Ericsson's screw propeller used for *Archimedes*	
1838		*Great Western* crossed Atlantic in 15 days	
1838		Part of Oxford Street tarred	
1839	Nasmyth's steam hammer	West Bute Dock, Cardiff	Anti-Corn Law League
1839	Watermark patent	Railway Act	Monmouthshire rebellion

	INDUSTRY	TRANSPORT	SOCIETY
1839			Hand loom Weavers' Commission set up
1839			County Police Act
1839			Owen's model village set up in Hampshire
1840	Electroplating invented	Swindon chosen for Great Western Railway workshops	First teachers' training college opened
1840	Temple Mill, Leeds	Railway Act	Penny post
1840		London–Southampton railway opened	Royal Agricultural Society
1840		Cunard Steamship Company	Transportation to New South Wales stopped
1840		P&O Steamship Company	
1841	Whitworth's standardized screw thread	Taff Vale Railway	
1841	Fox Talbot's calotype patent	Great Western railway completed	
1841	Jacquard loom adapted for lace-making		
1841	Superphosphate patent taken out		
1841	Shipbuilding yards founded at Govan by Robert Napier		
1842	Ransome's portable steam engine	Railways Act	Sanitary Conditions Report
1842	Bessemer's typesetting machine		Registrar of Friendly Societies appointed
1842			Mines Act
1842			Plug Plot Riots
1843	Thomas Hancock took out patent for vulcanizing rubber	Thames Tunnel completed	Governesses' Benevolent Institution
1843	Ransome's made its first all-iron plough	*Great Britain* launched	Health of Towns Commission set up
1843			*News of the World* published
1844	Whitworth's gear-cutting machine	Railways Act	Bank Charter Act
1844			Companies Act
1844			Rochdale Pioneers
1844			Factory Act
1844			Health of Towns Association
1844			Ragged School Union
1844			Health of Towns Report
1845	Compound steam engine invented by William McNaught	Albert Dock, Liverpool	Chartists' Land Company
1845		Canal Carriers Act	Lunacy Act

	INDUSTRY	TRANSPORT	SOCIETY
1845			Excise duty on glass lifted
1845			Town Improvement Company
1846	Electric Telegraph Company	Thomas Hancock made a solid rubber road vehicle tyre	Corn Laws repealed
1846		Gauge Act	Pupil-teacher system introduced
1846– 1847		Railway boom	
1847	Akroydon Mill, Halifax	Canal Carriers Act	Factory Act
1847	Linoleum industry founded in Kirkcaldy		
1848		Stanley Dock, Liverpool	Cholera epidemic
1848			Christian Socialism
1848			General Board of Health
1848			Queen's College, London, opened
1848			Public Health Act
1849	Usher's rotary steam plough		Navigation Acts repealed
c.1850	Latch needle invented		
1850	Lead-coated electric cable introduced	Britannia bridge over Menai Straits	Factory Act
1850	Patent for processing gold and silver from lead bullion		Public Libraries Act
1851	Liquid manure distributor invented	Underwater electric cable between Britain and France	Land Water Act
1851	Oil mining started in West Lothian		Amalgamated Society of Engineers
1851			Religious Worship Census
1851			Window tax abolished
1851			Great Exhibition at the Crystal Palace
1852		King's Cross Station built	Bilberry Reservoir collapsed
1852			Metropolitan Water Supply Act
1852			Patent Law Amendment Act
1853	Titus Salt's woollen mill, Bradford – founding of Saltaire		Transportation to Tasmania stopped
1853			Factory Act
1854	Coleman's Carrow Factory opened, at Norwich	London General Omnibus Company	
1854	Laxey waterwheel built, Isle of Man		
1854	Fowler's steam plough		
1855			Limited Liability Act

	INDUSTRY	TRANSPORT	SOCIETY
1856	Bessemer converter		County and Borough Police Act
1856	Aniline Dye produced by Sir William Perkin		Joint Stock Companies Act
1856	Britannia Agricultural Engineering Works, Bedford		British Medical Association
1857	Steam-driven generator used to produce electric light		Matrimonial Causes Act
1857			National Association for the Promotion of Social Sciences
1858	Hoffman's kiln introduced	*Great Eastern* launched	Cheltenham Ladies' College
1859		Brunel's Royal Albert Bridge	
1860			Bedford College formed
1861		HMS *Warrior*, with an iron hull, launched	
1862			Consolidation Act
1863	Fowler set up steam engine and plough works at Leeds		
1864	Paper-making using ground wood started	Brunel's Clifton Suspension Bridge	Factory (Extension) Act
1866		Transatlantic cable laid	
1867			Transportation to Western Australia stopped
1867			Factory (Extension) Act
1867			Marx's *Capital* published

Maps and Charts

Output of iron by regions, 1806

SOURCE: British Parliamentary Papers (1849), XXII, appendixes 25–6

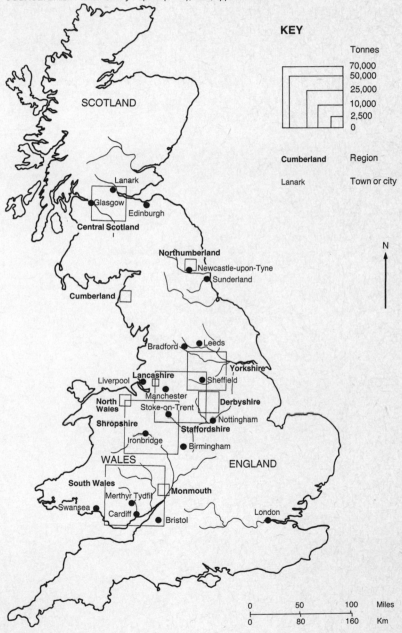

KEY

Tonnes

70,000
50,000
25,000
10,000
2,500
0

Cumberland   Region

Lanark   Town or city

N

SCOTLAND

Lanark
Glasgow
Edinburgh
Central Scotland

Northumberland
Newcastle-upon-Tyne
Sunderland

Cumberland

Bradford
Leeds
Yorkshire
Liverpool
Lancashire
Sheffield
Manchester
North Wales
Stoke-on-Trent
Derbyshire
Nottingham
Shropshire
Staffordshire
Ironbridge
Birmingham

WALES
ENGLAND

South Wales
Merthyr Tydfil
Monmouth
Swansea
Cardiff
Bristol
London

0	50	100	Miles
0	80	160	Km

The canal network, 1820

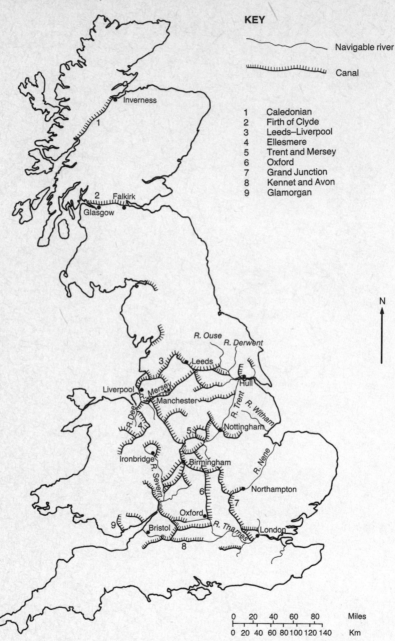

KEY

〜〜〜〜〜〜〜〜 Navigable river

⊥⊥⊥⊥⊥⊥⊥⊥⊥⊥⊥⊥ Canal

1   Caledonian
2   Firth of Clyde
3   Leeds–Liverpool
4   Ellesmere
5   Trent and Mersey
6   Oxford
7   Grand Junction
8   Kennet and Avon
9   Glamorgan

Inverness

1

2   Falkirk
Glasgow

N

R. Ouse
R. Derwent
3   Leeds
Liverpool   Hull
R. Mersey
Manchester   R. Trent
R. Witham
5   Nottingham
Ironbridge   Birmingham
R. Severn   R. Nene
6   Northampton
Oxford   7
9   Bristol   R. Thames   London
8

0   20   40   60   80   Miles
0 20 40 60 80 100 120 140   Km

Coalfields and industrial regions, 1820

KEY

Coalfield (approximate area mined by 1820)

Main industrial regions

Black Country Industrial region

Edinburgh Town or city

SCOTLAND

Central Scotland
Glasgow
Edinburgh
Ardrossan
Ayr
R. Clyde

North East
Newcastle-upon-Tyne
Sunderland
Workington
R. Wear
R. Tees

West Yorkshire
Bradford
Leeds
R. Calder
South Lancashire
Liverpool
Sheffield
Rotherham
Manchester
Don Valley
R. Trent

The Potteries
Stoke-on-Trent
Nottingham
East Midlands
Leicester
R. Severn
Birmingham
WALES
Black Country
ENGLAND

Merthyr Tydfil
South Wales
Llanelli
Swansea
Cardiff
Bristol
London
R. Thames

N

| 0 | 50 | 100 | Miles |
| 0 | 80 | 160 | Km |

Age distribution of the population of England and Wales, 1841

SOURCE: Censuses of England and Wales, 1841, 1981

KEY

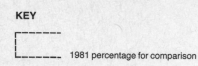

1981 percentage for comparison

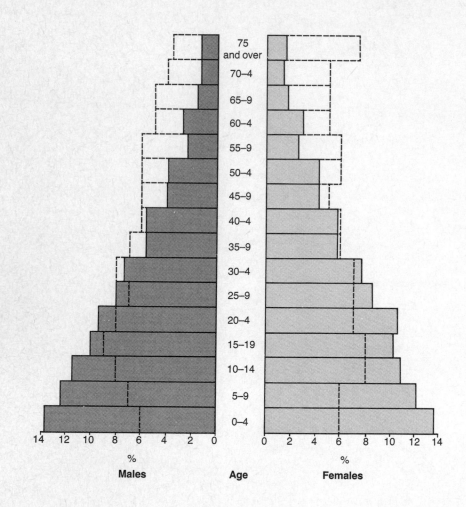

The main railway network, 1850

KEY

⌇ Main railway

SCOTLAND

Aberdeen

Perth · Dundee

Glasgow · Kirkcaldy

Edinburgh

Berwick

N

Carlisle

Newcastle-upon-Tyne

Darlington · Stockton

Whitby

Scarborough

Barrow-in-Furness · Lancaster

York

Preston · Leeds

Hull

Southport

Sheffield

Grimsby

Holyhead

Liverpool · Manchester

Crewe

Lincoln

Stoke-on-Trent · Derby

Nottingham

Birmingham

King's Lynn

Peterborough

Norwich

Great Yarmouth

Lowestoft

WALES

Rugby

Cambridge

Ipswich

Gloucester

ENGLAND

Colchester

Harwich

Merthyr Tydfil

Oxford

Swansea

Newport

Swindon

Cardiff

Reading

London

Whitstable

Bristol

Canterbury

Dover

Southampton

Lewes

Exeter

Bournemouth

Brighton

Torquay

Plymouth

| 0 | | 50 | | Miles |
| 0 | 50 | | 100 | Km |

CURRENCY CONVERSION TABLE

Pre-1971 (d = penny, s = shilling)		Decimal Coinage 1971 onwards (p = pence)
¼d	One farthing	0.1p
½d	One halfpenny (ha'penny)	0.2p
1d	One penny	0.4p
3d	Threepence	1.25p
6d	Sixpence	2.5p
1/–	One shilling	5.0p
2/–	One florin	10.0p
2/6d	Half a crown	12.5p
10/–	Ten shillings	50.0p
£1	One pound	£1 or 100p
£1.1s.0d.	One guinea	£1.05p